# FEDERAL ACQUISITION AND CONTRACT MANAGEMENT

**Eighth Edition**

---


**CLARK G. ADAMS, BSL, JD, CPCM**
**Past National President of NCMA and NCMA Fellow**



**Published By**

**AGU PRESS**

733 N. Dodsworth Avenue
Covina, California 91724

First Edition 1990
Second Edition 1992
Third Edition 1996
Fourth Edition 1999
Fifth Edition 2002
Sixth Edition 2006
Seventh Edition 2011
Eighth Edition 2014



Published and Distributed by:

AGU Press
733 N. Dodsworth Avenue
Covina, CA 91724
626-966-4576

**Library of Congress Control Number: 2014940637**

**ISBN 978-0-692-21879-2**

**10 9 8 7 6 5 4 3 2 1**

# PREFACE

The Federal Government continues to make changes to the Federal Acquisition Regulation (FAR). There have been 21 changes in those regulations since the publication of the Seventh Edition. The details of each of those changes have been included in this Eighth Edition. The Government's emphasis continues toward making the process simpler, adapting commercial practices and especially the technology age providing for more electronic capabilities.

Three major resources have been utilized in obtaining current data related to changes in the regulations. The Department of Defense's "Defense Acquisition Deskbook," which includes the FAR, as well as the Defense Federal Acquisition Regulation Supplement (DFARS), has been the most important source of data needed for this edition. The National Contract Management Association (NCMA) magazine, "Contract Management," and the Federal Acquisition Reports were vital in finding where the major changes occurred for incorporation in the text.

Considerable credit for publication of this Eighth Edition goes to Sheryl Ryan, Director of Editorial Operations at the American Graduate University, who has proofed all the changes, and provided many valuable suggestions.

Clark G. Adams
BSL, JD, CPCM
Past National President of NCMA and NCMA Fellow

Director, CGA Associates
Consulting in Government Acquisition
2821 Arizona Terrace, NW
Washington, DC 20016-2642

**Clark G. Adams**
**Author's Biographical Information**
**2014**

Clark G. Adams is Director of **CGA Consulting in Government Acquisition,** located at 2821 Arizona Terrace, NW, Washington, DC. 20016.

Mr. Adams took his education at the University of Utah, in Salt Lake City, Utah. He received the degree of Bachelor of Science of Law, BSL in 1950. He received the degree of Bachelor of Law, LL.B. in 1951. In 1969 he was awarded the degree of Juris Doctor, JD, from that University. As an attorney he was admitted to the Utah Bar, and has a broad and comprehensive background in the field of Government acquisition.

Mr. Adams has been active in the National Contract Management Association (NCMA), and was its first National President. In that role he was instrumental in establishing NCMA's Charter goals. The basic goal of NCMA is to provide access to increased knowledge and professionalism to those working in the field of Government Contract Management. This he believed would be of importance in lowering overall costs of Government. He remains dedicated to that principle.

From 1981 to 1994, Mr. Adams served in the United States General Accounting Office (GAO), currently named the Government Accountability Office (GAO), where he was an Assistant Director in the National Security and International Affairs Division. In that capacity, he supervised numerous reports for Congress.

While at GAO, Mr. Adams, because of his communication skills, was selected as an instructor to conduct courses for GAO auditors on Standards for Audits of Governmental Organizations, Programs, Activities, and Functions.

Prior to joining the GAO in 1981, Mr. Adams served as a Project Director of the original Cost Accounting Standards Board. He supervised the issuance of several Cost Accounting Standards which are in effect currently.

Prior to joining the Cost Accounting Standards Board in 1971, Mr. Adams worked for 19 years for the Rockwell International Corporation (formerly North American Aviation, Inc.). He was Vice President of Contracts and Pricing of the company's Los Angeles Aircraft Division.

Mr. Adams is currently on the faculty of American Graduate University. The subjects he teaches are "Pricing and Financial Management," "Government Contract Law," and "Contract Management and Administration."

# TABLE OF CONTENTS

## PART 1

## THE BASIC ELEMENTS OF FEDERAL CONTRACTING

### CHAPTER 1 – CONTRACT FUNDAMENTALS



### CHAPTER 2 – ELECTRONIC CONTRACTING



### CHAPTER 3 – THE ACQUISITION PROCESS

## CHAPTER 4 – CONTRACTING METHODS

## CHAPTER 5 – CONTRACT TYPES

# PART 2

# THE PREAWARD PHASE OF FEDERAL CONTRACTING

## CHAPTER 6 – DEVELOPING COMPETITIVE PROPOSALS

## CHAPTER 7 – SOURCE SELECTION PROCESS



## CHAPTER 8 – MANAGING CONTRACT RISK

## CHAPTER 9 – TOTAL OWNERSHIP COSTS



## CHAPTER 10 – CONTRACT COST AND PROFIT PRINCIPLES

## CHAPTER 11 – CONTRACT DOCUMENTATION

## CHAPTER 12 – FUNDAMENTALS OF NEGOTIATION

## PART 3

## THE POSTAWARD PHASE OF FEDERAL CONTRACTING

### CHAPTER 13 – CONTRACT PERFORMANCE

## CHAPTER 14 – DATA, PATENTS AND COPYRIGHTS



## CHAPTER 15 – CONTRACT TERMINATION AND CLOSEOUT

## CHAPTER 16 – CONTRACTUAL CHALLENGES



## APPENDICES

# PART 1

# THE BASIC ELEMENTS

# OF

# FEDERAL CONTRACTING

# CHAPTER 1

# CONTRACT FUNDAMENTALS

## NATURE OF GOVERNMENT CONTRACTING

### Introduction

The United States of America is unique among nations in many ways. Not the least of its uniqueness is the method or process by which the Federal Government obtains the supplies and services necessary for it to function. The method is generally referred to as the Acquisition Process or sometimes as the Procurement Process. It is by this process that the Government enters into contracts with the private sector of our country, as well as those in foreign countries, so that they may acquire those supplies and services. The objective of the acquisition process is to obtain the supplies, equipment and services that are needed to support Government programs, on time and at reasonable prices. When the decision has been made to outsource an acquisition rather than obtaining those supplies, equipment or services on an "in house" basis, agencies must ensure both the use of the proper contract vehicle and the right incentives necessary for contract success.

This text will follow the federal contracting process from its foundations and principles through various aspects and stages of contract acquisition and contract management, as prescribed by the statutes and regulations. The uniqueness of this process will become evident as one journeys through the subjects addressed herein.

### Legality of Government Contracts

The legal authority for the Government of the United States of America to enter into contracts with private citizens and non-government organizations is founded in the Constitution of the United States. This is the case even though that document does not contain any language which specifically authorizes such actions. The authority is derived from the simple statement in the Preamble of the Constitution that the Federal Government shall "*...provide for the common defense, promote the general Welfare, and secure the Blessings of Liberty....*" This thesis has been confirmed by legal opinion when in *United States vs. Tingey, (39 U.S.5 (Pet.) 114 (1831))* the court held that:

> "It is in our opinion, an incident to the general right of sovereignty; and the United States being a body politic, may, within the sphere of constitutional powers confided to it, and

through the instrumentality of the proper department to which these powers are confided, enter into contracts not prohibited by law, and appropriate to the just exercise of these powers.

Consistent with this authority, all Government contracts are made in the name of the United States of America and not in the name of the individual agency involved. In *United States vs Maurice, (26Fed. Cas.1211,1216(No.15747)(C.C.D. Va1823)* the court held that:

"...the government, therefore, is capable of contracting, and its contracts may be made in the name of the United States..."

In order for the contract to become a legal obligation of the U. S. Government the contract must be based on statutory authority. The Government may actually avoid any liability under contracts which are not supported by such authority. This concept has been upheld by legal opinion when in *New York Mail and Newspaper Transportation Co. vs. United States*, (*139 Ct. Cl. 751, 154 F. Supp. 271 (1957)*), the court held that:

"The authority of an officer to enter into a contract binding the United States must be found in some legally enacted provision of law."

## Congressional Authority

The statutory authority which provides the legal basis for a Government contract comes from the U.S. Congress. It is the Congress which creates the Executive Agencies, whether or not conceived by the President and the Cabinet. Congress drafts and passes the laws and statutes, called Authorization Acts, which establish the various Government agencies and the specific programs proposed by those agencies. Congress has derived this power from the Constitution, Article I, Section 8 – *General Powers of Congress*, where several of the parts therein state that Congress shall:

"1. ...lay and collect Taxes, Duties, Imposts and Excises, to pay the Debts and provide for the Common Defense and general Welfare of the United States;...;

"12. ...raise and support Armies,...;

"13. ...provide and maintain a Navy;

"14. ...make Rules for the Government and Regulation of the land and naval Forces;

"18. ...make all laws which shall be necessary and proper for carrying into Execution the foregoing Powers, and all other Powers vested by the Constitution in the Government of United States, or in any Department or Officer thereof."

**Fiscal Considerations**

In addition to the Authorization Acts which create an agency and its programs, Congress must also put into law an Appropriation Act which provides the funds with which that agency will function. Therefore, Government agencies cannot operate unless Congress appropriates the funds. This requirement is also derived from the Constitution where in Article I, Section 9 states:

> "...No money shall be drawn from the treasury, but in consequence of appropriations made by law;..."

Based upon the "need theory" (i.e., funds cannot be allocated except for need of the current year), the Appropriation Acts will specify the period of time for which those specific funds are available for use by the agency. The appropriations will be on a single year, multiple year, or no-year basis, the latter category being unrestrictive in nature. The predominant appropriation is on a single year basis. This approach requires the agencies to return annually to Congress and justify the budget desired for their operations and specific programs. There have been many recommendations that multi-year appropriations and related funding be approved on a regular basis for major multi-year programs (MYP) and projects. There is much to say for that approach as it would be of a significant savings for both the Government agencies and industry alike. There are several criteria MYPs must meet for the savings to be realistic. The minimum requirements must remain unchanged through the term of the procurement, the design must be stable, and the agency must ask for enough money to carry out the contract.

Once the funds have been appropriated by Congress, they are available for use by the Executive Branch. However, there are very definite strings attached to those funds. The following examples are some of the more binding strings.

Appropriated funds can only be spent within the scope of the authorization to be in compliance with 31 U.S. Code 628.

> "Except as otherwise provided by law, sums appropriated for the various branches and expenditure in the public service shall be applied solely to the objects for which they are respectively made, and for no others."

The appropriations are divided into three major categories: research and development (R&D), investment, and operations. R&D appropriations cover many phases of activities ranging from basic research and stopping short of full scale production. Investment appropriations are commonly referred to as procurement funds. They are concerned with the purchase of the Government's many assets both civilian and military. Operation appropriations are used for daily operations and maintenance expenses. These funds are used for such expenses as salaries, supplies, certain equipment, service contracts and training.

The funds must be obligated within the year for which they are authorized, in accordance with 31 U.S. Code 200(d).

> "No appropriation or fund which is limited for obligation purposes to a definite period of time shall be available for expenditure after the expiration of such period..."

The time period governing availability for obligation varies by the type of funding. Generally the time frames are three years for procurement funds, two years for Research, Development, Test & Evaluation (RDT&E), and one year for Operations & Maintenance (O&M).

In order to obligate the Government with regard to any appropriated funds, there must be a valid commitment by a contracting officer (i.e., offer and acceptance). This position is made clear in 31 U.S. Code 200, "*Documentary evidence of obligations*."

> "...no amount shall be recorded as an obligation of the Government of the United States unless supported by documentary evidence..."

With the ultimate goal of keeping expenditures within the obligated funds and preventing contracting officers from obligating more funds than those which were allotted, expenditures or contract obligations in excess of appropriated funds are prohibited by 31 U.S. Code 665(a).

> "No officer or employee of the United States shall make or authorize an expenditure from or create or authorize an obligation under any appropriation or fund in excess of the amount available therein; nor shall any such officer or employee involve the Government in any contract or other obligation, for the payment of money for any purposes, in advance of appropriations made for such purposes unless such contract or obligation is authorized by law."

There is an added limitation on the availability of funds for DOD agencies. With passage of the FY 91 Appropriation Act all procurement appropriation accounts must be closed-out at the end of the fifth fiscal year after the period of availability for the obligation ends. Under these procedures, when the period of availability for obligation ends, the balances of the appropriation remain in an expired category. These funds are available to liquidate obligations and fund valid upward obligation adjustments for five years. After five years all balances (obligated and unobligated) are canceled. Obligations outstanding after the five year period must be charged to a current appropriation account of the agency available for the same purpose.

**Budget Process**

The road leading up to an Appropriation Act is long and tedious. Each Government agency must develop its proposed budget for submission to the President through the Office of Management and Budget (OMB). That budget will be the culmination of a process that probably began several years earlier, when lower echelons began preparing and submitting their requests up the management ladder.

OMB will pass the President's budget on to Congress where the Congressional Budget Office (CBO) and the individual budget committees will review it in depth in preparation for setting targets and ceilings for the various federal functions. The budget will be dissected and sent to the various Senate and House of Representatives authorization and appropriation committees. These committees and their subcommittees will hold hearings, draft legislation and submit same to the House and Senate for debate and passage. The final budget must be approved by both legislative bodies before sending it back to the President for signature.

## AGENCY AND LEGISLATION INFLUENCES

### Government Agencies

It is the policy of the Government to rely generally on private commercial sources for supplies and services, if certain criteria are met, while recognizing that some functions are inherently governmental and must be performed by Government personnel. At the same time, they must give appropriate consideration to the relative cost in deciding between Government performance and contracting-out. Under the Economy Act (31 U.S.C. 1535), an agency may place orders with another agency for supplies and services that the servicing agency may be in a position or equipped to supply, render, or obtain by contract, if it is determined that it is in the best interest of the Government to do so (*FAR 17.5, Interagency Acquisitions Under the Economy Act*). When contracting-out, the agency issuing the contract will, by following the acquisition regulations and agency directives, exert the most influence on the terms, conditions and scope of the contract.

The Office of Management and Budget (OMB) and one of its subsidiaries, the Office of Federal Procurement Policy (OFPP) provides the Executive Branch with its policy and direction making capability for Government contracts. The OFPP became a permanent federal agency by the *Office of Federal Procurement Policy Act Amendment of 1988, Pub. Law 100-679.* The Act gave the OFPP Administrator oversight functions regarding executive agency procurement related regulations. For the Legislative Branch, Congress created the General Accounting Office (GAO) (now known as the Government Accountability Office) as its watchdog over all Government operations, including contracts.

### Legislation and Regulations

The Legislative and Judiciary Branches of the U.S. Government exert considerable influence on the creation and administration of federal contracts through the laws, statutes, acts, and legal decisions. Examples of some of the social and economic programs that have evolved from their actions and which have a direct bearing upon contracts are listed in Figure 1-1, *Federal Socioeconomic Programs*, pages 8 & 9.

# FEDERAL SOCIOECONOMIC PROGRAMS

**Acquisition of Foreign Buses**
*Pub. L. 90500 DOD Appropriations Act of 1969*
Act sets restrictions on appropriated funds for the purchase, lease, rent, or other acquisition of foreign-manufactured buses.

**Air Carrier, U.S. Flag (Fly America Act)**
*49 U.S.C. 1517; FAR 47.4*
Act requires federal employees and dependents, federal contractors, grantees, and others to use U.S. Government-financed international air travel.

**Black Colleges & Universities and Minority Institutions**
*DFARS 252.226-7000 & 7001*
Set-asides provided for contracts with historically black and minority colleges and universities.

**Blind and Other Handicapped Made Products (Javits Wagner O'Day Act)**
*41 U.S.C. 46-48; CFR Part 51; FAR 8.7*
Act requires mandatory purchase of products made by blind and other handicapped persons.

**Buy America Act**
*41 U.S.C. 10; Executive Order 10582 Dec. 17, 1954 as amended; FAR 25.1 & 25.2*
Act provides preference for domestic materials over foreign materials.

**Clean Air Act & Clean Water Act**
*42 U.S.C. 7401; 33 U.S.C. 1251; 40 CFR Part 15*
Federal agencies are prohibited from entering into contracts with companies convicted of criminal violation of air and water pollution standards.

**Contract Work Hours and Safety Standards Act**
*40 U.S.C. 327-333; FAR 22.3*
Act prescribes a 40-hour work week with payment of time-and-a-half for overtime, and health and safety standards for laborers and mechanics on public works.

**Convict Labor Act**
*40 U.S.C. 4082c2; Executive Order 11755, Dec. 29, 1973; FAR 22.2*
Act prohibits federal contractor employment of convict labor on Government contracts unless such convict labor has been authorized by the attorney general for development of occupational skills.

**Copeland Anti-Kickback Act**
*18 U.S.C. 874; 40 U.S.C. 276c; FAR 22.4*
Employees are prohibited from giving kickbacks on public works.

**Covenant Against Contingent Fees**
*41 CFR 1-1. 500-509; FAR 52.203-5*
Contracts obtained by a broker for a contingent fee are voided by the Government.

**Davis-Bacon Act**
*40 U.S.C. 276a; FAR 22.4*
Act prescribes minimum wages, benefits, and working conditions on federal construction contracts.

**Drug-free Workplace Act of 1988**
*Pub. L. 100-690; FAR 23.5*
Offerors for federal contracts exceeding the simplified acquisition threshold are required to certify that they provide a drug-free workplace.

**Duty-free Entry for Qualified Countries**
*DFARS 252.225-7008*
Act furthers economic and defense cooperation with qualifying nations such as NATO countries.

**Equal Employment Opportunity**
*Executive Order 11246 (Sept. 24, 1965); FAR 22.8*
Act prohibits discrimination based on race, color, religion, sex, and national origin.

**Figure 1-1**

# FEDERAL SOCIOECONOMIC PROGRAMS

**Fair Labor Standards Act of 1938**
*29 U.S.C. 201-219*
Act establishes minimum wage and hour standards for employees engaged in commerce or the production of goods for commerce.

**Federal Prison Industries**
*18 U.S.C. 4121-4128; FAR 8.601*
Act requires the mandatory purchase of specific supplies from Federal Prison Industries, Inc.

**Government Printing and Related Services**
*41 U.S.C. 501*
Acquisition of printing and printing related services must be made through the Government Printing Office unless specific exceptions are met.

**Gratuities**
*32 CFR 7.104-16; FAR 52.203-3*
The Government may terminate a contract if a gratuity is given to a Government employee to obtain a contract or favorable treatment.

**Hazardous Materials Identification and Material Safety Data**
*FAR 23.3*
Contractors must identify hazardous materials and provide safety data for delivery of hazardous material.

**Miller Act**
*40 U.S.C. 270 a-f; FAR 28.102*
Contractors are required to provide payment and performance bonds on Government construction contracts.

**Nondiscrimination Because of Age**
*Executive Order 11141, Feb. 12, 1964; FAR 22.9*
Act prohibits discrimination based on age except for bona fide occupational qualifications, retirement plans, or statutory requirements.

**Ocean Transportation by U.S. Flag Vessels**
*10 U.S.C. 2631 & 46 U.S.C. 1241; FAR 47.5*
All military and at least half of other goods must be shipped in U.S. flag ocean vessels.

**Rehabilitation Act**
*29 U.S.C. 793; FAR 22.14*
Contractors are required to take affirmative action to employ and advance in employment qualified handicapped individuals.

**Service Contract Act of 1965**
*41 U.S.C. 351-357*
Act provides wages, fringe benefits, and work conditions for service contracts for blue collar and some white collar workers.

**Small Business Act**
*15 U.S.C. 631-647, 41 U.S.C. 252(b), 10 U.S.C. 2301; FAR 19*
Act requires placement of a fair portion of Government contracts with small businesses.

**Socially Disadvantaged and Minority Firms**
*Section 8(a) of Small Business Act; FAR 19.8*
Section provides set-aside contracts and Government assistance to qualifying minority and other socially disadvantaged firms.

**Veterans, Employment Openings for**
*41 CFR 50-250 and Executive Order 11598*
Federal contracts must list job openings with state employment systems to assist veterans.

**Walsh-Healey Public Contracts Act**
*41 U.S.C. 35-45; FAR 22.6*
Act prescribes minimum wage, hours, age and working conditions for supply contracts.

**Figure 1-1 (continued)**

The *Federal Acquisition Act of 1977* initially authorized the formation of the Federal Acquisition Regulations System to establish the basis for the codification and publication of uniform policies and procedures for acquisition by all Executive agencies. The System consists of both the Federal Acquisition Regulation (FAR), which is the primary document, and agency acquisition regulations that implement or supplement the FAR. The General Services Administration (GSA) is responsible for establishing and operating the FAR Secretariat to publish and distribute the FAR. The FAR is published in the daily issue of the *Federal Register* and in cumulated form in the Code of Federal Regulations (CFR). The FAR is no longer issued in a print version. It is now on the Internet, at *www.acquisition.gov/far*. The current version of the FAR was issued in March 2005. The 2005 version of the FAR did not make any changes in the language of the document. It incorporated all updates made to the 2001 version, removed all headers and change indicators and changed the pagination so that future issues of the Federal Acquisition Circulars (FACs) will fit into the 2005 version. The Federal Acquisition Regulation (FAR) is issued in the Code of Federal Regulations (CFR) as Chapter 1 of Title 48.

Regulations like the FAR are subservient to the statutes. An example of this occurs when a need to release information about competition in a Federal procurement comes in conflict with the need to know under the Freedom of Information Act statute. Therefore, it is important to always remember, if an agency regulation conflicts with a Federal law, the Federal law will take precedence.

The FAR is the base document controlling the FAR System. The FAR, issued under the *Office of Federal Procurement Policy Act of 1974, Pub. L. 93-400 (41 U.S.C. 401)*, applies to all executive agencies as defined by the Act. Furthermore, it applies to all acquisitions made by such agencies with appropriated funds of: supplies; services, including research and development; and construction, alteration, repair and maintenance of real property. The FAR replaced the Federal Procurement Regulations (FPR), the NASA Procurement Regulations (NASAPR), and most of the Defense Acquisition Regulations (DAR). Actually, the DAR was the successor to the Armed Services Procurement Regulations (ASPR) which were developed in accordance with the *Armed Services Procurement Act of 1947.* The Federal Procurement Regulations (FPR), the non-DOD counterpart of the DAR/ASPR, were developed in accordance with Title III of the *Federal Property and Administrative Services Act of 1949.*

Overall management of the FAR System is vested jointly in the Secretary of Defense, the Administrator of General Services and the Administrator, NASA. Under their guidance, revisions to the FAR are prepared and issued through the coordinated action of two councils, the Defense Acquisition Regulations Council (DAR Council) and the Civilian Agency Acquisition Council (CAA Council) (*FAR 1.201-1, The Two Councils*).

The FAR revisions are distributed through the Code of Federal Regulations system and are issued as Federal Acquisition Circulars (FAC) which synopsize the changes and provide annotated pages of the revised text. Prior to issuance as an authorized revision, proposed additions, deletions and changed verbiage will be published in the *Federal Register* soliciting comments from all concerned. The various Executive Agencies are authorized, within the limits of Subpart 1.3, *Agency Acquisition Regulations,* of the FAR, to issue agency acquisition regulations and guidance to implement FAR policies and procedures within the agency. They may also issue supplements to the FAR to satisfy the specific needs of the agency. Those supplements cannot override the basic requirements of the FAR. Furthermore, the supplements are not to duplicate the basic FAR requirements.

When adopting acquisition regulations, agencies must ensure that they comply with the *Paperwork Reduction Act of 1988, Pub. L. 96-511 (44 U.S.C. 3501, et seq.),* which imposes a requirement on Federal Agencies to obtain approval from the Office of Management and Budget (OMB) before collecting information from ten or more members of the public. (*FAR 1.106, OMB Approval Under the Paperwork Reduction Act).* The *Regulatory Flexibility Act, 5 U.S.C. 601, et seq.,* applies when a law requires publication of a proposed regulation.

**Acquisition Initiatives**

The *Statement of Guiding Principles for the Federal Acquisition System*, as published in FAR 1.102, represents a concise statement designed to be user-friendly for all participants in Government acquisition.

> "(a) The vision for the Federal Acquisition System is to deliver on a timely basis the best value product or service to the customer, while maintaining the public's trust and fulfilling public policy objectives. Participants in the acquisition process should work together as a team and should be empowered to make decisions within their area of responsibility.
> (b) The Federal Acquisition System will: (1) satisfy the customer in terms of cost, quality, and timeliness of the delivered product or service by, for example: (i) maximizing the use of commercial products and services; (ii) using contractors who have a track record of successful past performance or who demonstrate a current superior ability to perform; and (iii) promoting competition; (2) minimize administrative operating costs; (3) conduct business with integrity, fairness, and openness; and (4) fulfill public policy objectives.
> (c) The Acquisition Team consists of all participants in Government acquisition including not only representatives of the technical, supply, and procurement communities, but also the customers they serve, and the contractors who provide the products and services.
> (d) The role of each member of the Acquisition Team is to exercise personal initiative and sound business judgment in providing the best value product or service to meet the customer's needs. In exercising initiative, Government members of the Acquisition Team may assume if a specific strategy, practice, policy or procedure is in the best interests of the Government and is not addressed in the FAR, nor prohibited by law (statute or case law), Executive order or other regulation, that the strategy, practice, policy or procedure is a permissible exercise of authority."

All participants in the System are responsible for making acquisition decisions that deliver the best value product or service to the customer. Best value must be viewed from a broad perspective and is achieved by balancing the many competing interests in the system. The result is a system which works better and costs less (*FAR 1.102-1, Discussion*).

### Acquisition Reform

Part of the *National Defense Authorization Act for Fiscal Year 2003, Title XIV,* signed into law on November 24, 2003, was the *Services Acquisition Reform Act of 2002 (SARA) (H.R. 1588).* Implementation of SARA was initiated by the Office of Management and Budget (OMB) calling each executive agency, except DOD, to appoint a Chief Acquisition Officer (CAO) and a Federal Chief Acquisition Officers Council. The council's objective is to identify acquisition best practices, coordinate multi-agency projects, and recommend procurement policy to OMB.

Under the SARA the Chief Acquisition Officer's (CAO) responsibilities include the following:

- Monitor and evaluate the performance of agency acquisition programs.
- Increase the use of full and open competition.
- Increase appropriate use of performance-based contracting.
- Develop an acquisition career management program to ensure an adequate procurement workforce.
- Manage the direction of acquisition policy for the agency.

A significant element of SARA is promoting the use of performance-based service contracts under $25 million that may be treated as contracts for commercial items. The contract will set forth each task the contractor must perform. Each task must be on a firm-fixed-price basis, be defined in measurable mission related terms, and identify the specific end products or services to be achieved.

## BASIC LEGAL CONSIDERATIONS AND PECULIARITIES OF GOVERNMENT CONTRACTING

### General Principles of Contract Formation and Performance

A generally accepted definition of a contract is, "an agreement which creates an obligation." The American Heritage Dictionary of the English Language defines a contract as, "an enforceable agreement." Black's Law Dictionary defines a contract as "an agreement between two or more persons which creates an obligation to do or not to do a particular thing."

The essentials of an enforceable contract are; competent parties, subject matter, legal consideration, mutuality of agreement, mutuality of obligation and for a legal purpose.

Prior to the creation of a contract, there must be an offer made by one party and an acceptance of that offer by another party. When making an offer, the first party is stating a willingness to perform an act in return for some form of "consideration." An offer may be unsolicited or in response to a specific request or solicitation by a potential customer. In the latter case, the offer must conform to the request in order to be responsive and considered for acceptance.

In contrast, unsolicited offers are not as structured. In either case, care should be taken to ensure that the details of the offer are clear and unambiguous. An offer may also be called a "bid" or a "proposal." Bids are usually firm offers in response to a solicitation and normally are not subject to negotiation. When the Government issues a Purchase Order it is making an offer which does not become a contract until accepted or filled by a vendor. It is normally accepted that vendors responding to a Request for Quote are submitting a quotation or "quote," and making a statement of "willingness," but not an offer.

Acceptance of an offer is established when the offeree makes known his or her agreement and concurrence with all the terms and conditions of the offer. Any conditional acceptance by an offeree is merely a counter offer and no contract is created unless the original offeror accepts the conditions. The date of acceptance is created at the time of oral acceptance or the date a letter, FAX, telegram or electronic transmission stating the acceptance are placed into the respective system.

The courts have upheld the position that without an offer and acceptance, there cannot be an “express contract.” Also, there cannot be an “implied contract” when the parties are negotiating toward an express contract but fail to finalize the deal. Furthermore, when the parties anticipate signing an express contract, there cannot be an implied contract for the same subject matter. *(Peninsula Group Capital Corp. v. United States, U.S. Court of Federal Claims No. 09-747C, August 6, 2010)*

Except for the "Firm-Bid Rule" in Federal Government procurements made by sealed bidding (discussed later in Chapter 4), an offer may be withdrawn up to the time of acceptance.

Consideration to be given or received as a result of a contract must be "something of value" to the contracting parties. That "something of value" may be monetary, something tangible, the performance of an act or function, or a combination of these. The courts do not judge the value of consideration; however, the law does not enforce a contract where there has been a promise without consideration. The one exception to this is referred to as the Doctrine of Estoppel. Under this doctrine, it has been found that a promise could be binding when the other party acts upon such a promise, even without consideration, when that other party would "suffer an injustice." Associated with this doctrine, an implied-in-fact contract may exist. Pursuant to an implied-in-fact contract, the Government may be held liable under the ordinary principles of equity and justice for the fair value of any benefits it retains. This is just another example of the reason the Federal regulations are firm in requiring that all contractual actions are documented and properly executed. They do not want to be subjected to claims for efforts that were not authorized.

## Government Contracting Authority and Responsibilities

The authority and responsibility to contract for authorized supplies and services are vested in the head of each Governmental agency. In order to provide the heads of executive agency with professional support, the position of Chief Acquisition Officer (CAO) has been established *(National Defense Authorization Act for Fiscal Year 2004, Pub. L. No. 108-136).* The CAO's role is to advise and assist those agency heads as to agency acquisition activities. The Act also provides the CAO with the authority to (a) increase the use of full and open competition in the acquisition of property and services, (b) increase the use of performance-based contracting, and (c) manage the direction of agency acquisition policy.

Contracts may be entered into and signed on behalf of the Government only by persons designated as contracting officers. Contracting officers are appointed in writing on a *Certificate of Appointment* (Figure 1-2, page 15) by agency heads or their designated agent. The certificate will clearly note any limitations on the individual contracting officer's authority (*FAR 1.6, Career Development, Contracting Authority, and Responsibilities*). In 2008, Contracting Officer Technical Representatives (COTR) became required to meet federal acquisition requirements that are very similar to those required of Contracting Officers. Information on the limits of the contracting officer's authority is readily available to the public and agency personnel.

There are situations where certain Government employees, who do not have such a warrant expressed by such a Certificate of Appointment, may bind the Government. Actual authority "to bind the Government" comes in two forms: express and implied. A CO with a Certificate has express authority. Certain other Government employees, without warrants, have implied actual authority to bind the Government. They are typically in higher echelon positions, the extreme example would be the President.

Contracting officers have authority to enter into, administer or terminate contracts and make related determinations and findings. Contracting officers may bind the Government only to the extent of the authority delegated to them. They are responsible for ensuring performance of all necessary actions for effective contracting, ensuring compliance with the terms of the contract, and safeguarding the interests of the United States in its contractual relationships (*FAR 1.602-2, Responsibilities*).

No contract will be entered into unless the contracting officer ensures that all requirements of law, executive orders, regulations, and all other applicable procedures, including clearances and approvals, have been met.

No Government contracting officer is authorized to enter into or modify a contract without consideration to the Government.

---

## *CERTIFICATE OF APPOINTMENT*

Under authority vested in the undersigned and in conformance with

Subpart 1.6 of the Federal Acquisition Regulation

is appointed

***Contracting Officer***

for the

***United States of America***

Subject to the limitations contained in the Federal Acquisition Regulations and to the following

Unless sooner terminated this appointment is effective as long as the appointee is assigned to

______________________________
(Organization)

______________________________
(Agency/Department)

______________________________
(Signature and Title)

______________________________
(Date) (No.)

Standard Form 1402

---

**Figure 1-2**

**Limitations and Restrictions in Government Contracting**

The Government's procurement community is charged with the task of expending public funds in a wise and prudent manner. Many federal laws and regulations place restrictions on the actions of Government personnel and contractors. Some of the basic rules are contained in Part 3 of the FAR, *Improper Business Practices and Personal Conflicts of Interest*, which prescribes policies and procedures for avoiding improper business practices and personal conflicts of interest and for dealing with their apparent or actual occurrence. A brief discussion of some of the more important restrictions follows. There is more detail in FAR Part 3.

As a general rule, no Government employee may solicit or accept, either directly or indirectly, any gratuity, gift, favor, entertainment, loan or anything of monetary value when it could create undue influence. That includes receiving something from anyone who has or seeks to obtain Government business with the employee's agency. It would include persons who conduct activities that are regulated by the employee's agency. Also included are persons who have interests that may be substantially affected by the performance or nonperformance of the employee's official duties. Certain limited exceptions may be authorized in agency regulations. The clause at FAR 52.203-3, *Gratuities*, will be contained in most contracts to impose these restrictions on the contractors, exposing them to legal action and possible contract termination should they be found guilty of these activities.

All Government agencies are required by Executive Order 11222 of 8 May 1965, and 5 CFR 735 to establish and prescribe "Standards of Conduct" for all employees within their agency.

With limited exceptions, solicitations for Firm-Fixed-Price (FFP) or Fixed-Price with Economic Price Adjustment (FPEPA) contracts will contain the provision at FAR 52.203-2, *Certificate of Independent Price Determination*. The bidders or offerors are certifying that they have not prepared their price proposals in collusion with another person or organization. Failure to submit the certificate, modification of the certificate or a false certification may be grounds for rejection of the proposal and even possible criminal or civil action.

The clause at FAR 1.107, *Certifications*, was created to implement the provisions of the *Clinger-Cohen Act of 1996, P.L. 104-106.* It prohibits the inclusion of a new certification requirement in the FAR for contractors or offerors unless is has been specifically imposed by statute or written justification before it is submitted to the Administrator for Federal Procurement Policy by the FAR Council and that written approval is received. To avoid any misunderstandings Congress has, from time to time, prescribed by statute that certain matters be the subject of certification or similar representation. Even the agencies appear to be relying more and more on contractor certifications to assist in policing procurement reform efforts. There is a broad range of certifications that affect a contractor's business practices. They include such broad ranging subjects as:

- Description of the contractor's business arrangement
- Status of the contractor's financial well being
- Accuracy, currency, and completeness of data and information
- Status regarding debarment or suspension
- Compliance with applicable laws
- Requests for Equitable Adjustment
- Past contractual performance

Practices that eliminate competition or restrain trade may be in violation of federal antitrust statutes and may warrant criminal, civil or administrative action against the participants. Examples of anti-competitive practices are collusive bidding, follow-the-leader pricing, rotating low bids, collusive price estimating systems, and sharing of the business.

Government contracting personnel must be sensitive to indications of unlawful behavior by offerors and contractors. The contracting officer (CO) will report any evidence of suspected antitrust violations in acquisitions for possible referral to the Attorney General. The CO will also notify the agency office responsible for contractor debarment and suspension, which are discussed later in Chapter 3, *The Acquisition Process*.

Any contractor arrangement to pay contingent fees for soliciting or obtaining Government contracts is considered contrary to public policy because such arrangements may lead to attempted or actual exercise of improper influence. In 10 U.S.C. 2306(b) and 41 U.S.C. 254(a), Congress affirmed this public policy but permitted certain exceptions. These statutes:

- Require in every negotiated contract a warranty by the contractor against contingent fees;
- Permit, as an exception to the warranty, contingent fee arrangements between contractors and bona fide employees or bona fide agencies; and
- Provide that, for breach or violation of the warranty by the contractor, the Government may annul the contract without liability or deduct from the contract price or consideration, or otherwise recover, the full amount of the contingent fee paid by the contractor.

Contingent fee means any commission, percentage, brokerage, or other fee that is contingent upon the success that person or concern has in securing a Government contract.

The Government seeks to eliminate any buying-in by offerors, because it may decrease competition or result in poor contract performance. The accepted definition of "buying-in" is when an offeror submits an offer below anticipated cost. The offeror will be expecting to increase the contract amount after award through unnecessary or excessively priced change orders, or the offeror hopes to receive a follow-on contract at artificially high prices. The intent is to recover losses incurred on the buy-in contract.

To minimize the chances of a buy-in, the Government may seek a price commitment covering as much of the entire program concerned as is practical. This may be done by using multiyear contracting. The solicitation will state that a price must be submitted only for the additional quantities. The option quantities, together with the firm contract quantity, will then equal the total program requirements.

Congress passed the *Anti-Kickback Act of 1986 (41 U.S.C. 51-58*) as a means of deterring subcontractors from making payments on any tier under any Government negotiated contract, as an inducement to or acknowledgement of the award of a subcontract or order. It also applies to prime contractors who are prohibited from soliciting, accepting or attempting to accept any kickbacks. Any such action creates a conclusive presumption that the payments have been included in the price of the subcontract or order and thus are ultimately borne by the Government.

Any person who knowingly makes or receives kickback payments is subject to criminal penalties. The Act requires contractors to have in place and follow reasonable procedures designed to prevent and detect violations of the Act. Contractors must also cooperate with any federal agency investigating a violation or suspected violation of the Act. The policies of the Act have been incorporated in the FAR at 3.502, *Subcontractor Kickbacks*. The clause at FAR 52.203-7, *Anti-Kickback Procedures*, will be inserted by contracting officers in solicitations and contracts exceeding the simplified acquisition threshold.

Contracting officers will insert the clause at FAR 52.203-6, *Restrictions on Subcontractor Sales to the Government*, in solicitations and contracts exceeding the simplified acquisition threshold. For the acquisition of commercial items, the clause with its Alternate I will be used. This is in accordance with 10 U.S.C. 2402 and 41 U.S.C. 253(g) which require that subcontractors will not be unreasonably precluded from making direct sales to the Government of any supplies or services made or furnished under a contract. However, this does not preclude contractors from asserting rights that are otherwise authorized by law or regulation. Contracting officers are careful to avoid any conflict of interest (COI) that might arise between Government employees' interests and their governmental duties. Contracting officers will not knowingly award a contract to a Government employee or to a business concern or other organization owned or substantially owned or controlled by one or more Government employees. An exception may be authorized only if there is a most compelling reason to do so, such as when the Government's needs cannot reasonably be otherwise met.

A conflict of interest situation also exists under conditions or circumstances wherein a person is unable or potentially unable to render impartial assistance or advice to the Government in light of other activities or other relationships with other persons. A COI situation also happens when, because of such relationships, one person is given an unfair competitive advantage. The underlying general concept of the term "unfair competitive advantage" is that people should not benefit from the exclusive access to information.

FAR Part 3, *Improper Business Practices and Personal Conflicts of Interest,* which is devoted entirely to the ethics of Government procurements, addresses the issue when it states:

> "Government business shall be conducted in a manner above reproach and, except as authorized by statute or regulation, with complete impartiality and with preferential treatment for none. Transactions relating to the expenditure of public funds require the highest degree of public trust and an impeccable standard of conduct. The general rule is to avoid strictly any conflict of interest or even the appearance of a conflict of interest in Government-contractor relationships. While many federal laws and regulations place restrictions on the actions of Government personnel, their official conduct must, in addition, be such that they would have no reluctance to make a full public disclosure of their actions." (FAR 3.101-1)

In 2007, FAR Part 3 was modified to substantially increase the ethics and compliance requirements of Government contractors with the addition of the new Subpart 3.10, *Contractor Code of Business Ethics and Conduct.* The basic theme of that clause is: (a) "contractors must conduct themselves with the highest degree of integrity and honesty," and (b) "contractors should have a written code of business ethics and conduct." The clause recommends that contractors establish a training program and an internal control system to ensure compliance. Subcontracts with major subcontractors will be required to comply with the requirements of FAR 3.10 by way of flow-down clauses.

Under Public Law 87-849, 18 U.S.C. 218, and Executive Order 12448, November 4, 1983, the President and the heads of executive agencies and military departments have the authority to declare void and rescind contracts under certain conditions. When there has been a final conviction of a contractor for bribery, conflict of interest, or any other violation of Chapter 11, 18 U.S.C. 201-224, the agency head or designated agent will consider the facts available. If appropriate, the agency head may declare the contract void and rescind the contract. In addition, the Government would recover any amounts expended and also recover any property transferred by the agency to the contractor. Rescission of a contract under this authority and a demand for recovery of amounts expended and property transferred therefore, is not a claim within the meaning of the *Contracts Disputes Act of 1978 (CDA*) (See Chapter 16, *Contractual Challenges*). Therefore, the CDA and associated FAR disputes procedures would not apply in these cases. The policies and procedures for exercising this discretionary authority are contained in FAR 3.7, *Voiding and Rescinding Contracts*. In addition, the agency may consider initiating debarment proceedings in accordance with FAR 9.4, *Debarment, Suspension, and Ineligibility*.

Offerors on contracts in excess of the simplified acquisition threshold are required to certify that they will maintain a drug-free workplace. The dollar limitation does not apply to contracts with individuals. Also exempt from the requirement are: (i) contracts for the acquisition of commercial items; (ii) contracts or parts of contracts that are to be performed outside the

United States; (iii) certain contracts by law enforcement agencies; and (iv) where application would be inconsistent with the international obligations of the United States or with the laws and regulations of a foreign country. This requirement was imposed by Public Law 100-690, *Drug-Free Workplace Act of 1988.* The FAR requirements are found in FAR 23.5, *Drug-Free Workplace.*

An offeror will not be eligible for contract award unless it certifies that it will provide a drug-free workplace by complying with the requirements of the law and regulations. The regulations require the publication and distribution of a statement notifying all employees that the unlawful manufacture, distribution, possession, or use of a controlled substance is prohibited in the contractor's workplace. The contractor is also required to establish a drug-free awareness program. In addition, the contractor must make a good faith effort to continue to maintain a drug-free workplace in accordance with the requirements.

The Government has several remedies if the contractor files a false certificate, fails to comply, or even fails to comply in good faith with the drug-free workplace requirements. The remedies include suspension of payments, termination of the contract, and debarment and suspension actions for any violation of the requirements. Contracting officers will implement the law by including the clause at FAR 52.223-6, *Drug-Free Workplace*, in solicitations and contracts.

## Ethics in Government Contracting

Maintaining integrity in the procurement of products and services is a responsibility of both the Government contracting agencies and their contractors. That is why, in December 2007, the Federal Acquisition Regulation (FAR) Council issued a rule imposing new ethics requirements on Government contractors with contracts exceeding $5 million and a period of performance exceeding 120 days. FAR 3.10, *Contractor Code of Business Ethics and Conduct*, became effective in December 2008. The features of the rule require contractors to perform the following:

- Create and publish a written code of business ethics and conduct
- Create an employee training program on the code
- Initiate an internal control system to promote compliance with the code
- Distribute and post agency inspector general posters

There is now a mandatory requirement for disclosure of violations of Federal criminal law involving fraud, conflicts of interest, bribery and gratuity violations and violations of the civil False Claims Act. Failure to knowingly disclose such violations could result in suspension and/or debarment.

While not focusing on the implementation or administration of an ethics compliance program, there are many statutes that offer direction about what should be in a contractor's ethics training program, some of which are:

- The False Claims Act (FCA), *31 U.S.C. 3729-3737*
- The Program Fraud Civil Remedies Act, *31 U.S.C. 3801-3812*
- The Procurement Integrity Act (PIA), *41 U.S.C. 423*
- The Anti-Kickback Act, *10 U.S.C. 2306a, 41 U.S.C. 254b*
- The Foreign Corrupt Practices Act, *31 U.S.C. 3729(a)(3)*
- The Truth in Negotiations Act, *41 U.S.C. 423(a)(1)*

Every Government contractor, regardless of size or number of contracts, should take the new ethics guidelines seriously. Compliance with them will influence the awarding of contracts for many years to come.

**Comparison of Governmental and Commercial/Private Contracting Factors**

There are some very significant differences between contracting with the Federal Government and contracts entered into by private parties or commercial organizations. Figure 1-3, *Comparison of Contracting Factors*, on pages 22 through 24 illustrates some of the more common differences.

One of the most important factors to consider is found in a comparison of the Federal Acquisition Regulation and the Uniform Commercial Code. The FAR is designed to incorporate governmental policies and statutes into regulatory directives. Those directives are designed to dictate how federal funds are to be controlled whenever the Government contracts-out for its supplies or services. The Uniform Commercial Code (UCC) does not have the same impact and clout as does the FAR. It is more a set of guides and best practices to be considered, exercised and contractually implemented by contracting parties in the private and commercial sectors.

The UCC is a complex statute which has been adapted for commercial practices in most states in the United States. The original sponsor of the UCC was the National Conference of Commissioners on Uniform State Laws. In most states the UCC is law by virtue of state by state enactment. The UCC is divided into eleven articles, each addressing a commercial area of law such as sales, commercial paper, letters of credit, bills of lading, and documents of title. Most of its provisions are not mandatory. In Federal contracts, the FAR, its supplements and various statutes will preempt the UCC. However, if the FAR rules do not address an issue in dispute concerning a Government prime or subcontract, the contracting parties can look to the UCC for guidance.

Many socioeconomic programs and policies are linked to the allocation and expenditure of Government funds. Some of those same programs and policies affect the commercial world of contracts, but not with the same intensity.

# COMPARISON OF CONTRACTING FACTORS

| GOVERNMENT | PRIVATE SECTOR |
| --- | --- |
| Contracting Party and Sovereign | Vis-à-vis Contracting |
| Monopsonistic buying power | Anti-Trust laws prevail |
| Funds available only through appropriations | Funds available from many legal sources |
| Procurement actions – set by laws, directives and policies, and procedures regulations | Set by individual company |
| Formal competition required | Company option |
| Can require cost or pricing data from suppliers | Strictly "off-the-shelf" or IAW price lists |
| Authority to audit books | "Forget it!" |
| **Authority of Contracting Agents** | |
| Must have actual authority<br>▪ Has limited authority<br>▪ Can commit only to limit of funds available<br>▪ Can contract only for what law allows | Only apparent authority<br>▪ Has "unlimited" authority<br>▪ Can commit to limit of anticipated funds<br>▪ Can contract for anything not prevented by law |
| Not legally bound by acts of unauthorized agents | Bound by acts of apparent agents |
| **Profit Margins** | |
| Fee/Profit negotiable | Built into "total price" |
| Ceiling on certain contracts | Only social impact felt |
| **Contract Clauses** | |
| Extensive contract "boiler-plate" clauses and many mandatory take-it-or-leave-it clauses | Only standard commercial code or those mutually agreed to by the parties |

**Figure 1-3**

## COMPARISON OF CONTRACTING FACTORS

| GOVERNMENT | PRIVATE SECTOR |
|---|---|
| **Copyrights & Patents** | |
| Go to Government if paid for by Government funds | Rights retained by owner |
| **Patent Infringement** | |
| Government indemnifies contractor from damages | Can seek damages and enjoin others from use of patented item |
| Compensation only to patent holder | |
| **Contract Termination** | |
| Terminate for convenience of Government | Uniform Commercial Code calls for assurance of adequate performance |
| Termination for failure to make progress | Normally not available |
| Compensation for excess reprocurement costs | Breach of contract – damages |
| No compensation for loss of anticipated profits | Breach of contract – damages |
| **Social & Economic Policies** | |
| Incorporated into contract thus become mandatory | Mostly social pressures. Some by law (e.g., Fair Employment Practices) |
| Penalties | Illegal in commercial contracts |
| Liquidated damages only if specified in contract | Same condition |
| Incentive Contracts | Unusual |
| Gratuities – Illegal | Company policy controls |

**Figure 1-3 (continued)**

## COMPARISON OF CONTRACTING FACTORS

| GOVERNMENT | PRIVATE SECTOR |
|---|---|
| **Conflicts of Interest – Individual & Organizational** | |
| Controlled by laws and regulations | Controlled by company policies |
| **Anti-trust Actions** | |
| Strict, well-defined, serious consequences | Not of same magnitude |
| Kickbacks – Illegal | Company policy controls |
| Contingent Fees – Illegal | Company policy controls |
| Congressional benefits from Government contracts are forbidden by laws and regulations | Members of Congress can have outside businesses |

**Figure 1-3 (continued)**

# CHAPTER 2

# ELECTRONIC CONTRACTING

---

## ASPECTS OF ELECTRONIC CONTRACTING

### Electronic Commerce

The world of commerce continues to change rapidly. This is largely because the technological developments that have occurred during the past few decades will continue to occur throughout the 21st century. Those technologies are having an impact upon the federal acquisition and contracting policies and procedures, especially when contracting by electronic means.

This chapter will address in broad terms many electronic contracting features. The Federal Acquisition Regulations (FAR) has already undergone numerous changes to incorporate electronic contracting into the federal process. A significant change has been the demise of the FAR in printed hard copy form. It is now available on the Internet at *www.acquisition.gov/far/* or *http://acquisition.gov*. Other changes range throughout the entire set of regulations, with the majority relating to the overall acquisition process. Since there are diverse topics affected, the specific applications will be detailed in the appropriate chapters throughout this text.

Electronic commerce (EC) is defined as "commercial activity that takes place by means of connected computers" (*Microsoft Press Computer Dictionary, 3rd ed., 1997*). Electronic commerce means "electronic techniques for accomplishing business transactions including electronic mail or messaging, World Wide Web technology, electronic bulletin boards, purchase cards, electronic funds transfer, and electronic data exchange." (*FAR 2.1, Definitions*)

Electronic commerce is the exchange of any business information by electronic means and in a paperless mode. Those means include such methods as: electronic data interchange (EDI), electronic mail (E-mail), electronic bulletin boards, facsimile transmissions (FAX), as well as the Internet and the Web. Electronic contracting employs the various methods of electronic commerce for the purpose of forming contracts and purchase agreements. Electronic data interchange, as used in the federal acquisition process, means "a technique for electronically transferring and storing formatted information between computers utilizing established and published formats and codes, as authorized by the applicable Federal Information Processing Standards."

### Policies

The policies and procedures for the establishment and use of electronic commerce in the federal acquisition process are contained in FAR 4.5, *Electronic Commerce in Contracting*. The requirement for this comes from Section 30 of the Office of Federal Procurement Policy (OFPP) Act (41 U.S.C. 426). The policy statement at FAR 4.502, *Policy*, dictates that "The Federal Government shall use electronic commerce whenever practicable or cost-effective."

Contracting officers are not restricted to EC but may supplement electronic transactions by using other media to meet their contractual needs.

Agencies must ensure that their systems, technologies, procedures and processes for electronic commerce:

- Are implemented uniformly throughout the agency, to the maximum extent practicable.
- Are implemented only after considering use of existing infrastructures.
- Facilitate access to acquisition opportunities by small business, small disadvantaged business and women-owned small business concerns.
- Provide widespread public notice of acquisition opportunities through the Government-wide point of entry.
- Comply with the standards noted above.

Furthermore, in compliance with the directive issued by the FAR Council as Federal Acquisition Circular (FAC) 97-27, all agencies must ensure that all electronic information technology (EIT) they purchase can be accessed by sensory and physically (e.g., visually) impaired Federal employees and members of the public. Also, FAC 97-27 established a new rule concerning performance criteria that EIT must meet to qualify for purchase by a Federal agency. The new rule identified the following EIT categories: software applications and operating systems; web-based information or applications; telecommunication products; video and multimedia products; self-contained, closed products (e.g., information kiosks, calculators, and fax machines); and desktop and portable computers.

Before using electronic commerce, agency heads must ensure that their agency systems are capable of ensuring authenticity and confidentiality commensurate with the risk and magnitude of the harm from loss, misuse, or unauthorized access to or modification of the information (*FAR 4.502(c)*).

One important element of any contractual agreement is there must be an offer and an acceptance wherein both parties have certain obligations to fulfill. It has been a tradition that a signature served to bind those parties to the agreement. Federal contracts were no exception to this procedure. The Government Accountability Office (GAO) has concluded that electronic data interchange (EDI) could create valid binding contractual obligations. The GAO further determined that electronic signatures have all the essential characteristics of hand-written signatures and therefore could be used to bind the parties.

The validity of electronic signatures, contracts, and records in electronic commerce (EC) was expressly provided by the Electronic Signatures in Global and National Commerce Act (*E-Sign) (Pub. L. 106-229*). E-Sign provides as follows:

With respect to any transaction in or affecting interstate or foreign commerce –

(1) a signature, contract, or other record relating to such transaction may not be denied legal effect, validity, or enforceability solely because it is in electronic form; and
(2) a contract relating to such transaction may not be denied legal effect, validity, or enforceability solely because an electronic signature or electronic record was used in its formation.

One interesting aspect of E-Sign since it is "technology neutral," is that one or both of the parties to any contractual transaction do not have to accept electronic signatures or records. They may insist that the transaction be recorded by paper-based means in a more traditional manner. When any contract or record is to be stored by electronic means it must accurately reflect the information originally contained in them. Also, the electronic record must be accessible to all people and capable of accurate reproduction.

To equate the electronic methods with paper methods, the regulations made two significant changes, noted by underlines, in FAR 2.101, *Definitions*. It defines "in writing," "writing," or "written" as "any worded or numbered expression that can be read, reproduced, and later communicated, and includes electronically transmitted and stored information." The clause defines "signature" or "signed" as "the discrete, verifiable symbol of an individual that, when affixed to a writing with the knowledge and consent of the individual, indicates a present intention to authenticate the writing. This includes electronic symbols."

The new electronic contracting approach known as electronic contract execution (ECE) is aimed at expediting the contracting process as well as reducing the "cost of doing business." It introduces high-speed, secure and controlled transactions that cut transaction times in half, reducing errors and operating costs.

## SmartPay Program

In 1988, the General Services Administration (GSA) established a commercial card program subsequently named *SmartPay*. The program was designed to simplify micropurchase payments. It is now a dominant method of payment within the Federal Government and is used regularly for small and medium-sized purchases. By using *SmartPay,* Government buyers have successfully achieved expedited payments to sellers, reduced paperwork and reduced costs per payment. This electronic purchase program has been considered very effective, has been enhanced significantly, and is now named *SmartPay2 (SP2).*

## Electronic Commerce in Contracting (FAR 4.5)

The Federal Acquisition Streamlining Act of 1994 (FASA) established the Federal Acquisition Computer Network (FACNET) with the intent of getting the Government's acquisition system into the cyberspace via the information technology age. The FACNET's general purpose was to get the Federal Government to be less dependent upon a paper driven acquisition process and to rely more upon electronic contracting. The concept was good, but the application, dependability and effectiveness left much to be desired.

In December 2007, the FAR Council removed all reference to FACNET. It has since been replaced by other electronic contracting systems, such as FedBizOpps.

**Electronic Contracting**

One of the major features of electronic contracting is the ability of buyers to be more active in seeking sources for goods and services, while sellers have the opportunity to market their goods and services at a relatively low cost. The process will enhance just-in-time contracting and inventory control. A prime example of this benefit is found in the ever increasing number of electronic catalogs. More and more commercial firms are developing a Web presence through home pages designed to market the firm and their products.

These electronic catalogs typically present descriptive information along with limited graphics of the products available. Many of these Websites permit on-line ordering and accept credit cards for payment. The increased usage of the Governmentwide commercial purchase card program makes these electronic catalogs a viable procurement tool.

In addition to consumer and industrial electronic catalogs being used to conduct market research and make purchases, a variety of them have been developed specifically for Government procurement personnel. Space does not permit the listing of all the governmental home pages.

Three of the largest and most important are: the General Services Administration (GSA) site at *www.gsa.gov*; the Defense Logistics Agency (DLA) maintains a site at *www.dla.mil*; and most importantly, *www.acquisition.gov*. As noted before, the latter is the site to access the FAR and its supporting documents.

One of the sub-sites that can be accessed at *www.acquisition.gov* was created in 2004 by the Office of Federal Procurement Policy. The Acquisition Center of Excellence (ACE) for Services is intended to provide a central repository in service contracting for both the public and private sectors. Initially it will provide information aimed at the following areas of service contracting: support services, equipment maintenance and repair, government-owned/contractor operated (GOCO) programs, information technology (IT) and telecommunications, and utilities.

A good example of the Government use of electronic cataloging process was announced by the Defense Logistics Agency (DLA). They plan an expanded Internet-based electronic mall, where all military customers and users could order spare parts and other logistics or operational support items electronically from vendors who are covered by long-term contractual arrangements.

## The Future

Electronic contracting is not only "here to stay," but it will continue to increase in usage and importance. It is bound to be a significant element in the Government's use of simplified acquisition procedures and the acquisition of commercial items and services. The ultimate goal is paperless purchasing. That would eliminate paperwork for all important documents, such as statements of work (SOW), requisitions, solicitations, purchase orders, invoices and payment documents.

One concern has to be protection of sensitive and classified information, both governmental and corporate. The issue prompted the government to establish the Federal Technical Data Solution (FedTeDS) website, *www.acq.osd.mil/scst/fedteds.htm.*Agencies are required to post sensitive contract information on that site. Contractors will be alerted to such posting via e-mail.

# CHAPTER 3

# THE ACQUISITION PROCESS

## EVOLUTION OF THE ACQUISITION PROCESS

Congress created the Commission on Government Procurement (COGP) in November 1969 when they passed Public Law 91-129. The Commission's charter was to study and recommend to Congress methods "to promote the economy, efficiency and effectiveness" of procurement by the executive branch of the Federal Government. Until recently, that has been the most comprehensive study of its kind on this subject. Subsequent studies looked at the system, but none were as thorough or complete until studies in 1991 and 1993.

In the first phase of the Commission study, some 400 procurement-related problems were identified and assigned for further study. Many of their recommendations have been carried out either by law or regulation. Of the many important and practical recommendations of the Commission, two essential ones dealing with the procurement process have been implemented.

With the April 1985 effectivity date for the Federal Acquisition Regulation (FAR), the COGP Recommendation (IB-1) for a government-wide uniform procurement regulation came into being. The COGP Recommendation (IA1a) dealing with Competitive Negotiation, and competition in general, was dealt with by Congress in 1984. Of the many procurement related laws that were passed by the 98th Congress, three in particular had a profound effect upon the federal contracting process concerning competition. Those laws were:

- The Competition in Contracting Act of 1984 (CICA), *Pub. L. 98-369 (Title VII)*
- The Small Business and Federal Procurement Competition Enhancement Act of 1984, *Pub. L. 98-577*
- The Defense Procurement Reform Act of 1984, *Pub. L. 98-525*

The first statute, CICA, shifted the emphasis from the method of procurement to the use of sources. Its foremost concern was "from whom you procure," rather than "how you procure." Previously, the law clearly stated that formal advertising was the preferred method over negotiated procurements. CICA emphasizes the use of competitive procurement procedures rather than contracting with a single source. The second act's purpose was to eliminate procurement procedures and practices that inhibit free and open competition. It also intended to foster opportunities for small businesses to participate in competitive procurements. The last act was an amalgamation of congressional initiatives designed to improve the effectiveness of the Department of Defense acquisition process.

The 1991 National Defense Authorization Act created a new study group called the Section 800 Panel. In December 1992 that panel issued a multi-volume report that proposed major revisions to the statutory requirements of the federal contracting process. Then in September 1993 the National Performance Review (NPR), created by the Administration, issued its report. The NPR had a goal of reinventing federal procurement by shifting from rigid rules to guiding principles and by fostering commercial procurement practices. NPR's report made twenty additional recommendations for improvement in the procurement area.

A direct outgrowth from these two important reports is found in the Federal Acquisition Streamlining Act (FASA) of 1994 *(Pub. L. 103-355)*. FASA contained the most extensive changes in Federal Government contracting since the three 1984 laws previously noted were enacted. It repealed, or substantially modified, more than 225 provisions of law that affected the contracting and acquisition system. Some of the more significant areas affected include a simplified acquisition threshold, electronic commerce, commercial items, the Truth in Negotiations Act (TINA), contract formation, bid protests and debriefings, contract administration, and small businesses. Each of these is addressed later in the related areas of the text.

## ACQUISITION STRATEGY AND PLANNING

### Acquisition Strategy

Prior to implementing any procurement action, the Acquisition Team should develop an acquisition strategy to serve as a roadmap to be followed from program initiation through post-production support. A primary goal in developing an acquisition strategy must be minimizing the time and cost of satisfying an identified and validated need, consistent with common sense and sound business practices. The acquisition strategy needs to include all of the critical events that will be used to govern the management of the program. It must link program decisions to demonstrated accomplishments in development, testing, initial production and ultimately life-cycle support. The acquisition strategy must be tailored to meet the specific needs of each individual program.

### Market Research (*FAR Part 10*)

One of the key steps in implementing the acquisition strategy and initiating the acquisition plan will be the performance of a thorough market research effort. This is the action taken to improve a purchasing organization's understanding of the market from which they procure their supplies and services. One of the major objectives is to determine if commercial items or non-developmental items are available to meet the Government's needs or could be modified to meet those needs. FAR Part 10, *Market Research*, prescribes the policies and procedures for federal agencies when conducting market research to arrive at the most suitable approach to acquiring, distributing, and supporting supplies and services.

Market research includes understanding the industry, manufacturing processes and external factors that affect the market. One technique of market research is a market survey to find sources to manufacture or supply a product or service. Another important benefit is to get a better focus on the current market price for a product or service. This will add significant credence to the budgeting exercises. It will also aid any cost or price analysis performed on bids and offers received during the solicitation and acquisition process. Agencies are encouraged to document the results of their market research efforts in a manner appropriate to the size and complexity of the acquisition.

**Planning Policy**

All Government agencies of the Executive Branch are required to comply with Part 7 of the FAR, *Acquisition Planning*. "Acquisition planning," means the process by which the efforts of all personnel responsible for an acquisition are coordinated and integrated through a comprehensive plan for fulfilling the agency need in a timely manner and at a reasonable cost. It includes developing the overall strategy for managing the acquisition.

In late 2010, the Department of Defense established *affordability requirements* that will have the same force as high-priority performance requirements. They will have an impact on both the planning process and the acquisition process.

FAR Part 7 prescribes the policies and procedures for developing acquisition plans and determining whether to use commercial or Government resources for the acquisition of supplies or services. It sets the guidelines for gathering information to aid in planning the most advantageous quantities of supplies to be bought. Guidelines for deciding whether it is more economical to lease equipment rather than buy it are also included.

**Integrated Product Teams**

An early effort in implementing the acquisition strategy and plan will be setting up an integrated product team (IPT). The IPT will be composed of representatives from all of the appropriate functional disciplines working together to build a successful program. The teams function in a spirit of teamwork, with the participants empowered and authorized, as much as possible, to make commitments for the organization they represent. That teamwork is essential to the integrated and concurrent development of the product and its associated processes.

To be fully effective, integrated product teams should be formed as soon as possible at the beginning of the program. That way the IPT can be utilized in performing as many acquisition functions as possible, including oversight and review of the acquisition process and subsequent program.

## Planning for Competition

The Executive Agencies must perform acquisition planning and conduct market surveys to promote full and open competition. When less than full and open competition is permitted by FAR Part 6, *Competition Requirements*, they must still obtain competition to the maximum extent practicable. They must, of course, do this with due regard to the nature of the supplies or services to be acquired. The market surveys will help the agencies find out what qualified sources are capable of satisfying the Government's requirements.

The plan must address all the technical, business, management and other significant considerations that will control the acquisition. The contents of each plan will vary, depending upon the nature, circumstances and stage of the acquisition. One important feature of the plan will describe how competition will be sought, promoted and sustained throughout the course of the acquisition. When full and open competition is not contemplated, the plan must address, in detail, how they will apply the authority contained in FAR 6.302, *Circumstances Permitting Other Than Full and Open Competition*, which permits such action. A further discussion of the plan is contained in Chapter 7, *Source Selection Process*.

The subject of planning and its relationship to competition is clearly stated in Competition Communiqué 6-87, for Navy and Marine Corps Competition Advocates, issued by Rear Admiral R.M. Moore, SC, USN, Competition Advocate General. The following is a quote from that communiqué:

> "Planning for competition must begin in the early conceptual stages of the program; it must be part and parcel of the program's acquisition strategy if the real benefits of competition are to be achieved. Competition planning must not only involve the current procurement, but also must be an inherent element of the plan for all procurements scheduled by the program office or requirements activity. Each procurement should provide or preserve needed building blocks for eventual competition. Competition can only be assured if it is the planned strategy of the program."

## Risk Management

Another important element of acquisition planning is establishing a risk management program early in the planning cycle. It is advisable to establish a "risk management team" composed of representatives from all of the disciplines that will be involved during the acquisition process. Even during the life of a program it is advisable to examine the various program elements for any new risks that may have come into being.

In the federal acquisition process, risk is a measure of the ability to achieve overall program objectives within defined cost, schedule, and technical constraints. There are two components of risk: (1) the probability of failing to achieve a particular outcome; and (2) the consequences of failing to achieve that outcome.

Risk management is the act or practice of controlling risk. The practice includes risk planning, assessing risk areas, developing risk-handling options, monitoring risks, and documenting the program. Risk management must be proactive. Risk reduction measures must be included in cost-performance trade-offs, where applicable. Likewise, technical risks must be assessed when reviewing proposed changes to a design or system. For more information on risk management, please see Chapter 8, *Managing Contract Risk*.

### Multiple Sources

The *1986 DOD Authorization Act (Pub. L. 99-145)* added a requirement concerning multiple sources to the acquisition plans for major DOD programs. Before beginning full-scale development of a major program (or major subsystem), the Secretary of Defense must prepare an acquisition strategy. The Secretary must also submit a report detailing the strategy to the House and Senate Armed Services Committees. The acquisition plan must include provisions to set up and maintain competitive alternative sources from the beginning of full-scale development through the end of production. Such sources must be capable of developing or producing systems which serve a similar function and compete effectively with each other, but need not be identical.

When determined that maintaining multiple sources is inappropriate, the Secretary of Defense may, after proper notice to Congress, waive the application of the requirement. This may be done in one of three manners. The waiver may apply to either phase of the procurement if it would cause unacceptable delay or be adverse to national security interests. It could apply only to the full-scale development phase if it would neither materially reduce technological risks nor improve the design in proportion to the additional cost. Or, it could apply to the production phase if maintaining multiple sources would increase the total program cost.

This aspect of multiple sourcing is not related to multiple award contracts associated with indefinite-delivery/indefinite-quantity contracts discussed in Chapter 5, *Contract Types*.

### Acquisition Streamlining

Federal Acquisition Circular (FAC) 84-39 published approved changes to FAR Part 7, *Acquisition Planning*, to institutionalize the implementation of acquisition streamlining. It is now the requirement that the various departments and agencies include acquisition streamlining into their acquisition planning process. Acquisition streamlining is any effort taken to be sure that only necessary and cost effective requirements are included in solicitations and contracts. Acquisition streamlining policies and procedures apply to the design, development and production of new systems or the modification. It also applies to existing systems that involve redesign of the system or subsystems.

The goal of acquisition streamlining is to exclude requirements that do not add to the operational effectiveness and suitability of the system, or effective management of its acquisition, operation or support. The obvious exceptions would be those requirements mandated by law or established agency policy. When the development of a system is started, the system-level requirements will be specified in terms of mission-performance, operational effectiveness, and operational suitability. "How-to-design" specifications are to be avoided whenever possible. Furthermore, the specifications, standards and related documents are to be tailored as much as possible to the unique circumstances of individual acquisition programs.

During all acquisition phases, solicitations and contracts are to state management requirements in terms of results needed rather than detailed "how-to-manage" procedures. The authority and accountability for determining which requirements should be incorporated in a system acquisition contract will be delegated to the Government program manager, subject to appropriate reviews within the agency.

DODD 5000.1, *The Defense Acquisition System*, DODI 5000.2, *Operation of the Defense Acquisition System,* and the *Defense Acquisition Guidebook*, contain policy direction on acquisition streamlining performance requirements, the technical package, and the contracting strategy (*DFARS 207.1, Acquisition Plans*).

**Simplified Acquisition Procedures (*FAR Part 13*)**

The Federal Acquisition Streamlining Act of 1994 (FASA) established a simplified acquisition threshold (SAT) of $100,000 which has been raised to $150,000. Agencies must use simplified acquisition procedures to the maximum extent practicable for all purchases of supplies or services not exceeding the simplified acquisition threshold, including purchases at or below the micro-purchase threshold of $3,000. The SAT goal is to streamline the acquisition process by reducing administrative costs, improving opportunities for small, small disadvantaged, and women-owned small business concerns to obtain a fair proportion of Government contracts, promoting efficiency and economy in contracting, and avoiding unnecessary burdens for agencies and contractors.

When conducting simplified acquisitions, agencies are directed to use the Government-wide commercial purchase card and electronic purchasing techniques to the maximum extent possible. They are also directed to make maximum use of electronic commerce when practicable and cost-effective (*FAR 13.003, Policy*). The policy is also for agencies to utilize innovative approaches in awarding contracts using simplified acquisition procedures.

In a simplified acquisition, when an agency will be requiring written proposals addressing unique Government requirements, the agency should advise offerors the evaluation factor weights, even though it is not required by the FAR *(Finlin Complex, Inc., B-288280, October 2001).*

# COMPETITION REQUIREMENTS

## Policies and Procedures

FAR Part 6, *Competition Requirements*, was added to the FAR as a result of the *Competition in Contracting Act (CICA)*. This part prescribes the policies and procedures the Executive Agencies must follow in promoting full and open competition in the acquisition process. It also prescribes how the agencies are to provide for the three directed categories of acquisition. Those three are: full and open competition; full and open competition after exclusion of sources; and procurement when made by other than full and open competition. The term "full and open competition," when used with respect to a contract action, means that all responsible sources are permitted to compete.

For purchases not exceeding the simplified acquisition threshold, contracting officers may solicit from one source if the CO determines that the circumstances of the contract action deem only one source reasonably available *(FAR 13.106-1(b), Soliciting Competition)*. That does not relieve contracting officers from promoting competition to the maximum extent practicable in all situations.

## Full and Open Competition (*FAR 6.1*)

The statutory requirement for full and open competition found in 10 U.S.C. 2304, applies to the Department of Defense, the Coast Guard and the National Aeronautics and Space Administration, while 41 U.S.C. 253 applies to all other Executive Agencies. Both of these permit certain limited exceptions, as discussed later in this Chapter. Contracting officers must promote and provide for full and open competition through the use of one of the following procedures:

- Sealed bidding
- Competitive proposals
- Combination of competitive procedures
- Other competitive procedures
  - Selection of architect-engineer contracts under Pub. L. 92-582 (*40 U.S.C. 541*)
  - Competitive selections of basic and applied research proposals for award (*FAR Part 35, Research and Development Contracting*)
  - Use of multiple award schedules issued under the procedures set up by the Administrator of General Services (GSA) consistent with the requirement of 41 U.S.C. 259(b)(3)(A).

## Full and Open Competition After Exclusion of Sources (*FAR 6.2*)

Agencies may exclude one or more sources from participation in a contract action under the circumstances noted below. Even after such exclusion, the contracting officer will still use the competitive procedures prescribed above.

Agencies may exclude a particular and alternative source or sources for the supplies or services being acquired. To do so the agency head will make a determination that one of the following situations would exist.

- It would increase or maintain competition and likely result in reduced costs.
- The Government would have a facility available for furnishing the supplies or services in case of a national emergency or industrial mobilization.
- The action would be establishing or maintaining an essential engineering, research, or development capability to be provided by an educational or other non-profit institution or a federally funded R&D Center.

In addition, the exclusion action could ensure continuous availability of a reliable source of supplies or services and satisfy projected needs based on a history of high demand, or satisfy a critical need for medical, safety or emergency supplies. Any such actions will be supported by a Determination and Findings (D&F). A D&F will be a document originated by the contracting officer that is supporting a decision that had been made or action taken. The D&F will be signed by the head of the agency or designee and will become a permanent record in the procurement file. D&F's are also discussed in Chapter 5.

To fulfill the statutory requirements relating to small business concerns (*FAR 19.5, Set-Asides for Small Business*) contracting officers may set aside solicitations to allow only such business concerns to compete, giving consideration to the recommendations of agency personnel having cognizance of the agency's small business programs.

## Other Than Full and Open Competition (*FAR 6.3*)

10 U.S.C. 2304(c) authorizes, under certain conditions, the Department of Defense, Coast Guard, and National Aeronautics and Space Administration to contract without providing full and open competition. 41 U.S.C. 253(c) grants that authority to the other Executive Agencies.

Contracting without providing full and open competition, or full and open competition after exclusion of sources, is a violation of one of those statutes. As noted in the next section, some exceptions are permitted.

Each contract awarded under one of these exceptions must cite the U.S. Code that applies to that exception.

The contracting officer cannot use either of the following reasons to issue a contract without providing for full and open competition. The lack of planning by the required activity is not an acceptable excuse. Neither are concerns related to the amount of funds available to the agency for the acquisition of supplies or services.

When not providing for full and open competition, the contracting officer must solicit offers from as many potential sources as is practicable under the circumstances.

**Circumstances Permitting Other Than Full and Open Competition (*FAR 6.302*)**

There are only seven (7) situations that permit procurements to be made under the third group, other than full and open competition. Those seven are discussed in the following paragraphs.

**Only One Responsible Source and No Other Supplies or Services Will Satisfy Agency Requirements (*FAR 6.302-1*)**

Full and open competition is not required when the supplies or services needed by an agency are available from only one responsible source. For DOD, NASA, and the Coast Guard, the requirement applies when only one or a limited number of responsible sources can be solicited, and no other type of supplies or services will satisfy the agency requirements (*U.S.C. 2304(c)(1); 41 U.S.C. 253(c)(1)*).

This authority may be used in situations such as the following:

- The required supplies or services are available from only one source (i.e., sole source).
- Follow-on contracts for the continued development or production of a major system or highly specialized equipment, including major components thereof, may be awarded to the original source. This is permitted when it is likely that competitive procedures would cause the Government to incur substantial duplication of cost not expected to be recovered through competition.
- This authority may also be cited if full and open competition would create acceptable delays in fulfilling the agency's requirements.

The acceptance of an unsolicited research proposal from one source is authorized, provided it demonstrates a unique and innovative concept. Unsolicited proposals are discussed later in Chapter 4, *Contracting Methods*.

Awards may be made to only one source where there is the existence of patent rights, copyrights, secret processes, the control of basic raw material, or similar circumstances.

Utility services (power, gas, water, etc.) may be procured from only one source, when circumstances dictate.

A "sole source" contract may be awarded when the agency head has determined, under their standardization program, that only one source is available. That source will have the specified makes or models of technical equipment and parts that will satisfy the agency needs for additional units or replacement items.

Written justification and approvals must support the use of this exception.

**Unusual and Compelling Urgency (*FAR 6.302-2*)**

This reason is cited when an agency's need for a supply or service is of such an unusual and compelling urgency that the Government's operations would be seriously impaired, financially or otherwise, without those supplies or services. The agency is then permitted to limit the number of sources from which it solicits bids or proposals, under the authority of 10 U.S.C. 2304(c)(2) or 41 U.S.C. 253(c)(2).

This statutory authority requires that offers be solicited from as many potential sources as is practicable under the circumstances. Furthermore, a written justification and approval must support use of this authority, even if produced after contract award due to time restrictions.

**Industrial Mobilization; Engineering, Developmental, or Research Capability; or Expert Services (*FAR 6.302-3*)**

Full and open competition is not necessary for award of a contract to a particular source or sources in all cases. It can be waived in order to maintain a facility, producer, manufacturer, or other supplier available for furnishing supplies or services in case of a national emergency or to achieve industrial mobilization. An exception can be made to establish or maintain an essential engineering, research, or development capability to be provided by an educational or other nonprofit institution or a federally funded research and development center or to acquire the services of an expert for any current or anticipated litigation or dispute (*10 U.S.C. 2304(c)(3)*).

Contracts awarded under these statutory authorities will be supported by written justifications and approvals.

**International Agreement (*FAR 6.302-4*)**

Other than competitive procedures are permitted when the terms of an international agreement, or a treaty between the United States and a foreign government or international organization, so dictate. The same holds true when written direction is received from a foreign Government which is repaying the agency for the cost of the acquisition of the supplies or services for that Government (*10 U.S.C. 2304(c)(4); 41 U.S.C. 253(c)(4)*).

Written justifications and approvals which are discussed below must support the use of this exception by all agencies except DOD, NASA and the Coast Guard.

### Authorized or Required by Statute (*FAR 6.302-5*)

The procedures for full and open competition need not be followed, when a statute expressly authorizes or requires that the acquisition be made through another agency or from a specified source. This is also possible when the agency's need is for a brand-name commercial item for authorized resale (*10 U.S.C. 2304(c)(5); 41 U.S.C. 253(c)(5)*). The brand-name authorized exception may be used only for the purchase of brand-name commercial items for resale through commissaries or other similar facilities.

Part 8 of the FAR, *Required Sources of Supplies or Services*, deals with the acquisition of supplies and services from or through Government supply sources. Sources such as Federal Prison Industries, Inc. (*FAR 8.6*) and Printing and Related Supplies (*FAR 8.8*) are solicited under this exception to full and open competition.

Written justifications and approvals must support the use of this exception.

### National Security (*FAR 6.302-6*)

This exception is cited when the disclosure of an agency's needs would compromise the national security, unless they are permitted to limit the number of sources from which they solicit bids or proposals. In those circumstances full and open competition procedures are not required under the authority of 10 U.S.C. 2304(c)(6), or 41 U.S.C. 253(c)(6).

This authority is used when the disclosure of the Government's needs would violate security requirements. The authority may not be used merely because the acquisition is classified or because access to classified matter is needed in order to submit a proposal and ultimately perform the contract. Therefore, solicitation of offers from as many potential sources as is practical under the circumstances, is required by this statute.

A written justification and the necessary approvals must support the use of this exception.

### Public Interest (*FAR 6.302-7*)

Full and open competition need not be provided for when the agency head determines that it would not be in the public interest in the particular acquisition concerned *(10 U.S.C. 2304(c)(7); 41 U.S.C. 253(c)(7))*.

This authority may be used when none of the other exceptions noted above apply. When this authority is used, written determinations and findings will be made by the agency head. In addition, Congress will be notified in writing of such a determination, not less than thirty (30) days before award of a contract. The agency head may also require the contracting officer to prepare a justification to support the determination.

### Justifications (*FAR 6.303*)

A contracting officer (CO) must not begin negotiations for a sole source contract, unless justified in writing, when required by one of the authorities cited in FAR 6.302, *Circumstances Permitting Other Than Full and Open Competition*. Neither should the CO start negotiations for a contract resulting from an unsolicited proposal. Additionally, the CO should not award any other contract without providing for full and open competition without such a written justification.

The contracting officer must certify to the accuracy and completeness of the justification. Obtaining approvals from higher authorities as required FAR 6.304, *Approval of the Justification*, may also be required by the agency. Written justifications and approvals are not required when a statute expressly requires that a procurement be made from a specified source.

The justifications are made on either an individual or class basis. However, justification for contracts awarded under FAR 6.302-7, *Public Interest*, will only be on an individual basis. The contracting officer must be sure that each contract action taken under the authority of a class justification is within the scope of that justification as approved. The contract file will be documented accordingly.

The justification must contain enough facts and rationale to justify the use of the specific authority cited. Each justification will include such things as:

- Nature and description of the action being approved.
- A description of the supplies or services, including their estimated value, required to meet the agency's needs.
- An identification of the statutory authority permitting other than full and open competition.
- A demonstration that the proposed contractor's unique qualifications or the nature of the acquisition requires use of the authority cited.
- A description of efforts made to ensure that offers are solicited from as many potential sources as is practicable.
- A determination by the contracting officer that the expected cost to the Government will be fair and reasonable.
- A description and results of the market research, conducted under FAR Part 10, *Market Research*, or a statement of the reasons it was not conducted.
- Any other information required by FAR 6.303-2, *Content*, as well as other facts supporting the use of other than full and open competition.

### Sealed Bidding and Competitive Proposals (*FAR 6.4*)

Contracting officers may use either sealed bidding, or competitive proposals, when contracting by means of full and open competition or full and open competition after exclusion.

When appropriate, either one may be used when contracting for other than full and open competition. These processes are discussed in more detail in Chapter 4, *Contracting Methods*.

Contracting officers will solicit sealed bids when all of the following conditions exist. First of all, there must be enough time to permit the soliciting, submission and evaluation of sealed bids. Next in importance is when the award will be made on the basis of price and other price-related factors. Sealed bids are used when it will not be necessary to conduct discussions with the responding offerors about their bids. Lastly, they will use sealed bidding procedures when there is a reasonable expectation of receiving more than one sealed bid.

Competitive proposals under negotiation procedures may be requested by contracting officers if sealed bids are determined to be inappropriate because the conditions described above are not present.

### Competition Advocates (*FAR 6.5*)

Section 20 of the *Office of Federal Procurement Policy Act* requires the head of each Executive Agency to appoint a competition advocate for the agency and for each procuring activity of the agency. The advocate must be someone other than the senior procurement executive of the agency. The person may not be assigned duties that would conflict with the duties and responsibilities for the advocate as specified in the FAR.

Each agency competition advocate will, among other things, have the following responsibilities:

- Be responsible for challenging barriers to the promotion of full and open competition in the acquisition of supplies and services by the agency.
- Review the contracting operations of the agency and identify and file reports with the agency senior procurement executive. The reports will identify opportunities and actions taken to achieve full and open competition, and any condition or action that has the effect of unnecessarily restricting competition.
- Recommend goals and plans for increasing competition.

## SPECIALIZED COMPETITION ACTIONS

### Small Business Programs (*FAR Part 19*)

There are numerous programs, created by a large variety of congressional mandates and executive orders, which affect the manner in which the Government deals with organizations that are classified as small businesses. These "small business programs" are concerned with providing contracting opportunities for the following organizations:

- Small business concerns
- Small disadvantaged business concerns
- Women-owned small business concerns
- HUBZone small business concerns

It is the Government's policy to provide maximum practical opportunities in its acquisitions to these types of concerns. Furthermore, they must also have the maximum practicable opportunity to participate as subcontractors in the contracts awarded by any executive agency, consistent with efficient contract performance (*FAR 19.201, General Policy*).

**Set-Asides for Small Business (*FAR 19.5*)**

In support of the stated policy, the Government may set-aside the award of certain acquisitions exclusively to small business concerns. Set-asides for acquisitions may be either total or partial. Total or partial set-asides may be conducted by using either sealed bids or competitive proposals.

A determination to make a set-aside may be a unilateral decision by the contracting officer. It may also be a joint determination made in concurrence with the recommendation of the procurement center's Small Business Administration representative. Once a product or service has been acquired successfully by a contracting officer (CO) on the basis of a small business set-aside, future requirements for that particular product or service will normally be acquired by that CO on the basis of a repetitive set-aside.

A contracting officer may set aside an individual acquisition or class of acquisitions. This may be done in the interest of maintaining or mobilizing the Nation's full productive capacity. It may be done in the event of war or for national defense programs. The set-asides are also for assuring that a fair proportion of Government contracts is placed with small business concerns.

Each acquisition of supplies or services that has an anticipated value exceeding $3,000, but not over $150,000, is automatically reserved exclusively for small business concerns. However, the contracting officer need not impose a set-aside if unable to obtain offers from two or more small business concerns that are competitive with market prices and cannot meet the required quality and delivery requirements of the services or goods being purchased. Total set-asides for small business participation, for acquisitions over $150,000, are made when there is a reasonable expectation that offers will be received from at least two (2) responsible small business concerns offering the products of other small business concerns. The contracting officer must also be sure that they will result in reasonable prices.

In partial set-asides the contracting officer will award the non-set-aside portion first using normal contracting procedures. The set-aside portion will be awarded as provided in the solicitation. Except for offers on the non-set-aside portion of partial set-asides, offers received from concerns that do not qualify as small business concerns will be rejected.

In 1997 Congress passed *The Historically Underutilized Business Zone (HUBZone) Act, (15 U.S.C. 631)* which created the HUBZone Contracting Program. The purpose of the HUBZone Program is to provide federal contracting assistance for qualified small business concerns located in historically underutilized business zones. Participating agencies must set aside acquisitions exceeding the simplified acquisition threshold for competition restricted to HUBZone small business concerns when there is a reasonable expectation that: (1) offers will be received from two or more HUBZone small business concerns; and (2) award will be made at a fair market price (*FAR 19.1305, HUBZone Set-Aside Procedures*). All federal agencies that employ one or more contracting officers are required to participate.

Significant solicitation and contract FAR clauses used by contracting officers are: *Notice of Total Small Business Set-Aside* at 52.219-6 and *Notice of HUBZone Set-Aside or Sole Source Award* at 52.219-3. In addition, contracting officers must insert the clause at 52.219-14, *Limitations on Subcontracting*, in solicitations and contracts for supplies, services, and construction, if any portion of the requirement is to be set aside or reserved for small business and the contract amount is expected to exceed $150,000.

**Leader-Follower Contracting**

With a diminishing industrial base confronting the Federal Government, the concept of leader-follower contracting has been getting serious consideration for certain acquisitions. The technique is considered to be extraordinary and limited to special circumstances. It does not have broad support from industry since some companies stand to receive less business because of it. FAR 17.4, *Leader Company Contracting*, contains the requirements and procedures applicable to leader-follower contracting.

The leader-follower technique hopes to achieve one or more of the following: reduced delivery times, better geographic dispersion of suppliers, maximum use of scarce tooling or special equipment, economies in production and elimination of proprietary data usage problems.

Under the concept, a developer or sole producer of a product or system is designated to be the leader company. In that role it will furnish assistance and know-how under an approved contract to one or more designated follower companies. They may then also become a source of supply. The contracting officer may award a prime contract to a leader company, compelling it to subcontract a designated portion of the required end item(s) to a specified follower company and to assist it to produce the required end item(s).

Under the second method a contract may be awarded to a leader company for the required assistance to a follower company. In addition, a prime contract may be awarded to the follower company for production of the items. The third method is to award a contract to a follower company, obligating it to subcontract with a designated leader company for the required assistance.

The contracting officer must be sure that any contract awarded under this concept contains a firm agreement regarding disclosure, if any, of contractor trade secrets, technical designs or concepts, and specific data, or software, of a proprietary nature.

Leader-follower contracting usually will be carried out after the concept definition and full scale development stages of an acquisition. It could be used for limited rate initial production (LRIP) prior to competitive award of full scale production contracts. If that does occur, the leader and follower companies would be competing for the major production role. They would split the total volume, such as a 60/40 ratio, depending upon the outcome of the competition. The Government must try to prevent a "happy follower" syndrome from developing within the competition. That is where one of the companies would be willing to accept the smaller position to get the business and not compete hard for the larger role.

**Planning for the Purchase of Supplies in Economic Quantities (*FAR 7.2*)**

Federal agencies are required to purchase supplies in quantities, where practicable, that will result in a total cost and unit cost that is most advantageous to the Government. However, they must not buy quantities that exceed those reasonably expected to be needed by the agency.

Contracting officers may insert the provision at FAR 52.207-4, *Economic Purchase Quantity – Supplies*, in solicitations for supply contracts. This provision invites offerors to respond and state an opinion on whether the quantity of the supplies proposed in the solicitation is economical. If applicable, they may recommend a quantity or quantities which would be more advantageous to the Government from an economic standpoint. The recommendations must include a quotation of the total price and the unit price for supplies procured in each recommended quantity.

The intent of the economic purchase quantity data is to assist inventory managers in establishing and evaluating economic order quantities for supplies under their cognizance. When the contracting officer determines that the Government should be ordering an item of supply in different quantities the inventory manager or requirements development organization must concur. The solicitation for the item will then be amended or canceled and a new requisition would be released.

**Commercial Contracting**

The Federal Acquisition Streamlining Act (FASA) of 1994 (*Pub. L. 103-355*) expanded the definition of commercial items and set forth a statutory preference for them in developing contractual requirements. The Act requires that, to the maximum extent practicable, contract requirements and market research must facilitate the use of commercial items. When commercial items are not available, there is a preference for nondevelopmental items previously developed by or for the Government.

FASA also exempts commercial item acquisitions from a number of unique Government statutes and requirements that ordinarily would apply to federal procurements. Nineteen laws impacted by FASA include: *Walsh-Healey Act, Drug-Free Workplace Act, Contingent Fees, Clean Air Act, Anti-Kickback Act, Procurement Integrity Act, Cost Accounting Standards, Truth in Negotiations Act.*

The requirements for commercial contracting are contained in FAR Part 12, *Acquisition of Commercial Items*. Contracting officers must use the policies unique to the acquisition of commercial items prescribed in Part 12 in conjunction with the policies and procedures for solicitation, evaluation and award prescribed in Part 13, *Simplified Acquisition Procedures*, Part 14, *Sealed Bidding*, or Part 15, *Contracting by Negotiation*, as appropriate for the particular acquisition.

The contracting officer may also use the streamlined procedure for soliciting offers for commercial items prescribed in FAR 12.603, *Streamlined Solicitation for Commercial Items*. For acquisitions of commercial items exceeding the simplified acquisition threshold of $150,000 but not exceeding $6,500,000, including options, contracting activities must employ the simplified procedures authorized by FAR 13.5, *Test Program for Certain Commercial Items*, to the maximum extent practicable.

The primary definition of a commercial item in FAR 2.101, *Definitions*, is:

> "Any item, other than real property, that is of a type customarily used by the general public or by non-governmental entities for purposes other than governmental purposes, and: (i) has been sold, leased, or licensed to the general public; or (ii) has been offered for sale, lease, or license to the general public."

Acquisition of commercial products begins with the agency defining their needs stated in functional terms in sufficient detail so that market research and analysis can be used to help determine whether commercial products, distribution systems, and logistic support are available to fill those needs. Consistent with statutes and exemptions noted above, and the requirements of FAR Part 6, *Competition Requirements*, agencies will acquire commercial products or distribution systems whenever they satisfy the Government's needs. Exceptions will be found in FAR Part 8, *Required Sources of Supplies and Services*. Furthermore, as specified in FAR 12.101, *Policy*, the agencies will require prime contractors and subcontractors at all tiers to incorporate, to the maximum extent practicable, commercial items or non-developmental items as components of the contractual items to be supplied to the Government.

Contracting officers may only use firm-fixed-price or fixed-price with economic price adjustment contracts when acquiring commercial items. However, indefinite-delivery contracts may be used where the prices are established based on a firm-fixed-price or fixed-price with economic price adjustment basis.

**Performance-Based Acquisition (*FAR 37.6*)**

As the Government strives to stay within its reduced budgets, the various agencies continue to seek less costly means of obtaining its supplies and services. One such concept is a return to performance-based acquisition. Performance-based acquisition (PBA) is the preferred method for acquiring services (FAR 37.102, *Policy*).

Performance-based acquisition methods are intended to ensure that the contractually required performance quality levels are achieved. Also, the total payments to the contractor are related to the degree of services performed in accordance with the contractual standards. Performance-based contracts will:

- Describe the requirements in terms of results rather than the methods of performance of the work in a performance work statement (PWS);
- Use measurable performance standards (i.e., terms of quality, timeliness, quantity, etc.) and quality assurance surveillance;
- Specify procedures for reductions of fee or for reductions to the price of a fixed-price contract when services are not performed or do not meet contract requirements; and
- Include performance incentives where appropriate. (*FAR 37.601, General*)

A performance-based acquisition may be described as one structured around the purpose of the program with the contractual requirements set forth in clear, specific, and objective terms with measurable outcomes. A PBA performance work statement must define the requirements in clear, concise language identifying specific work to be accomplished. As prescribed in FAR 37.602-1 (*Performance Work Statement*), when preparing a statement of work for a PBA program, the agency must, to the maximum extent practicable:

- Describe the work in terms of "what" is to be the required output rather than either "how" the work is to be accomplished or the number of hours to be provided;
- Enable assessment of work performance against measurable performance standards;
- Rely on the use of measurable performance standards and financial incentives in a competitive environment to encourage competitors to develop and institute innovative and cost-effective methods of performing the work; and
- Avoid combining requirements into a single acquisition that is too broad for the agency or a prospective contractor to manage effectively.

The types of contracts used in performance-based acquisition can vary significantly. Where services can be defined objectively and risk of performance is manageable, a fixed-price contract may be appropriate. Performance incentive provisions, either positive or negative or both, should be considered to encourage contractors to increase efficiency and maximize performance. The selection of contract type and any incentives should be made to motivate contractors to perform at optimal levels.

## PUBLICIZING CONTRACT ACTIONS

### Policy for Publicizing

Contracting officers must publicize the opportunities available for private parties and commercial organizations to vie for Government contracts. In addition, they must publicize certain information about the award of contracts. The purpose of publicizing these contract actions is threefold. It will increase competition. Industry participation in meeting Government requirements will be broadened. It will aid small business concerns, veteran-owned small business concerns, service-disabled veteran-owned small business concerns, HUBZone small business concerns, small disadvantaged business concerns, and women-owned small business concerns in obtaining contracts and subcontracts.

The policies and procedures for publicizing contract opportunities and award information are prescribed in FAR Part 5, *Publicizing Contract Actions*. The term "contract action" refers to an action resulting in a contract, including actions for additional supplies or services outside the existing contract scope. It does not include actions that are within the scope and under the terms of the existing contract, such as contract modifications issued pursuant to the Changes clause, or funding and other administrative changes.

Basically, procurement rules require an agency to publicize the availability of a forthcoming solicitation. This will allow the agency to get full and open competition for the procurement. In order to make it easier for potential vendors, the Contracting Officer has to select a category under which the procurement will be publicized on *FedBizOpps*.

For any part of the FAR that requires the publishing of a contract action, the contracting officer must transmit such notice to the Governmentwide Point of Entry (GPE). The GPE is the single point where Government business opportunities greater than $25,000 can be accessed electronically by the public. The GPE is located on the Internet at *http://www.fedbizopps.gov*.

### Dissemination of Information (*FAR 5.1*)

Proposed contract actions are publicized for the following purposes to:

- Increase competition at the prime or subcontract level;
- Broaden industry participation; and
- Meet socio-economic policies by assisting small businesses in obtaining contracts and subcontracts

By publicizing, opportunities are offered to all sources. Proposed contract actions that exceed $25,000 must be publicized through the Governmentwide Point of Entry (GPE), known as FedBizOpps (*www.fedbizopps.gov*). Proposed contract actions expected to exceed $15,000 but not $25,000 must be publicized by displaying a notice in a public place or by electronic means. There are exceptions to the publication requirements at FAR 5.202 and FAR 5.301.

Electronic dissemination available to the public at the contracting office may be used to satisfy the public display requirement. Contracting offices utilizing electronic systems for public posting must periodically publicize the methods for accessing such information.

Additional methods of dissemination include: preparing handouts listing proposed contracts; working with local trade associations; submitting brief announcements to various mass communication media for free publication; and placing paid advertisements in newspapers and other communication media. Paid advertising will be placed only when it is expected that effective competition cannot be otherwise obtained. Written authorization by the head of an agency is required for approval to publicize contract actions by means of paid advertisements in newspapers (*44 U.S.C. 3702*). Unless the agency head determines otherwise, advance written authorization is not required to place advertisements in media other than newspapers. Orders for paid advertisements may be placed directly with the media or through an advertising agency (*FAR 5.502, Authority* and *FAR 5.503, Procedures*).

**Publicizing and Response Time (*FAR 5.203*)**

Whenever an agency is required to publish a notice or synopsize a proposed contract action, it must be published on the Governmentwide Point of Entry (GPE) at least fifteen (15) days before issuance of the solicitation. Except for the acquisition of commercial items, they must allow at least thirty (30) days response time for receipt of bids or proposals from the date of issuance of the solicitation if the proposed contract action is expected to exceed the simplified acquisition threshold. If the contract action is categorized as research and development, they must allow at least forty five (45) days response time.

Notwithstanding the above, contracting officers must establish solicitation response times which will afford potential offerors a reasonable opportunity to respond for each contract action, including actions for which the notice of proposed contract action and solicitation information is accessible through the GPE. In so doing, the contracting officer will consider the circumstances of the individual procurement, such as complexity, commerciality, availability and urgency.

**Publicizing Subcontract Opportunities**

When it is in the Government's interest and significant subcontracting opportunities exist, contracting officers may publish in the GPE the names and addresses of prospective offerors. Prime contractors and subcontractors are encouraged to publicize subcontracting opportunities stemming from their Government business under the guidance of FAR 5.206, *Notices of Subcontracting Opportunities*.

In order to increase subcontracting opportunities for qualified HUBZone small business, small disadvantaged women-owned business, veteran-owned small business, and service-disabled veteran-owned small business concerns, the GPE synopses must be clear and concise descriptions of the supplies or services needed. Such information will allow interested parties to make informed business judgments as to whether they can participate in a Government contract. Synopses of subcontract opportunities should be prepared and submitted in accordance with FAR 5.207, *Preparation and Transmittal of Synopses*.

In addition to publicizing solicitations, contracting officers must synopsize in the GPE awards of all contracts exceeding $25,000 that are likely to result in the award of any subcontracts (*FAR 5.301, General*). Classified contract actions exempted under FAR 5.202(a) are excluded from this requirement.

**Exceptions to Publicizing**

The conditions under which contracting officers need not submit notice of contract actions for publication in the GPE are defined in FAR 5.202, *Exceptions*. Some of the more significant exceptions are as follows:

- Disclosure would compromise the national security.
- The Government would be seriously injured if the agency complied with the specific time periods.
- Upon written direction of a foreign Government funding the acquisition.
- Under terms of an international agreement or treaty.
- When the contract action is expressly authorized or required by a statute to be made through another Government agency.
- For utility services other than telecommunication services and only one source is available.
- Under the terms of an existing contract that was previously synopsized.
- The contract action is for an amount not expected to exceed the simplified acquisition threshold and the contract action will be made through GPE.
- Orders under indefinite-delivery contracts.
- For actions under the Small Business Innovation Development Act of 1982.
- Under an unsolicited proposal for a unique and innovative concept.
- For perishable subsistence supplies.
- For brand name commercial items for resale.
- Contracts performed in outlying areas outside the United States.
- For services in support of government litigation.

# CONTRACTOR QUALIFICATIONS

## Responsible Prospective Contractors

The law requires that contracts must be awarded to responsible contractors (*10 U.S.C. 2305(c); 41 U.S.C. 253*). The regulatory policy is clearly defined in FAR 9.103(a), which states: "Purchases shall be made from, and contracts shall be awarded to, responsible prospective contractors only." Criteria for determining responsibility are set forth in the laws, FAR 9.1, *Responsible Prospective Contractors*, and Comptroller General and court decisions.

Responsibility determinations are performed by contracting officers. They have the delegated authority to determine which prospective contractors are sufficiently competent, qualified, and eligible to perform the work under a forthcoming contract. There are two primary factors of consideration the contracting officer will use in the decision process. The first is whether a contractor will complete the contract in a satisfactory and timely manner. The other is whether the contractor meets collateral statutory and regulatory qualification criteria, such as socio-economic goals.

Contracting officers will apply the standards detailed in FAR 9.104, *Standards*, to determine that a prospective contractor is responsible. However, a contracting officer has broad discretion in finding a bidder responsible. The courts have been differential to a CO's decision in these matters. In determining that there has been a "satisfactory record". of integrity and business ethics, the CO will determine that the prospective contractor possesses basic honesty and trustworthiness and that the Government can rely on it to perform the contract. The contracting officer will give the greatest weight to any adjudicated matters where there is a history of repeated, pervasive, and significant violations.

The contracting officer must also decide if any special factors are to be used to determine the responsibility of the vendors or if the general responsibility factors noted below will be sufficient. When making such a decision the contracting officer may be open to second-guessing by protesters. To offset possible protests, contracting officers should coordinate nonresponsibility determinations based upon integrity and business ethics with the agency's legal counsel. A Government Accountability Office (GAO) decision confirmed that contracting officers have great discretion when making these decisions. When a protester challenged the contracting officer's decision to use a sealed bid acquisition, the GAO considered the reasonableness of the contracting officer's decision to not use special responsibility factors and agreed with the agency. "The protester's mere disagreement with the contracting officer's judgment does not make the determination unreasonable *(Tennessee Apparel Corporation, B-253178.3, B-253178.4, 1993)*."

Some of the more significant detailed criteria for determining responsibility and the source of the factors are discussed below:

1. In contracts for the manufacture or furnishing of supplies in an amount exceeding $10,000, the contractor must be the manufacturer of, or a regular dealer in, the supplies to be manufactured or used in the performance of the contract (*Walsh-Healey Act, 41 U.S.C. 35*).
2. A contractor who is qualified as a manufacturer may be awarded the contract even though the intention is to subcontract the work (*34 Comp. Gen. 595 (1955)*).
3. Contractors must have adequate financial resources, or the ability to obtain resources as required during performance of the contract (*FAR 9.104-1(a)*).
4. Prospective contractors must be able to comply with the required or proposed delivery or performance schedule, they must take into consideration all existing business commitments, commercial as well as governmental (*FAR 9.104-1(b)*).
5. The prospective contractor must have the necessary organization, experience, skills, equipment and facilities, or the ability to obtain them (*FAR 9.104-1(e)*).
6. A prospective contractor must have a satisfactory performance record, with emphasis placed on the quality of their products and services (*FAR 9.104-1(c)*).
7. Prospective contractors must have a satisfactory record of integrity and business ethics (*FAR 9.104-1(d)*). This includes satisfactory compliance with the law, including tax, labor and employment, environmental, antitrust, and consumer protection laws.
8. Federal employees are not eligible to provide supplies or services to the government, unless the needs of the Government cannot be met in any other way (*27 Comp. Gen. 735 (1948)*).
9. A prospective contractor's compliance with limitations on subcontracting shall take into account the time period covered by the contract base period or quantities plus option periods or quantities, if such options are considered when evaluating offers for award (*FAR 9.104-3(a)*).

An important factor affecting the determination of responsibility is the question of bankruptcy. In accordance with the provisions of FAR 42.903, *Solicitation Provision and Contract Clause*, contracting officers must insert the clause at 52.242-13, *Bankruptcy*, in all solicitations and contracts exceeding the simplified acquisition threshold. While a contractor cannot be precluded from award simply because it is in or has filed for Chapter 11, it will force the contracting officer to determine that the offeror has the ability to obtain the necessary financial resources necessary for performance of the contract. This is in keeping with the criteria listed in paragraph 3 above.

Detailed provisions for determining responsibility are made in FAR 9.1, *Responsible Prospective Contractors*. They essentially task the contracting officer to make an affirmative finding that the prospective contractor is a responsible bidder under the established criteria. This will be done by examining information in the file about the contractor. The CO will also make appropriate inquiries of the contractor. When considered necessary, the CO will conduct preaward surveys of plants and facilities.

The contracting officer's signing of a contract constitutes a determination that the prospective contractor is responsible with respect to the contract. Certain actions must be taken when an offer, on which an award would otherwise be made, is rejected because the prospective contractor is found nonresponsible. The contracting officer will make, sign and place in the contract file a determination of responsibility, which will state the basis for the determination and rejection.

Responsibility for small business concerns is determined by the Small Business Administration (SBA). It has the statutory authority to certify the competency of any small business concern as to capacity, competency, capability, credit, integrity, perseverance and tenacity. Contracting officers will accept SBA Certificates of Competency (COC) as conclusive, unless they have "substantial doubt," about the small business.

Part 19 of the FAR, *Small Business Programs*, provides the regulations for those concerns.

## Qualification Requirements

The policies and procedures regarding qualification requirements and the acquisitions that are subject to such requirements are contained in FAR 9.2, *Qualification Requirements*. The term "qualification requirements" means a requirement for testing or other quality assurance demonstration that must be completed by a prospective contractor before being awarded a contract.

An agency responsible for setting up the qualification requirement will urge manufacturers and other potential sources to demonstrate their ability to meet the standards specified for qualification. When possible they will give enough time to arrange for qualification before award.

In acquisitions subject to qualification requirements, the contracting officer will use presolicitation notices when appropriate, to advise potential suppliers before issuing solicitations involving qualification requirements. The notices will identify the specification containing the qualification requirement. They will designate an allowable period, consistent with delivery requirements, for prospective offerors to demonstrate their abilities to meet the standards specified for qualification. The notice will be publicized in the GPE in accordance with FAR 5.204, *Presolicitation Notices*. Whether or not a presolicitation notice is used, the general synopsizing requirements of FAR 5.2, *Synopses of Proposed Contract Actions*, will apply.

The contracting officer will insert the applicable provision at FAR 52.209-1, *Qualification Requirements*, in solicitations when the acquisition is subject to a qualification requirement. If a qualification requirement applies, the contracting officer will consider offers identified as meeting the requirement. Contractors on the applicable Qualified Parts List (QPL), Qualified Manufacturers List (QML), or Qualified Bidders List (QBL) will also be considered in the evaluation process. They will also consider an offeror that can satisfactorily demonstrate to the contracting officer that it or its product can meet the standards for qualification before the date specified for award.

**First Article Testing and Approval**

First article testing and approval ensures that the contractor can furnish a product that conforms to all requirements for acceptance. The policies and procedures for first article testing and approval are contained in FAR 9.3, *First Article Testing and Approval.*

The term "first article" relates to preproduction models, initial production samples, test samples, first lots, pilot lots or pilot models. Testing and evaluating the first article is to determine conformance with specified contract requirements either before or in the initial stage of production.

Before requiring testing and approval, the contracting officer must consider the following. What will be the impact on cost or time of delivery? Will there be a risk to the Government of foregoing such a test? Furthermore, what is the availability of other, less costly, methods of ensuring the desired quality?

The contracting officer will insert the clause at 52.209-3, *First Article Approval – Contractor Testing*, with any applicable alternates, in solicitations and contracts when the contract will require first article approval and the contractor is to conduct the first article testing. The clause at 52.209-4, *First Article Approval – Government Testing*, and any applicable alternates, will be used when first article approval applies and the Government will be responsible for conducting the first article testing.

Before first article approval, the purchase of materials or components, or start of production, is normally at the sole risk of the contractor. To reduce this risk, the contracting officer must provide enough time in the delivery schedule for acquisition of materials and components, and for production after receipt of first article approval. When Government requirements prevent this action, the contracting officer may, before approval of the first article, authorize the contractor to acquire specific materials or components. Authority to start production to the extent essential to meet the delivery schedule may also be granted. Costs incurred based on this authorization are allocable to the contract for progress payments and termination settlements in the event that the contract is terminated for the convenience of the Government.

**Debarment, Suspension and Ineligibility**

The policies and procedures relating to debarment and suspension of contractors and offerors are in FAR 9.4, *Debarment, Suspension and Ineligibility.* FAR 9.4 applies equally to all Executive Branch agencies when debarment, suspension or other Governmentwide exclusion is initiated under the Nonprocurement Common Rule. Every agency will honor exclusionary actions, debarments and suspensions by other agencies.

All agencies must establish procedures to implement these policies. They are encouraged to set up methods for coordinating their debarment and suspension actions with other agencies. The

General Services Administration (GSA) compiles and maintains the consolidated list of all contractors that have been debarred, suspended, proposed for debarment, or declared ineligible by the Government Accountability Office (GAO) or other agencies. The excluded parties list system is produced in accordance with FAR 9.404. The list is available to Government agencies through the System for Award Management (SAM). The electronic version of the list is updated daily.

In accordance with FAR, 9.405, *Effect of Listing,* contracting officers must request and obtain written approval from higher authority before conducting any ordering activities with contractors who have been debarred, suspended, or proposed for debarment which:

- Exceed the guaranteed minimum for indefinite quantity contracts;
- Are placed under optional use of Federal Supply Schedule contracts, blanket purchase agreements, or basic ordering agreements; or
- Add new work, exercise options, or otherwise extend the duration of the contract

Contractors debarred, suspended, or proposed for debarment are excluded from receiving contracts. A contractor debarred, suspended, or otherwise prohibited from entering into a federal procurement is also ineligible for grants, cooperative agreements and other nonprocurement activities. Agencies may not solicit offers from, award contracts to, or consent to subcontracts with such contractors. Waiver of this restriction is permitted when the acquiring agency's head or a designee determines there is a compelling reason for such action. Those contractors are also excluded from acting as agents or representatives of other contractors. Contractors listed as ineligible on the basis of statutory or other regulatory procedures are excluded from receiving contracts and, if applicable, subcontracts, under the conditions and for the period set forth in the statute or regulation. Agencies may not solicit offers from, award contracts to, or consent to subcontracts with such contractors under those conditions and for that period.

Prime contractors are prohibited from awarding subcontracts valued at $30,000 or more to any firm that has been suspended, debarred, or proposed for debarment unless there is a compelling reason to do so (FAR 52.209-6, *Protecting the Government's Interest When Subcontracting with Contractors Debarred, Suspended, or Proposed for Debarment*). Any prime contractor that intends to subcontract with one of those firms must provide the following safeguards to the Government:

- The contracting officer must be notified in writing of the planned action.
- Disclose its knowledge of the reasons for the subcontractor being listed with an exclusion in SAM.
- Explain its compelling reasons for doing business with that firm.
- Disclose how it will protect the Government’s interests.

Agencies may continue contracts or subcontracts in existence at the time a contractor becomes debarred, suspended or proposed for debarment. If the situation warrants it, some type of termination action will be taken. Existing contracts will not be renewed or extended with those contractors without compelling reasons.

**Debarment (FAR 9.406)**

Debarment relates to action taken by a debarring official to exclude a contractor from Government contracting and Government-approved subcontracting for a reasonable, specified period. A contractor so excluded is "debarred."

An agency's debarring official may debar a contractor for any of the following causes, as described in FAR 9.406-2, *Causes for Debarment*.

(a) Conviction of or civil judgment for:
   (1) Commission of fraud or a criminal offense in connection with: (i) obtaining; (ii) attempting to obtain; or (iii) performing a public contract or subcontract;
   (2) Violation of Federal or State antitrust statutes relating to the submission of offers;
   (3) Commission of embezzlement, theft, forgery, bribery, falsification or destruction of records, making false statements, tax evasion, violating Federal criminal tax laws, or receiving stolen property;
   (4) Intentionally affixing a label bearing a “Made in America” inscription to a product sold or shipped to the United States or its outlying areas, when the product was not made in the United States or its outlying areas; or
   (5) Commission of any other offense indicating a lack of business integrity or business honesty that seriously and directly affects the present responsibility of a Government contractor or subcontractor.

(b) The debarring official may debar a contractor, based upon a preponderance of evidence, for:
   (1) Violation of the terms of a Government contract or subcontract so serious as to justify debarment, such as: (i) willful failure to perform in accordance with the terms of one or more contracts; or (ii) a history of failure to perform, or of unsatisfactory performance of, one or more contracts.
   (2) Violations of the Drug-Free Workplace Act of 1988 (*Pub. L. 100-690*), as indicated by: (i) the offeror’s submission of a false certification; (ii) the contractor’s failure to comply with its certification; or (iii) such a number of contractor employees having been convicted of violations of criminal drug statutes occurring in the workplace, as to indicate that the contractor has failed to make a good faith effort to provide a drug-free workplace.
   (3) Commission of an unfair trade practice as defined in FAR 9.403, *Definitions*.

(c) Any other cause of so serious or compelling a nature that it affects the present responsibility of a Government contractor of subcontractor.

Debarments are imposed for periods that are commensurate with the seriousness of the cause(s) but generally not more than three (3) years. If a suspension precedes a debarment, the suspension period must be considered in determining the debarment period. The debarring official may extend the debarment for an additional period. That may be done if, based upon new facts and circumstances, the official determines that the extension is necessary to protect the Government's interest.

In contrast, the debarring official may reduce the period or extent of debarment upon the contractor's request. Any such action must be supported by documentation. Reasons for such an action may be newly discovered material evidence, or the reversal of the conviction or judgment upon which the debarment was based. There could also be a bona fide change in ownership or management or elimination of other causes for which the debarment was imposed.

It is the debarring official's responsibility to determine whether debarment is in the Government's interest. The debarring official may, in the public interest, debar a contractor for any of the causes noted above, using the procedures in FAR 9.406-3, *Procedures*. The existence of a cause for debarment, however, does not necessarily require that the contractor be debarred; the seriousness of the contractor's acts or omissions and any remedial measures or mitigating factors should be considered in making any debarment decision. Before arriving at any debarment decision, the debarring official should consider factors such as those listed in Figure 3-1, *Factors to Be Considered in Debarment or Suspension*, on page 59.

**Suspension (FAR 9.407)**

Suspension is action taken by a suspending official to disqualify a contractor temporarily from Government contracting and Government-approved subcontracting. A contractor so disqualified is "suspended." A suspension is a temporary debarment. Suspension allows the Government to keep a contract from a company it thinks has done something wrong, while the Government decides whether or not to bar the contractor from receiving a contract. Since suspension and possible debarment are such serious penalties, the contracting officer must suspend the contractor only if it has good proof of a wrongdoing. Therefore, the CO must obtain accurate information before taking such actions.

# FACTORS TO BE CONSIDERED IN DEBARMENT OR SUSPENSION

---

1. Whether the contractor had effective standards of conduct and internal control systems in place at the time of the activity which constitutes cause for debarment or had adopted such procedures prior to any Government investigation of the activity cited as a cause for debarment.

2. Whether the contractor brought the activity cited as a cause for debarment to the attention of the appropriate Government agency in a timely manner.

3. Whether the contractor has fully investigated the circumstances surrounding the cause for debarment and, if so, made the result of the investigation available to the debarring official.

4. Whether the contractor cooperated fully with Government agencies during the investigation and any court or administrative action.

5. Whether the contractor has paid or has agreed to pay all criminal, civil, and administrative liability for the improper activity, including any investigative or administrative costs incurred by the Government, and has made or agreed to make full restitution.

6. Whether the contractor has taken appropriate disciplinary action against the individuals responsible for the activity which constitutes cause for debarment.

7. Whether the contractor has implemented or agreed to implement remedial measures, including any identified by the Government.

8. Whether the contractor has instituted or agreed to institute new or revised review and control procedures and ethics training programs.

9. Whether the contractor has had adequate time to eliminate the circumstances within the contractor's organization that led to the cause for debarment.

10. Whether the contractor's management recognizes and understands the seriousness of the misconduct giving rise to the cause for debarment and has implemented programs to prevent recurrence.

The existence or nonexistence of any mitigating factors or remedial measures noted on this list is not necessarily determinative of a contractor's present responsibility. Accordingly, if a cause for debarment exists, the contractor has the burden of demonstrating, to the satisfaction of the debarring official, its present responsibility and that debarment is not necessary.

**Figure 3-1**

Upon adequate evidence, an agency's suspending official may suspend a contractor suspected of any of the following situations:

- Commission of fraud or a criminal offense in connection with (i) obtaining, (ii) attempting to obtain, or (iii) performing a public contract or subcontract.
- Violation of federal or state antitrust statutes relating to the submission of offers.
- Commission of embezzlement, theft or forgery, bribery, falsification or destruction of records, making false statements, or receiving stolen property.
- Violations of the Drug-Free Workplace Act of 1988.
- Intentionally affixing a label bearing a "Made in America" inscription to a product not made in the United States.
- Commission of an unfair trade practice as defined in FAR 9.403.
- Commission of any other offense indicating a lack of business integrity or business honesty that seriously and directly affects the present responsibility of a Government contractor or subcontractor.

An indictment for any of the above noted causes is adequate evidence for suspension. Furthermore, the suspending official may, upon adequate evidence, also suspend a contractor for other causes. Those are usually of so serious or compelling a nature that they affect the present evaluation of the "responsibility" of a Government contractor or subcontractor.

The existence of a cause for suspension does not necessarily require that the contractor be suspended. The suspending official should consider the seriousness of the contractor's acts or omissions and may, but is not required to, consider remedial measures or mitigating factors, such as those set forth in FAR 9.406-1(a), see Figure 3-1 on page 59.

A suspension will be for a temporary period, pending completion of an investigation of the causes of suspension and any following legal proceedings, unless ended sooner by the suspending official. If legal proceedings are not begun within twelve (12) months after the date of the suspension notice, the suspension will be terminated. An Assistant Attorney General may request and receive an extension for up to an additional six (6) months.

### Certification

For awards expected to exceed $30,000, offerors are required to certify whether they or their principals are presently suspended, debarred, or proposed for debarment. The certification includes a disclosure of convictions of a crime or civil judgment for commission of fraud or other criminal offenses connected with efforts to obtain or perform federal, state or local contracts. The certificate also extends to violations of federal statutes and numerous other crimes.

Obviously, negative information or false certification could cause an offeror to be declared non-responsible with sufficient grounds for elimination from award consideration.

The contracting officer will insert the clause at FAR 52.209-5, *Certification Regarding Responsibility Matters*, in solicitations for procurements expected to exceed the simplified acquisition threshold.

## Organizational Conflicts of Interest

FAR 9.5, *Organizational and Consultant Conflicts of Interest*, prescribes responsibilities, general rules, and procedures for identifying, evaluating and resolving organizational conflicts of interest. It also provides examples to aid contracting officers in applying those rules and procedures to individual contracting situations.

The FAR definition of an "organizational conflict of interest" reads:

> "Organizational conflict of interest" means that because of other activities or relationships with other persons, a person is unable or potentially unable to render impartial assistance or advice to the Government, or the person's objectivity in performing the contract work is or might be otherwise impaired, or a person has an unfair competitive advantage.

An "organizational conflict of interest" (OCI) can exist due to the nature of the work to be performed under a Government contract. Without some restriction on future activities, it could result in an unfair competitive advantage to the contractor or impair the contractor's objectivity in performing the contract work. The burden of identifying and mitigating an OCI lies first with vendors, but ultimately the burden falls upon the contracting officer (CO). During the solicitation stage of a procurement, contracting officers must focus on mitigating significant organizational conflicts of interest and not just any type of OCI. Proof of a significant potential OCI requires real "hard facts." The CO must exercise common sense, good judgment, and sound discretion in assessing whether a potential OCI exists.

An OCI may involve either a profit or nonprofit organization and occur in any kind of acquisition. However, organizational conflicts of interest are more likely to occur in contracts involving the following situations:

- Management support services.
- Consulting or other professional services.
- Contractor performance of or assistance in technical evaluations of Governmental requirements and offers and performance of other contractors.
- Systems engineering and technical direction work performed by a contractor that does not have overall contractual responsibility for development or production.

The general rules prescribing limitations on contracting as a means of avoiding, neutralizing, or mitigating OCI situations that might otherwise exist in an acquisition are described in FAR 9.505, *General Rules*. The limitations described cover the following situations:

- A contractor that provides systems engineering and technical direction for a system but does not have overall contractual responsibility for its development, its integration, assembly, and check-out, or its production. Normally, such a contractor will not be awarded a contract to supply the system or any of its major components. Furthermore, that contractor will not be a contractor or consultant to a supplier of the system or any of its major components.
- In most cases a contractor that prepares and furnishes complete specifications covering non-developmental items, to be used in a competitive acquisition, will not be allowed to furnish those items, either as a prime contractor or as a subcontractor, for a reasonable period of time.
- When a contractor prepares, or assists in preparing, a work statement to be used in competitively acquiring systems or services (or provides material leading directly, predictably, and without delay to such a work statement) they will not be permitted to supply the system, major components of the system or the services. Exceptions to this would be when the contractor is the sole source or has participated in the development and design work. An exception would also include the case where more than one contractor has been involved in preparing the statement of work.
- Contracts involving technical evaluations of other contractors' offers or products or consulting services can cause an organizational conflict of interest situation. This will occur when a contractor is to evaluate, or advise the Government concerning its own products or activities, or those of a competitor, without proper safeguards to ensure objectivity and protect the Government's interests.
- In contracts where a contractor will have access to proprietary information of other companies in performing advisory services for the Government, the contractor must enter into a written agreement with the other companies. In the agreement the parties will state their intent to protect each other's information from unauthorized use or disclosure for as long as it remains proprietary. They will also agree to refrain from using the information for any purpose other than that for which it was furnished. The contracting officer will obtain copies of those agreements and ensure that they are properly executed.

One prime example where unfair advantage exists is found in Service/Support contracts where an organization has its personnel in residence with a Government agency. It is not important whether or not they have access to the agency's acquisition data, their very presence will make them suspect. If they are allowed to compete on a procurement and actually receive the contract award, other offerors will most likely file a protest. Therefore, in order to avoid a potential conflict of interest situation, that organization should be excluded from any competitive solicitation.

When, as a condition of award, a contractor's eligibility for future prime contract or subcontract awards will be affected, the solicitation must contain a proposed OCI clause. The clause will specify both the nature and duration of the proposed restraint. The resulting contract will contain the final OCI clause as negotiated by the contracting officer and the successful offeror. The duration of the restraint imposed by such a clause must be limited to a fixed term. The term must be long enough to avoid circumstances of unfair competitive advantage or potential bias. The contracting officer will use the information contained in FAR 9.507-1, *Solicitation Provisions*, and FAR 9.507-2, *Contract Clause*, as guidance in preparing and negotiating the respective clauses.

Conflict of interest restrictions apply to organizations and individuals. Consultants to the Government and Government contractors are specifically addressed in the *DOD Appropriations Act of 1989, Pub. L. 100-463*. All contractors are encouraged to consider carefully the potential for conflicts of interest in all of their activities associated with federal procurement.

**Procurement Integrity**

FAR Part 3, *Improper Business Practices and Personal Conflicts of Interest*, was expanded by one of the provisions of the Office of Federal Procurement Policy (OFPP) Act Amendments of 1988 (*Pub. L. 100-679*). FAR 3.104, *Procurement Integrity*, was created to implement Section 27 of the OFPP Act (the Procurement Integrity Act) (*41 U.S.C. 423*). The Act and FAR 3.104 contain significant restrictions on Government personnel and contractors alike on matters relating to the procurement process. FAR 3.104-2, *General*, cites several other statutes and regulations that deal with the same or related prohibited conduct. All parties participating in the procurement/acquisition process must be thoroughly familiar with and adhere to all of the provisions spelled out in FAR 3.104.

During the conduct of any federal agency procurement action of $10,000,000 or more, competing contractors, their personnel and agents have the following limitations imposed upon them. They cannot discuss or offer employment with any procurement official of that agency. They are generally prohibited from soliciting or obtaining from any official or employee of a federal agency proprietary or source selection information. The prohibitions on gifts and gratuities to federal employees are emphasized.

In the same manner, federal procurement officials have the same limitations placed upon them. They cannot solicit or accept employment, gifts or gratuities. There are also post-employment restrictions on those officials. As cited in FAR 3.104-2, there are certain prohibited activities by former Government employees, including representation of a contractor before the Government in relation to any contract or other particular matter involving specific parties on which the former employee participated personally and substantially while employed by the Government. However, nothing in the regulations prohibit a former official from a federal agency from accepting compensation from any division or affiliate of a contractor that does not produce the same or similar products or services.

Federal procurement officials cannot disclose any proprietary or source selection information regarding a procurement, directly or indirectly, to any person other than someone authorized by the head of the agency or the contracting officer.

The sanctions for violating the laws are severe for both Government and contractor personnel. Criminal and civil penalties, and administrative remedies, may apply to any conduct which violates these statutes and regulations. The administrative remedies, which include contract termination, suspension and debarment, in some cases can be even more of a deterrent. Few contractors will want to jeopardize their opportunity to participate in future Government procurements, which the administrative penalties could cause to happen.

**System for Award Management (SAM)**

The General Services Administration's (GSA) Office of Governmentwide Policy is consolidating the governmentwide acquisition and award support systems into one new system – the System for Award Management (SAM).

Automation of the federal procurement and awards processes has evolved over time through development of systems to perform individual steps in the process. Paper-based systems and business processes were automated as the internet became widely available. These systems were adopted across the Federal Government and are now managed under one organization. The Integrated Acquisition Environment (IAE) manages these systems and their system capabilities have been organized around six key functional areas.

SAM is currently being developed in phases. Phase 1, released in July 2012, includes the capabilities found previously in Central Contractor Registration (CCR)/Federal Agency Registration (FedReg), Online Representations and Certifications Application (ORCA), and the Excluded Parties List System (EPLS). Upcoming releases to SAM will include the capabilities found today in the electronic Subcontracting Reporting System (eSRS)/FFATA Subaward Reporting System (FSRS), the Catalog of Federal Domestic Assistance (CFDA), Federal Business Opportunities (FBO), Wage Determinations On Line (WDOL), Federal Procurement Data System (FPDS), and the combination of Past Performance Information Retrieval System (PPIRS), Contractor Performance Assessment Reporting System (CPARS), and the Federal Awardee Performance and Integrity Information System (FAPIIS).

# ACQUISITION OF MAJOR SYSTEMS

## OMB Circular A-109

Office of Management and Budget (OMB) Circular No. A-109, *Major System Acquisition*, established policies to be followed by executive branch agencies in the acquisition of major systems. A "major system" as described in FAR 2.101, *Definitions*, means "that combination of elements that will function together to produce the capabilities required to fulfill a mission need. The elements may include hardware, equipment, software, or any combination thereof, but exclude construction or other improvements to real property."

The policies and procedures to be followed by Government agencies and departments in acquiring major systems are prescribed in FAR Part 34, *Major System Acquisition*, which implements the relevant acquisition policies of OMB Circular No. A-109. The Department of Defense (DOD) has implemented the system acquisition policies and procedures through the DOD 5000 series consisting of DOD Directive 5000.1, *The Defense Acquisition System*, DOD Instruction 5000.2, *Operation of the Defense Acquisition System*, and the Defense Acquisition Guidebook which contains detailed procedures for acquiring major systems (https://acc.dau.mil).

It is the expressed policy of the Government to promote innovation and full and open competition in the development of major system concepts. This is done by expressing agency needs and major system acquisition program objectives in terms of the agency's mission and not in terms of specified systems to satisfy needs. They also focus agency resources and special management attention on activities conducted in the initial stage of major programs. It is also the policy to sustain effective competition between alternative system concepts and sources for as long as it is economically beneficial to the Government and practicable for the agency to do so.

The type of contract to be utilized in a major system acquisition can be critical. A cost-plus-fixed-fee contract normally should not be used in development of a major system once preliminary exploration, studies, and risk reduction have indicated a high degree of probability that the development is achievable and the Government has established reasonably firm performance objectives and schedules. On the other hand, contracts containing technical performance incentives may be particularly appropriate, both in the development phase (when performance objectives are known and the fabrication of prototypes for test and evaluation is required) and the production phase (if improved performance is attainable and highly desirable to the Government).

System acquisitions normally designated as major are those programs that:

- Are directed at and critical to fulfilling an agency mission;
- Entail the allocation of relatively large resources; and
- Warrant special management attention.

Individual agency heads are given authority to establish additional criteria and relative dollar thresholds for determining what constitutes a major system, and to establish the acquisition process and procedures for their agency.

Typical major system acquisition programs will include such projects as:

- Federal office buildings
- Hospitals
- Energy programs
- Transportation systems
- Defense systems
- Space programs
- Automated information systems

## Major System Acquisition Cycle

The acquisition process is iterative in nature. Fundamental to the entire process is an agency's Mission Analysis process. Each agency has one or more national mission responsibilities. When analysis identifies a deficiency in existing agency capabilities or an opportunity to establish new capabilities in response to a technologically feasible opportunity, a mission need statement will be submitted to the agency head for approval. Such approval allows the agency to initiate budget requests.

With full authority to explore alternative system design concepts, solicitations will be formally issued in terms of mission needs. Industrial and not-for-profit organizations will be requested to provide alternative system design concepts to satisfy those needs.

Parallel short-term contracts are awarded for those concepts that show some promise and are selected for further exploration. This allows the Government and contractor to expand on those concepts and also reduce any technical uncertainties found in those solutions.

The second major decision point involves selection of a limited number of the alternative systems for further exploration to assure the mission need and program objectives will be met.

Competitive demonstration contracts are let to verify that the chosen concepts are sound, perform in an operational environment, and provide a basis for selection of the system design concept(s) to be continued into full-scale development.

With verification that the chosen system design concept(s) is sound and the risks are acceptable, and when the mission need and program objectives are reaffirmed, the agency head may authorize full-scale development (FSD) and limited production.

FSD will include test and evaluation of the initial production system. Following satisfactory test results and reconfirmation of the mission need and program objectives, the agency head may authorize full production.

As production systems become available, they are deployed into operational use, thereby providing the capability originally identified in the Mission Need Statement. This new capability then becomes a factor in the continuing cycle of mission analyses for the agency.

In every acquisition program there are certain core issues that must be addressed at the appropriate milestone. Those issues would include program definition, program structure, program design, program assessments and periodic reporting. The proper authorities will tailor these issues to minimize the time it takes to satisfy an identified need consistent with common sense, sound business management practice, applicable laws and regulations, and the time sensitive nature of the requirement itself. Tailoring may be applied to various aspects of the acquisition process, including program documentation, acquisition phases, timing and scope of decision reviews, and decision levels.

# CHAPTER 4

# CONTRACTING METHODS

---

## ACQUISITION BY SEALED BIDDING

### General Nature of Sealed Bidding

The current regulations governing procurement by sealed bidding are in FAR Part 14, *Sealed Bidding*. Sealed bidding is a method of contracting that employs competitive sealed bids and public opening of the bids and awards, as prescribed in the regulation. Fundamental to sealed bidding are the principles that an invitation to bid is a call for offers or bids, and is not itself an offer. In addition a bid may NOT be withdrawn or modified after the opening of bids. This later principle is referred to as the "Firm-Bid Rule."

Sealed bidding is required whenever the conditions of FAR 6.401(a), *Sealed Bidding and Competitive Proposals*, are met. The next paragraph summarizes those conditions. This requirement will apply to any proposed contract action entered into under FAR Part 6, *Competition Requirements*. The sealed bidding procedures may be used for classified actions if their use does not violate agency security requirements (*FAR 14.103-1, General*).

Sealed bidding can operate efficiently only when all of the following conditions are present:

- There is a complete, detailed and realistic specification or purchase description.
- There are two or more suppliers available, willing, and able to compete effectively for the Government's business.
- Selection of the successful bidder can be made, without discussions of the bid, on the basis of price or price-related factors alone.
- Enough time is available to prepare a complete statement of the Government's needs and the terms under which it will do business (i.e., the solicitation) and to permit bid submission and evaluation.

If any of the above conditions are not present, a contract should be solicited under one of the alternatives to the requirement for sealed bidding in 10 U.S.C. 2304 or 41 U.S.C. 253 as discussed below.

The purpose of competitive bidding statutes is to "give all persons equal right to compete for Government contracts; to prevent unjust favoritism, or collusion or fraud in the letting of contracts for supplies; and thus to secure for the Government the benefits which arise from competition" (*U.S. vs. Brookridge Farm, Inc. (10$^{th}$ Cir. 1940) 11 F.2d 461, 463*).

# STANDARD FORM 33 – SOLICITATION, OFFER AND AWARD

**SOLICITATION, OFFER AND AWARD**

1. THIS CONTRACT IS A RATED ORDER UNDER DPAS (15 CFR 7900) ▶ RATING | PAGE OF PAGES

2. CONTRACT NUMBER | 3. SOLICITATION NUMBER | 4. TYPE OF SOLICITATION ☐ SEALED BID (IFB) ☐ NEGOTIATED (RFP) | 5. DATE ISSUED | 6. REQUISITION/PURCHASE NUMBER

7. ISSUED BY CODE | 8. ADDRESS OFFER TO *(If other than item 7)*

NOTE: In sealed bid solicitations "offer" and "offeror" mean "bid" and "bidder".

**SOLICITATION**

9. Sealed offers in original and ______ copies for furnishings the supplies or services in the Schedule will be received at the place specified in item 8, or if hand carried, in the depository located in ______ until ______ *(Hour)* local time ______ *(Date)*

CAUTION - LATE Submissions, Modifications, and Withdrawals: See Section L, Provision No. 52.214-7 or 52.215-1. All offers are subject to all terms and conditions contained in this solicitation.

10. FOR INFORMATION CALL ▶ | A. NAME | B. TELEPHONE *(NO COLLECT CALLS)* AREA CODE / NUMBER / EXT. | C. E-MAIL ADDRESS

**11. TABLE OF CONTENTS**

| (X) | SEC | DESCRIPTION | PAGE(S) | (X) | SEC | DESCRIPTION | PAGE(S) |
|---|---|---|---|---|---|---|---|
| | | PART I - THE SCHEDULE | | | | PART II - CONTRACT CLAUSES | |
| | A | SOLICITATION/CONTRACT FORM | | | I | CONTRACT CLAUSES | |
| | B | SUPPLIES OR SERVICES AND PRICES/COSTS | | | | PART III - LIST OF DOCUMENTS, EXHIBITS AND OTHER ATTACH. | |
| | C | DESCRIPTION/SPECS./WORK STATEMENT | | | J | LIST OF ATTACHMENTS | |
| | D | PACKAGING AND MARKING | | | | PART IV - REPRESENTATIONS AND INSTRUCTIONS | |
| | E | INSPECTION AND ACCEPTANCE | | | K | REPRESENTATIONS, CERTIFICATIONS AND OTHER STATEMENTS OF OFFERORS | |
| | F | DELIVERIES OR PERFORMANCE | | | | | |
| | G | CONTRACT ADMINISTRATION DATA | | | L | INSTRS., CONDS., AND NOTICES TO OFFERORS | |
| | H | SPECIAL CONTRACT REQUIREMENTS | | | M | EVALUATION FACTORS FOR AWARD | |

**OFFER *(Must be fully completed by offeror)***

NOTE: Item 12 does not apply if the solicitation includes the provisions at 52.214-16, Minimum Bid Acceptance Period.

12. In compliance with the above, the undersigned agrees, if this offer is accepted within ______ calendar days *(60 calendar days unless a different period is inserted by the offeror)* from the date for receipt of offers specified above, to furnish any or all items upon which prices are offered at the set opposite each item, delivered at the designated point(s), within the time specified in the schedule.

| 13. DISCOUNT FOR PROMPT PAYMENT *(See Section I, Clause No. 52.232-8)* ▶ | 10 CALENDAR DAYS (%) | 20 CALENDAR DAYS (%) | 30 CALENDAR DAYS (%) | CALENDAR DAYS(%) |
|---|---|---|---|---|

| 14. ACKNOWLEDGMENT OF AMENDMENTS *(The offeror acknowledges receipt of amendments to the SOLICITATION for offerors and related documents numbered and dated)*: | AMENDMENT NO. | DATE | AMENDMENT NO. | DATE |
|---|---|---|---|---|
| | | | | |

15A. NAME AND ADDRESS OF OFFEROR | CODE | FACILITY | 16. NAME AND TITLE OF PERSON AUTHORIZED TO SIGN OFFER *(Type or print)*

15B. TELEPHONE NUMBER: AREA CODE | NUMBER | EXT. | ☐ 15C. CHECK IF REMITTANCE ADDRESS IS DIFFERENT FROM ABOVE - ENTER SUCH ADDRESS IN SCHEDULE. | 17. SIGNATURE | 18. OFFER DATE

**AWARD *(To be completed by Government)***

19. ACCEPTED AS TO ITEMS | 20. AMOUNT | 21. ACCOUNTING AND APPROPRIATION

22. AUTHORITY FOR USING OTHER THAN FULL OPEN COMPETITION: ☐ 10 U.S.C. 2304 (c) ☐ 41 U.S.C. 253 (c) | 23. SUBMIT INVOICES TO ADDRESS SHOWN IN *(4 copies unless otherwise specified)* ▶ ITEM

24. ADMINISTERED BY *(If other than Item 7)* | 25. PAYMENT WILL BE MADE BY CODE

26. NAME OF CONTRACTING OFFICER *(Type or print)* | 27. UNITED STATES OF AMERICA *(Signature of Contracting Officer)* | 28. AWARD DATE

IMPORTANT - Award will be made on this Form, or on Standard Form 26, or by other authorized official written notice.

AUTHORIZED FOR LOCAL REPRODUCTION
Previous edition is unusable

STANDARD FORM 33 (REV., 9-97)
Prescribed by GSA - Far (48 CFR) 53.214 (c)

**Figure 4-1**

An unsuccessful bidder has no remedy to compel an award to himself, to prevent an award to another bidder, or to recover damages for failure to be awarded a contract. However, the Court of Claims said that a low bidder would have the right to recover its expenses of preparing a bid if an arbitrary and capricious solicitation of bids with no intention to use them were proved (*Heyer Prod. Co. vs. U.S. (Ct. Cl. 1959) 140F Supp. 409 and 177F Supp. 251*).

Failure to comply with formal advertising (sic., sealed bidding) requirements renders the resulting contract invalid (*New York Mail and Newspaper Transp. Co. vs. U.S. (Ct. Cl. 1957) 154F Supp. 271).* The general requirements for sealed bidding specify that no award shall be made as a result of that acquisition unless:

- Bids are solicited as required by FAR 14.2, *Solicitation of Bids*;
- Bids are submitted as required by FAR 14.3, *Submission of Bids*;
- The contracting officer meets the requirements of FAR 1.602-1(b), which states that: "No contract shall be entered into unless the contracting officer ensures that all requirements of law, executive orders, regulations, and all other applicable procedures, including clearances and approvals, have been met";
- The requirements of FAR Part 6, *Competition Requirements*, have been met; and
- The award is made to the responsible bidder whose bid conforms to the invitation for bids and is most advantageous to the Government, considering only price and price-related factors identified in the invitation, as provided in FAR 14.4, *Opening of Bids and Award of Contract.*

Only two types of contracts are authorized for use when acquisition is made by sealed bids. They are Firm-Fixed-Price (FFP) and Fixed-Price with Economic Price Adjustment (FPEPA) contracts (*FAR 14.104, Types of Contracts*). These are discussed in detail in Chapter 5, *Contract Types*.

### The Invitation for Bids

The general function of the invitation for bids (IFB) is to state the Government's requirements for supplies and services. It must also state any special factors to be used in bidding and evaluation of bids.

Contracting officers are directed to prepare invitations for bids and contracts using the Uniform Contract Format outlined in FAR 14.201, *Preparation of Invitations for Bids* (see Figure 4-3, page 89). Upon award, the contracting officer will not physically include Part IV, *Representations and Instructions*, of the format in the resulting contract, but will retain it in the contract file. It may be incorporated in the contract by reference. Award may be made by acceptance of a bid on the award portion of Standard Form 33, "*Solicitation, Offer, and Award*" (see Figure 4-1, page 70). Standard Form 26, "*Award/Contract*" (see Figure 11-1, page 252), may be used for supplies or services in which sealed bids were received on the Standard Form 33.

## STANDARD FORM 1447 – SOLICITATION/CONTRACT

**SOLICITATION/CONTRACT**
BIDDER/OFFEROR TO COMPLETE BLOCKS 11, 13, 15, 21, 22, & 27

1. THIS CONTRACT IS A RATED ORDER UNDER DPAS (15 CFR 700) | RATING | PAGE OF

2. CONTRACT NO.
3. AWARD/EFFECTIVE DATE
4. SOLICITATION NUMBER
5. SOLICITATION TYPE ☐ SEALED BIDS (IFB) ☐ NEGOTIATED (RFP)
6. SOLICITATION ISSUE DATE

7. ISSUED BY CODE

8. THIS ACQUISITION IS ☐ UNRESTRICTED OR ☐ SET ASIDE: % FOR:
☐ SMALL BUSINESS
☐ WOMEN-OWNED SMALL BUSINESS (WOSB) ELIGIBLE UNDER THE WOSB PROGRAM
☐ HUBZONE SMALL BUSINESS
☐ EDWOSB
☐ SERVICE-DISABLED VETERAN-OWNED SMALL BUSINESS
☐ 8(A)
NAICS:
SIZE STANDARD:

NO COLLECT CALLS

9. (AGENCY USE)

10. ITEMS TO BE PURCHASED *(BRIEF DESCRIPTION)*
☐ SUPPLIES ☐ SERVICES

11. IF OFFER IS ACCEPTED BY THE GOVERNMENT WITHIN ____ CALENDAR DAYS (60 CALENDAR DAYS UNLESS OFFEROR INSERTS A DIFFERENT PERIOD) FROM THE DATE SET FORTH IN BLOCK 9 ABOVE, THE CONTRACTOR AGREES TO HOLD ITS OFFERED PRICES FIRM FOR THE ITEMS SOLICITED HEREIN AND TO ACCEPT ANY RESULTING CONTRACT SUBJECT TO THE TERMS AND CONDITIONS STATED HEREIN.

12. ADMINISTERED BY CODE

13. CONTRACTOR OFFEROR CODE FACILITY CODE

14. PAYMENT WILL BE MADE BY CODE

TELEPHONE NUMBER ____ DUNS NUMBER ____

☐ CHECK IF REMITTANCE IS DIFFERENT AND PUT SUCH ADDRESS IN OFFER

SUBMIT INVOICES TO ADDRESS SHOWN IN BLOCK

15. PROMPT PAYMENT DISCOUNT

16. AUTHORITY FOR USING OTHER THAN FULL AND OPEN COMPETITION ☐ 10 U.S.C. 2304 ( ) ☐ 41 U.S.C. 253 ( )

| 17. ITEM NO. | 18. SCHEDULE OF SUPPLIES/SERVICES | 19. QUANTITY | 20. UNIT | 21. UNIT PRICE | 22. AMOUNT |
|---|---|---|---|---|---|
| | | | | | |

23. ACCOUNTING AND APPROPRIATION DATA

24. TOTAL AWARD AMOUNT *(FOR GOVERNMENT USE ONLY)*

25. CONTRACTOR IS REQUIRED TO SIGN THIS DOCUMENT AND RETURN ____ COPIES TO ISSUING OFFICE. CONTRACTOR AGREES TO FURNISH AND DELIVER ALL ITEMS SET FORTH OR OTHERWISE IDENTIFIED ABOVE AND ON ANY CONTINUATION SHEETS SUBJECT TO THE TERMS AND CONDITIONS SPECIFIED HEREIN.

26. AWARD OF CONTRACT: YOUR OFFER ON SOLICITATION NUMBER SHOWN IN BLOCK 4 INCLUDING ANY ADDITIONS OR CHANGES WHICH ARE SET FORTH HEREIN, IS ACCEPTED AS TO ITEMS:

27. SIGNATURE OF OFFEROR/CONTRACTOR

28. UNITED STATES OF AMERICA *(SIGNATURE OF CONTRACTING OFFICER)*

NAME AND TITLE OF SIGNER *(TYPE OR PRINT)* | DATE SIGNED

NAME OF CONTRACTING OFFICER | DATE SIGNED

AUTHORIZED FOR LOCAL REPRODUCTION
PREVIOUS EDITION NOT USABLE

**STANDARD FORM 1447** (REV. 2/2012)
Prescribed by GSA - FAR (48 CFR) 53.214(d)

**Figure 4-2**

The contents of an invitation for bid (IFB) should always include the following data:

- Provisions Concerning Supplies or Services
  - Description of supplies or services
  - Time of delivery or performance
  - Place of delivery
  - Contractual provisions
- Provisions Concerning Bidding and Evaluation of Bids
  - Bond and other guaranty requirements
  - Time of acceptance of bids
  - Telegraphic bids
  - Affiliate bids
  - Special technical qualifications
  - Significant factors and subfactors to be used in evaluation of bids
  - Price and price-related factors and the relative importance of each

Contracting officers may use the simplified contract format in lieu of the uniform contract format noted above. The simplified format may be used for supplies and services procured under a firm-fixed-price or fixed-price with economic price adjustment contracts. The contracting officer has flexibility in preparing and organizing the simplified solicitation. Standard Form (SF) 1447, *Solicitation/Contract* (see Figure 4-2, page 72), is used as the first page of the solicitation. The subsequent pages will include only the essential information needed by the bidders. Clauses required by the FAR must be included. Additional clauses will be included only when they are considered absolutely necessary to the particular acquisition (*FAR 14.201-9, Simplified Contract Format*).

After issuance of an invitation for bids, but before the time of bid opening, it may become necessary to make changes to the IFB. Typical changes involve quantities, specifications, delivery schedules, opening dates, etc., or to correct a defective or ambiguous invitation. Such changes will be accomplished by issuance of an amendment to the IFB. Standard Form 30, *"Amendment of Solicitation/Modification of Contract"* (see Figure 13-1, page 316), is issued for supply and service contracts and is optional for construction contracts (*FAR 14.208, Amendment of Invitation for Bids*).

Any amendment to an IFB must be sent, before time for bid opening, to everyone to whom invitations were furnished. When submitting bids, offerors must acknowledge all amendments that have been issued. This requirement is waived when notice has been received that a bid will not be submitted. Failure to acknowledge an amendment may cause a bid to be non-responsive.

An IFB will not be canceled before bid opening unless cancellation is clearly in the public interest. An example is, if there is no longer a requirement for the supplies or services, or where amendments to the IFB would be of such size that a new invitation would be desirable. When an invitation is canceled, bids which have been received will be returned unopened to the bidders. In addition, a notice of cancellation will be sent to all who received the original IFB. When bids have been received electronically, the contracting officer must ensure that the data is not viewed and also purge the data from primary and backup data storage systems (*FAR 14.209, Cancellation of Invitations Before Opening*).

**Solicitation of Bids**

FAR 2.101 defines solicitation as "any request to submit offers or quotations to the Government." Consistent with the needs of the Government for obtaining supplies and services, IFBs will allow bidders enough time to prepare and submit their bids. As a general rule, bidding time will be not less than thirty (30) calendar days (*FAR 14.202-1, Bidding Time*).

Invitations for bids (or presolicitation notices) will be mailed, or otherwise delivered, to enough prospective bidders to elicit adequate competition. Contracting officers must encourage maximum response to solicitations by small business, small disadvantaged business concerns, women-owned small business concerns, and HUBZone small business concerns when appropriate.

Bidders mailing lists will be maintained by each contracting activity to insure access to adequate sources of supplies and services. This rule need not be followed, however, when (i) the requirements of the contracting officer can be obtained through the use of simplified acquisition procedures, (ii) the requirements are nonrecurring, or (iii) electronic commerce methods are used which transmit solicitations or presolicitation notices automatically to all interested sources participating in electronic contracting with the purchasing activity. When electronic bids are authorized, the solicitation must specify the electronic commerce method(s) that bidders may use (*FAR 14.202-8, Electronic Bids)*. Lists may be established as a central list for use by all contracting offices within the contracting activity, or as local lists maintained by each contracting office. All eligible and qualified suppliers who have submitted bidders mailing list applications will be placed on the appropriate bidders mailing list (*FAR 14.205, Presolicitation Notices*). Any source that the purchasing activity considers capable of filling the requirements will also be sent an invitation.

In addition to maintaining and using bidders lists, procuring activities must also publicize the release of an IFB. Display in public places of unclassified invitations is required by regulation. Information releases to newspapers, magazines, and trade journals for free publicity are common. Paid advertising, while possible, is not the general rule. Also see *Publicizing Contract Actions*, on page 49.

**Submission of Bids (*FAR 14.302*)**

Before going to the effort of preparing a “bid” or “proposal” an organization must first consider whether or not it should even “bid” on a solicitation. There are numerous factors to take into consideration before making any efforts and expenditures, such as: Is the program related to their "line of business?" Are there resources available (budget and manpower) to make the bid and later perform the contract? What is their competitive advantage in this line of business and especially this program? What are the "risks" if they do win the contract? These are just some broad questions management must consider. The "Bid/No-Bid" questions relate to proposals for negotiated contracts as well.

A bid is an offer to enter into a contract under the terms of the IFB. The FAR definition for a "bid" is, "any response to a solicitation, including a proposal under a negotiated acquisition." In order for a bid to be considered for award of the contract, it must be "responsive." That means it must comply in all material respects with the IFB. It must comply, both as to the method and timeliness of submission and to the substance of any resulting contract. Thus, all bidders will stand on equal footing. The FAR definition of "bidder" is "any entity that is responding or has responded to a solicitation, including an offeror under a negotiated acquisition."

A bidder/offeror that combines line items on a bid, rather than giving all prices as required in the IFB, does not necessarily make the bid nonresponsive when the bid commits the bidder to provide the work as requested at a price that is lowest in all plausible circumstance. Bidders may properly combine line items. The real issue is whether the quoted prices are the lowest of all bidders and whether the bidder is obligated to do the work specified in the IFB (*D.B.I. Waste Systems, Inc., B-285049, July 10, 2000*).

Unless permitted by the IFB, telegraphic bids will not be accepted by the Government. Telegraphic bids are authorized only when there will not be enough time for bidders to use the prescribed forms or prices are subject to frequent changes. Unless prohibited or otherwise restricted by agency procedures, contracting officers may authorize facsimile bids. Some factors that the contracting officer must consider before authorizing facsimile bids are: (i) anticipated bid size and volume, (ii) urgency of the requirement, and (iii) adequate administrative procedures and controls for handling such bids. One major concern in the use of facsimile transmittals is safeguarding the bids until bid opening. If facsimile bids are authorized, contracting officers may, after bid opening, request the apparently successful bidder to provide the complete, original signed bid (*FAR 14.202-7, Facsimile Bids*).

Contractors are encouraged to fill out, execute and submit the form designated by the IFB. However, failure to use prescribed forms is not grounds for rejecting a bid if it is otherwise responsive. If a bidder uses its own bid form or a letter to submit a bid, the bid may be considered only if: (i) the bidder accepts all the terms and conditions of the invitation, and (ii) award on the bid would result in a binding contract with terms and conditions that do not vary from the terms and conditions of the invitation. Bids submitted by electronic commerce may be considered only if the electronic commerce method was specifically stipulated or permitted by the solicitation (*FAR 14.301, Responsiveness of Bids*).

Bids must be submitted in such a manner that they will be received in the designated office and not later than the exact time set for bid opening. Bids will be considered "late bids" if received after the exact time for opening. Late bids, late bid modifications, or late withdrawal of bids will be considered only under very limited circumstances (*FAR 14.304, Submission, Modification, and Withdrawal of Bids*). Consideration of late offers is permitted if the Government has mishandled the offer.

While not a frequent occurrence in the sealed bid process, a bidder who has submitted the lowest bid, may request that its bid be revised upward. An agency can allow such a correction if the intended bid is within a narrow range of uncertainty and also would still be the lowest bid. The GAO supported that position when it held:

> "An agency may permit correction of a bid where clear and convincing evidence establishes both the existence of a mistake and the bid actually intended. In addition, where the mistake has a calculable effect on the bid price and that effect can be determined by a formula evident from the bidder's work papers, the overall intended bid may be ascertained by taking into account the effects of the error on other bid calculations based on the mistaken entry. Moreover, correction may be allowed, even when the intended bid price cannot be determined exactly, provided there is clear and convincing evidence that the amount of the intended bid would fall within a narrow range of uncertainty and would remain low after correction." (*Roy Anderson Corporation, B-292555; B-292555.2, October 10, 2003*)

Under the "Firm-Bid Rule," a bid may be withdrawn or modified by any method authorized by the solicitation, if notice is received in the designated office not later than the exact time set for bid opening. Upon withdrawal of an electronically transmitted bid, the data received must not be viewed and must be purged from primary and backup data storage systems. After bid opening time a bid may not be withdrawn or modified, except under very limited circumstances (*FAR 14.303, Modification or Withdrawal of Bids*).

**Opening and Recording Bids**

All bids and bid modifications received before the time of opening are kept in a locked box, a safe or in a secured, restricted-access electronic bid box. They must remain unopened until the time set for bid opening (*FAR 14.401, Receipt and Safeguarding of Bids*).

At the time designated for opening, all unclassified bids that were received are publicly opened. When practical, they will be read aloud by the bid opening official. Information necessary for bid evaluation is entered on a Standard Form 1409, *Abstract of Offers*. For construction project bids, Optional Form 1419, *Abstract of Offers – Construction*, is used to record the information. Except for classified procurements, these abstracts are open for public inspection. Classified bids and abstracts are not accessible to the general public (*FAR 14.402-2, Classified Bids*). Only those with the proper clearance and the appropriate need-to-know will be allowed to participate in the bid opening.

Contracting officers are responsible for the protection of proprietary information supplied by bidders. Bids accompanied by descriptive literature upon which the bidder has imposed restrictions, must not be publicly disclosed. However, such restrictions may make the bid non-responsive (*FAR 14.404-4, Restrictions on Disclosure of Descriptive Literature*).

**Rejection of Bids**

Statutes on competitive bidding provide that all bids may be rejected when it is determined that such action is in the best interests of the Government (*10 U.S.C. 2305(c)* and *41 U.S.C. 253*).

Preservation of the integrity of the competitive bid system dictates that after bids have been opened, award must be made to that responsible bidder who submitted the lowest responsive bid. An exception would be if there is a compelling reason to reject all bids and cancel the invitation (*FAR 14.404, Rejection of Bids*).

Individual bids may be rejected under any of the following situations:

- The contracting officer must reject as non-responsive, any bid that does not conform to the essential requirements of the IFB. Whatever is wrong with your bid must not affect the price, the time of delivery, or the quantity or quality of the end item to be delivered (*30 Comp. Gen. 179 (1950)*).
- Conditioned bids modifying the requirements are usually rejected.
- Bids from contractors that are ineligible, debarred, suspended, or proposed for debarment are rejected "*unless a compelling reason determination is made*" (*FAR 9.4, Debarment, Suspension, and Ineligibility*).
- Bids received from contractors not meeting the standards of responsibility set forth in FAR 9.1, *Responsible Prospective Contractors*, will be rejected.
- Bids that are submitted on an "all or none" basis may be rejected when so provided in the IFB.
- When the cover letter accompanying the bid has language making the bid ambiguous, the bid is not an "unequivocal promise" and therefore must be rejected.
- Bids that are unsigned in the legal sense, that is, one which is not legally binding on the bidder, will be rejected.
- Where the IFB requires a bid guarantee, failure to furnish the guarantee makes the bid nonconforming and it will be rejected.
- If addenda to an IFB contain provisions affecting price, quantity, or quality of the work, a bid that fails to acknowledge the addenda must ordinarily be rejected.
- Bids that limit the rights of the Government under any contract clause will be rejected.
- A bid that does not include an acknowledgment of a material amendment must be rejected as nonresponsive, since the bidder would not be obligated to comply with the terms of the amendment.
- A bid that states an alternate not specified in the IFB will be rejected.

- If a bid appears to be ambiguous, that is, it may have two or more reasonable interpretations, and the rule that an ambiguity be resolved against the party creating it is not applicable, the bid cannot be accepted (*40 Comp. Gen. 393 (1961)*). However, any bid containing a pricing ambiguity will not be rejected automatically when they are low under all reasonable interpretations of the intended price.
- In a total small business set-aside, bids from non-small businesses will be rejected.
- In a total small business set-aside, a small business must make a representation that "all end items to be furnished will be manufactured by a small business concern." The small business must perform fifty percent (50%) of the cost of manufacturing the supplies, including the cost of the materials. Also, they must do the final end item manufacturing (*13 CFR 121.3-2(r)*).

**Cancellation of Invitations After Opening (*FAR 14.404-1*)**

To preserve the integrity of the competitive bid system, it is customary that, after bids have been opened, award should be made to the responsible bidder who submitted the lowest bid. However, there may be a compelling reason to reject all bids and cancel the invitation. The GAO has ruled that there is a valid reason for canceling a solicitation when all bids received are found to be unreasonably high (*Quality Inn and Suites Conference Center, B-283468, October 20, 1999*). Every effort must be made to anticipate changes in a requirement before the date of opening and all prospective bidders must be notified of any resulting modification or cancellation.

Invitations may be cancelled and all bids rejected before award and after bid opening when the agency head determines in writing that a number of conditions exist. Some of the more important conditions are as follows:

- Inadequate or ambiguous specifications were cited in the invitation;
- The specifications have been revised;
- The supplies or services are no longer required;
- There is a lack of funding;
- All otherwise acceptable bids received are at unreasonable prices;
- Only one bid is received and the contracting officer cannot determine the reasonableness of the bid price;
- The bids were not independently arrived at in open competition, were collusive, or were submitted in bad faith;
- No responsive bid has been received from a responsible bidder; or
- For other reasons, cancellation is clearly in the public's interest.

## Mistakes in Bids (*FAR 14.407*)

The general concept is that the "Firm-Bid Rule" is paramount for mistakes claimed by offerors. In a few cases, contractors have been allowed to withdraw or correct erroneous bids. However, this is a rare occurrence and should not be relied upon.

After the opening of bids, contracting officers (CO) will examine all bids for mistakes. In cases of apparent mistakes, the CO must request from the bidder a verification of the bid, calling attention to the suspected mistake. This will also be done when the contracting officer has reason to believe that a mistake may have been made. If the bidder alleges a mistake, the matter must be resolved before award of the contract.

A contractor's desire to correct its bid under the "mistake-in-bid" situation will usually fall under one of two situations: (1) where a loser wants to lower its price in order to win the award; or (2) where a winner wants to raise its bid and still remain the low bidder. Because "mistake-in-bid" situations can have the potential of fraud on the part of the bidder, the regulations make it very difficult for the first situation to be accepted by the Government. That bidder must present clear and convincing evidence of both the existence of the mistake and the bid that was actually intended. This is where good records and work papers are very important.

Relief of a mistake is available under the following conditions:

- Clerical mistakes apparent on the face of a bid may be corrected by the contracting officer before award, if the CO has first obtained verification of the bid actually intended (*FAR 14.407-2, Apparent Clerical Mistakes*).
- The contracting officer can give a bidder an opportunity to cure any deficiency resulting from a minor informality or irregularity in a bid. That is one which is merely a matter of form and not substance. Also, the contracting officer may waive any such deficiency where it is to the advantage of the Government. However, the waiver must not be prejudicial to other bidders (*FAR 14.405, Minor Informalities or Irregularities in Bids*).
- The departments and agencies are authorized to make certain administrative determinations concerning mistakes in bids, other than those noted above, alleged by the bidders after opening of the bids but before award. However, the authority to permit correction of bids is limited to bids that, as submitted, are responsive to the IFB. The authority may not be used to permit correction of bids that will make them responsive. The details on these administrative determinations are contained in FAR 14.407-3, *Other Mistakes Disclosed Before Award.*
- Withdrawing bids in cases of mistakes disclosed and proved before award is generally allowed on the theory that the Government may not "snap up" an offer it knows to be erroneous.
- Where the mistake was made by a subcontractor or vendor, relief has been denied in some cases on the theory that it was the bidder's responsibility to discover the mistake (*19 Comp. Gen. 207 (1939)*).

- When a mistake in a contractor's bid is not discovered until after award, the mistake may be corrected by supplemental agreement. This may be done only if correcting the mistake would make the contract more favorable to the Government. Furthermore, it must not change the essential requirements of the specification (*FAR 14.407-4, Mistakes After Award*).
- A low bidder may correct its bid upward if its worksheets reasonably establish clear and convincing evidence of the mistake in the intended bid and the bid remains low after the upward correction (*GAO, Reliable Mechanical Inc., B-282874.2, September 13, 1999*).

Mistakes in bids and contracts are classified as unilateral or mutual mistakes. In a unilateral mistake, it usually means that the Government does not have notice of the mistake. In mutual mistakes for sealed bid procurements, it often means that the Government was aware of the bidder's mistake before award. Whereas for negotiated procurements, it sometimes means the contract failed to reflect the common understanding of the parties.

Authority to grant relief is vested in the Government Accountability Office (GAO) with broad delegations of authority to grant relief passed down to the Department of Defense (DOD) and the General Services Administration (GSA). The subject of mistakes in contracts is discussed in Chapter 16, *Contractual Challenges*.

**Award**

The regulation requires that award will be made with reasonable promptness. This is done by giving written or electronic notice to the responsible bidder whose bid conforms to the invitation and will be most advantageous to the United States. Only the total price and price related factors that were included in the invitation are considered (*FAR 14.408, Award*).

Standard Form 33 (Figure 4-1, page 70) provides that sixty (60) calendar days will be allowed for award unless the bidder states a longer period. Those bids which only allow a shorter time will be rejected.

The several lowest bidders will be requested, before expiration of their bids, to extend the time for bid acceptance if administrative difficulties prevent award within the specified time. Under some circumstances, completion of the acquisition after cancellation of the invitation for bids may be appropriate (*FAR 14.404-1(d) & (e), Cancellation of Invitations After Opening*). As an example, a bidder can be allowed to revive an expired bid if that bidder had complied with all previous agency extension requests (*GAO, Consultants, Ltd., B-286688-2 May 16, 2001).*

During the evaluation of bids, the contracting officer must consider such items as price, options, economic price adjustments, transportation costs, equal low bids and other areas controlled by regulations and laws.

After opening of bids, the Government has the right, but not the duty, to exclude bidders whose bid is unrealistically low. It is not mandatory that the Government notify such bidders to warn them that their bids are unrealistically low (*CTA, Inc. v. The United States, U.S. Court of Federal Claims (COFC) No. 97-864C, August 31, 1997*).

Prompt payment discounts will not be considered in the evaluation of bids. However, any discount offered will form a part of the award. They will be taken by the payment center if payment is made within the discount period specified by the bidder (*FAR 14.408-3, Prompt Payment Discounts*).

Although the above language suggests a broad discretion on the part of the contracting officer, that is really not the case. Bids may not be evaluated upon the basis of experience or other qualifications as long as the low bidder qualifies as a responsible bidder and submits a responsive bid (*37 Comp. Gen. 51 (1957)*).

Except as authorized by law, a contract may not be awarded as a result of a set-aside for one of the small business programs, or under an 8(a) program, if the cost to the awarding agency exceeds the fair market price for the efforts solicited. Fair market price will be determined in accordance with the directions contained in FAR 19.202-6, *Determination of Fair Market Price*. The 8(a) program is discussed later in this chapter.

From time to time, the Government will decide that having certain options available in a particular program will be to its advantage. Such options would grant the Government the unilateral right in the contract by which, for a specified time, it may elect to purchase additional supplies or services called for by the contract, or may elect to extend the term of the contract. The solicitation will contain appropriate option provisions and clauses, so that bidders will be aware of the need to bid accordingly.

There are special provisions in FAR 17.2, *Options*, for evaluating bids received under IFBs with options for additional quantities or time periods. The contracting officer will evaluate offers for those options when it has been determined before soliciting bids that the Government will likely exercise the options. Otherwise, the contracting officer may not evaluate those offers or bids. Any determination that evaluation would not be in the best interests of the Government must be approved at a level above the CO. It would not be in the best interest of the Government to add to the base bid price two option items when the Government could only exercise one or the other (*GAO, Kringer Construction, Inc., B-286960, March 15, 2001*).

When an invitation for bids (IFB) does not contain an economic price adjustment clause, bids received which quote a price and contain an economic price adjustment provision with a ceiling will be evaluated. That evaluation will be made on the maximum possible economic price adjustment of the quoted base price. Bids which contain an economic price adjustment without a ceiling will be rejected, unless a clear basis for evaluation exists (*FAR 14.408-4, Economic Price Adjustment*).

Where the IFB contains an economic price adjustment clause and no bidder takes exception to its provisions, bids are evaluated based on the prices quoted without any adjustment. Bidders who respond with some change to the economic price adjustment provisions run the risk of being rejected.

Bids subject to the Buy American Act that offer supplies from abroad, will still be evaluated. This is done by increasing the foreign bid price, transportation costs and duty by more than 6% if the domestic offer is from a large business concern. The increase would be 12% if comparison is with a small business concern (*FAR 25.105, Determining Reasonableness of Cost*).

When two or more low bids are equal in all other respects, award will be made in accordance with FAR 14.408-6, *Equal Low Bids*, which sets the following order of priority:

- Concerns which qualify as small business concerns that are also labor surplus concerns.
- Other small business concerns.
- Other business concerns.

If, after going through the priority process, two or more bidders remain eligible for award, the award will be made by a drawing of lot limited to those bidders (*FAR 14.408-6(b)*).

Award will be made by furnishing the successful bidder with a properly executed award document or a Notice of Award (NOA). A Notice of Award does not need to be in a specified format. An official letter signed by the contracting officer is all that is necessary. The NOA must, however, be specific in the details it contains. It should include the contract number, its effective date, authorized funding provided, and the initial tasks to be performed by the contractor. This assumes that full contract go-ahead has not been granted. The main purpose of an NOA is to provide expedited contractual go-ahead to a contractor. It provides time for the formal contract document to go through its drafting and execution process. The award is effective when received by the contractor.

**Notification to Bidders**

The contracting officer will notify the successful bidder with reasonable promptness, in writing or electronically, the notice of award.

Within three days after contract award the contracting office must notify, in writing or electronically, unsuccessful bidders that their bids were not accepted. The normal procedure is to notify them before the contract is awarded. Such advance notice is especially helpful for small businesses that may wish to contest not only the award, but also the small business status of the winner. Advance notice is not always possible. The urgency of the requirement may necessitate award without delay, which could prevent the contracting officer from sending out advance notices to unsuccessful bidders. FAR 15.503, *Notification to Unsuccessful Offerors*, gives guidance on issuing notifications. When requested by an unsuccessful bidder, the contracting officer must furnish the name and address of the successful bidder and the contract price.

Contracting officers must consider all protests or objections to the award of a contract, whether received before or after award. When a written protest of an award is received, award will not be made until the matter is resolved. Unless the contracting officer can fully justify one of the following conditions, award will be delayed. The CO must show that the items to be procured are urgently required, or that delivery or performance will be unduly delayed by failure to make the award promptly. Alternatively, it must be shown that a prompt award will otherwise be advantageous to the Government. Protests are discussed later in this chapter.

No bidder has an enforceable right to prevent award to another bidder, to compel an award to itself, or to recover damages for losing an award (*U.S. vs. Gray Line Water Tours of Charleston, 4th Cir. 1962, 311 F.2d 779*).

### Announcement of Contract Awards (*FAR 5.303*)

Contracting officers must make information available on awards over $4 million, unless another dollar amount is specified in agency acquisition regulations. This must be done in sufficient time for the agency concerned to announce it by 5:00 p.m. Washington, DC time on the day of award. The timing is set to be made after the closing of the New York Stock Exchange. Contracts excluded from this reporting requirement include: (1) those placed with the Small Business Administration under Section 8(a) of the Small Business Act; (2) those placed with foreign firms when the place of delivery or performance is outside the United States and its outlying areas; and (3) those for which synopsis had been exempted. Agencies shall not release information on awards before the public release time of 5:00 p.m. Washington, DC time.

Agencies may also release information on contract awards to the local press or other media. When local announcements are made for contract awards in excess of the simplified acquisition threshold, they shall include a statement that the contract was awarded after competition by sealed bidding, the number of offers solicited and received, and the basis for selection (e.g., the lowest responsible bidder). For awards after negotiation, either by price or design competition, the statement will include identifying the type of competition, and in general terms, the basis for selection.

### Miscellaneous Sealed Bidding Facets

The contracting officer may, after expiration or rejection of a bid, request or permit reinstatement of a bid and make a valid award to that bidder. This situation may occur when the contracting officer determines that lower priced and responsive bids are rejected because the bidders are found to be non-responsible contractors and thus ineligible for award of a contract.

If the contracting officer believes it appropriate to do so, negotiations may be held with the eligible low bidder to reduce the price (*Leitman vs. U.S. (1945) 104 Ct. Cl. 324*). This situation, while remotely possible, is not a common occurrence. However, it could result from budget and funding restraints that were not anticipated.

If changes are to be made to a contract entailing additional work of any considerable magnitude, consideration must be given to obtaining competitive bids (*30 Comp. Gen. 34 (1950)*). The theory here is the contract should not be modified for efforts that are clearly out of scope of the original contract. .

Sealed bidding is not legally required of prime contractors in their procurement actions (*37 Comp. Gen. 315 (1957)*).

## ACQUISITION BY TWO-STEP SEALED BIDDING

### Fundamentals

Two-step sealed bidding procedures are defined in FAR 14.5, *Two-Step Sealed Bidding*. This process is a combination of competitive procedures designed to obtain the benefits of sealed bidding where adequate specifications are not available. It is extremely useful in procurements requiring technical proposals, especially those for complex items. Unless other factors require the use of sealed bidding, the two-step method may be used in preference to negotiations when conditions are right (*FAR 14.502, Conditions for Use*).

### Two-Step Process

Step one consists of the request for a technical proposal without pricing. Those proposals submitted will undergo evaluation and, if necessary, discussion to determine the acceptability of the supplies or services offered. The request for technical proposals is less formal than the IFB, yet it follows the same procedures noted in Sealed Bidding above.

Step two is confined to those bidders who submitted acceptable technical proposals in step one (*FAR 14.503, Procedures*). At this point, the method converts to the standard sealed bidding concepts. The IFB must state that each bidder will submit a price proposal that supports both the specifications used in step one and the bidder's own acceptable technical proposal. During step two, the agency will not place a synopsis of the procurement in the Governmentwide Point of Entry (GPE) as an acquisition opportunity. Furthermore, it will not be publicly posted as is done in a typical sealed bid acquisition. However, the names of firms that submitted acceptable proposals in step one will be listed in the GPE for the benefit of prospective subcontractors.

Bids submitted in step two will be evaluated and awards will be made under the normal sealed bidding procedures. Therefore, any award will be made without further discussions with the bidders.

# ACQUISITION BY NEGOTIATION

## General Nature of Negotiated Contracts

The policies and procedures governing contracting for supplies and services by negotiation are detailed in FAR Part 15, *Contracting by Negotiation*. FAR Part 15 underwent major revisions in 1997 and again in 2001. This text will discuss the major aspects of contracting by negotiation as impacted by those changes.

The term "negotiation" as applied to the acquisition process, means contracting through the use of either competitive or other than competitive proposals and discussions between the contracting officer and the offerors. Any contract that is awarded without using sealed bidding procedures is a negotiated contract. Contracting officers are not required to explain in writing their rationale for choosing to use competitive proposals rather than sealed bidding (*FAR 6.401, Sealed Bidding and Competitive Proposals)*. Negotiation is a procedure that includes the receipt of proposals from offerors and permits discussions and bargaining. FAR 15.002, *Types of Negotiated Acquisition*, cites two types of such acquisitions: sole source and competitive.

The essential elements of sealed bidding procedures apply to negotiated procurements. Those elements include amendments to solicitations, late proposals and modifications to proposals, publication in the Governmentwide Point of Entry (GPE), and the treatment of procurement information, protests and mistakes. As with sealed bids, facsimile proposals may be authorized by contracting officers, using the same criteria for authority and control. One difference will be that all offerors may be requested to provide the original signed proposal.

A significant difference between the two acquisition methods is the application of the "Firm-Bid Rule" which is present in sealed bidding acquisitions. Offerors are allowed to make changes to their proposals up to the conclusion of negotiations or the common cut-off date. Proposal changes are either "modifications" or "revisions." A proposal modification is a change made to a proposal before the solicitation closing date and time, or made in response to an amendment, or made to correct a mistake at any time before award. A proposal revision is a change to a proposal made after the solicitation closing date, at the request of or allowed by a contracting officer, as the result of negotiations.

## Presolicitation Notices and Information Exchange

The Government publishes presolicitation notices in the Governmentwide Point of Entry (GPE) as prescribed in FAR 5.204, *Presolicitation Notices*, as one of the preliminary steps to a negotiated procurement. The notices provide a general description of the scope or purpose of a forthcoming acquisition. It allows the Government to develop sources for acquisition and permit the solicitation from potential offerors of preliminary information based on general description of effort involved. The notices give those prospective offerors the opportunity to submit preliminary proposal information which then allows the Government to advise those interested firms about their potential to be viable competitors. Details of this procedure are described in FAR 15.202, *Advisory Multi-Step Process*. Even with the use of presolicitation notices, the contracting office is still required to synopsize the notice prior to issuance of any resulting solicitation.

The entire process is dependent upon the free flow of information between Government agencies and industry. Agencies are encouraged to promote exchange of information from the earliest identification of a requirement through receipt of proposals. The purpose of this is to improve the understanding of Government requirements and industry capabilities. FAR 15.201, *Exchanges With Industry Before Receipt of Proposals*, recommends the following techniques designed to promote early exchanges of information:

- Industry or small business conferences
- Public hearings
- Market research
- One-on-one meetings with potential offerors
- Presolicitation notices
- Draft request for proposals (RFPs)
- Requests for information (RFIs)
- Presolicitation or preproposal conferences
- Site visits

After release of the solicitation, the Contracting Officer will be the focal point of any exchange of information with potential offerors. When specific information about a proposed acquisition, that would be necessary for the preparation of proposals, is disclosed to one or more offerors, that information must be made available to the public as soon as possible. While trying to avoid creating an unfair competitive advantage, care must be taken to protect the offeror's confidential information.

The net result of this preliminary activity is either the issuance of a formal solicitation in accordance with standard procedures or the cancellation or postponement of the activity. Such drastic action will be taken if information obtained during this period indicates the wrong requirements are being specified. It might even be a case of "you just can't get there from here."

**Solicitation of Proposals and Information**

The requirements for preparation of requests for proposals (RFPs) or requests for information (RFIs) for negotiated acquisitions are in FAR 15.2, *Solicitation and Receipt of Proposals and Information*. RFPs are normally prepared on Standard Form 33, "*Solicitation, Offer and Award*" (see Figure 4-1, page 70). Standard Form 1447, *Solicitation/Contract* (see Figure 4-2, page 72), may be used if the contracting officer elects to use the simplified contract format and may be used in place of Standard Form 26 (see Figure 11-1, page 252) or Standard Form 33.

Contracting officers are encouraged to use a uniform contract format to facilitate preparation of the solicitation and resulting contract (*FAR 15.204, Contract Format).* When contracting in a sole source environment, the request for proposals should be tailored to remove unnecessary information and requirements. When contracting in a competitive environment agencies are encouraged to minimize the complexity of the solicitation, the evaluation, and the source selection decision. At the same time they maintain a process designed to foster an impartial and comprehensive evaluation of offerors' proposals, leading to selection of the proposal representing the best value to the Government (*FAR 15.002, Types of Negotiated Acquisition).* "Best value" means the expected outcome of an acquisition that, in the Government's estimation, provides the greatest overall benefit in response to the requirement (*FAR 2.101, Definitions).* Best Value will be discussed again in Chapter 7, *Source Selection Process*.

As part of the effort to minimize the complexity of the procurement process and economize on federal spending while seeking the best value, agencies are encouraged to define their requirements in terms that will enable and encourage offerors to supply commercial and nondevelopmental products, as well as provide offerors of such products an opportunity to compete in procurements.

In its part to simplify the procurement process, the General Services Administration (GSA) has developed a new tool to allow contractors to submit their proposals electronically. They have created eOffer, a common template that guides its vendors through the process of submitting offers. The process is automated for electronically signing and submitting completed proposals to the Contracting Officer. GSA created eMod as part of eOffer to allow contractors to submit modification requests electronically. eOffer can be accessed online at http://www.eoffer.gsa.gov/.

The details of the prescribed format are outlined in FAR 15.204-1, *Uniform Contract Format*, and shown here in Figure 4-3, *Uniform Contract Format,* page 89. Part IV, *Representations and Instructions*, will not be physically included in the resulting contract.

Section K, Representations, certifications, and other statements of offerors or respondents *(Reps and Certs)*, will normally be incorporated by reference in the definitized contract. FAR 4.12, *Representations and Certifications,* prescribes the policies and procedures for requiring submission and maintenance of Reps & Certs via the Online Representations and Certifications Application (ORCA). Contracting Officers are relieved from filing a paper copy of a contractor's Reps & Certs in the CO's office files. However, archived records from the ORCA must be included in the contract file to satisfy documentation requirements.

FAR permits the use of annual representations and certifications by contractors. This applies to both sealed bidding and negotiated procurements. The decision to use the annual "Reps and Certs" will be made by the Contracting Officers in accordance with agency procedures. The solicitation will contain FAR 52.204-8, *Annual Representations and Certifications*.

The details for the application request for proposals (RFPs) in negotiated acquisitions are found in FAR 15.203, *Request for Proposals.* It is not mandatory that RFPs be issued on a Standard Form 33. An RFP in letter format may be used for acquisitions conducted under the authority of FAR 6.302, *Circumstances Permitting Other Than Full and Open Competition.*

Some agencies may have regulations that prohibit the use of letter RFPs. When a letter RFP is used, Contracting Officers must still follow other solicitation requirements. A letter RFP must be clear and concise and contain all the relevant information found in a standard RFP. Whether the RFP is issued on Standard Form 33 or in letter format, the very minimum information must include:

- RFP number and date
- Name and address of contracting officer
- Type of contract contemplated
- Quantity, description, and required delivery dates for the item
- Applicable certifications and representations
- Anticipated contract terms and conditions
- Instructions to offerors and evaluation criteria
- Proposal due date and time
- Other relevant information, such as incentives, variations in delivery schedule, cost proposal support, and data requirements

Electronic commerce may be used to issue RFPs and to receive proposals, modifications and revisions. The RFP must specify the electronic commerce method or methods that offerors may use. Contracting officers may decide to issue RFPs and also authorize receipt of proposals, modifications, or revisions by facsimile. In either of these methods, offerors may be required to provide complete, original signed proposals at a later date.

In determining sources to be solicited, contracting officers basically utilize the same types of resources used for sealed bidding. Offeror mailing lists are maintained, and unclassified procurements are synopsized in the Government Point of Entry. An additional source is information about R&D contractors which frequently comes from technical and project personnel within the Government.

An important attachment to the solicitation is the statement of work (SOW). The preparation and use of a clear and complete statement of work is essential to sound contracting as well as the initial pricing by the offerors. SOWs must be individually tailored by technical, program management, and contracting personnel to attain the desired degree of flexibility for contractor creativity. This is important for the submission of proposals and later in contract performance. Work statements are discussed in more depth in Chapter 11, *Contract Documentation.*

## UNIFORM CONTRACT FORMAT

(For use with Solicitation of Offers)

### Part I – The Schedule

| | |
|---|---|
| Section A | Solicitation/contract form |
| Section B | Supplies or services and prices/costs |
| Section C | Description/specifications/statement of work |
| Section D | Packaging and marking |
| Section E | Inspection and acceptance |
| Section F | Deliveries or performance |
| Section G | Contract administration data |
| Section H | Special contract requirements |

### Part II – Contract Clauses

| | |
|---|---|
| Section I | Contract clauses |

### Part III – List of Documents, Exhibits and Other Attachments

| | |
|---|---|
| Section J | List of attachments |

### Part IV – Representations and Instructions

| | |
|---|---|
| Section K | Representations, certifications, and other statements of offerors or respondents |
| Section L | Instructions, conditions, and notices to offerors or respondents |
| Section M | Evaluation factors for award |

**Figure 4-3**

**Oral Solicitations and Presentations**

In appropriate cases, proposals or quotations may be solicited orally. Oral solicitation is appropriate for small purchases. It may also be used when the processing of a written solicitation would delay the furnishing of the supplies or services to the detriment of the Government.

Oral amendments to solicitations are often a necessary evil. There will be situations when time does not allow an agency the opportunity to formally amend a solicitation. Oral amendments, however, are certainly not the preferred method of amending a solicitation, so great care must be taken not to do something that would invalidate the whole solicitation.

Use of oral solicitations does not relieve the contracting officer of following the other applicable portions of the regulations. Any resulting contract must be prepared on the prescribed contract form for signature by both parties.

In the same manner, solicitations may request that offerors make oral presentations that could substitute for or augment written information. This could be an effective way to streamline the source selection process. They may occur at any time in the acquisition process, but they are subject to the same restriction as written information regarding timing and content. The solicitation may require offerors to submit part of their proposals through oral presentations. Oral presentations provide an important opportunity for dialogue among the parties (*FAR 15.102, Oral Presentations*).

**Selection of Candidates for Negotiation**

Contracting officers are responsible for selecting those offerors with whom the government will enter into discussions and negotiation. The following Comptroller General decision will influence their choice of candidates.

> "All parties within competitive range should be negotiated with to obtain the best contract for the Government." (*Comptroller General Decision B-161334*)

It is the contracting officer's responsibility to establish the competitive range, by utilizing those proposals; that meet the Government's technical requirements, that are within the price range envisioned and, otherwise, comply with all the essential aspects of the RFP.

**Contract Award Without Discussions**

Awarding a contract on the basis of initial proposals, without discussion, is a technique of negotiated procurement which can prove very useful. When one offeror's proposal is so clearly superior to those of the other offerors, the Government may award the contract without proceeding further with the negotiation process. Such an award can reduce the time it takes to get an offeror on contract. It will also reduce the cost of the procurement to the Government and offerors alike. While potentially beneficial, special rules exist governing how and when such awards can be made. Failure to follow the rules will probably result in successful protests which will offset the anticipated savings in costs and time.

In order to avoid the possibility of such a protest, a statement such as the following needs to be included in the solicitation.

> "Proposals may be evaluated, and award made, without discussions with the offerors (other than discussions conducted for the purpose of minor clarification)."

Authority to award contracts without discussions is found in the Competition in Contracting Act of 1984 (CICA). The specific authority is found at *10 U.S.C. 2305(b)(4)(A)(ii)*, which reads as follows:

> "The head of the agency shall evaluate competitive proposals and award a contract –
>
> ****
>
> (ii) without discussions with the offeror (other than discussions conducted for the purpose of minor clarification) when it can be clearly demonstrated from the existence of full and open competition or accurate prior cost experience with the product or service that acceptance of an initial proposal without discussions would result in the lowest overall cost to the United States."

Major elements of the Competition in Contracting Act (CICA) are implemented in FAR 15.306, *Exchanges With Offerors After Receipt of Proposals*. The clause states that if award will be made without conducting discussions, offerors may be given the opportunity to clarify certain aspects of their proposals, such as the relevance of their past performance information and adverse past performance information to which they have not previously had an opportunity to respond and clarify. They may also be given the opportunity to resolve minor or clerical errors.

Award may be made without discussions if the solicitation states that the Government intends to evaluate proposals and make the award without discussions. If the solicitation contains such a notice and the Government later determines that it will be necessary to conduct discussions, the contracting officer must document the contract file with the rationale for taking that action.

Other elements of CICA, as implemented by FAR 15.306, are discussed later in Chapter 7, *Source Selection Process*.

**Notifications to Offerors**

In any procurement not using simplified acquisition procedures, where it appears the period of evaluation of proposals is likely to exceed thirty (30) days, the contracting officer must take some immediate actions. One important action relates to any proposal which has been found unacceptable. The CO must provide prompt notice of that fact to the source submitting the proposal. This will also apply to situations where a limited number of suppliers have been selected for additional discussion. The contracting officer must notify offerors promptly in writing when their proposals are being excluded from the competitive range or otherwise eliminated from the competition. The notice must state the basis for the determination and that a proposal revision will not be considered (*FAR 15.503, Notifications to Unsuccessful Offerors*).

Those offerors that have been excluded from the competitive range, or otherwise excluded from the competition before the award has been made and announced, may request a debriefing. They have to request the debriefing in writing to the contracting officer, and within 3 days after receipt of the notice of exclusion. They may even request that the debriefing not be held until after the award has been made. The contracting officer must make every effort to debrief the unsuccessful offeror as soon as practicable. The debriefings may be done orally, in writing, or by any other method acceptable to the contracting officer. The timing of the debriefing must be in the best interests of the Government (*FAR 15.505, Preaward Debriefing of Offerors*).

The contracting officer must award a contract with reasonable promptness to the successful offeror who was selected in accordance with the evaluation criteria specified in the solicitation. As with sealed bids, all proposals received in response to a solicitation may be rejected. Such action can be taken only if the agency head makes a written determination that one of the following situations exists. One situation is when all otherwise acceptable proposals received are at unreasonable prices. Also when the proposals were not independently arrived at in open competition, were collusive, or were submitted in bad faith. Another important reason would be if a cost comparison shows that performance by the Government would be more economical. As with many other things, it could be for the reason that cancellation is in the best interest of the Government.

Purchasing offices conduct debriefings to provide unsuccessful offerors with some insight as to why they were not chosen to perform the contract. This will advise them of the Government's evaluation of the significant factors contained in their proposals that led to their elimination. They should cite determinative deficiencies and weaknesses to support their position. Adequate debriefings can provide the basis upon which offerors may improve future proposals, which eventually will be of benefit to the Government.

When a contract is awarded on some basis other than price, unsuccessful offerors will be debriefed upon a written request to the contracting officer. Timing of the debriefing is important to all parties. The sooner it is conducted, the earlier the "lessons learned" knowledge gained from the debriefing will get applied. To the maximum extent practicable, the debriefing should occur within five days after receipt of the written request (*FAR 15.506, Postaward Debriefing of Offerors*).

### Announcement of Contract Awards (*FAR 5.303*)

Just as noted before in the sealed bidding process, contracting officers must make information available on awards over $4 million, unless another dollar amount is specified in agency acquisition regulations. This must be done in sufficient time for the agency concerned to announce it at 5:00 p.m. Washington, DC time on the day of award. As with sealed bidding, the timing is set to be after the closing of the New York Stock Exchange. Contracts excluded from this reporting requirement include those placed with: (1) the Small Business Administration under Section 8(a) of the Small Business Act; and (2) with foreign firms when the place of delivery or performance is outside the United States or its possessions. Agencies may not release information on awards before the public release time of 5:00 p.m. Washington, DC time.

Agencies may also release information on contract awards to the local press or other media. When local announcements are made for contract awards in excess of the simplified acquisition threshold (SAT) they will include the information prescribed by FAR 15.503, *Notifications to Unsuccessful Offerors*. After competitive negotiation (either price or design competition) it will include a statement to that effect, and in general terms the basis for selection.

### Postaward Conferences

A very important management tool for both the contractor and all affected Government agencies is a postaward conference. These conferences aid all personnel to achieve a clear and mutual understanding of all contract requirements and to identify and resolve any potential problems. The sessions are not to be used to alter the final agreements arrived at during any negotiations leading to the contract. The contracting officer (CO) may make commitments or give directions within the scope of the CO's authority. The CO will put in writing and sign any commitments or directions, whether or not it changes the contract. Any change to the contract that results from a postaward conference must be made by a contract modification for it to be legal.

The prime contractor is responsible for conducting any postaward conference with their subcontractors. The size and responsibility of each subcontractor will determine which ones would benefit from such a conference. In the interest of fostering a team type environment, it would normally be appropriate to invite Government representatives to attend the conference with the subcontractors. Those Government representatives who attend such a subcontractor conference must remember that the Government does not have privity of contract with the subcontractor. Therefore, they should be cautious in their actions while in attendance and resolve any issues with the prime contractor at a later time.

Postaward conferences are held at the discretion of the contracting officer. FAR 42.5, *Postaward Orientation*, provides the guidance for selecting contracts for the conferences.

# ALTERNATE CONTRACTING METHODS

## Modular Contracting (*FAR 39.103*)

Federal agencies, in their acquisition of information technology, may make use of modular contracting techniques. Modular contracting is defined as:

> "use of one or more contracts to acquire information technology (IT) systems in successive, interoperable increments."

Modular contracting is intended to reduce program risk and to motivate contractor performance while meeting the Government need for timely access to rapidly changing technology. To avoid obsolescence, a modular contract for information technology should, to the maximum extent practicable, be awarded within 180 days from the date the solicitation was issued. Otherwise, cancellation of the solicitation should be considered.

When using modular contracting, an acquisition system of information technology may be divided into several smaller acquisition increments or modules. That would allow for easier management of the increments, address complex IT objectives incrementally, and provide for delivery, implementation, and testing of workable systems or solutions in discrete increments.

The characteristics of each increment will vary depending upon the type of IT being acquired and the nature of the system being deployed. For each increment, the CO will choose the appropriate contracting technique that facilitates the acquisition of subsequent increments. An increment/module is an economically and programmatically separate segment that has a substantial programmatic use, even if no additional segments are acquired (*P.L. 104-106, Clinger-Cohen Act*). Therefore, each contract will be structured to ensure that the Government is not required to procure additional increments.

## Bundled Contracts

The contracting agency may consolidate two or more requirements for supplies or services, previously provided under separate contracts, into a solicitation for a single contract; referred to as a bundled contract. This will be done when it is likely that those requirements would be unsuitable for award to a small business concern due to any of the following factors or combination thereof:

- The diversity, size, or specialized nature of the elements of the performance specified;
- The aggregate dollar value of the anticipated award; or
- The geographical dispersion of the contract performance sites.

Due to the potential impact on small business participation, the head of the agency must conduct market research to determine whether bundling is necessary and justified (*FAR 7.107, Additional Requirements for Acquisitions Involving Bundling*). The agency must identify and quantify anticipated benefits and explain how their impact would be measurably substantial.

## Multi-Year Contracting (*FAR 17.1*)

Multi-year contracting is a special contracting method to acquire known requirements in quantities and total cost not over planned requirements for up to 5 years unless otherwise authorized by statute, even though the total funds ultimately to be obligated may not be available at the time of contract award. This method may be used in sealed bidding or contracting by negotiation (*FAR 17.104, General*). Multi-year contracting is a flexible contracting method which can be applied to a wide range of acquisitions.

Some of the objectives of multi-year contracting include one or more of the following:

- Lower costs
- Enhancement of standardization
- Reduced administration efforts in the placement and administration of contracts
- Stabilization of contractor work forces
- Broadening of the competitive base of firms

Selection of the contracting method will be governed by the nature of the requirement. The multi-year procedure is compatible with sealed bidding, including two-step sealed bidding and negotiation. The type of contract to be used will also depend upon the nature of the requirement as well as the longer performance period involved. Profit objectives should be commensurate with contractor risk and financing arrangements.

All program years in multi-year contracting, except the first, are subject to cancellation. For each program year subject to cancellation, the contracting officer must establish a cancellation ceiling in accordance with FAR 17.106-1(c), *Cancellation Procedures*.

In determining what the cancellation ceilings should be, the CO must estimate reasonable preproduction or startup, labor learning, and other nonrecurring costs that would be incurred by an "average" prime contractor or subcontractor. The CO would determine which of these costs would be applicable to, and which normally would be amortized over, the items or services to be furnished under the multi-year requirements.

The contracting officer must establish cancellation dates for each program year's requirements. Those dates will be influenced by production lead times and also the date by which funding for those requirements can reasonably be established. Cancellation ceilings and dates may be revised after issuing the solicitation.

When issuing the solicitation for multi-year contracts, the contracting officer must include at least the following factors to be used in the evaluation process:

- The requirements, by item of supply or service for the first program year, and the multi-year contract, including the requirement for each program year.
- Criteria for comparing the lowest evaluated submission on the first program year to the lowest evaluated submission on the multi-year requirements.
- Notice that if the Government determines before award that only the first program year requirements are needed, the evaluation of price or estimated cost and fee will consider only the first year.
- A statement that award will not be made on less than the first program year requirements.
- The cancellation ceiling will not be an evaluation factor.

**Options (*FAR 17.2*)**

Contracting officers may include options in both sealed bidding and contracting by negotiation, when it is in the best interest of the Government. Before incorporating option(s) in a sealed bidding acquisition, the contracting office must make a written determination that there is a reasonable likelihood that the option will be exercised. The clause *Evaluation of Options* (*FAR 52.217-5))* will then be incorporated in the solicitation.

Solicitations that contemplate options must include appropriate provisions and clauses to provide for the exercise of the options including the basis for their evaluation. When appropriate, offerors must be informed when it is anticipated that the Government may exercise the option at time of award.

Contracting officers have an extensive list of provisions and clauses to choose from when contemplating the use of options. They are found at FAR 17.208, *Solicitation Provisions and Contract Clauses*.

Contracts awarded with option provisions must specify the limits on the purchase of additional supplies or services, including the time period within which the option may be exercised. That period must provide the contractor adequate lead time to ensure continuous production. In compliance with FAR 17.207, *Exercise of Options*, the contracting officer may exercise options only after making the determination that:

- Funds are available;
- The requirement covered by the option fulfills an existing Government need;
- The exercise of the option is the most advantageous method of fulfilling the Government's need, price and other factors considered;
- The option was synopsized in accordance with FAR Part 5, *Publicizing Contract Actions* unless exempted by 5.202(a)(11) or other appropriate exemptions in FAR 5.202, *Exceptions*;
- The contractor is not listed in the System for Award Management Exclusions;

- The contractor's past performance evaluations on other contract actions have been considered; and
- The contractor's performance on this contract has been acceptable, e.g., received satisfactory ratings.

# UNSOLICITED PROPOSALS

**Fundamentals**

The policies and procedures for submission, receipt, evaluation and acceptance of unsolicited proposals are outlined in FAR 15.6, *Unsolicited Proposals*. The term "unsolicited proposal" means a written proposal that is submitted on the initiative of the offeror with the intent of receiving a contract with the Government.

To be a valid unsolicited proposal it must meet the following criteria:

- It must be innovative and unique.
- It must have been independently originated and developed by the offeror.
- The proposal must have been prepared without Government supervision, endorsement, direction or direct Government involvement.
- It must include sufficient detail so the Government can determine that its support would be worthwhile and meet the agency's mission.
- The proposal must contain sufficient cost and pricing information for evaluation.
- It has overall scientific, technical, or socioeconomic merit.
- It is not responding to a previously published requirement.
- It was not an advance proposal for a known agency requirement that could be acquired by competitive methods.
- It was not submitted in response to a formal or informal request for proposals.

An exception to those limitations would be when responding to a publicized agency request constituting a general statement of needs. A Broad Agency Announcement (BAA) issued by an agency and publicized through the Governmentwide Point of Entry (GPE) is an example of such a statement of needs. NASA makes use of statements called NASA Research Announcements (NRA) or Announcements of Opportunity (AO). These types of announcements are unlike an RFP. They usually do not contain a statement of work or specifications to which offerors are to respond. BAAs, NRAs and AOs provide for the submission of competitive project ideas which have been conceived by the offerors but are related to the subject matter in the announcement. It is the Government's policy to encourage the submission of new and innovative ideas in response to these types of announcements. However, when those ideas do not fall under the topic areas publicized under those programs or techniques, the ideas may be submitted as unsolicited proposals.

## Evaluation

Before the receiving agency initiates a comprehensive evaluation, they will determine that the proposal is a valid unsolicited one, relates to the agency's mission, and contains sufficient technical and cost information for evaluation. It must also be approved by a responsible official or other representative who is authorized to contractually obligate the offeror. The proposal which meets the requirements will be acknowledged and undergo the evaluation process. If a proposal is rejected because of not meeting those basic requirements, the agency must promptly inform the offeror in writing of the reasons for rejection and the proposed disposition of the unsolicited proposal.

Evaluators of unsolicited proposals will consider the factors listed below. There may be other factors used by the evaluators which are specifically appropriate for the particular proposal (*FAR 15.606-2, Evaluation*).

- Unique, innovative and meritorious methods, approaches or concepts demonstrated by the proposal;
- Overall scientific, technical or socio-economic merits of the proposal;
- Potential contribution of the effort proposed to the agency's specific mission;
- The offeror's capabilities, related experience, facilities, techniques or unique combinations of these which are integral factors for achieving the proposal objectives;
- The qualifications, capabilities and experience of the proposed principal investigator, team leader or key personnel critical in achieving the proposal objectives; and
- The realism of the proposed cost.

Agencies frequently return unsolicited proposals to offerors as unacceptable for a contract award. This is most often done when one of the following situations exists: (1) what has been proposed by the submitting organization is available to the Government without restriction from another source; (2) when the proposed efforts closely resemble a pending competitive acquisition requirement; (3) when it does not relate to the activity's mission; or (4) when the proposal does not demonstrate an innovative and unique method, approach or concept, or is otherwise not deemed a meritorious proposal.

## Acceptance and Award

Under limited circumstances contracting officers may accept for negotiation an unsolicited proposal without providing for full and open competition. Based upon a successful negotiation they may award a contract for the proposed efforts. However, they can only do this when all of the following conditions exist:

- There is a favorable comprehensive evaluation of the proposal.
- The proposal was not returned for any of the reasons stated above.
- The agency's technical office sponsoring the contract adequately supports the non-competitive action and also furnishes the necessary funds.
- The contracting officer complies with the synopsis requirements of FAR 5.2, *Synopses of Proposed Contract Actions*.
- The contracting officer has executed any justifications needed and obtained appropriate approvals, and has complied with FAR 6.3, *Other Than Full and Open Competition*.

Government personnel may not use any data, concept, idea, or any other part of an unsolicited proposal as the basis, or even part of the basis, for a solicitation or in negotiations with any other firm than the one that submitted the unsolicited proposal. That restriction will not be effective if the original offeror agrees to such use or that material was also available from another source (*FAR 15.608, Prohibitions*).

## CONTRACT AWARD PROTESTS

### Protest Principles (*FAR 33.1*)

Under certain conditions unsuccessful bidders and offerors in pursuit of Government business may protest Governmental contract award actions. They make their protests because they believe that the Government has not followed the prescribed procedures for the solicitation, evaluation and award of a contract. The right to file a protest is administrative since no contractual relationship exists between the protester and the Government.

There are two types of protests, those filed challenging the provisions of a solicitation before contract award and those challenging the actual award of the contract. Any interested party may file a protest. As defined in FAR 33.101, *Definitions*, to be an "interested party," the protester must be an actual or prospective offeror who has a direct economic interest in the acquisition that would be affected by the award of a contract or by failure to award a contract. Actual or prospective bidders have the standing to sue the Government over a solicitation, however, no bidder can file a protest until a solicitation has been issued.

Furthermore, to be a valid protest, the objection must be timely and in writing. Protests and documentation related thereto may also be filed by facsimile, and to provide that, subject to restrictions where a protective order has been issued, all filings may be filed by electronic means. Protests may be filed to take exception to Governmental actions in any one of the following situations:

- A solicitation or other request by an agency for offers for a contract for the procurement of property or services.

- The cancellation of the solicitation or other request.
- An award or proposed award of the contract.
- A termination or cancellation of an award of the contract, if the written objection contains an allegation that the termination or cancellation is based in whole or in part on improprieties concerning the award of the contract. (*FAR 33.101, Definitions*).

From time to time the Government finds it necessary to issue an amendment to the solicitation prior to the due date for proposal submission. It is understandable that such an amendment will have an impact on the proposal offerors intend to submit. The basic rule is that a protest against an amendment to a solicitation must be filed before the due date for submission of proposals on the original solicitation.

However, when the amendment has been issued just a few days prior to the solicitation date, that could be impossible. GAO rulings in the past have determined that in most cases the offers did not have to be filed by the due date for offers but within 10 days of the amendment.

There is another situation that can trigger a protest to a solicitation. This is when a company, intending to submit an offer, discovers an obvious error in the solicitation. They must file their protest to the Court of Federal Claims (COFC) prior to the deadline for submission of offers. The COFC is the only federal court empowered to hear both pre- and post- award bid protests.

There are several limiting factors for determining if a protester has standing as an interested party. The decisions of the Comptroller General and the Boards of Contract Appeal provide guidance for this. The following are examples that control that standing:

- An offeror who submits a late proposal is not an interested party for protest purposes. Generally, to be an interested party, a protester must be in line for award if the protest is sustained. However, even a protester not in line may be an interested party if he seeks cancellation of the solicitation and resolicitation of the requirement. In that case, if successful, the protestor would be able to compete again. A party who submits a late proposal does not have standing to protest the evaluation of proposals or any changes in the terms of the solicitation that result from proposal evaluation. Such issues affect only the parties that remain in the competition (*Comp. Gen. B-220680.3*).
- A bidder/offeror who is nonresponsive for other than non-correctable technical deficiencies, may be considered an interested party. If the protest is sustained, the protester would most likely be eligible to participate in reopened negotiations or the resolicitation of the requirement. This is a different situation than the protester who submits a late bid or proposal.
- One exception does exist from the "interested party" rule. When a bidder or offeror wants to protest the terms of a solicitation before the bids or proposals are due, filling a protest can often affect its right to remain in the competition. It still will be considered a valid protest (*ViON Corporation, GSBCA No. 11292-P (1991)*).

- An offeror who sees an obvious error in a solicitation must protest it to the Court of Federal Claims prior to submission of any offors.

There are several questions a company must ask itself before filing a protest. They include: (1) do you believe that you were *prejudiced* against; (2) how *important* is this contract/program to your company; (3) how will it *impact your relationship* with your customer, especially if you have other contracts/programs; (4) what are the chances *you will win* the protest; and (5) if you do win, what are the odds on *winning the contract*?

The successful bidder (awardee) to the solicitation is considered an interested party to the protest. It is only natural the awardee intervene in any protest that has been filed by a disappointed bidder that is seeking to challenge the contract award. In so doing, they will be supporting the contracting decision being protested. The awardee will be entitled to participate in the protest procedure by reviewing the protest file and providing comments supporting the contracting decision.

**Protest Process**

Contracting officers must consider all protests or objections to the award of a contract and to seek legal advice in their efforts to effectively handle the situation. This applies whether the protest is submitted before or after contract award. Neither does it matter if filing was directly with the agency, the Government Accountability Office (GAO) or the Federal Courts. For protests filed directly with the courts, as noted above, both pre-award and post-award protests are filed at the Court of Federal Claims. When handling a protest, the courts can consider whether or not the protestor actually has standing to raise the protest, and also whether or not the protestor could win the award. When going to the courts a protester must seek an injunction to prevent the Government from awarding the contract or permitting further performance while the protest is pending.

When an oral objection is made the parties will make an effort to resolve the issue in that manner. If they cannot resolve the matter informally, the contracting officer will request a written confirmation of the protest. The protest may be filed by hand delivery directly to the contracting officer, via postal services or by electronic means, such as facsimile or e-mail. When done electronically, it would be advisable to verify the protest was actually received by the CO. Whichever mode of delivery is used, the protestor must adhere to the timeliness requirements. The CO will notify the protester in writing of the final decision on the protest.

In the process of handling contractor protests and other claims, contracting officers' decisions must be their personal and independent decision. While they will almost always ***consult*** with experts, management and lawyers, it is still ***their*** final decision. When an issue is complex and highly technical it creates a difficult situation for the CO. In a recent decision, the Court of Federal Claims (COFC) invalidated a contracting officer's final decision because the judge concluded the decision was of the agency lawyers and not the personal and independent decision of the CO. The court stated that ". . . if other government officials are consulted, including government attorneys, a contracting officer may not forsake his duties, but rather must insure that his decisions are the product of his personal and independent judgment. . . ." (*Fireman's Fund Ins. Co. v. U.S. 92 Fed. Cl. 598 (2010)*)

The Government encourages interested parties wishing to protest, to seek resolution within the agency before filing directly with the GAO or the courts. However, that is not a mandatory rule. A protest must be filed within ten (10) calendar days of when the protestor learns of the bases for a protest, or should have known, whichever is earlier. Timeliness in filing the protest is very important. The rules on timeliness are predicated on a simple principle. Participants in Government procurements are entitled to proceed on the assumption that procurements are being conducted lawfully, until actual or constructive notice of a transgression become apparent.

Protests filed directly with the contracting agency must follow the procedures set forth in FAR 33.103, *Protests to the Agency*. When a protestor only files with the agency and before award, the contracting officer will delay award, pending resolution of the matter. However, award may be made anyway, if it is determined that contract award is justified for urgent and compelling reasons or is determined to be in the best interest of the Government. Either of these "go-ahead" actions must be fully documented and the written justification will be part of the contract file. Justification or determination will be approved at a level above the contracting officer, or by another official pursuant to agency procedures.

Upon receipt of a protest within 10 days after contract award or within 5 days after a debriefing date offered to the protester, whichever is later, the contracting officer will immediately suspend performance, pending resolution of the protest within the agency, including any required independent reviews. If continued performance is deemed necessary, the same actions noted for preaward will be followed.

For protests filed directly with the GAO, the protester has one (1) day to furnish a copy of the complete protest to the contracting officer. In some solicitations a different official or location is designated to receive protests. Failure to furnish that copy within the one day limit will likely result in dismissal of the protest by the GAO (*FAR 33.104, Protests to GAO*).

Contractors are advised to obtain a copy of the Government Accountability Office's guide, *Bid Protests at GAO: A Descriptive Guide (GAO-06-797SP)*, which provides an informal overview of GAO's bid protest regulations. The *Eighth Edition*, issued in 2006 to replace the April 2003 issue, incorporated the April 2005 changes to the bid protest regulations.

When an agency receives notice from GAO of a protest filed directly with GAO, they may not award the contract, unless authorized by agency procedures. The normal procedure requires approval by the head of the contracting activity. That approval is based upon a written finding that the interests of the United States are significantly affected by urgent and compelling circumstances that will not permit awaiting the decision of the Comptroller General. Furthermore, they will not make the contract award until the agency has notified GAO of the finding.

When an agency receives notice of a protest filed directly with GAO, within ten (10) calendar days after award, different rules apply. The contracting officer will immediately suspend performance or terminate the awarded contract. However, notwithstanding the protest, contract performance may be authorized in the best interests of the Government, under the same provisions cited above. A protester does not have an opportunity to challenge the Government's determination to override or lift a suspension. Any challenge to such a determination must be filed as a separate action in federal court. That filing will have to show that the Government's findings were arbitrary and capricious or in violation of law. When it is necessary to suspend performance or terminate the awarded contract, the contracting officer will attempt to negotiate a mutual agreement on a no-cost basis.

The GAO must notify the agency of a protest within ten (10) calendar days after award of the protested acquisition. Otherwise, the automatic stay provisions will not be invoked. Normally the contracting officer will neither suspend performance nor terminate the awarded contract when it is not in the best interest of the Government. The same two exceptions apply in these cases.

Based upon the merits and findings of a protest, the GAO may declare the successful protester is entitled to the costs of filing and pursuing the protest. Those costs would include reasonable attorneys' fees, and costs for bid and proposal preparation. After such an award, the costs may be paid by the agency out of funds available for the acquisition of supplies or services.

For the protester to recover those costs, it will generally be required to prove that the agency violated a statute or regulation and that the protester was prejudiced by that violation. However, if the protester is given an opportunity to win the award of the contract, the GAO will not award any bid or proposal preparation costs. No specific provisions exist that allow for the recovery of bid or proposal costs at the agency level. Although, if it becomes clear that the agency has unduly delayed in taking corrective action in a clearly meritorious protest, the agency may have to pay a protester’s costs.

Any offeror or other interested party may protest the small business representation of an offeror in a specific offer. After offers are open, the contracting officer may question the small business representation in a specific offer and file a contracting officer's protest.

Protests received, whether timely or not, and any contracting officer's protest will be promptly forwarded for resolution to the SBA Regional Office for the geographical area where the principal office of the concern in question is located (*FAR 19.302, Protesting a Small Business Representation or Rerepresentation*).

For a good understanding of the best process for filing a bid protest with the Government Accountability Office (GAO), it is recommended that the protestor go to “*Bid Protests at GAO: a Descriptive Guide*” (*GAO-06-797SP*), which provides an overview of GAO’s bid protest regulations (*http://www.gao.gov/decisions/bidpro/bid/d03539sp.htm*).

# SMALL PURCHASES AND OTHER SIMPLIFIED PURCHASE PROCEDURES

## Basic Concepts

The FAR policy states that simplified acquisition procedures (SAP) are to be used to the maximum extent practicable for all purchases of supplies or services not exceeding the simplified acquisition threshold (*FAR 13.3, Simplified Acquisition Methods*). The current simplified acquisition threshold (SAT) is $150,000. The basic purpose for the simplified acquisition procedures is to:

- Reduce administrative costs;
- Improve opportunities for small, small disadvantaged, and women-owned small business concerns to obtain a fair proportion of Government contracts;
- Promote efficiency and economy in contracting; and
- Avoid unnecessary burdens for agencies and contractors.

Contracting officers may not use simplified acquisition procedures to acquire supplies and services if the anticipated award will exceed the simplified acquisition threshold. They are encouraged to use innovative approaches to the maximum extent practicable in awarding contracts using the SAP. However, they are not encouraged to break up a procurement just to use the simplified acquisition procedures.

Contracting officers must solicit a reasonable number of sources to promote competition to the maximum extent practicable. This is to ensure that the purchase is advantageous to the Government, based, as appropriate, on either price alone or price and other factors including the administrative cost of the purchase. An unspoken benefit of such competition is reducing the chance of protests.

## Micro-Purchases (*FAR 13.2*)

The Federal Acquisition Streamlining Act (FASA) established a micro-purchase threshold of $3,000 and authorized purchases not greater than that amount to be made without obtaining competitive quotations. Micro-purchases are excluded from small business set-aside requirements and Buy America Act provisions.

Agencies are encouraged to use the Governmentwide commercial purchase card and electronic purchasing techniques to the maximum extent practicable. The agency heads are encouraged to delegate micro-purchase authority to individuals who will be using the supplies or services being purchased. The individuals delegated this authority, while not warranted, are contracting officers within the scope of the FAR.

To the maximum extent practicable, micro-purchases must be distributed equitably among qualified suppliers. These purchases may be awarded without soliciting competitive quotations if the contracting officer, or individual authorized to make micro-purchases, considers the price to be reasonable (*FAR 13.203, Purchase Guidelines*).

**Governmentwide Commercial Purchase Card (*FAR 13.301*)**

A Governmentwide commercial purchase card is authorized for use in making and/or paying for purchases of supplies, services, or construction. The card may be used by contracting officers and other individuals designated to use them. Agencies are encouraged not to limit the use of these cards to micro-purchases, but use them for greater dollar amounts. The Governmentwide commercial purchase card may be used to:

- Make micro-purchases;
- Place a task or delivery order; or
- Make payments, when the contractor agrees to accept payment by the card.

**Purchase Orders (*FAR 13.302*)**

Except when issued as an unpriced purchase order, all purchase orders will be issued on a firm fixed-price basis. The purchase order must include any discounts offered by the supplier, specify quantities ordered, prescribe inspection and delivery requirements and contain a definite calendar date by which delivery of supplies or performance of services are required. Normally the contracting officer's signature will appear on the purchase order. Facsimile signatures may be used in the procedure of purchase orders by automated methods.

Unpriced purchase orders are orders where the price is not established at the time of issuance. They may be used only when it is impractical to obtain pricing in advance of issuance of the purchase order, and the purchase is for: (1) repairs to equipment requiring disassembly to determine the nature and extent of repairs; (2) material available from only one source and for which cost cannot readily be established; or (3) supplies or services for which prices are known to be competitive, but exact prices are not known.

Unpriced purchase orders may be issued in writing or electronically. They must contain a realistic monetary limitation which will be subject to adjustment when the firm price is established. It is incumbent upon the contracting officer to follow up on each purchase order to ensure timely pricing.

**Blanket Purchase Agreements (*FAR 13.303*)**

The blanket purchase agreement (BPA) is a simplified method of filling anticipated repetitive needs for supplies or services. The BPA process establishes "charge accounts" with qualified sources of supply. BPAs should be established for use at the level responsible for providing supplies for its own operations or other offices, installations, projects, or functions. Blanket purchase agreements may only be used for purchases that are otherwise authorized by law or regulation. Individual purchases normally may not exceed the simplified acquisition threshold. However, agency regulations may establish a higher threshold consistent with the FAR.

The existence of a BPA does not of itself justify purchasing from only one source or avoiding small business set-asides. Contracting officers must ensure the maximum practicable competition when purchasing with the use of BPAs. Also, the use of BPAs does not exempt the agency from responsibility for keeping obligations and expenditures within available funds.

Under FAR 13.303-2(c), *Establishment of BPAs*, agencies may set up BPAs with Federal Supply Schedule contractors so the agencies can make better use of those schedules. The agencies can access the General Services Administration (GSA) on-line shopping service for purchases from the schedule(s) that best meet their needs (*FAR 8.404, Use of Federal Supply Schedules*).

Purchases under blanket purchase agreements usually will be made electronically, or orally when it is not considered economical or practical to use electronic methods. A paper purchase document may be issued if necessary to ensure the parties all agree to the details of the transaction.

### Imprest Funds and Third Party Drafts (*FAR 13.305*)

Imprest funds and third party drafts are cash funds of a fixed amount set up by an advance of funds. They do not carry an appropriation charge. They are provided to a duly appointed cashier to effect immediate cash payments of relatively small amounts for authorized purchases of supplies and non-personal services. Each purchase using imprest funds or third party drafts must be based upon an agency's approved method of ensuring that adequate funds are available for the purchase. Normally, purchases will be placed orally and without soliciting competition if prices are considered reasonable.

Imprest funds may be used for small purchases when the transaction is not in excess of $500. Third party draft transactions may not exceed $2,500. The use of either of these also must be considered advantageous to the Government, and their use complies with any additional conditions established by the agency. These funds are used for such items as local delivery charges, postage, C.O.D. charges, travel advances, travel expenses and transportation charges.

### Fast Payment Procedure (*FAR 13.4*)

The fast payment procedure provides for payment for supplies based on the contractor's submission of an invoice. This procedure allows payment under limited conditions to a contractor prior to the Government's verification that supplies have been received and accepted. A part of that invoice is a representation that the supplies have been delivered to a post office, common carrier or point of first receipt by the Government.

Title to the supplies will vest in the Government upon delivery to the post office or common carrier for mailing or shipment to destination. Title will also pass upon receipt by the Government when shipment is by means other than the Postal Service or common carrier.

Under this procedure individual orders cannot exceed $30,000. However, executive agencies may establish higher dollar limitations for specified activities or items. The purchasing instrument will be a firm-fixed price contract, a purchase order, or a delivery order for supplies. Another condition for use is when the delivery of supplies is to occur at locations where there is both a geographical separation and a lack of adequate communications facilities between Government receiving and disbursing activities that will make it impractical to make timely payment based on evidence of Government acceptance.

A system must be in place to ensure there is: (1) documented evidence of contractor performance under fast payment acquisitions; (2) timely feedback to the contracting officer in case of contractor deficiencies; and (3) identification of suppliers who have a current history of abusing the fast payment procedure. The supplier must agree to replace, repair or correct supplies not received at the destination, damaged in transit or not conforming to purchase requirements.

## CONTRACTING WITH THE SMALL BUSINESS ADMINISTRATION

Under the authority of Section 8(a) of the Small Business Act (*15 U.S.C. 637(a)*), the Small Business Administration (SBA) may enter into all types of contracts with other federal agencies. The SBA may enter into subcontracts with eligible small business firms which will perform the contracted effort. The Act established what is referred to as the "8(a) program," and SBA's subcontractors are referred to as "8(a) contractors." FAR 19.8, *Contracting With the Small Business Administration (The 8(a) Program)*, sets forth the process of the 8(a) program. It describes how the program relates to the federal agencies, and the working relationship between the SBA and the agencies' contracting officers. Included in that relationship is the selection of acquisitions for participation in the 8(a) Program. Agencies must avoid unnecessary and unjustified bundling of orders that would preclude small business participation as contractors. Under SBA rules the size standard for a procurement is in effect on the date when the solicitation is issued, not when contract award is made.

The SBA has entered into "delegation of authority" agreements with a significant number of federal agencies. The agreements are expected to substantially streamline the 8(a) program's contracting process. As noted above, the SBA has served as the "middleman" when federal agencies wanted to contract with an 8(a) company for goods and services. Under the delegation agreements, federal agencies will be able to contract directly with the 8(a) companies. The SBA will then be resolving the issues as to whether a business is a qualified 8(a) firm and whether it is responsible. When an agency intends to place 8(a) contracts with the SBA, their notification must include the following:

- Any special restrictions on the contract;
- Identification of all known 8(a) businesses that have expressed interest in the contract;
- Identification of all SBA field offices interested in the acquisition under the 8(a) program;
- A request, if appropriate, that a requirement with an estimated contract value under the applicable competitive threshold be awarded as an 8(a) competitive contract; and
- A request, if appropriate, that a requirement with a contract value over the applicable competitive threshold be awarded as a sole source contract.

Selecting the small business concerns for participation in the 8(a) program is the responsibility of SBA. Small business concerns applying for the 8(a) program must be at least fifty one percent (51%) unconditionally owned, controlled and managed by socially and economically disadvantaged individuals who are of good character and citizens of the United States. In addition, they must be able to demonstrate a potential for success in the proposed procurement. They must have been in operation for two years prior to acceptance into the program. Small businesses can remain in the 8(a) program for nine years. However, they are expected to make maximum efforts to obtain non-8(a) contracts while in the program. The SBA will base its selection upon the criteria in *13 CFR 124.101-112*. There is a statutory provision requiring that all 8(a) manufacturing contracts worth more than $6.5 million be awarded through competition among 8(a) firms. The threshold for competing service contracts and other non-manufacturing contracts under the program is $4 million. Contracts may be awarded to the SBA for performance by eligible 8(a) firms on either a sole source or competitive basis.

Small business owners who are interested in doing business with the Federal Government will need to remain fully competitive. To do this, they will need to adapt to and master electronic commerce because so much of the Government's acquisition needs will be publicized in that media. To assist them in this matter, the SBA's website (*http://classroom.sba.gov*) provides training resources and links to information on Government contracting, federal procurement, and how to get loans.

Pub. L. 100-656, *Business Opportunity Development Reform Act of 1988*, requires termination of an 8(a) contract when ownership or control of the 8(a) concern is transferred. However, the Administrator of the Small Business Administration has the authority to waive the termination under certain conditions.

Pricing of an 8(a) contract will be performed, in accordance with FAR 15.4, *Contract Pricing*, by the agency's contracting officer. The CO may request the SBA to get certified cost or pricing data from its contractor if required by Part 15.4. The contracting officer will estimate the fair market price of the work to be performed by the 8(a) contractor in accordance with the instructions in FAR 19.807, *Estimating Fair Market Price*. In estimating the fair market price for an acquisition other than for repeat business, the contracting officer will use cost or price analysis and consider commercial prices for similar products and services, available in-house cost estimates, data (including cost or pricing data) submitted by the SBA or the 8(a) contractor, and data obtained from any other Government agency.

Funding for the 8(a) contract normally comes from the contracting agency. An exception would be if the contract that is awarded contains business development expenses. These would be classified as start-up costs, training, and similar investment or learning costs in excess of those normally incurred by established business concerns engaged in the same business. Those business development costs will be funded by the SBA.

Small businesses operating under a "long term" contract are required to recertify their size status: (1) when a contract option is exercised; (2) when the small business is purchased by or merged with another business; or (3) at the end of the first five years of a contract. A "long term" contract is one that exceeds five years. The recertification process is intended to determine that the contractor still qualifies as a small business for future contracts; it will not have any effect on a contract in place.

In 2008 the SBA added a new small business procurement preference category in addition to the socially and economically disadvantaged small businesses (the 8(a) program), covered above and the historically underutilized business zone (HUBZone) small businesses (Chapter 3, page 45). The new category deals with contracts with service-disabled veteran-owned small business concerns. This will give such veterans many of the advantages available to the other two small business categories. In general, the three programs are similar, however, each has its own peculiar criteria. The contracting officer may set-aside or restrict the procurement to only one of these three types of small business programs. The CO might even decide to give preference to one of them over the others. To go into detail about the similarities, differences and set-aside criteria of the three programs would require more detailed information than essential for this text.

# CHAPTER 5

# CONTRACT TYPES

## TYPES AND KINDS OF CONTRACTS

### Types of Contracts

The term "Type of Contract" refers to the method provided in the contract for compensating the contractor for supplies or services to be provided to the Government. There are two basic types of contracts: the Fixed-Price (FP) type and the Cost-Reimbursement (CR) type. FAR Part 16, *Types of Contracts*, describes the types of contracts that may be used by contracting officers in acquisitions. It prescribes policies and procedures and provides guidance to the contracting officers in their selection of a contract type that would be appropriate to the circumstances of an acquisition they are contemplating.

The selection of contract type is generally a matter for negotiation and requires the exercise of sound judgment. Type of contract and pricing are interrelated and should be considered together in negotiation. Because the type of contract should reflect the degree of risk to both the contractor and the Government, use of an appropriate type is of primary importance (*FAR 16.1, Selecting Contract Types*).

One factor in selecting contract type in a procurement is the amount of responsibility the contractor will assume for performing the work. In addition, they must consider the level of incentive to be provided to the contractor for performing the work efficiently and effectively. The relative advantages and disadvantages of the several contract types are shown in Figure 5-1, page 112, *Contract Types – Theoretical Advantages and Disadvantages*.

One of the primary objectives of the Government should be to make maximum use of the type of contract that includes reasonable contractor risk and provides the contractor with the greatest incentive for efficient and economical performance.

Several basic contract types are described in the following paragraphs. Some of the types authorized by the regulation will not be covered, either because they are special contracts with narrow application or because they are designated more properly as procurement methods than as contract types.

A firm-fixed-price contract, which best utilizes the basic profit motive of business enterprise, will be used when the risk involved is minimal or can be predicted with an acceptable degree of certainty. All contracts resulting from sealed bidding must be either a firm-fixed-price contract or a fixed-price contract with economic price adjustment. When a reasonable basis for firm pricing does not exist, other contract types should be considered.

# CONTRACT TYPES
# THEORETICAL ADVANTAGES AND DISADVANTAGES

| Contract Type | Advantages to Government | Disadvantages to Government | Advantages to Contractor | Disadvantages to Contractor |
|---|---|---|---|---|
| Firm-Fixed Price | ▪ Shifts total risk to contractor<br>▪ Minimum administration<br>▪ Simplifies budget process<br>▪ Some degree of price competition<br>▪ Uniformity of bid evaluation<br>▪ Contractor responsible for management<br>▪ Well-defined work statement and specifications | ▪ Presolution of design problems<br>▪ Price must always contain some contingencies<br>▪ No in-process control of work<br>▪ Less visibility of cost data<br>▪ Complete formality for changes | ▪ Potential for higher profit<br>▪ Minimum government control<br>▪ Well-defined specifications<br>▪ Better cost estimates<br>▪ Less financial audit | ▪ Total assumption of financial and technical risks<br>▪ Risk of liability for work in process<br>▪ Requires vigilance to institute change claims<br>▪ Government does not accept cost contingencies |
| Fixed-Price with Economic Price Adjustment | ▪ May result in adjustments<br>▪ Contractor responsible for management | ▪ Increased administrative costs<br>▪ Poor choice of index distorts | ▪ Spreads risk | ▪ Contains absolute ceiling<br>▪ Poor index distorts<br>▪ Escalation limited to industry-wide contingencies<br>▪ Contingencies within contractor control excluded |
| Fixed-Price Incentive (cost only) | ▪ Spreads risk<br>▪ Less reason for contingencies in price<br>▪ Encourages efficiency<br>▪ Contractor responsible for management<br>▪ No ceiling on incentive for efficiency | ▪ No ceiling on profit<br>▪ Increased administration costs<br>▪ Must budget to ceiling price<br>▪ Minimum control of work in process<br>▪ Complex negotiations<br>▪ Precludes technical direction<br>▪ Limits technical innovation | ▪ Potential for higher profit for higher risks<br>▪ Rewards good management<br>▪ Less Government control | ▪ Price ceiling<br>▪ Detailed accounting records<br>▪ Government verification of costs<br>▪ Complex negotiations<br>▪ Government tends to treat as cost type contract controls, cost principles, and so forth |

**Figure 5-1**

# CONTRACT TYPES
# THEORETICAL ADVANTAGES AND DISADVANTAGES

| Contract Type | Advantages to Government | Disadvantages to Government | Advantages to Contractor | Disadvantages to Contractor |
|---|---|---|---|---|
| Fixed-Price Multiple-Incentive (also see FPI cost only) | ▪ Motivates contractor to surpass performance targets | ▪ Complex administration<br>▪ May increase costs<br>▪ Unbalanced incentives may result in undesirable trade-offs<br>▪ Contract must be specific | ▪ Spreads cost and profit risk | ▪ Incentive measurements may be inaccurate<br>▪ Delays in profit determination<br>▪ Changes difficult to administer |
| Fixed-Price Redeterminable | ▪ High possibility of downward adjustment | ▪ Little motivation for cost reduction<br>▪ Prompt price redetermination required<br>▪ Prospective pricing period must conform to contractor's system<br>▪ Not used until negotiation of firm fixed-price not satisfactory | ▪ Reduces risks | ▪ May include absolute ceiling<br>▪ More detailed accounting<br>▪ Government verification of accounting records<br>▪ High possibility of downward adjustment |
| Cost | ▪ No fee | ▪ No motive to reduce costs<br>▪ Government partially responsible for management | ▪ Minimum risk | ▪ No fee |
| Cost Sharing | ▪ No fee<br>▪ Bears only a portion of cost<br>▪ Motivates for cost reduction | ▪ Limited to certain R&D cases<br>▪ Limits competition<br>▪ Must show conclusive evidence of probability of commercial benefit | ▪ Government participation in commercial development | ▪ Cost share may be excessive |

**Figure 5-1 (Continued)**

# CONTRACT TYPES
# THEORETICAL ADVANTAGES AND DISADVANTAGES

| Contract Type | Advantages to Government | Disadvantages to Government | Advantages to Contractor | Disadvantages to Contractor |
|---|---|---|---|---|
| Cost-Plus-Incentive-Fee | ▪ Shared risk<br>▪ Motivates for cost effectiveness through bonus-penalty arrangement<br>▪ Shares in-process control of work<br>▪ Limited price contingencies<br>▪ Cost visibility | ▪ Overrun costs<br>▪ High administrative costs<br>▪ Complex negotiations<br>▪ High risks<br>▪ Reduced opportunity to manage | ▪ Limited risk<br>▪ Possibility of increased fee<br>▪ Assures recovering costs<br>▪ Rewards good management | ▪ Reduced fee because of reduced risk<br>▪ Absolute limit on fee<br>▪ Disallowance of certain normal business costs<br>▪ Government engagement<br>▪ Complexity of negotiations |
| Cost-Plus-Multiple-Incentive-Fee | ▪ Establishes relative value of cost, performance, and schedule<br>▪ Motivates for superior performance achievement | ▪ Unbalanced incentives may result in undesirable trade-offs<br>▪ Complex administration | ▪ Spreads cost and profit risk<br>▪ Incentive trade-off decisions | ▪ Incentive measurement may be inaccurate<br>▪ Delays in profit determinations<br>▪ Changes difficult to administer |
| Cost-Plus-Fixed-Fee | ▪ Control of delivery schedule<br>▪ Ease of governmental redirection of effort<br>▪ Maximum control of work<br>▪ Emphasizes performance objectives | ▪ Low motivation for cost efficiency<br>▪ High risk<br>▪ Not for development of major systems once exploration indicates engineering development feasible<br>▪ Maximum administrative burden<br>▪ Funding uncertainties<br>▪ Settlement of final costs is prolonged | ▪ Low cost and technical risk<br>▪ Risk of loss of Government property borne by Government | ▪ Maximum Government controls and reporting<br>▪ Disallowance of certain normal business costs<br>▪ Lower fees because of lower risks |
| Cost-Plus-Award-Fee | ▪ Shared risk<br>▪ Motivates for superior performance achievement<br>▪ Cost visibility | ▪ High administrative costs<br>▪ High cost risks | ▪ Limited risk<br>▪ Assures recovering<br>▪ Delays in profit<br>▪ Complex negotiations<br>▪ Spreads cost and profit risk<br>▪ Rewards good management | ▪ Subjective award measurement & determination<br>▪ Changes difficult to administer<br>▪ Complexity of negotiations |

**Figure 5-1 (Continued)**

A cost-reimbursement contract may only be used under the following conditions: (1) the contractor's accounting system is adequate for determining costs applicable to the contract; and (2) appropriate Government surveillance during performance will provide reasonable assurance that the contractor is using efficient methods and effective cost controls. The use of cost-reimbursement contracts is prohibited for the acquisition of commercial items (*FAR 16.301-3, Limitations*).

The basic types of contracts authorized in the regulation may be used in combination when that would make a contract better fit the circumstances of the procurement. This means that a single contract might have both fixed-price and cost-reimbursement features. Any proposed combinations would have to meet the basic test; that is, it must promote the best interests of the Government.

However, such a combination must not cause problems with which the contractor's accounting methods could not cope, since it is mandatory that the costs of the different efforts must be segregated. The use of cost-plus-a-percentage-of-cost (CPPC) contracting is strictly forbidden by statute (*10 U.S.C. 2306(a)* and *41 U.S.C. 254(b)*). Prime contracts, other than firm-fixed-price contracts, are also prohibited from issuing CPPC subcontracts.

Contracting officers must document the contract file with a statement showing why a particular contract type was selected. Exceptions to this requirement are: (1) fixed-price acquisitions made under simplified acquisition procedures, unless required by agency procedures, (2) contracts on a firm-fixed-price basis other than those for major systems or research and development; and (3) awards on the set-aside portion of sealed bid partial set-asides for small business.

## Kinds of Contracts

The term "Kinds of Contracts" refers to what is being procured by the Government. The three basic kinds of contracts are for supplies, services and construction. Research and development (R&D) contracts frequently are for both supplies and services. R&D contracts are given separate attention in the regulation and have attained near-equal status with the other three.

## Other Transactions

"Other transactions" are instruments other than contracts, grants or cooperative agreements. Basically, there are two types of "other transactions." The first type is used for basic, applied, and advanced research projects. They have generally been used to enter into dual-use research projects. This first type is authorized by 10 U.S.C. 2371 – *Research Projects.*

The second type of "other transactions" is used for prototype projects directly relevant to weapons or weapon systems proposed to be acquired or developed by the Department of Defense. The second type is authorized under Sections 845/804 – *Prototype Projects*, of Public Law 103-160 and Public Law 104-201, as amended.

These "other transactions" should not be used when it would be more appropriate to use a standard contract, grant or cooperative agreement.

**Determinations and Findings (*FAR 1.7*)**

A Determination and Finding (D&F) constitutes a special form of written approval required by statute (*10 U.S.C. 2310*) or regulation as a prerequisite to the taking of certain contracting actions. Requirements for specific types of D&F's will be found with the appropriate subject matter. One example is found in FAR Part 16, *Types of Contracts*, where a D&F will be required before entering into certain types of contracts. D&F's are required by FAR 6.302-7, *Public Interest*, the authority to cite public interest as reason for contracting by other than full and open competition. These topics are discussed in Chapter 3, *The Acquisition Process*.

The "determination" is a conclusion or decision supported by the "findings." Findings are statements of fact or rationale essential to support the determination. The findings must cover each requisite of the statute or regulation to support the determination and be consistent with the determination.

When a D&F is required, it must be signed by the appropriate official in accordance with the agency's regulations. Authority to sign or delegate signature authority for the various D&F's will be found in the applicable FAR part citing a requirement for the document.

## FIXED-PRICE CONTRACTS

**Firm-Fixed Price Contracts (FFP) (*FAR 16.202*)**

In a firm-fixed-price (FFP) contract, price is agreed to before a definitive contract is awarded and remains firm for the life of the contract. However, a contract may be modified pursuant to a clause in the contract. The price is not subject to adjustment by reason of the cost experience of the contractor in performance of the contract. The contractor accepts full cost responsibility when agreeing to this type of contract. This relates to the acceptance of risk by both the contractor and the Government. The contractor is confident that risks can be managed to the degree that effective performance will result in a profit. The contracting officer accepts the risk that the contractor could overrun so severely that bankruptcy occurs resulting in a default situation.

Ultimate profit from the FFP contract is directly related to the cost of doing the work; that is, how effectively the contractor controls costs and manages the total contract effort. In the terminology of an incentive contract, the sharing arrangement in a FFP contract is 0/100. This means that the Government does not share at all, but the contractor accepts 100% of any difference between estimated and actual costs. The contractor assumes complete responsibility, in the form of profits or losses for all contract costs.

The FFP contract is suitable for acquiring commercial items or for acquiring other supplies or services, on the basis that reasonably definitive design or performance specifications are available and fair and reasonable prices can be established at the outset. Specifications are discussed in detail in Chapter 11, *Contract Documentation.*

### Fixed-Price Contracts with Economic Price Adjustment (FPEPA) (*FAR 16.203*)

The fixed-price with economic price adjustment (FPEPA) contract provides for the upward and downward revision of the stated contract price upon the occurrence of certain contingencies which are specifically defined in the contract.

The fixed-price contract with economic price adjustment (FPEPA) may be used when the contracting officer determines that price adjustment provisions are necessary, either to protect the contractor or the Government against significant economic fluctuations in labor or material costs or to provide for contract price adjustments should the contractor change its established prices.

Use of this type of contract is appropriate when serious doubt exists as to the stability of market or labor conditions which will exist during the extended period of contract performance. The FPEPA contract is also used when contingencies which would otherwise be included in the contract price can be identified and covered separately by a price adjustment clause. FAR 16.203, *Fixed-Price Contracts with Economic Price Adjustment*, describes the details of these contracts.

The first technique, price adjustments based on established prices, will normally be restricted to industry wide contingencies while price adjustments based on labor or material costs will be limited to other contingencies beyond the control of the contractor. When using the established price approach, adjustments are based on an increase or decrease from an agreed-upon level in published or otherwise established prices. This could be applied to specific items or price levels of contract end items.

The second technique makes adjustments based on labor or material costs, using the Actual Cost Method. Adjustments are based on an increase or decrease in specific costs of labor or material actually experienced by the contractor during performance of the contract. The schedule of the contract will describe in detail the types of labor and materials subject to adjustment. The related labor rates, including any fringe benefits that are adjustable will also be stated. Unit prices of materials, which may increase or decrease, and the quantities of labor and specified materials allocable to each unit of supplies to be delivered under the contract will also be identified.

Adjustments based on labor or material costs, using the Cost Index Method, is the last technique. Here an increase or decrease from specified labor or material cost standards or indices will prompt the adjustment. The standards or indices are largely dependent upon two general series published by the U.S. Department of Labor, Bureau of Labor Statistics. These are the

Industrial Commodities portion of the Wholesale Price Index (WPI) for material and the Wage and Income Series by Standard Industrial Classification (SIC) for labor. Normally, not more than two indices will be used in the contract. One will be used for labor, both direct and indirect. Another index will be used for direct and indirect material. Like the previous method, these will be specified in a clause of the contract, with the parameters for adjustment.

**Fixed-Price with Redetermination Contracts (FPR) (*FAR 16.205 & 16.206*)**

There are two distinct types of fixed-price redetermination (FPR) contracts, one prospective and the other retroactive. One type, fixed-price contracts with prospective price redetermination (*FAR 16.205*), provides for the negotiation of fixed prices to be used in a prospective period. It can be described as a series of two or more firm fixed-price contracts negotiated at stated times during performance. A FPR contract with prospective redetermination may be used in acquisitions of quantity production or services when it is possible to negotiate a fair and reasonable firm fixed price for an initial period, but not for subsequent periods of contract performance. Normally, the initial period will be the longest with subsequent periods at least 12 months long.

The other type, fixed-ceiling-price contracts with retroactive price redetermination (*FAR 16.206*), provides for adjusting contract price after performance. Therefore, it is completely retroactive. In two respects, this contract type is a fixed-price incentive (FPI) contract. A ceiling price is negotiated initially and actual, audited, contract costs are used as a basis for price revision. However, there is one significant difference. The degree of the contractor's cost responsibility, in terms of a share formula, is defined as an incentive contract. This FPR, however, makes the degree of cost responsibility a matter of negotiation at the time of price redetermination which occurs after work has been completed. A great deal depends on a subjective evaluation of the manner in which the contractor has performed. In other words, a revised price reflecting both cost and profit consideration is negotiated at the time of price redetermination. With an FPI contract, only final costs are negotiated; final profit is determined mathematically in accordance with the contract share formula.

Thus, except for the price ceiling, the contractor does not have a calculable, positive incentive for cost control. This contract type does not foster the cost conscious climate generally present when contract management clearly sees that higher costs mean lower profits. For this reason, the regulation limits use of this type to small dollar ($150,000 or less), short term contracts for research and development.

**Firm-Fixed-Price, Level-of-Effort Term Contracts (FFP-LOE) (*FAR 16.207*)**

The firm-fixed-price level-of-effort (FFP-LOE) term contract describes the scope of work in general terms, usually calling for investigations or studies in a specific research and development area. It obligates the contractor to devote a specified amount of labor hours (level-of-effort) over a stated period of time for a fixed dollar amount, normally $150,000 or less.

The normal deliverable of the contract is submission by the contractor of reports which show the results achieved through application of the required level-of-effort; however, payment is based on effort expended rather than on results achieved. This type of contract can be a useful tool, particularly in those research and development areas where the work cannot be clearly defined and the level-of-effort desired can be identified and agreed upon in advance of performance.

**Fixed-Price Incentive Contracts (FPI) (*FAR 16.204 & 16.403*)**

The fixed-price incentive (FPI) contract is a compromise between a firm-fixed-price arrangement and a cost reimbursement one. This is a fixed-price type contract with provision for adjustment of profit and establishment of the final contract price by a formula based on the relationship which final negotiated total cost bears to the total target cost.

A FPI contract is appropriate where cost uncertainties exist and there is the possibility of cost reduction and/or performance improvements by giving the contractor a degree of cost responsibility and a positive profit incentive.

The firm target type of incentive contract (FPIF) is appropriate where a target cost, target profit and ceiling price and formula for establishing final profit and price can be negotiated at the outset. This arrangement will provide a fair and reasonable incentive and a ceiling that provides for the contractor to assume an appropriate share of the risk.

The successive target type of incentive contract (FPIS) is appropriate for use whenever available cost and pricing information is not sufficient to permit the negotiation of realistic firm targets at the outset. The FPIS type of contract is used infrequently. It is designed for some situations involving procurement of the first and second production quantity of a newly developed item, or for long lead time requirements for a follow-on quantity before design or production stability has been achieved. When an FPIS contract is used, a firm contract should be negotiated before the first contract end item is delivered. The new contractual arrangement could be either FFP or FPIF.

When the contract is completed, the contractor submits a statement of costs incurred in performance of the contract. This is audited by the Government to determine allocability to the contract and to point out any costs which may not have been necessary in the performance of the contract or are otherwise questionable. The contractor's cost statement and the advisory report by the Government auditor are the starting points in the analysis and negotiation of the proposal for the final settlement of contract price.

A discussion of FPI incentive arrangements follows later in this chapter.

### Fixed-Price Award Fee Contracts (FPAF) (*FAR 16.404*)

Under certain circumstances a fixed-price contract may be used with award-fee provisions similar to those in a cost-plus-award-fee (CPAF) contract. In negotiating this type of contract, a fixed price (including normal profit) will be established plus the award fee criteria. The typical performance criteria of quality, timeliness, technical ingenuity and effective management can be applied but not cost incentives since the fixed-price arrangement should be incentive enough. Upon contract completion, any award fee earned will be paid in addition to the fixed price.

These contracts are best used when the Government wishes to motivate a contractor and other incentives cannot be used because contractor performance would not be measured in an objective manner. Before entering into a FPAF contract, the contracting office must show that the administrative costs of conducting award-fee evaluations are not expected to exceed the expected benefits and that procedures have been established for conducting the award-fee evaluation. Unlike a CPAF contract, a FPAF contract will rarely if ever contain a base fee in addition to the award fee. A base fee would be incompatible with the fixed-price concept.

Award fee contracting works best when the criteria are specifically applied, such as:

- When the contracting parties have a clear and comprehensive understanding of what is required from the contract in terms of final results (i.e., products and services).
- When those results can be measured against clear and unambiguous criteria and also objectively evaluated.
- When the Government personnel assigned to the program are well trained in the execution and administration of award-fee contracts.
- Where the available resources are adequate for the contractor to perform the contract properly and those resources are available throughout the life of the contract.
- Where the contracting parties exhibit a conscientious and consistent implementation of the contractual requirements throughout the entire contract period.

See the discussion of cost-plus-award-fee contracts later in this chapter. The process will be almost identical for fixed-price contracts with award fees.

## COST-REIMBURSEMENT CONTRACTS

### Cost Contracts (*FAR 16.302*)

The cost contract is a cost-reimbursement type contract under which the contractor receives no fee. The Government agrees to reimburse the contractor for all allowable and allocable costs incurred in performance of the contract.

Cost allowability is determined in accordance with the principles in FAR Part 31, *Contract Cost Principles and Procedures*, and any specific provisions of the contract. Because of the no-profit feature, this type of contract has limited appeal. Generally, use is restricted to either research contracts with educational institutions or other nonprofit organizations and contracts providing facilities to contractors.

### Cost-Sharing Contracts (*FAR 16.303*)

A cost-sharing contract is a cost-reimbursement type contract, for use in research and development procurements, under which the contractor is reimbursed for an agreed-upon portion or percentage of the allowable costs. The contractor agrees to absorb a portion of the costs of performance in the expectation of substantial compensating benefits. The Government agrees to reimburse the contractor for a predetermined percentage of the allowable and allocable costs of contract performance. The contractor receives no fee for the efforts expended.

Cost-sharing contracts are commonly used when the contractor will have a commercial interest in the final contract end item. However, there have been several instances where competing contractors have been forced to spend considerable sums of company funds during initial development stages. The end items in those programs were definitely for use by the Government and not of a commercial nature.

### Cost-Plus-Incentive-Fee Contracts (CPIF) (*FAR 16.304 & 16.405-1*)

The cost-plus-incentive-fee (CPIF) contract is a cost-reimbursement type contract with the provision for a fee which is adjusted by formula in accordance with the relationship which total allowable costs bear to target cost. Under this type of contract initial negotiations will establish the target cost, a target fee, a minimum and maximum fee, and a fee adjustment formula (or share ratio). After performance of the contract, the fee payable to the contractor is determined in accordance with the formula. The formula provides, within limits, for increases above target fee when total allowable costs are less than target cost and decreases below target fee when total allowable costs exceed target cost. The provision for increase or decrease in the fee is designed to provide an incentive for maximum effort on the part of the contractor to manage the contract effectively.

A CPIF contract should be used where the uncertainties of performance preclude use of a fixed-price type contract. However, those uncertainties may not be great enough to justify use of a cost-plus-fixed-fee contract. CPIF contracts are suitable for procurements for advanced engineering or operational systems development and for first production items. A CPIF contract injects an incentive sharing formula into what otherwise would be a cost-reimbursement situation with a 100/0 share.

A detailed discussion of CPIF incentive arrangements follows later in this chapter.

**Cost-Plus-Award-Fee Contracts (CPAF) (*FAR 16.305 & 16.405-2*)**

The cost-plus-award-fee (CPAF) contract is a cost reimbursement type of contract with special fee provisions. It provides a means of applying incentives in contracts which are not susceptible to finite measurements of performance necessary for structuring incentive contracts. The fee established in a CPAF contract consists of two parts. The first is a Base Fee, which may be zero, or will be a fixed amount, set at the inception of the contract, that does not vary with performance. The other is an Award Fee pool, an amount paid in addition to the base fee. This pool of dollars is designed to provide motivation for excellence in contract performance in areas such as quality, timeliness, ingenuity and cost effectiveness. Award fee may be earned by the contractor in whole or in part. The amount of award fee to be paid is based upon a subjective evaluation by the Government of the quality of the contractor's performance, judged in light of evaluation criteria set forth in the contract.

Base fees are paid in the same manner as the fixed-fee of a cost-plus-fixed-fee contract. They are independent of the award criteria. Not all CPAF contracts will have a base fee.

A CPAF arrangement is suitable for contracts where mission feasibility is established but measurement of achievement must be by subjective evaluation rather than objective measurement. A CPAF contract is appropriate for work which would have been placed under another type of contract if the performance objectives could be expressed in advance by definitive criteria measuring actual performance.

A further description of CPAF applications follows later in this chapter.

**Cost-Plus-Fixed-Fee Contracts (CPFF) (*FAR 16.306*)**

The cost-plus-fixed-fee (CPFF) contract is a cost-reimbursement type of contract which provides for the payment of a fixed fee to the contractor. The fixed fee, once negotiated, does not vary with actual costs expended. However, it may be adjusted as a result of any subsequent changes in the work or services to be performed under the contract. Because the fixed fee does not vary in relation to the contractor's ability to control costs, the cost-plus-fixed-fee contract provides the contractor with only a minimum incentive for effective management control of costs.

The CPFF contract type is designed chiefly for use in research or exploratory development when the level of contractor effort required is unknown. It is also intended for use in advanced development efforts whenever it is required by the nature of the work. Generally, the dollars involved are significant, work specifications cannot be defined precisely, and the uncertainties of performance are so great that a firm price or an incentive arrangement cannot be set up at any time during the life of the contract. The Government agrees to reimburse the contractor for all allowable and allocable costs incurred in performance of the contract. In addition, the Government agrees to pay the contractor a fixed number of dollars above the costs as fee (profit) for doing the work.

Cost-plus-fixed-fee contracts are the most common of all the cost-reimbursement contracts. However, they are not to be used for the acquisition of commercial items.

Allowability of costs is governed by Part 31 of the Federal Acquisition Regulation and the specific terms of the contract. The fee dollars change only when there is a change in the scope of work resulting from a modification to the contract. In practice, this contract is at the opposite end of the spectrum from the FFP contract, where price is fixed and a dollar of cost incurred by the contractor means a dollar less profit. If, in the terminology of incentive contracting, the firm-fixed-price contract is depicted as one having a 0/100 share, the CPFF type will be described as one with a 100/0 share.

The cost-plus-fixed-fee contract can be drawn in one of two "forms": Completion or Term. The "*Completion Form*" is one which describes the scope of work to be done as a clearly defined task(s). There is a definite goal or target expressed and a specific end-product or service required. This contract form normally requires the contractor to complete and deliver the specified end-product or service as a condition for payment of the entire fixed-fee. The goal is to have the contractor perform all the tasks within the estimated cost, if possible. In the event the work cannot be completed within the estimated cost, the Government has two options. It can elect to accept that which has been completed or require continued effort by the contractor without an increase in fee. Normally, the latter option is available only if the contracting officer increases the estimated cost and funding.

The "*Term Form*" is one which describes the scope of work to be done in general terms. It obligates the contractor to devote a specified level-of-effort for a stated period of time. Under this contract form, the final fixed-fee is payable at contract completion on certification by the contractor that it has expended the specified level-of-effort. The contracting officer must concur with the contractor's claim and agree performance was satisfactory to the Government. Renewal for further periods of performance will be a new acquisition involving new cost and fee arrangements.

Normally, the completion form of contract is preferred over the term form because of differences in obligation assumed by the contractor. The completion form works best when the tasks or specific milestones can be defined with precision.

In response to criticism from the Government Accountability Office (GAO) of Department of Defense (DOD) incentive and award fee contracting results, one branch, the Air Force Air Armament Center (AAC) has taken a new approach. They have devised the cost-plus-fixed-fee with performance incentive (CPFF-PI) contracts. The incentive fee portion is typically only 30% of the fee pool earned in periods during the life of the contract, typically every 12 months. The remaining 70% can be earned at the end of the contract in the typical CPFF manner. This concept gives the Government the option to pay the incentive fee portion only for overall satisfactory performance. It remains to be seen if this practice is effective; if it is, other branches should follow suit.

# OTHER CONTRACTUAL ARRANGEMENTS

## Time and Materials Contracts (T&M) (*FAR 16.601*)

The time and materials (T&M) type of contract provides for the procurement of supplies or services on the basis of direct labor hours and materials. Labor will be provided at specified fixed hourly rates, which include wages, overhead, general and administrative expense and profit. Material is provided at cost, plus material handling costs where appropriate.

The contract is designed to be used in those situations where the amount or duration of work cannot be predicted. Therefore, total costs cannot be estimated realistically. The Government uses T&M contracts to buy, repair and overhaul services. In those situations the conditions of items for repair cannot be forecast with confidence. This type of contract does not offer the contractor any positive profit incentive to control the cost of materials or to manage the labor force effectively. Therefore, surveillance by the contracting officer will be required to give reasonable assurance that efficient methods and effective cost controls are being used by the contractor.

The contracting officer may at any time, by written order, make changes within the general scope of the contract. Examples of those changes may include: description of services to be performed, time of performance, place of performance of the services, and place of delivery. Such changes could result in an equitable adjustment in the ceiling price, hourly rates, delivery schedule or other affected items (*FAR 52.243-3, Changes – Time-and-Materials or Labor Hours*).

Time-and-materials contracts should only be used when the CO determines it is not possible at the time of placing the contract to make an accurate estimate of the extent or duration of the work to be performed or to the anticipated costs. This decision must be documented in a determinations and finding (D&F) stating that no other contract type would be suitable. Also, the contract will include a ceiling price above which the contractor exceeds at its own risk.

## Labor-Hour Contracts (LH) (*FAR 16.602*)

The labor-hour (LH) type of contract is a variant of the time and materials type. It differs only in that materials are not supplied by the contractor. The application and concerns associated with T&M contracts are also appropriate with this type of contract.

## Letter Contracts (*FAR 16.603*)

A letter contract is a written preliminary contractual instrument which authorizes immediate commencement of the manufacture of supplies or performance of services. With this document the contractor is given a binding commitment so that work can be commenced immediately. Letter contracts are issued for the convenience of the Government. They are frequently used when it is not possible to negotiate a definitive contract in sufficient time to meet the Government's procurement needs. They are very useful when the nature of the work involved prevents the preparation of definitive requirements, specifications and reliable cost or pricing data.

Letter contracts will include an agreement between the Government and the contractor as to the date by which definitization is expected to be completed and a schedule to meet that goal (*FAR 52.216-25, Contract Definitization*). That date must be prior to the expiration of 180 days from the effective date of the letter contract, or forty percent (40%) of performance of the work, whichever occurs first. In extreme cases, an additional period may be authorized. The maximum liability during a letter contract will be the estimated amount necessary to cover the contractor's requirements for funds before definitization. However, the liability will not exceed fifty percent (50%) of the estimated cost of the definitized contract (*FAR 52.216-24, Limitation of Government Liability*). Furthermore, the contractor will not be allowed to bill fee (cost type contract) or profit (fixed price contract), while under a letter contract. Obviously there is a great incentive for the contractor to cooperate and get the contract definitized.

### Indefinite Delivery/Definite Quantity Contracts (ID/DQ) (*FAR 16.502*)

This type of contract provides for delivery of a definite quantity of specific supplies or services for a fixed period. Actual deliveries or performance at designated locations will be made upon order of the contracting officer. The definite quantity type of contract is suitable for use where it is known in advance that a definite quantity of supplies or services will be required during a specified period. They must be regularly available or be available after a short lead time.

Advantages of this type of contract are that it permits stocks in storage depots to be maintained at minimum levels. It permits direct shipment by the seller to the ultimate user.

### Indefinite Delivery/Requirements Contracts (IDR) (*FAR 16.503*)

This type of contract provides for filling all actual purchase requirements of supplies or services during a specified contract period. Deliveries or performance will be scheduled by the timely placement of orders with the contractor. These instruments are also known as "Call Contracts." They may be used for procurements where it is impossible to determine in advance the precise quantities of the supplies or services that will be needed during a definite period of time. Funds are obligated by each delivery order, not by the contract itself.

An important aspect of a requirements contract is that there is no guarantee of ever getting an order. The Government guarantees no more than that it will purchase all of its requirements for the subject matter of the contract from the contractor during the contract term. It is incumbent upon the Government to give the contractor a good faith estimate of what those requirements will probably be. However, if no requirement arises, there will not be any orders to fill.

The requirements contract is appropriate for acquiring any supplies or services when the Government anticipates recurring requirements but cannot predetermine the precise quantities of supplies or services that will be needed during a definite period.

**Indefinite Delivery/Indefinite Quantity Contracts (ID/IQ) (*FAR 16.504*)**

This type of contract has the same features and applicability as the requirements contract. The major difference is the indefinite delivery/indefinite quantity (ID/IQ) contract must provide that the Government will procure or order and the contractor furnish at least a stated minimum quantity of supplies or services within a maximum limit. The limits may be expressed as a number of units or as dollar values. The contract may also require the contractor to furnish, if so ordered, any additional quantities, not to exceed a stated maximum. ID/IQ contracts work well when it is not practical to determine precisely defined and priced services and supplies at the time of contract award. To ensure that the contract is binding, the minimum quantity must be more than a nominal quantity, but not exceed the amount that the Government is fairly certain to order. When the Government does not order the established minimum quantities, the contractor may be able to receive compensation for the difference between the amount ordered and the minimum specified in the contract.

The contracting agency must conduct market research before placing an indefinite delivery/indefinite quantity task or delivery order valued above the simplified acquisition threshold of $150,000.

The contracting officer should, to the maximum extent practicable, give preference to making multiple awards of indefinite quantity contracts under a single solicitation for the same or similar supplies or services to two or more sources. Multiple award contracts help to balance the benefits found in competing well-defined requirements with the need for streamlined acquisition processes.

**Basic Agreements (B/A) (*FAR 16.702*)**

A basic agreement (B/A) is not a contract. It is a written instrument of understanding executed between an Executive Department or procuring activity and a contractor. It sets forth the negotiated contract clauses which will be applicable to future procurements entered into between the parties during the term of the agreement. The use of a basic agreement contemplates that coverage of a particular procurement action will be accomplished by the execution of a formal contractual document.

Any ensuing contracts with that contractor will incorporate, by reference or appendage, clauses agreed upon in the basic agreement. Basic agreements may be used with negotiated fixed-price or cost-reimbursement type contracts. Basic agreements are appropriate for use when past experience and future plans indicate that a substantial number of separate contracts may be entered into with a contractor during the forthcoming year. They are useful when substantial recurring negotiating problems exist with a particular contractor.

Basic agreements will neither cite appropriations to be charged nor to be used alone for the purpose of obligating funds. In addition, they will not in any manner, provide for or imply any agreement on the part of the Government to place future orders or contracts with the contractor. Furthermore, they will not be used in any manner to restrict competition.

### Basic Ordering Agreements (BOA) (*FAR 16.703*)

A basic ordering agreement (BOA) is not a contract. It is a document which is similar to a basic agreement. However, it also includes a description, as specific as practicable, of the supplies to be furnished or services to be performed when ordered. The BOA will include a description of the method for determination of the prices to be paid to the contractor. Either the specific terms and conditions of delivery or a description of the method of their determination will be set forth in the BOA. The BOA will list one or more activities which are authorized to issue orders under the agreement. Any activity so named may issue orders to the holder of the BOA specifying the supplies or services required.

Each BOA will specify the point at which each order becomes a binding contract. For example, the agreement may provide that issuance of an order gives rise to an immediate contract. A contract may arise when a contractor fails to reject the order within a specific number of days. Also a contract may be formed when the contractor accepts the order in a specified manner, such as a postcard, telegram, letter or signing and returning a copy of the order. The contracting officer will neither make a final commitment nor authorize the contractor to begin work on a BOA order until prices have been established, unless within the exception noted in FAR 16.703(d)(3).

Basic ordering agreements are used as a means of expediting procurement where specific items, quantities, and prices are not known at the time of executing the agreement. They are useful when past experience or future plans indicate that a substantial number of requirements for items or services will result in procurements from the contractor during the forthcoming year.

## INCENTIVE CONTRACTING

### Introduction to Incentive Contracting

The profit motive is the real essence of incentive contracting. There is an implied assumption by the Government that a contractor will have more motivation in performing the contract if there is a chance to increase profits. By accepting an incentive contract the contractor is agreeing, at least superficially, with the Government.

Therefore, the objective in an incentive contract is to motivate the contractor or subcontractor to earn more profit. The added earnings will be gained by achieving better performance and controlling contract costs. Such results are in the best interest of both the prime contractor and the Government. The technique is to adjust the contractor's profit by comparing the value of the completed contract to the cost and performance goals set in the contract. The profit adjustments may be positive (i.e., reward), negative (i.e., penalty) or a combination of the two.

There are three categories of incentives: cost, schedule and performance. Though separately identified, they all relate to some aspect of the contractor's performance under the contract: Each one will ultimately influence the amount of profit earned. Contractor performance is one of the basic precepts of award fee contracts, as discussed later in this chapter.

The incentive arrangements can be either overlapping or compartmentalized. The sum of the incentive factors, in either a maximum gain or loss mode, may exceed the maximum fee or minimum fee limits in the contract. That is an overlapping arrangement. However, that does not permit the contractor to receive more than the contractual limitations on fees. When the sum of the incentive factors equals the maximum or minimum fee limits, it is a compartmentalized incentive.

The application of incentives to performance-based contracts (PBC), which were discussed in Chapter 3, *The Acquisition Process*, has become extremely popular. The incentive features may be positive or negative. Whatever, they must create a proper balance of objective incentives between cost, schedule and performance. Those performance incentives must focus on the contractor's efforts toward the desired performance standards and be capable of being measured objectively. As in any contractual relationship it is essential that the contractor fully understands what is most important to the Government.

## Selection and Negotiation of Contract Type

As discussed at the beginning of this chapter, the selection of contract type follows the guidelines set forth in FAR 16.1, *Selecting Contract Types*. In addition, the contracting officer will apply the appropriate criteria described in FAR 16.4, *Incentive Contracts*, when initiating an incentive contract. The Government usually determines the type of contract and the incentive criteria desired in each procurement action prior to issuing the solicitation.

The request for proposal (RFP) will indicate that a fixed-price-incentive (FPI), cost-plus-incentive-fee (CPIF), cost-plus-award-fee (CPAF) or other type of contract is contemplated. It will also contain a representative list of the several incentive criteria expected to be in the contract. These factors are usually negotiable and may need adjustments to be compatible with the conditions of the individual procurement. As an example, in R&D contracting the nature of the work makes the selection of contract type very critical. Those contracts usually lack definitive requirements and technical objectives are difficult to quantify. The inability to measure risk frequently necessitates the selection of a CPAF or CPFF contract.

The former *DOD/NASA Incentive Contacting Guide* presented the following guidance for use in the selection and negotiation of the proper type of contract and its incentive criteria. The advice is still very appropriate.

> "The best structured incentive arrangements may become completely ineffectual if the type of contract and the contract price in combination are so unrealistic as to eliminate any possibility of the contractor's earning increased profit through cost savings or performance improvement."

With that guidance in mind, the selection of incentive criteria requires that consideration be given to the following guidelines:

- It is mandatory that multiple incentive contracts include cost incentives (*FAR 16.402-1(a)*).
- The three incentive types (cost, schedule, and performance) must be balanced.
- Emphasis on any type of incentive must be based on the nature of the program, its requirements and the type of contract.
- The contractor must have an opportunity to perform trade-offs between the several types of incentives.
- The cost criteria must provide the contractor with a real incentive to be cost conscious.
- Any incentives on schedule for delivery or completion must be realistic and the reward or penalty must be significant.
- Any performance criteria must be measurable, significant, important to the mission and limited in number.

## COST INCENTIVES

### Basic Concepts of Cost Incentives

Of the three types of incentive parameters – cost, schedule and performance – the straight cost incentive receives the widest application. Conceptually, it is the simplest of the three. It is an arrangement by which the contractor's profit or fee increases or decreases as the actual incurred allowable costs fall below or above the contract target cost.

To augment that simple concept and write an effective contract, it is not enough merely to include "some" cost incentive arrangement. The arrangement must be written so it offers the contractor a real incentive to meet or better cost objectives. The incentives must offer the contractor rewards commensurate with the risks assumed. Furthermore, the arrangement must not create a situation in which cost is either overemphasized or underemphasized relative to other procurement objectives. Satisfaction of these criteria requires that each cost incentive fee arrangement reflects the characteristics and problems of a particular procurement and an individual contractor.

## Cost Sharing Incentive Arrangements

Constructing cost incentives for Government contracts is not complicated, but it is complex with several moving elements to consider at the same time to arrive at the desired conclusion. In constructing a cost incentive, it is mandatory that one have access to graph paper. The vertical axis would usually represent the *fee* under a cost-plus-incentive-fee (CPIF) contract or the *profit* under a fixed-price-incentive (FPI) contract; while the horizontal axis will represent the *contract cost*. As the cost, estimated or actual, shifts along the horizontal axis, the fee or profit on the vertical axis will be adjusted according to the share ratio agreed upon.

The process of how the contractor's profit or fee is adjusted based upon cost performance is called the sharing arrangement or share ratio. The ratio is usually specified in the contract in dollars and cents. However, it basically relates to the percentage difference that actual costs incurred vary from the target cost in the contract. The sharing can also be described as a fraction, showing how the variance (overrun or underrun) will be shared by the buyer and seller.

To illustrate the concept, an 80/20 share ratio means that the buyer retains eighty percent (80%) of any underrun. The seller receives the remaining twenty percent (20%) of the underrun as additional fee or profit. In an overrun situation, with an 80/20 share ratio, the contractor's fee or profit gets reduced by twenty percent (20%) of any funded overrun. The sharing arrangement will operate within the maximum and minimum fee or profit limitations specified in the contract.

## Fixed-Price-Incentive (FPI) – Cost Only (*FAR 16.204 & 16.403*)

The fixed-price-incentive (FPI) contract is often preferred over a CPIF contract by both the Government and contractors. In 2010 the Defense Department initiated actions to put more of their programs into FPI type contracts. That action will place more burdens upon contractors forcing them to be more proactive in controlling costs, as they will have to absorb losses for overruns.

There are certain prerequisites for FPI contracts for that condition to exist. The degree of technical uncertainty should be the primary criterion for the choice between selection of a CPIF or an FPI contract. In addition, the mutual confidence the parties have in the cost or pricing information will play an important role. FPI contracts are not good when the available cost or pricing information and performance specifications prevent negotiation of firm targets and firm ceiling prices. FPI contracts are really appropriate when there is a reasonable expectation of technical success within stated, measurable limits.

The FPI contract should include relatively firm design, specifications and performance requirements. They will permit the contractor to operate without detailed control or technical direction. Events or direction outside control of the contractor should not have an adverse impact upon performance and schedule goals.

The ingredients of a fixed-price-incentive (FPI) contract shown in Figure 5-2, *FPI Cost Incentive Structure*, illustrate the relationship of the FPI ingredients.

- Target Cost – The amount against which the final costs are measured.
- Target Profit – A reasonable profit for target cost at target performance.
- Target Price – The combination of target cost and target profit.
- Ceiling Price – The Government's maximum dollar liability.
- Sharing formula ratio – The arrangement for establishing final price.
- Ceiling Cost (aka Breakpoint of Point of Total Assumption (PTA)) – The dollar amount of a FPI contract at which point the share formula converts to a firm-fixed-price arrangement.

**FPI COST INCENTIVE STRUCTURE**

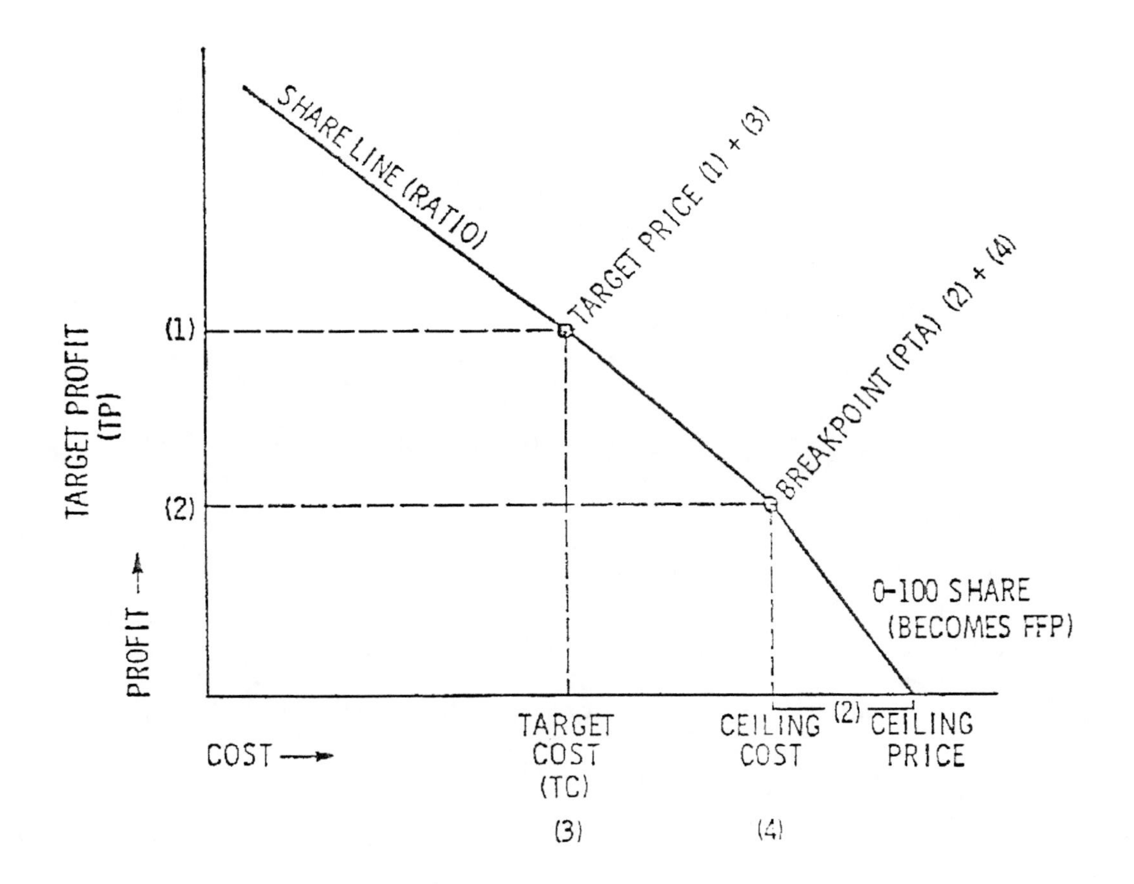


**Figure 5-2**

## FPI Structuring Techniques

There are several techniques for structuring a fixed-price-incentive contract during the course of the negotiations. The following technique is often used and is the one most favored by the author. The parties will negotiate target cost, target profit, ceiling price and sharing ratio individually. While this seems simplistic, it is very advisable to base final negotiation upon simultaneous agreement of all elements of the price. This is an excellent procedure when all elements are properly evaluated and combined.

To illustrate this process use Figure 5-3, *FPI Cost Incentive Example*, page 133, as an example. Then we have to assume that the negotiation results in agreement that the following are reasonable:

Target Cost: $10,000,000
Target Profit: $ 1,050,000
Target Price: $11,050,000
Ceiling Price: $12,000,000 (or 120% of Target Cost)
Share Ratio: 65/35

Using the above negotiated factors, the next important step will be for the contracting parties to establish the cost ceiling or Point of Total Assumption (PTA). The following formula was used to find the PTA used in examples shown in Figures 5-2 and 5-3.

$$\text{Cost Ceiling (PTA)} = \frac{\text{Ceiling Price} - \text{Target Price}}{\text{Government's Share}} + \text{Target Cost}$$

$$= \frac{\$12{,}000{,}000 - \$11{,}050{,}000}{.65} + \$10{,}000{,}000$$

$$= \frac{\$950{,}000}{.65} + \$10{,}000{,}000$$

$$\text{Cost Ceiling (PTA)} = \$1{,}461{,}538.40 + \$10{,}000{,}000 = \$11{,}461{,}538.40$$

Therefore, if the contractor's costs exceed $11,461,538.40, the share ratio changes from 65/35 to 0/100. This has the effect of converting the contract from an FPI arrangement to an FFP one. If the contractor's costs exceed the ceiling price of $12,000,000, all such costs become a loss to the contractor. Costs incurred in excess of the ceiling price are not reimbursed by the Government.

## FPI COST INCENTIVE EXAMPLE

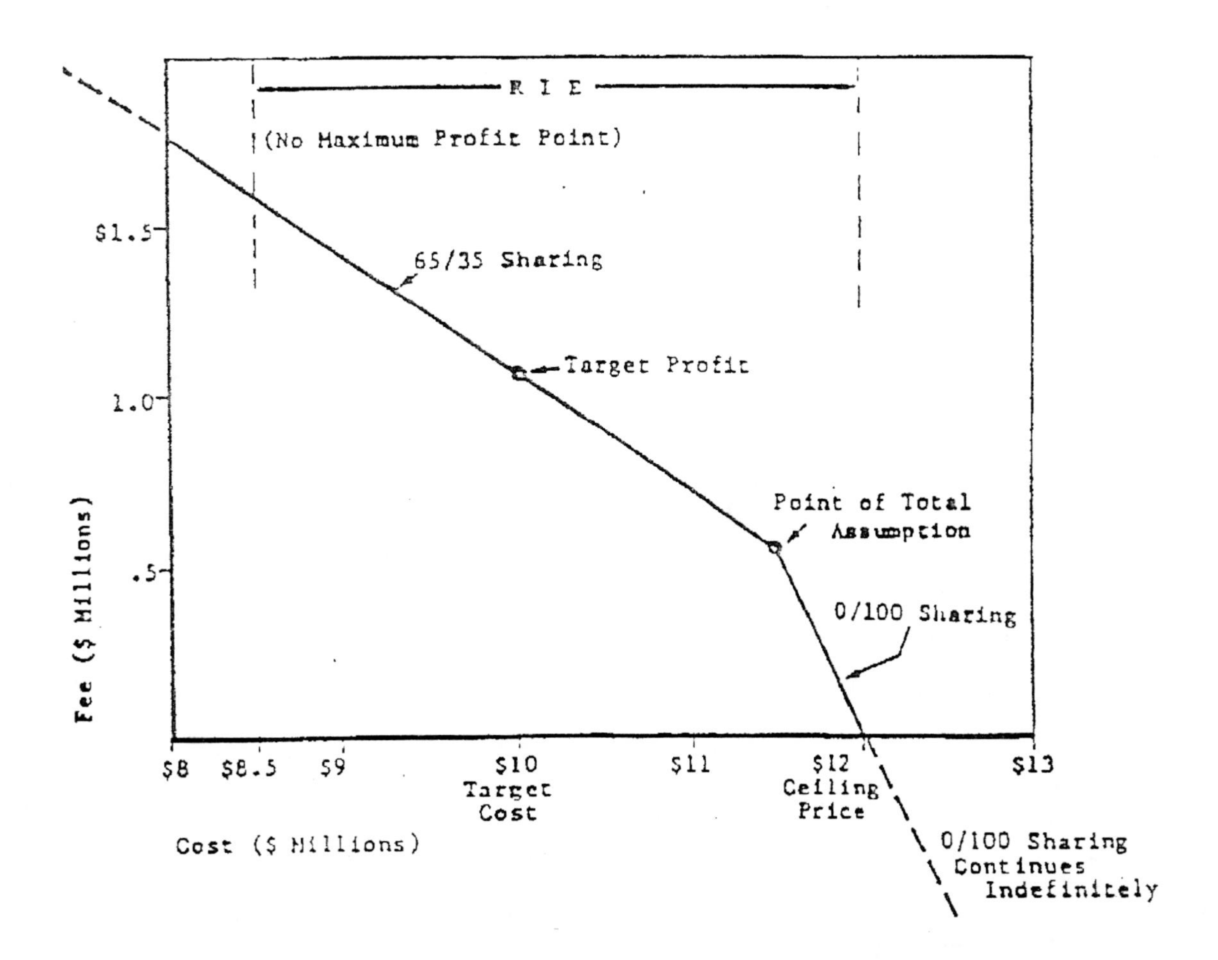


Figure 5-3

### Cost-Plus-Incentive-Fee – Cost Only

The cost-plus-incentive-fee (CPIF) contract (*FAR 16.304 & 16.405-1*) is very effective where there are significant uncertainties in successful contract performance and estimated costs. Those uncertainties do not encourage use of any type of fixed-price contract. Positive profit incentives are likely to provide much more motivation for contractors to be cost effective than in a CPFF environment. Therefore, the motivation features of CPIF contracts are appropriate for efforts that fall between the spectrum of fixed-price and cost-plus type contracts.

There are several characteristics which distinguish CPIF contracts from FPI contracts. There is no ceiling price in a CPIF contract. In the CPIF situation, the Government reimburses costs in accordance with the regulations and the terms and conditions of the contract. In FPI contracting, final cost is established in accordance with a negotiated agreement. Under a CPIF contract, the final "allowable" costs are applied to the incentive formula to determine the final fee earned. Also the maximum fee the contractor can receive is subject to the statutory limits noted below.

In a FPI contract the "negotiated final costs" are applied to the incentive formula to determine the amount of earned profit. Furthermore, there are no regulatory limits on profit with fixed-price type contracts.

The following are the ingredients of a cost-plus-incentive-fee (CPIF) contract.

- Estimated Cost – The Government's maximum cost exposure for the contract. This usually equates to the target cost at the beginning of the contract. An exception to this exists when there are non-fee bearing costs included in the estimated cost.
- Target Cost – This is the most probable cost for performance by the contractor.
- Target Fee – A reasonable fee to be paid for target performance.
- Maximum Fee – The maximum amount of fee payable regardless of cost performance. The initial maximum fee may be subject to statutory limits.
- Minimum Fee – The minimum amount of fee payable regardless of cost performance. It may be a negative fee.
- Share Formula (aka share-ratio) – The arrangement for setting final fee payable at contract completion.

Note: The maximum fee and minimum fee amounts equate to the outer limits of the Range of Incentive Effectiveness (RIE).

**Statutory Fee Limitations**

The regulations (*FAR 15.404-4, Profit*) are very explicit about the fee a contracting officer can negotiate in cost-plus-fixed-fee contracts. The following statutory limitations are imposed by 10 U.S.C 2306(e) and 41 U.S.C. 254(b) and are spelled out in FAR 15.404-4(c)(4)(i). For experimental, developmental, or research work, the fee may not exceed 15 percent of the contract's estimated cost, excluding fee. For architect-engineer services for public works or utilities, the contract price or the estimated cost and fee for production and delivery of designs, plans, drawings, and specifications may not exceed 6 percent of the estimated cost of construction of the public work or utility, excluding fee. For all other CPFF contracts, the fee may not exceed 10 percent of the contract's estimated cost, excluding fee.

**CPIF Structuring Techniques**

As noted before, there are several techniques for structuring FPI (cost-only) contracts. There are even more techniques for structuring CPIF contracts. The use of a structured approach for determining profit or fee prenegotiation objectives provides a discipline for ensuring that all relevant factors are being considered by the parties. No attempt is made here to identify all the variations used to reach agreement under a CPIF (cost-only) contract. The following are four of the most common examples for developing a negotiating position.

- The first task is to establish a target cost. Then you use predetermined percentages for all other elements. An example of this is a Target Fee of 7%, Maximum Fee of 10% (+3%), Minimum Fee of 4% (−3%), Sharing Ratio of 85/15, RIE ±20%. This technique is representative of many earlier incentive structures. A variation of this method is first negotiate both target cost and target fee. Then let all the other factors "fall-out" on the basis of predetermined or arbitrary percentage or within the equal ratios.
- You may set target cost and target fee, and then apply a confidence factor to the sharing ratio. You set them above and below target cost to previously selected maximum and minimum fees. This will allow the Range of Incentive Effectiveness (RIE) to be an automatic fall-out. With this arrangement the RIE may vary on each side of the target cost. That will depend upon the respective share ratio and fee level established. This approach is a little better than the one above, where the so-called "confidence factor" is usually subjective in nature. It seldom reflects the actual conditions that could be reasonably estimated for cost results above and below target cost.
- In the third case, you establish target cost, target fee, Range of Incentive Effectiveness (RIE) and the sharing ratio. Then you let the maximum and minimum fees "fall-out." This technique is superior to either of the above techniques. However, it assumes that the sharing ratio and the RIE have been evaluated and represent an expression of "value to the Government." This has not always been the case.
- The last approach is to establish through cost analyses the most probable cost (target), the most optimistic cost (minimum), and the most pessimistic cost (maximum). Then you select a reasonable fee for each of these. After that you calculate the sharing ratio between maximum fee and target and between target and minimum fee. The advantage here is that these values aid in setting the prenegotiation position based on the evaluation of the contractor's proposal. This is possible because you have been separately evaluating each of the essential ingredients of the incentive pricing arrangement.

Figure 5-4, *CPIF Cost Incentive Structures*, page 136, illustrates two CPIF incentive fee structures. The top example illustrates a cost incentive with an 80/20 cost share, and the bottom graph illustrates a contract with a 90/10 share ratio. It is evident from the graphs how much difference a cost share ratio can make.

## CPIF COST INCENTIVE STRUCTURES

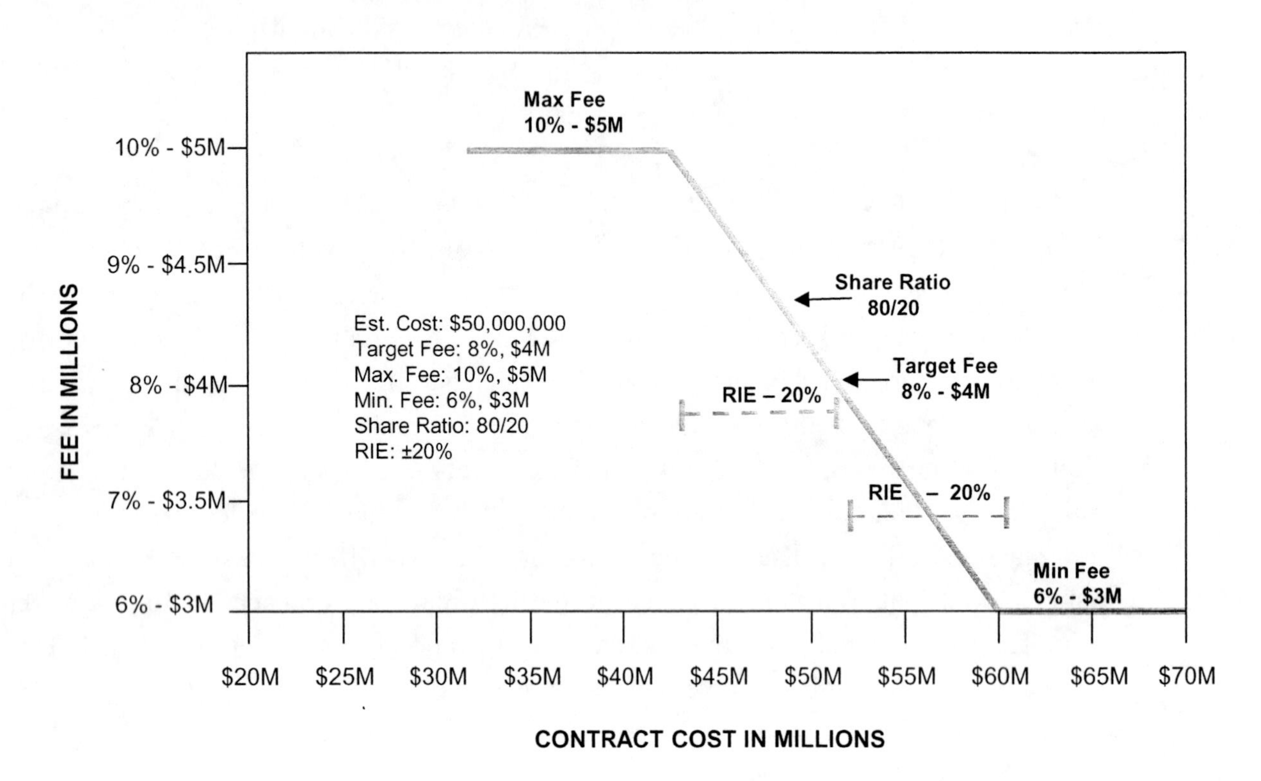


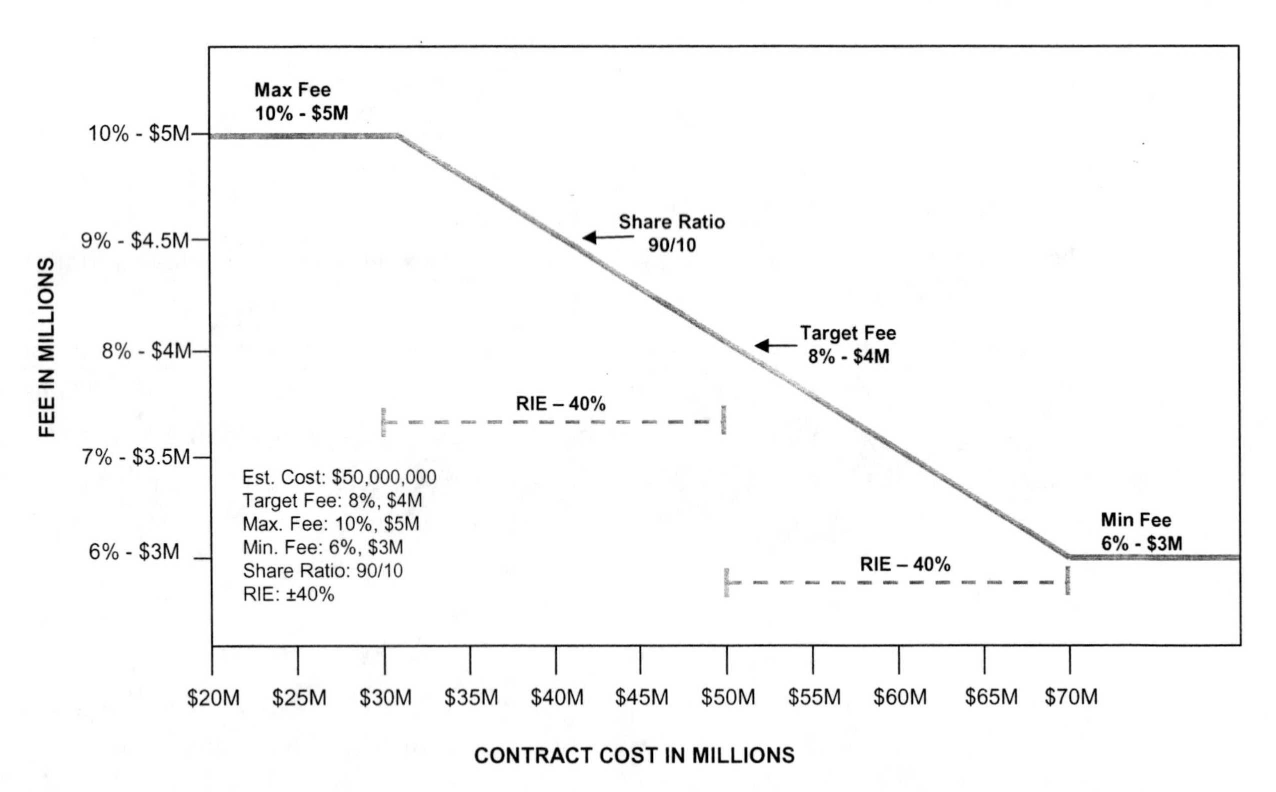


**Figure 5-4**

**Range of Incentive Effectiveness**

It is an accepted principle that cost incentive provisions in incentive type contracts, both CPIF and FPI, should be effective over the entire range of possible costs incurred. The idea is to reduce the chance that the incentive provisions will run out at an early point in contract performance. That would create a non-incentivized situation where the contractor will place little or no emphasis on cost control. Equally to be avoided is extending the sharing arrangement beyond the reasonable limits of probable cost outcomes. Doing so would have the effect of reducing the fee pool in the "actual" incentive range.

The application of this principle assumes that the maximum fee, when and if earned, will be reward for an outstanding job. Conversely, the cost at which minimum fee is paid will represent a low level of accomplishment.

Range of Incentive Effectiveness (RIE) is an evaluation of what costs are likely to be. The RIE will be expressed either as high to low costs, or most pessimistic to most optimistic costs. RIE is a judgment of the range of probable costs. It is not an estimate of the range of possible costs above and below that range. The RIE is the product of cost and price analysis. It is a conclusion reached after analysis of facts and cost projections. RIE is that conclusion translated into dollars of target cost, share lines and either price ceiling or fee floor and fee ceiling. It operates in both CPIF and FPI environments.

## MULTIPLE INCENTIVES

**Basic Concepts of Multiple Incentives**

Multiple incentive contracting combines the motivation for technological progress, timely delivery and effective cost control. It has the ultimate objective of attaining an appropriate balance between performance, schedule and cost control. Therefore, lowest cost is not the controlling goal in multiple incentives. In contrast, in a cost-only incentive contract the emphasis is on the attainment of the stated performance achievement at the lowest cost.

The sound application of multiple incentive contracting relates profit motivation in a quantitative manner directly to the goals of the contracting parties. Multiple incentives must identify the alternative technical levels of performance. The incentives must place the relative value on the alternatives as they are affected by the interrelationship between cost, performance and schedule decisions. The objective is to emphasize the proper application of multiple incentives. Multiple incentives can be useless, even detrimental, if improperly developed or inappropriate for a particular program and contract. Therefore, the contracting parties must avoid "standard incentive parameters" and tailor the incentives to the immediate program taking into consideration the possible risks that the program may encounter during the period of performance.

Multiple incentives should be negotiated within a structure which gives appropriate weight to basic procurement and program objectives. This includes a balancing of the range of cost and performance goals. The proper balancing of objectives achieves two important results. First it communicates the Government's goals to the contractor. It also establishes the contractor's profit in direct relationship to the value of the combined level of performance in all areas. However, the interrelationship of the various incentive features must provide the opportunity for trade-offs by the contractor, rather than competing with each other.

All multiple incentive contracts must include a cost incentive. Otherwise the contractor might ignore any cost controls to earn additional performance or schedule incentives. This would not be in the best interest of the Government. Neither is it the basic premise of incentive contracting. Even a firm-fixed-price contract has a cost sharing ratio, expressed as 0/100. The sharing arrangement for a cost-plus-fixed-fee contract at 100/0 is the direct opposite. Specifically, all performance weighting and schedule targets are eventually reduced to a profit base. For this reason, all performance elements and schedule criteria automatically relate to a cost sharing ratio of some kind.

## Multiple Incentive Structuring (*FAR 16.402-4*)

The multiple incentive contract should reflect the importance to the Government of various cost, schedule and performance outcomes. This is done by relating the dollar value to the results, through the profit assigned, to each part of the multiple incentive structure.

It is reasonable to assume that the contractors' management make trade-offs during the prenegotiation phase. Similar trade-offs are made at the negotiation table and during the contract budget effort. Later trade-offs are limited to relatively minor decisions. That could change if major difficulties occur.

The techniques, as proposed by the former *DOD/NASA Incentive Contracting Guide,* used in structuring a multiple incentive contract, suggested a seven-step procedure summarized as follows:

- **Step I** is to identify those key parameters whose improvement will add to overall mission accomplishment.
- **Step II** is the formulation of minimum and maximum levels of performance (RIE) for each parameter selected. The minimum must be high enough to satisfy the mission, while the maximum should not be so high that it is unattainable.
- **Step III** is rating the performance parameters by weighting each parameter according to its relative importance. The weights are then assigned to the maximum performance level. The sum of the weights (of maximum levels) of each of the parameters should be 100. The minimum level for each parameter is scored as Zero. Then, the number of points assigned to target performance for each parameter is chosen.

- **Step IV** is the evaluation of the performance arrangement. There are several tools available to aid in this evaluation. Actual performance is measured against performance point curves, incentive fee curves, performance ordering tables and performance nomographs. An analysis using these tools will assist technical personnel in selecting the best technical combination possible.
- **Step V** relates the Government cost estimates with the technical combinations selected in Step IV. Estimates such as range of probable cost and target cost are arrived at through a cooperative effort between procurement and technical personnel. At this point, an in-house estimate is probably not final, but it will serve to set up a cost-performance relationship. That relationship can be useful for the initial Government negotiation position as well as for RFP planning and preparation and later proposal evaluation.
- **Step VI** is the development of the cost-performance relationship. This step is an iterative process for developing the cost versus fee (profit) curve. The curve is compared to the performance structure(s), as developed in Steps I through IV. This process uses cost versus performance trade-off curves, cost-performance-schedule ordering tables, and cost-performance-fee nomographs.
- **Step VII** is the final analysis of the entire incentive structure. This includes analyzing the trade-off curves, tables and nomographs from Step VI. The purpose is to determine acceptability of the cost-performance trade-offs (value statements) developed.

Figure 5-5, *CPIF – Multiple Incentives*, on page 140 is an example of a compartmentalized CPIF multiple incentive contract. This example has straight share lines covering cost, performance and schedule elements. At appropriate stages during the life of the contract, the contractor's actual performance will be compared to the performance criteria contained in the Incentive Fee Plan. Results of that comparison are plotted against a graph similar to example (A) in Figure 5-5. The results of the performance rating are then transferred to the composite graph similar to (B) in the figure.

In this example the performance score is shown by the broken line above the solid cost incentive share ratio line. If the contractor has not met the scheduled delivery dates a schedule incentive loss will occur. That loss is also defined in the Incentive Fee Plan. The results are plotted in example (B) as the broken line below the cost incentive line. This process is frequently delayed until the contract is physically complete.

The following criteria were used in Figure 5-5:

| | |
|---|---|
| Cost Range: | $8M - $12.5M |
| Target Cost: | $10M |
| Target Fee: | $800K (8%) |
| Maximum Fee: | $1,400K (14%) |
| Minimum Fee: | $240K (2.4%) |
| Cost Sharing: | 80/20 |
| Performance Incentive: | +$200K (IAW – Performance Requirements) |
| Schedule Incentive: | –$60K (IAW – Schedule Requirements) |

## CPIF – MULTIPLE INCENTIVES

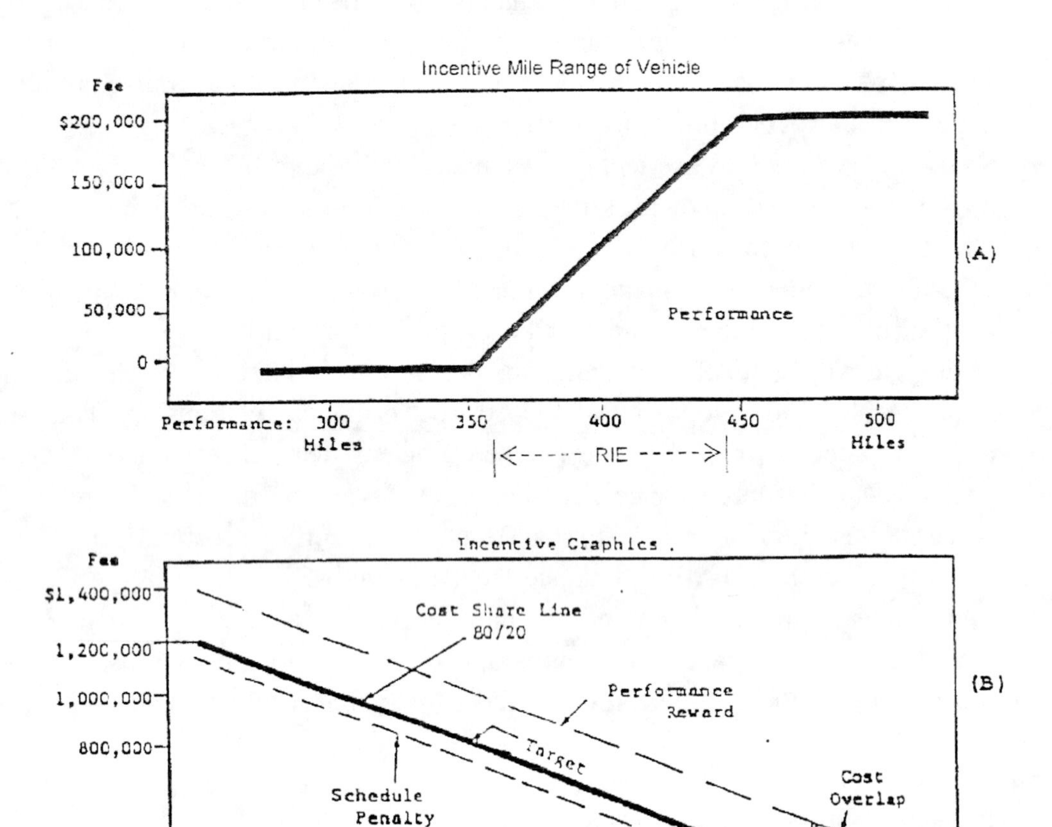


**Figure 5-5**

The structure for Fixed-Price multiple incentive (FPI) contracts can have either rewards-penalty or rewards-only features. Figure 5-6, *FPI Rewards-Penalty,* on page 141 illustrates the rewards-penalty concept and Figure 5-7, *FPI Rewards-Only*, on page 142 illustrates the rewards-only concept. Both illustrations use the following criteria.

Target Cost: $10M
Target Profit: $1,050K (10.5%)
Ceiling Price: $12M (120% of Target Cost)
Share Ratio: 65/35
Performance Penalty: $350K (3.5%)
Penalty-Rewards: $420K (4.2%)

## FPI REWARDS-PENALTY

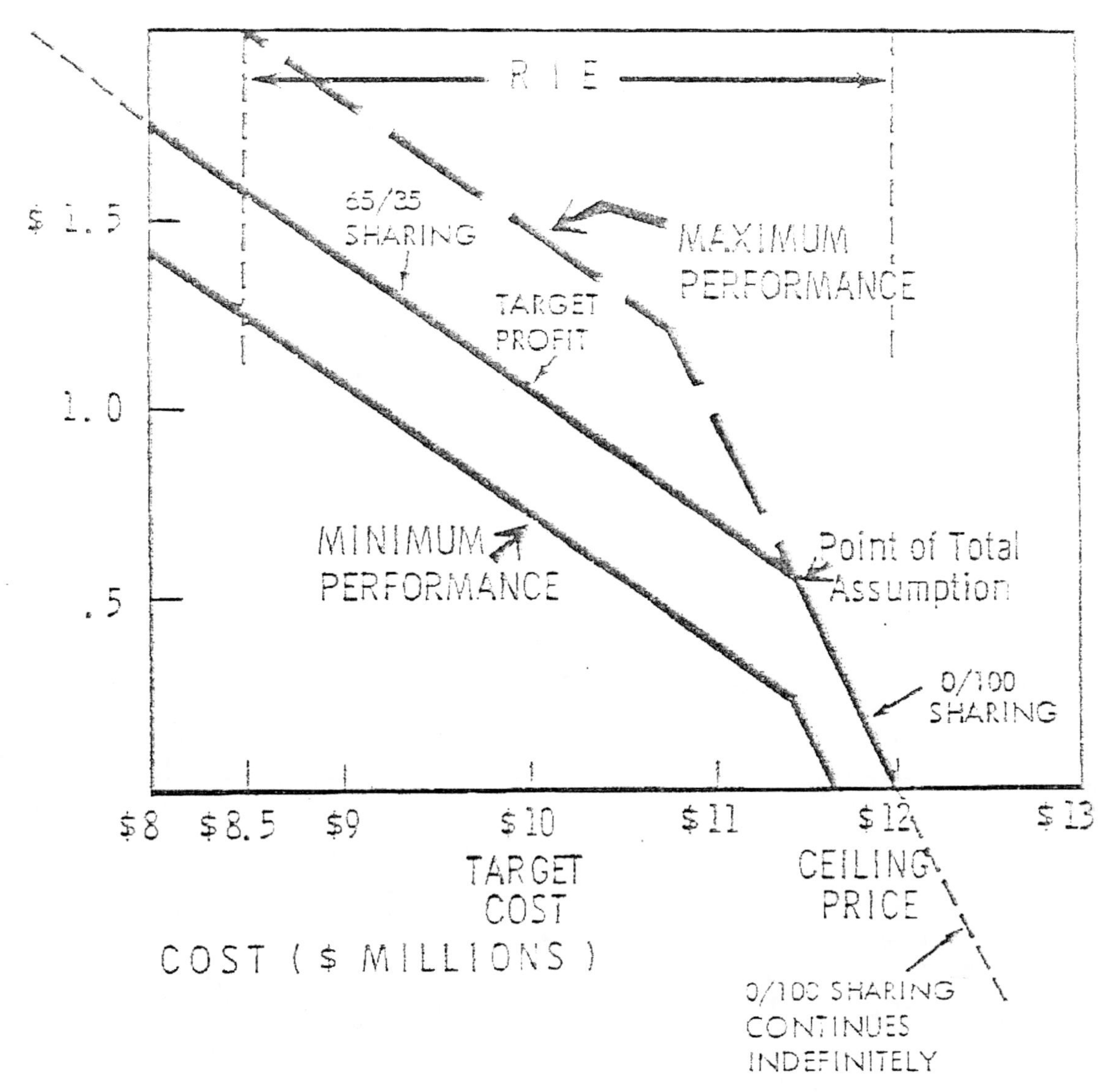


**Figure 5-6**

**FPI REWARDS-ONLY**

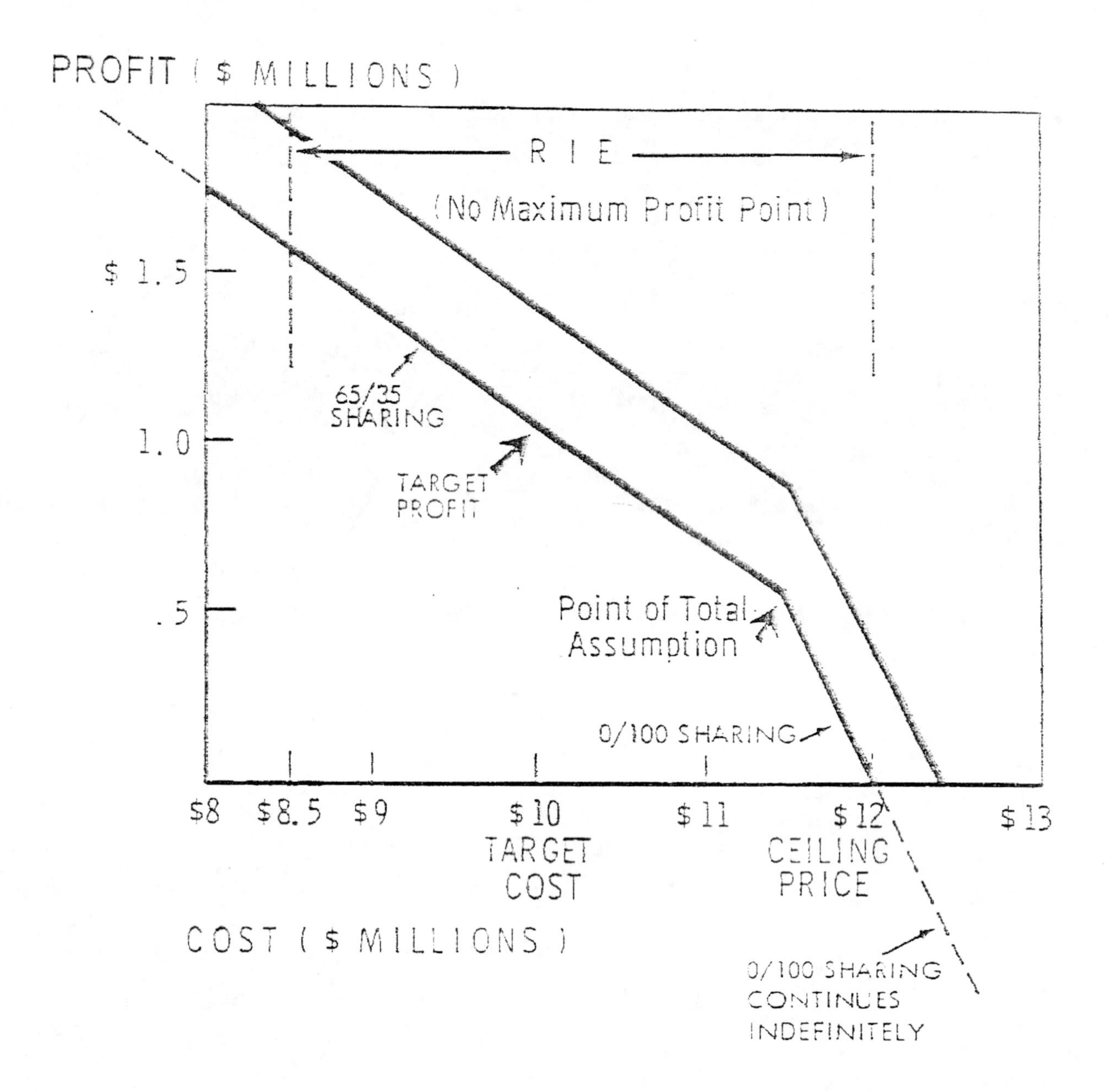


**Figure 5-7**

**Performance Incentives (*FAR 16.402-2*)**

The application of performance incentives can be the most important motivator the Government can impose upon its contractors. Performance incentives may be applied to selected contract end items and their specific product characteristics or other specific elements of the contractor's performance. The incentives selected should relate the profit or fee to results achieved by the contractor when compared with specific targets.

With service contracts, criteria for measurements are usually evaluated in an objective manner. Therefore, the tasks for measurement must be both relevant to the services to be provided and controllable by the contractor. Technical performance incentives are commonly used in major systems contracts, during both development and production.

Technical performance criteria may involve a variety of characteristics that contribute to the overall performance of the end item. Examples of such criteria are: missile range, aircraft speed, engine thrust or vehicle maneuverability. Therefore, the incentives on individual technical characteristics must be balanced so that no one of them is exaggerated to the detriment of the overall performance of the end item.

**Delivery Incentives (*FAR 16.402-3*)**

Delivery or schedule incentives can be either positive (reward) or negative (penalty). The Government will usually require a negative incentive to emphasize the importance of the contractual delivery date. However, the Government will use a positive incentive if it is willing to pay a premium for early delivery. The reward incentive is also used when the Government has an urgent need for the item and hopes a positive incentive will motivate the contractor to accelerate the delivery schedule.

For several reasons it may be very difficult to determine and assign realistic schedule incentives. It is hard to calculate the true monetary impact a schedule delay will have upon the Government's operations. The objectives may not remain constant. The effect of any change cannot be forecast with reasonable accuracy. Furthermore, the impact of an actual schedule delay could easily exceed the total contract value. An example of the latter situation would be when there is a contractor responsible for delivery of a small but critical hardware item for installation on a launch site. What is the cost impact if the item delays the launch of the space shuttle for several days? That cost could be more than the company's entire assets.

Many equitable adjustments to contracts involve schedule changes as well as cost adjustments. Contractors can make trade-offs between cost and schedule throughout the entire contract period of performance. Including schedule incentives in a contract will encourage such actions.

Schedule delivery dates are listed in contracts in several ways. They frequently use calendar dates, such as 20 Jan 99. Some agencies like to use an acronym, like *150 DAC*, which means 150 days after contract award. Others use *150 ADAD* which means 150 days after date of award document.

A number of days after a specific event or program milestone, such as Final Systems Test plus 15 days, is another technique.

## AWARD FEE CONTRACTING

### Award Fee Contracts

Government agencies are tending to have more contracts where award fees are utilized than other incentive arrangements that they had in past years. This partially relates to the reduced budgets available and smaller staffs to perform the necessary close surveillance of contractor performance. They now have to place more reliance upon the contractors to perform their contractual obligations.

Award fee can be incorporated into both fixed-price and cost-reimbursement contracts. Fixed-price-award-fee contracts were discussed previously in this chapter. Another contract type, performance-based contracts, which can be either fixed-price or cost-reimbursable, can incorporate award fee provisions. These were also addressed earlier in this chapter and in Chapter 3, *The Acquisition Process*. Following is an in-depth discussion of cost-reimbursement award-fee contracts.

## COST-PLUS-AWARD-FEE CONTRACTS

### Basic Concepts of Cost-Plus-Award-Fee (CPAF) Contracts

The cost-plus-award-fee (CPAF) contract is a Cost-Reimbursement type of contract with special incentive fee provisions. It provides a means of applying incentives in contracts which are not susceptible to development of firm measurable objectives for cost, technical and management performance. FAR 16.405-2 *(Cost-Plus-Award-Fee Contracts)* provides guidance for the application of CPAF contracts.

FAR 16.405-2 states that the CPAF contract is suitable for use when the following conditions exist:

- The work to be performed is such that it is neither feasible nor effective to devise predetermined objective incentive targets applicable to cost, technical performance, or schedule.
- The likelihood of meeting acquisition objectives will be enhanced by using the flexibility to evaluate both actual performance and the conditions under which it was achieved.

- Any additional administrative effort and cost required to monitor and evaluate performance are justified by the expected benefits.

A cost-plus-award-fee (CPAF) arrangement fits in the spectrum of approved contract types between cost-plus-fixed-fee (CPFF) and cost-plus-incentive-fee (CPIF) contracts. It is improper to use a CPAF contract as an administrative technique to avoid a CPFF contract when the CPFF criteria are appropriate. Furthermore, do not use a CPAF contract to avoid the effort of establishing objective targets, when a CPIF type of contract is really the proper type of contract.

In contrast to a CPIF contract, the CPAF contract provides that the contractor's earned fee is determined subjectively. Designated Government personnel make periodic, after-the-fact, evaluations of the contractor's performance. Cost-plus-award-fee contracts have a base fee, a maximum fee and an award fee pool. Only the latter is subject to the evaluation process. The award fee determination is subject to special checks and balances which provide procedural safeguards. Their purpose is to protect both the Government and the contractor from arbitrary or capricious evaluations.

The ingredients of CPAF contracts are:

- *Estimated Cost* – The Government's maximum cost exposure for the contract.
- *Base Fee* – A fixed fee which does not vary with performance and is not subject to the evaluation process. The base fee is equivalent to the fixed-fee in a CPFF contract and gets similar treatment. Not all CPAF contracts will have a base fee included in the fee arrangement.
- *Award Fee* – A fee determined on a subjective basis, following evaluation of performance measured against the performance criteria in the contract. The total award fee pool is divided into several equal segments extending over the contract period of performance. Each segment is individually evaluated with award made after each period. Award fee may be earned in whole, in part or may even be zero, depending upon the subjective evaluation.
- *Maximum Fee* – Base fee plus the total award fee pool. The maximum fee as negotiated will not exceed the regulatory limits on CPAF contract fees, as noted before.
- *Performance Criteria* – The criteria used by the contracting officer or other designated official in rating the contractor's performance for each evaluation period.
- *Fee Payment Plan* – The Schedule clause that specifies the method and frequency by which the contractor may invoice awarded fees.

**Award Criteria and Evaluation**

Award fee evaluation plans and subjective measurement systems are more effective when developed before start of the contract effort. Both contractor and Government personnel should fully understand the evaluation plan and the techniques for assessing the contractor's performance. Sometimes the plans and procedures are included within the Schedule of the contract. Often they are incorporated into the contract by a separate contractual exhibit.

To evaluate the contractor's performance, the Government team may use performance criteria that are extensively defined, or as brief as these:

- Effective business, contract management and cost control
- Soundness of technical approach to problems and effectiveness of problem solutions
- Effectiveness of final assembly and factory check-out
- Successful attainment of mission objectives
- Efficient utilization of labor force
- Responsiveness to Government's requirements
- Reliability and quality control effectiveness

The parties must fully understand the meaning and intent of each criterion. Whenever there is doubt about any of the criteria the parties should enter into discussions to resolve any issues.

All CPAF contracts must provide for evaluations to be performed at stated intervals during the life of the contract. That way the contractors are periodically informed of the quality of their performance and the areas where improvement will be expected. Partial payment of fee will generally correspond to the evaluation periods. At the beginning of each award fee period, the Government will notify the contractor about the specific areas of concentration to be observed during that segment. During the evaluation period, selected Government personnel will have the assignment to maintain a "score card" on the contractor's performance. At the end of each period they will rate the contractor against the specific criteria using the data gathered.

A typical award fee plan will contain subjective levels of evaluation that the award determination official or committee will apply to the several criteria. Each level will have a percentage range within which they will assign a value. That assigned value is then applied to the award fee available for the period under evaluation. The fee actually awarded will be in direct ratio to the points earned. The following is an example of possible levels and percentage ranges:

| Evaluation Level | Range of Performance Points |
|---|---|
| Superior | 91 to 100 |
| Above Average | 81 to 90 |
| Average | 71 to 80 |
| Below Average | 61 to 70 |
| Unsatisfactory | 0 to 60 |

Summaries of the evaluations are usually furnished to the contractor to allow for comments and observations on the evaluator's findings. This gives the contractor a chance to appeal the award fee recommendations. The contractor will try to qualify or justify actions taken during the performance of that period. After consideration of the contractor's comments, the fee evaluation official or board will make a unilateral award fee decision. The contracting officer sends that decision to the contractor in writing. That decision is not subject to further official discussions. The determination and methodology for determining the award fee to be paid to the contractor are unilateral decisions made solely at the discretion of the Government. The contractor cannot appeal it under the disputes procedures.

### Award Fee Adjustments

Award fee adjustments are increases only. The potential award fee (fee pool) should be an amount which will provide motivation for excellence in the areas described in the performance criteria. However, the decision to pay an amount of the "variable incentive" fee, whether it is all, part or none, is a unilateral determination made by the Government.

The base fee is normally payable at least on a monthly basis, in the same manner as the fixed-fee in a CPFF contract. The award fee is generally determined on a quarterly or semi-annual basis. After the award fee is determined the contract is modified to cite the amount awarded and funds allocated. The modification will permit the contractor to submit an invoice for payment. In some contracts, a provision will permit portions of the fee not awarded during any period to be available for award in later periods. This provision is always exercised at the discretion of the contracting officer.

The Department of Defense has authorized contracting officers to make provisional award fee payments on a case-by-case basis. There are some restrictions in that:

- They may not be made more than once a month.
- They are limited to no more than 50 percent of the award fee available for the initial award fee evaluation period.
- They are limited to no more than 80 percent of the award fee available for the current period.

Also, contracting officers are required to collect any overpayment made on provisional award fees.

### Combination CPAF Contracts

Some CPAF contracts provide for a combination incentive measurement plan and a combination fee. They are frequently used where cost control is largely under the control of the contractor. When the arrangement is mostly an award fee and subjective in nature, it is identified as a CPAF/IF contract. There the performance criteria carry more weight than the cost elements. If the cost-based incentive was predominant, it is identified as a CPIF/AF contract. Actually, an award fee can be suitable for incorporation into other types of contracts, such as an FPI/AF arrangement. Whatever combination, well defined criteria are essential.

The structuring methods, graphics and criteria for combination CPAF contracts would be similar to conventional incentives. Award fees fit into either a compartmentalized or overlapping structure.

# PART 2

# THE PREAWARD PHASE

# OF

# FEDERAL CONTRACTING

# CHAPTER 6

# DEVELOPING COMPETITIVE PROPOSALS

---

## PROPOSAL FUNDAMENTALS

### Organizing for Proposal Development

In the world of Government contracting, proposals are the "point of sale" for companies seeking to do business with the Federal Government. The majority of such business comes through the route of proposals. Except for sole source acquisitions, those proposals will be in for some very stiff competition. Even in sole source situations there is no excuse for a company to submit an inadequate and half-hearted proposal. Common courtesy demands that a responsive and effective proposal be submitted at all times. Therefore, a great deal of attention must be given to developing a good proposal organization within the management structure.

Any business which hopes to do a significant amount of Government business should have a good, strong and permanent group of individuals dedicated to the acquisition of new business through the development of "winning" proposals. The size of a company, plus the nature of its business and volume of proposals will determine the make-up of its proposal organization. Regardless of size, the proposal group should have the attention of top management.

Each proposal should have its individualized team. Using the proposal organization as its nucleus, the team will draw upon specialists in the multiple disciplines needed to cover all areas of the proposal.

### Proposal Preparation Procedures

Every company must have specific, well-defined and detailed policies and procedures for the development and submission of proposals. Without them, there could be a great waste of time, talent and money. Even more tragic, there would be fewer contracts won.

One important procedure recommended for all significant proposals is the issuance of a Proposal Plan which will serve several functions. The Proposal Plan will contain the overall outline to be followed in writing the proposal and the schedule for the proposal process. The plan will set up the basis for the budget to be allocated and become the basic control document to monitor progress being made.

The bid and proposal (B&P) budget assigned for each proposal must be realistic. Comparison must be made to the expected business which may be earned. In order to optimize the return on investment, funding for a proposal should be maintained within the guidelines established by management.

The proposal funds will typically come from one of three sources. Direct charges to a contract will be made when a contractor is required, as a contract deliverable, to submit a proposal for the next phase of the program. Indirect costs, called bid and proposal (B&P) costs, will be used for all other proposal efforts. However, those indirect charges will only be made up to their reimbursable limits allowed by the Government. Virtually every major contractor is placed under a negotiated ceiling for reimbursable bid and proposal (B&P) and independent research and development (IR&D) costs. Smaller contractors are subject to a formula mathematically limiting these costs (*FAR 31.205-18, Independent Research and Development and Bid and Proposal Costs*).

Once the authorized or negotiated B&P limits have been reached, further proposal costs will come from company funds. Great care must be exercised by all parties concerned that B&P costs are allocated to the proper accounts. Improper charging will subject the costs to disallowance by the Government.

Successful proposals like any successful program depend upon effective management and control. There must be proper advance planning and definite goals set. Realistic schedules must be made and then closely monitored. As with any team effort, well defined and detailed procedures are needed for directing the proposal team. The B&P budget will require constant monitoring. To all this we need to add effective team work and management surveillance.

## Pre-Proposal Activities

Probably the most important pre-proposal activity a company must undertake will be deciding which new business opportunities to pursue. More bid opportunities are available than can be pursued. Due to limitations on new business funds and manpower, bid/no-bid decisions must be made very carefully. There are some very basic criteria that need to be considered in making that decision. Correct answers to the following questions are important. What is the probability of actual program occurrence? What are the odds that your company will win the competition? What are the projected sales and profits from the enterprise? What is the synergistic relationship this program will have with your other programs and projects? Will this program enhance your company's long-range objectives?

Once the preliminary bid decision is made, early organization, planning, scheduling and technical development is essential. Effective customer relations begin well in advance of receipt of the request for proposal (RFP) or request for quote (RFQ). Furthermore, an efficient information gathering program is mandatory if you are to prepare worthwhile, timely and effective proposals.

It is important to know when to start your pre-proposal activities. Too early a start can be just as useless as a late start. The marketing activities should provide the key information necessary to make that decision. Remember that in the majority of cases, there is little chance of winning when there has been no advance knowledge of the program described in the RFP. Much of the advance information will be gathered from trade journals, Congressional budget activities, the Federal Register and FedBizOpps. An analysis must be made of the Government's programs and budgets and where they are headed. Then a determination must be made to see how they match the company's line of business and aspirations. An early decision is then made regarding which programs to pursue and which to pass. The pursue decision must not be irreversible. Later developments and information regarding the program and your competitive position could easily turn a bid decision into a no-bid one. That could occur even after considerable efforts have already been expended.

Decide early in the game "WHY" you should win and build it into your pre-proposal activities. Some of the early actions should include organizing the team, developing schedules and setting strategies. Drafting a "strawman" RFP and preparing a mock proposal will create a baseline for future reference when the official RFP is issued. Taking an initial cut at a make-or-buy plan and developing a good team of subcontractors is a great time saver. The same can be said for developing parametric cost estimates of the expected program.

Be sure to submit comments on draft solicitations so that your recommendations are known to the Government. Also, attendance at presolicitation conferences is a must. The intelligence to be gained from them is invaluable and could have a significant impact upon the remainder of your proposal activities.

### Analysis of Procurement Requests

Immediately upon receipt of an RFP or RFQ, the proposal team should make a thorough analysis of the real requirements and their impact upon the company and its operations. Make a comparison between the contract terms and conditions, statement of work, data requirements, deliverables and the complete technical data package with those which were developed in the strawman RFP.

After receipt of the solicitation, a formal bid/no-bid decision must be made quickly. Good answers to questions like those in Figure 6-1, *Bid/No-Bid Decision Questions*, on page 154 are necessary for a bid decision to be made. As a word of advice, don't bid unless you are out-to-win. Then develop a real win strategy and build that strategy into the entire proposal activity. Be sure your proposal schedule is aimed at "on-time" submission with adequate time for possible re-writes and of course management reviews.

## BID/NO-BID DECISION QUESTIONS

The following are typical questions that require positive answers when making a bid/no-bid decision for a new proposal.

1. Is the program related to the immediate and long range business objectives of the firm?
2. When it is necessary to develop new capabilities, are they compatible with the long range plans of the firm?
3. How much advance information did the company have on the project or program?
4. What is the priority and importance of the program; and its relationship to present and future programs?
5. What is the projected funding profile for the program?
6. Is there a real requirement? If this is for a subcontract, has the prime actually made a make-or-buy decision? Is this "window dressing" for a "make" decision already made?
7. What are your current capabilities for performing the project? What resources are currently available; what must be acquired; and how will they be secured? Is it possible to augment the current capabilities by acquiring additional personnel, consultants, subcontracting, new facilities and equipment?
8. What capital expenditures will be needed? How do they relate to the company's plans?
9. Can this program be phased into the current projects using existing resources of personnel and facilities?
10. What are the estimated total sales and profit?
11. What is the effect of the program on technical advances, product development, enhancement of the firm's overall reputation and competitive position?
12. How many competitive programs are there?
13. What is our competitive position; who are the competitors?
14. Who are the key customer personnel? What has been our past experience with this agency? What is the company's reputation and working relationship with the customer?

**Figure 6-1**

# THE PROPOSAL

## Proposal Format and Preparation

Various proposals will differ in their scope and tone depending upon the RFP and the size of the proposal. The basic content and format should be essentially the same no matter what the size or scope. That is basically true whether or not it is an unsolicited proposal or one in response to an RFP. Each company should develop its own standard basic proposal format and techniques as long as they remain responsive to Government requirements.

One very basic premise in the preparation and development of any proposal being submitted to the United States Government is: all offers must be submitted in the **English** language and the proposed value made in **U.S.** currency.

The basic format for most Government proposals will contain the following three major elements:

- Technical Proposal
- Management Proposal
- Cost Proposal

Those three basic elements are frequently enhanced by separate documents or volumes. Examples of these include the Executive Summary and various plans addressing subjects such as: program management, subcontract management, systems engineering, testing, quality assurance, training and logistics. Each individual section or element of the proposal should follow the same general format which will contain an introduction, the body of the proposal, a summary of key points, and any appendices. The actual format may be dictated by the instructions contained in the RFP. Be sure to follow it to the letter.

## Writing the Proposal

Writing any proposal is a significantly formidable task, depending upon the size and complexity of the project. The degree of competition involved will also be an influence. Quality control for proposals is just as important as it is for hardware, and must not be ignored. An effective team effort by all elements of the company is required for the development of an effective proposal. However, don't hesitate to seek clarification of any conflicting directions or other types of ambiguities. Some general hints suitable for most proposals are listed in Figure 6-2, *General Proposal Hints,* on page 156.

## GENERAL PROPOSAL HINTS

---

- Establish the preparation plan and stick to it
- Develop "WIN" message and themes
- Control design and program plans
- Assume evaluators do not know your company
- Show rationale for everything
- Control subcontractor participation
- Lay on the services for the team
- Be intimately aware of latest customer directive, instruction or specification in a given discipline
- Don't deviate from the customer expressed (and unexpressed) wishes, specs or requirements
- Follow RFP religiously! When in doubt, overkill!
- Be sure that RFP stated criteria is applied to every applicable proposal response
- If a commitment is made to pursue a particular approach – go all the way in your description. Do not try to get by with the use of buzz words, summaries, etc.
- Use illustrations profusely – control them in designated display rooms
- Use stand-alone philosophy – minimize references
- When evaluation criteria is given – believe it
- Don't try to con the readers – they will find you out
- Make sure the words in the write-ups match the music in the cost proposal
- Do not insult readers – do not "lecture" or talk down
- Avoid any semblance of arrogance
- Emphasize ability to find things easily
- Package proposal as attractively and professionally as possible

**Figure 6-2**

Organized work is essential to effective proposal writing. Here are some suggestions to help in getting started:

- Divide the subject matter into its logical parts.
- Develop an outline of how you will cover the subject.
- Isolate those tasks that are already available.
- Isolate those tasks that will require more research or special care.
- Identify areas where additional help is needed to meet schedules.

Be sure to write the proposal to inform and convince the reviewers, not "snow them." Remember that the proposal is a selling document, so keep in mind the old selling philosophy that you:

- Tell them what you are going to tell them,
- Tell them what you want them to know, then,
- Tell them what you told them.

There are numerous proposal writing theories and techniques espoused by various proposal professionals. The four effective techniques selected for discussion here are: single-author, annotated outline, storyboard, and graphic.

**Single-Author Method**

A professional writer, the author, will analyze the requirements of the RFP and draft a compatible outline of the proposal. The author will interview available specialists in the functional disciplines associated with the requirements. Then, in isolation, the writer will prepare the initial draft which will be reviewed by the specialists and management, prior to the final draft being prepared.

The single-author method is a cost effective proposal method, best used for small proposals. Typically, small management, technical and "off-the-shelf" projects can effectively use this method. It is also a good approach for proposals of an unsolicited nature.

**Annotated Outline Method**

Based upon the analysis of the RFP, the team leaders will initiate a basic outline for the proposal. They will build on that outline with a detailed outline, called an annotated outline. The annotated outline will be expanded through several iterations. This will be repeated until it is clear to all writers what issues, facts and approaches are to be taken. The initial and final drafts of the proposal will grow from the annotated outline. Figure 6-3, *Annotated Outline,* on page 158, illustrates the growth pattern from the basic to an annotated outline.

The annotated outline method is ideal for large proposals. It is appropriate for use when the team is unfamiliar with the storyboard method and not well enough prepared for the graphic method.

# ANNOTATED OUTLINE

| BASIC OUTLINE | DETAILED OUTLINE | DETAILED ANNOTATED OUTLINE |
|---|---|---|
| **OVERVIEW** (Introduction)<br><br>**1.0 PROGRAM MANAGE-MENT APPROACH**<br><br>1.1 Program Management<br><br>1.2 Management of Systems Engineering<br><br>1.3 Configuration and Data Management<br><br>1.4 Program Controls<br><br>**2.0 TECHNICAL APPROACH**<br><br>2.1 Analytical Methodologies<br><br>2.2 Design Methodologies<br><br>2.3 Preliminary Candidate Concepts<br><br>3.0 **APPROACH TO ECONOMIC, SERVICE, AND RISK EVALUATION**<br><br>3.1 Economic Evaluation Approach<br><br>3.2 Service Evaluation Approach<br><br>3.3 Risk Evaluation Approach<br><br>**4.0 EMHS SUPPORT APPROACH**<br><br>4.1 Human Factors Support<br><br>4.2 Training Support<br><br>4.3 Maintainability Support | **OVERVIEW** (Introduction)<br><br>**1.0 PROGRAM MANAGE-MENT APPROACH**<br><br>1.1 Program Management<br><br>Philosophy of Program Office Approach<br><br>Interfacing with Service<br><br>Program Advisory Committee<br><br>1.2 Systems Engineering<br><br>1.3 Configuration and Data Management<br><br>1.4 Program Controls<br><br>**2.0 TECHNICAL APPROACH**<br><br>2.1 Analytical Methodologies<br><br>Goals and Objectives<br><br>Environmental Factors<br><br>Technical Environment<br><br>Social Environment<br><br>2.2 Design Methodologies<br><br>Design Objectives<br><br>Alternate Design Concepts<br><br>Subsystem Definition | **OVERVIEW**<br><br>Objective and Scope; XCO's Qualifications<br><br>Management Approach; Program Organization<br><br>Study Flow Logic; Responsiveness and Flexibility<br><br>**1.0 PROGRAM MANAGE-MENT APPROACH**<br><br>1.1 Program Management<br><br>Philosophy of Program Office Approach<br><br>XCO experience in program management shows a full-time, dedicated Program Office is needed, with specialists representing each major discipline. High placement of Program in XCO organization shows a high level of interest in the study objectives.<br><br>Interfacing with Service<br><br>XCO recognizes need for effective communication techniques, and their influence on Program success. Use mutually agreed methods of reporting and communicating to permit fast response to customer guidance. |

Figure 6-3

## Storyboard Method

When properly managed, the storyboard method of proposal writing should result in a neat, easy-to-read, persuasive set of documents. This method is a very systematic and orderly way to prepare proposals. The real challenge is to make it all hang together and flow easily from beginning to end.

The storyboard method calls for making each sales point a controversial, dramatic point and then defending that point. An outline is developed by the team leaders. The outline is then expanded into a series of "Action-Phrase Topics." These are not just headings but assertions, that is, the sales points to be utilized by the writers.

Each Action-Phrase Topic is assigned to a writer who will develop a brief "thesis statement" and a listing of the main points to be covered. When this is approved by the team leaders, the writer will then expand upon those points. The writer will use minimal wordage and also sketch any illustrations needed to support the statement. After further approvals, the text is developed and the illustrations refined. This is a straight-forward assembly of refined and approved modules.

This combination of text and illustration is referred to as a module. The final proposal document is a straight-forward assembly of refined and approved modules.

It is the considered opinion of some proposal professionals that neither the storyboard nor the graphic method should be attempted unless the team is in a strong technical position. The storyboard method, sometimes referred to as the motion picture industry approach, is a preferred technique for forcing sales orientation. This can be important when the inclination of the proposal team is towards preparing a technical report instead of a proposal.

## Graphic Method

The graphic method of proposal writing is ideal for a sophisticated team which has the time and talent to rework well developed write-ups solely for the sake of maximizing persuasive and effective communications.

The process begins with the same initial stage of the Annotated Outline method. From the annotated outline, the team leaders will select the main sales points. Each of these will then be developed into a graphic, which will be posted and displayed with all the others.

These displays will provide each team member with an overview of how the proposal is developing. Writers will be assigned to each graphic to develop the text which will accompany it in the document. This technique can be thought of as "show and tell" through the use of modules. It is sometimes referred to as the Madison Avenue approach.

## Proposal Introduction and Summaries

The Introduction of any proposal is very important. Normally, it is the only part of a proposal actual read by ALL reviewers.

Some of the main functions of an Introduction are as follows:

- Summarize information about the origin and scope of the proposal.
- Give a brief summary of the program, its purpose, goals and basic problems.
- Provide general information on the requirements of the RFP and how the interests of the company relate to it.
- Furnish an analysis of the problem and the company's proposed solution.
- Summarize the major elements of the proposal.

In large proposals the Introduction may be a separate volume from the rest of the proposal. Final Summaries are used to summarize all the points developed in detail in the technical and management volumes and to make the final "sales pitch." A very effective approach is to develop an "Executive Volume," which will serve as both the Introduction and Final Summary. Some solicitations will require an Executive Volume be submitted as one of the proposal deliverables.

Appendices are attached to proposals to further expand or discuss in more detail significant areas of the proposal which might be of interest to only a limited group of the reviewers. The appendices may contain required plans covering subjects like management, systems engineering, subcontracting, small business/small disadvantaged business, and quality assurance. They are also used to provide the data from trade studies, computer analyses and classified material from other volumes.

Appendices should be used with care and discrimination. Unless noted in the RFP, appendices normally will not be used in the official evaluation process. In some cases appendices not required by the solicitation could be a detriment to the total score earned.

## Proposal Review and Submission

At various stages of preparation and writing, each element of the proposal must be reviewed by the proposal leaders. When they are satisfied that the writers and editors are on the right track, outside help should be obtained. That help should come from experienced persons who have not been involved in the writing. They will review the RFP requirements and critique the proposal. The intent is to make sure the proposal is responsive to the RFP, that it is readable and error free. In addition, they are looking to see if the proposal really sells the company and its solution of the Government's needs. The group, commonly called a "red team," will make use of the evaluation criteria in the RFP and score the proposal. In doing this they give an evaluation as if they are the Government reviewers.

After all reviews have been conducted, a series of final management approvals must be made. The level of these will depend upon company policy. Authorization to submit the proposal is sought by this process. Transmittal should be by a letter from a company executive showing a commitment to the project. This is also the time to be assured that all personnel associated with the proposal have signed their Procurement Integrity Certificate so that the program manager or proposal leader can prepare the company certificate to be submitted to the Government contracting officer when requested.

Remember that timely submission is extremely important. The time, date and place for submission are just as critical for proposals as it is for sealed bids. Late delivery can cause all of your efforts to have been a complete waste of resources.

## TECHNICAL PROPOSALS

### Technical Proposal Objectives

The primary objective of the technical proposal is to demonstrate to the customer that you fully understand its problems and goals. The technical proposal also shows that you are proposing the best and most cost effective solution to achieve those goals. To do this, the technical proposal must accurately interpret the customer's requirements and define your approach to satisfy them. It must clearly describe the selected concept or design and its operation, and provide the rationale for your selection.

### Key Elements of Technical Proposals

An overview of the contractual tasks and how you will perform them is the key to a good proposal. A detailed description of the technical approach is an important element. The description must at least include the following type of information:

- An operational diagram
- Block diagrams of systems, subsystems and hardware
- Photographs of any existing hardware
- A definition of system/subsystem engineering concepts
- A description of cost, time and performance trade-offs used in developing the proposed solution
- Identification of known risk areas, and your proposed method of mitigating them

In supporting the description of the technical approach, the proposal must also address these programmatic features:

- Work breakdown structure and its relationship to the work statement and project tasks
- Technical support and test plans
- Program plans and schedules

- The company's related experience
- Efforts to be subcontracted
- Key technical personnel and their expertise

Remember, the idea is to show why your company is technically best suited to get the contract. Figure 6-4, *Do's and Don'ts for Technical Proposals*, on page 163 lists several helpful ideas for the writing of technical proposals. There is one important factor that must be remembered. There must be a very close correlation between the various tasks described in the technical volume and the costs associated with those tasks. One criteria of the evaluation process is the realism of the costs proposed. If the costs, schedule and technical tasks do not match-up the evaluators will give a very poor score for cost realism. They will even question the total costs quoted as being under-quoted which will not be to your advantage.

## MANAGEMENT PROPOSALS

### Primary Purpose of Management Proposals

The primary purpose of management proposals is to explain in precise detail how the company intends to manage the proposed program when awarded the contract. Therefore, a key element of the management proposal is a good description of the type of management which the company intends to provide. The organizational structure contemplated and the relationship of program management to top management is also needed. Management proposals continue to gain importance in the evaluation and source selection process. So they deserve the same attention to detail as is given the technical proposal.

### Proposal Content

Management proposals must show that you fully comprehend the managerial requirements of the solicitation. In addition, you must show how your organization will manage the effort in the way that best meets those requirements. Depending upon the scope of the efforts and requirements stated in the RFP, the proposal will, among other things, include:

- Program control systems and techniques
- Master plans and schedules
- Make-or-buy plans
- Managerial support plans (i.e., cost control, quality control, subcontract management, configuration management, data management, etc.)
- Record of company's past performance
- Resumes of managerial personnel

The company's track record in cost and schedule control is an important source selection factor. Therefore, adequate coverage of those elements is vital to a good management volume.

# DO'S AND DON'TS FOR TECHNICAL PROPOSALS

---

## – DO –

- Play back customer's preferred solutions
- Have a general section for senior people and great details for specialists
- State important conclusions up-front
- Put massive test, trade-off and supporting data in appendices
- Never assume readers will automatically accept your position
- Avoid technical arrogance, false claims, glib statements, etc.
- Use the building block approach without insulting the readers' intelligence
- Balance coverage of the whole subject
- Use illustrations profusely
- When strong in an area layout all the details
- Overkill in areas of known weakness
- Be responsive to the RFP requirements
- Audit proposal for responsiveness – use a responsiveness checklist

## – DON'T –

- Deviate from RFP requirements
- "Parrot" the RFP
- Have an imbalance between Tasks and Phases
- Fail to show enough "how"
- Include far-out or incredible ideas
- Assume the evaluators know your technology, products, programs or the company
- Know less than your subcontractors

**Figure 6-4**

# COST PROPOSALS

## Pricing Principles

The price for any supply or service is based on the accepted concepts of demand, competition, costs, profit, and benefits derived. Demand is what the customer is willing to pay for an item. Pricing a product or service in relationship to the competition's pricing also requires consideration.

Relative to the ultimate price is an understanding of what additional costs will be incurred by providing the supply or service. Therefore, knowledge of the total economic cost of the effort is extremely important. Total economic cost is the summation of non-variable, semi-variable and variable costs. These cost factors are illustrated in Figure 6-5, *Cost Variability,* on page 165.

- Non-variable or fixed costs are those which are the same in total amount, regardless of the volume of output.
- Semi-variable costs will vary with increases or decreases in output but not in a direct relationship to changes in production or effort.
- Variable costs will vary in direct relationship to changes in output of either labor or materials.

Consideration must also be given to opportunity or alternative costs. This decision concerns the proper and economic application of the company's resources. Fundamentally, it is a question of the expected return on investment (ROI). That is, will the expenditures of resources for this project be to our advantage? Conversely, can we make a better use of those resources elsewhere? The combination of all cost factors in relation to a specific product or service at a particular time, determines the firm's competitive position.

How much the contract will increase the firm's total economic profit is another point to consider. Profit on any contract is the difference between "out-of-pocket" costs for performing the effort and the total income received. However, the true profit will be the "economic profit." That is the difference between the additional costs (both variable and selected semi-variable) incurred to perform the contract and the total income from the contract.

The final proposed price will also take into account certain short and long range benefits. These are benefits which the firm will secure from the contract or program. They more than likely will be peculiar to that firm and may be very intangible.

# COST VARIABILITY

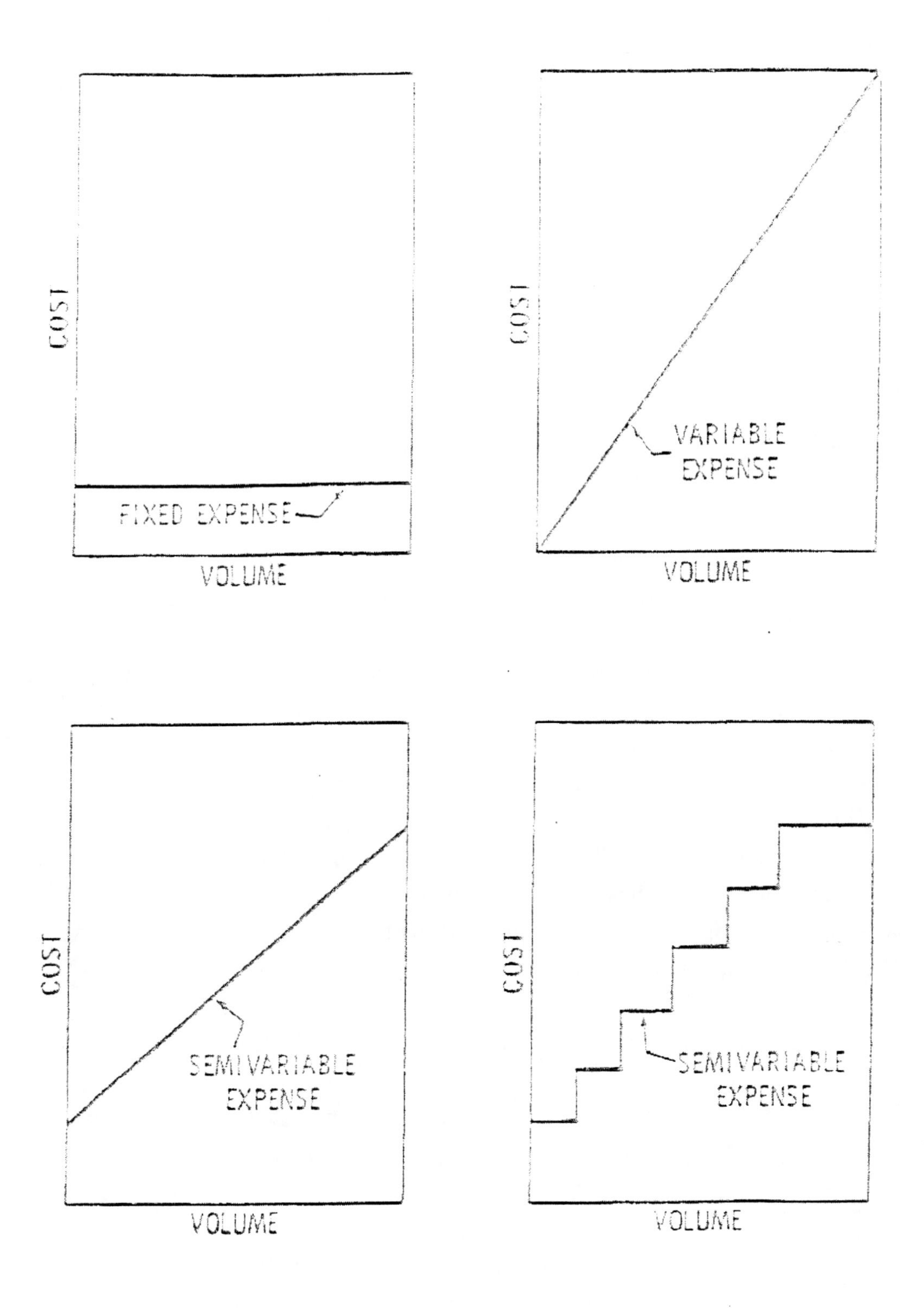


**Figure 6-5**

### Types of Pricing Techniques

The Economic Pricing Theory assumes that a firm wishes to maximize profits and that it is a normally efficient organization. Most organizations will utilize one of the following techniques which may or may not maximize profit on a specific effort and at that instance.

- ***Marginal Pricing*** – A price which is less than the estimated full average costs, but is in excess of the variable costs to perform the work.
- ***Market Pricing*** – A price which is in excess of the estimated costs of performance, plus a "reasonable profit."
- ***Average Cost Pricing*** – A price based upon a combination of direct costs, overhead and expected profit.

### Cost Proposal Format

Cost proposals are of equal importance with the technical and management volumes. The purpose of the cost proposal is to present costs in such detail that the prospective customer will be convinced of the reasonableness of those costs proposed. The customer will use the cost proposal to establish the credibility of the contractor. They will cross check it with the technical and management proposals, to determine if the contractor has a real understanding of the nature of the work, its scope and its problems.

The Government will be looking at the absolute cost of each proposal. They desire to see what their total cost exposure would be from each offeror. They will also be looking at cost realism. This relates to the reasonableness of the costs proposed and the rationale for those costs as described in the proposals. Which of these criteria will carry the most weight will depend upon the nature and phase of the program in question.

A typical cost proposal will contain most of the following features, unless they are required by the RFP to be located in other volumes.

- Title page and introduction, relating the proposal to the RFP or explaining the nature of an "unsolicited" proposal.
- Statement of work (SOW), work breakdown structure (WBS) and incentive plan.
- Funding profile and requirements for incrementally funded programs.
- Contractual terms and conditions (T&Cs) which differ in any respect from those in the RFP.
- Certifications and representations as required by the RFP.
- Explanations and conditions associated with the cost proposal.
- Cost and profit summary.
- Cost breakdown by elements of cost: direct and indirect labor, material, subcontracts, other direct costs, overhead and general and administrative.

- The basis of the estimated utilized
- Supporting data for any of the above.

**Cost Estimating Process**

Estimating is the practice or technique of applying analytical judgment factors to known or historical cost data or historical facts and predicted conditions. The analysis data is then used as a basis for the prediction of future costs.

The cost estimate serves two main purposes. It supports the technical and management proposal in seeking new contracts and additional effort on current contracts. In addition, it forms a sound basis for the control of the project or effort after award. Cost estimates are required under the following circumstances:

- Supplies or services with which the firm has had no previous experience.
- Supplies or services where the previous experience has been of the same or similar type.
- A follow-on to an existing contract.
- Engineering change proposals (ECPs) to an existing contract.
- Spare parts that are not procured or produced concurrently with the contract line item.

All estimates are guesses as to what something will cost in the future. Their accuracy is essential to securing the contract initially and not losing money on the contract when awarded. Estimating techniques vary according to the size of the proposal and the nature of the work. The following are three common estimating methods.

- ***Quick Quote Method*** – Sometimes referred to as "Committee Quoting," the Quick Quote is made when representatives of interested departments are brought together to develop the cost estimate. Their inputs will be based upon experience, knowledge of product, and knowledge of market conditions. Its main advantages are speed of response and low cost.
- ***Estimating by Comparison*** – Comparable components or processes are used as a guide, and judgment factors are applied as to any complexity factors. This method is convenient for use when the requirements for the new item or service are very similar to previous ones and relatively few adjustments need be made.
- ***Detailed Estimating*** – This is estimating from the bottom-up. A thorough and detailed analysis is made of all components, processes, assemblies, functions and activities. This is translated into labor, material, tooling, equipment and facility requirements. Labor rates, material prices and overhead or burden rates are applied to determine the estimated cost for each element. The development of total cost by this method is labor

intensive, requires the efforts of personnel form the various disciplines to be employed and is very time consuming. In many cases, preliminary design effort is necessary before starting the estimating process.

- A combination of these techniques is frequently used when preparing large cost proposals.

Basic to the entire proposal efforts, in support of the quoting methods described on pages 157 and 159, is the Basis of Estimate (BOE) supporting the cost estimates used in preparing the proposal. The BOE provides the Government with the rationale behind every component of the proposed price. It also provides the credibility for those components through detailed justification and analysis based on the best data available. The essential elements of the BOE are:

- Proposal and company information
- Description of the task proposed
- Assumptions and considerations employed
- Estimating method applied
- Rationale and justification for each cost element
- Distribution of the costs in the proposal

The estimating process involves many organizations and individuals working together. Initially, a complete and thorough review of the statement of work (SOW) and related documents is necessary. They must integrate the SOW requirements with the program schedule, work breakdown structure (WBS) and company accounting and budget systems.

Each company's WBS will be unique to the specific program/operation being proposed. In some cases the basic structure may be dictated by the request for proposals (RFP) being quoted. Whatever, the WBS must be designed to identify the various organizations and major systems that comprise the first level of management under the top system. Then there will be the several layers of subsystems and operations broken down to whatever level is needed for clear understanding of the costs. Work breakdown structures must directly correlate with work statement requirements.

The team leaders must prepare a detailed Proposal Package for personnel assigned to provide estimates. They should then hold a kick-off meeting with all personnel associated with the proposal. This is the time to explain such things as: program mission, program schedule, proposal requirements, estimating ground rules and the proposal schedule.

At the same time, vendors and subcontractors will be solicited for their quotes and proposals. The team will review and critique their estimates. They must then consolidate and integrate the data received. Pricing the labor and material estimates and applying rates as necessary will come next. After several pricing iterations they will reduce all data to comply with the RFP requirements. All that is left to do is to obtain managerial approval, publish and submit the proposal on schedule.

Some of the general factors to be considered in cost proposals are as follows:

- Previous estimates should be used in making or checking current estimates of similar items.
- Previous cost history of like or similar items provides an excellent basis of comparison.
- Give careful consideration to expected future costs of labor, material and overhead.
- Consideration must be given to the anticipated use of buildings, computers, machinery, tools, and equipment in the product development, production and test.
- Quantities to be manufactured must be estimated.
- Time available to perform the required effort, especially for production activities.
- The efficiency of the available labor force will have a direct cost relationship.
- The competitive environment requires careful consideration.
- The possibility of follow-on or co-related business must be taken into consideration.
- Generous proportions of ***EXPERIENCE*** and ***JUDGMENT*** are needed in any estimating situation.

With considerations to the above listed factors, the estimating process makes use of sources and techniques such as the following:

- Use of unchanged historical data by basing the estimate on the actual last cost of an identical or similar item.
- Projecting past actual costs of identical or similar items over future time periods.
- Use of rough yardsticks or relationship to some other cost element, such as: (1) production hours per pound of the item; (2) lines of software code; (3) relationship between production and inspection; (4) relationship between design and drafting and design check; and (5) test hours per number of components.
- Projecting cost trends for labor and material based on past indices of labor rates or material prices.
- Use of complexity factors (or numerical ratios), by comparing what is currently being proposed to previous or current items.

Most estimates use several of these examples. ***JUDGMENT*** is used in varying degrees in every phase of the estimate process. How much labor will be needed, what factors to employ, and the time to complete a task are typical of the areas needing good sound judgment.

# SPECIAL COST CONSIDERATIONS

## Cost or Pricing Data

The requirement for cost or pricing data in Government contracts has origin in Public Law 87-653 (*10 U.S.C. 2306(f)*), enacted in 1962; which is known as the Truth in Negotiations Act (TINA). The 1987 amendments to the Truth in Negotiations Act contained in Public Law 99-550 define cost or pricing data as follows:

> "Cost or pricing data means all information that is verifiable and that, as of the date of the agreement on the price of the contract (or the price of a contract modification), a prudent buyer or seller would reasonably expect to affect price negotiations. Such term does not include information that is judgmental, but does include the factual information from which a judgment is derived."

In 2010 there was an amendment to the FAR to clarify the terms "cost or pricing data," "certified cost or pricing data," and "data other than certified or pricing data." Under the final rule, "cost or pricing data" means, in part, all the facts that can reasonably be expected to contribute to the soundness of estimated future costs and to the validity of determinations of cost already incurred. The rule states that, "certified cost or pricing data," means, in part, cost or pricing data that were required to be submitted in accordance with FAR 15.403-4 and 15.403-5, and have been certified, or are required to be certified, in accordance with FAR 15.406-2. "Data other than certified cost or pricing data" means, in part, pricing data, cost data, and judgmental information necessary for the contracting officer to determine a fair and reasonable price or price realism. (FAR Case 2005-036, 75 *Federal Register* 53135, August 30, 2010)

FAR 15.402, *Pricing Policy*, prescribes the cost and price negotiation policies and procedures applicable to initial and revised pricing of: (1) negotiated prime contracts (including subcontract pricing under them when required); and (2) contract modifications, including modifications to contracts awarded by sealed bidding. It is the Government's policy that contracting officers will purchase its supplies and services from responsible sources at fair and reasonable prices. When establishing the reasonableness of the offered prices, contracting officers are directed not to obtain more information than is necessary. To the extent that the Truth in Negotiations Act, as implemented by FAR 15.402, permits, the contracting officer will generally use the following order of preference in determining the type of information required:

- No further information from the offeror if the price is based on adequate price competition.
- Information other than certified cost or pricing data.
- Certified cost or pricing data

Cost or pricing data consists of all facts which prudent buyers and sellers would reasonably expect to significantly affect price negotiations. Cost or pricing data are factual, not judgmental, and are therefore verifiable. While they do not indicate the accuracy of the contractor's judgment about estimated future costs or projections, they do include data forming the basis for that judgment. Cost or pricing data are more than historical accounting data; they are all the facts that can be reasonably expected to contribute to the soundness of estimates of future costs and to the determinations of costs already incurred. They also include such factors as:

- Historical accounting data
- Vendor quotations
- Nonrecurring costs
- Changes in production methods
- Changes in production or procurement volume
- Data supporting projections of business prospects
- Make-or-buy decisions
- Unit cost trends such as those associated with labor efficiency
- Estimated resources to obtain business goals
- Other management decisions which could reasonably be expected to have a significant bearing on the costs of the proposed contract

**Submission of Certified Cost or Pricing Data**

When submitting their proposals to the Government, contractors must comply with FAR 15.403, *Obtaining Certified Cost or Pricing Data*, and its subclauses. That subpart requires submission of, either actually or by specific identification in writing, certified cost or pricing data to support certain cost proposals. That data will enable the Government to perform cost or price analysis and ultimately negotiate fair and reasonable prices for the supplies or services.

Certified cost or pricing data will be obtained only if the contracting officer concludes that none of the exceptions in FAR 15.403-1, *Prohibition on Obtaining Certified Cost or Pricing Data,* applies. Certified cost or pricing data may not be obtained for acquisitions at or below the simplified acquisition threshold. Certified cost or pricing data will be required, in accordance with FAR 15.403-4, *Requiring Certified Cost or Pricing Data*, when any of the following actions are expected to exceed the threshold in effect at the time of agreement on price: (1) award of any negotiated contract (except for undefinitized actions such as letter contracts); (2) award of a subcontract at any tier, if the contractor and each higher tier subcontractor have been required to furnish certified cost or pricing data; or (3) modification of any sealed bid or negotiated contract covered by (2), whether or not certified cost or pricing data were initially required. The threshold for obtaining certified cost or pricing data is currently $700,000. Contracting officers may obtain certified cost or pricing data for pricing actions below that threshold provided the action exceeds the simplified acquisition threshold.

If certified cost or pricing data are not required because an exception applies, or an action is at or below the certified cost or pricing data threshold, the contracting officer must make a price analysis to determine the reasonableness of the price and need for further negotiation. The contracting officer may require submission of information other than certified cost or pricing data only to the extent necessary to determine reasonableness of the price or cost realism. Information other than certified cost or pricing data means, "any type of information that is not required to be certified, in accordance with FAR 15.403-4, that is necessary to determine price reasonableness or cost realism." If, after receipt of offers, the contracting officer concludes there is insufficient information available to determine price reasonableness and none of the exceptions applies, then certified cost or pricing data may be obtained.

Contracting officers will specify in the solicitation the overall cost and pricing data requirements. First, there will be a notice of whether or not cost or pricing data are required. The notice should also state whether or not certification will be required. If complete data are not necessary, then the CO will specify the extent of cost or pricing data required. Lastly, the solicitation will include a statement specifying the form in which the data must be submitted. By submitting a proposal and later being selected for negotiation, the offeror is granting the contracting officer, or an authorized representative, certain access rights. At any time prior to contract award the CO may request and get information and data utilized in preparing the cost proposal. The data which the CO will have the right to examine includes books, records, documents and other types of factual information. It does not matter what form the data is in or whether such supporting information is specifically referenced or included in the proposal. This authority is designed to give the Government enough information so an adequate evaluation can be made of the proposed price.

Under certain conditions the certificate may not be required. Where the negotiated price is based on adequate price competition the contracting officer may waive the requirement. Adequate price competition may exist even where price is not a primary factor in evaluation of proposals, regardless of the type of contract contemplated by the Government. Some form of cost data may be required to determine cost realism to ensure that the offerors adequately understand the scope of the work.

Exceptions to certified cost or pricing data requirements and the standards for applying the exceptions are specified in FAR 15.403-1, *Prohibition on Obtaining Certified Cost or Pricing Data*. Contracting officers are prevented from requiring submission of certified cost or pricing data, when the CO determines that prices agreed upon were based on: (1) adequate price competition; (2) prices set by law or regulation; (3) a commercial item being acquired; (4) a waiver has been granted; or (5) modification to a contract or subcontract for commercial items.

Unnecessarily requiring certified cost and pricing data is not in the best interest of either the Government or the offerors. It could extend the procurement lead time as well as waste both contractor and Government resources.

Upon completion of negotiations, contractors may be required to certify as to their cost or pricing data submitted during negotiations. They will be certifying that to the best of their knowledge and belief, the cost or pricing data submitted was current, accurate, and complete as of the date the contractor and the Government agreed on price. Certification will be done, in accordance with FAR 15.406-2, *Certificate of Current Cost or Pricing Data*, using a certificate similar to the one shown in Figure 6-6 below. The requirement will apply to the negotiation of modifications to any contract which involves aggregate increases and/or decreases in costs plus applicable profits which exceed $700,000.

---

## CERTIFICATE OF CURRENT COST OR PRICING DATA

THIS IS TO CERTIFY THAT, TO THE BEST OF MY KNOWLEDGE AND BELIEF, THE COST OR PRICING DATA (AS DEFINED IN SECTION 2.101 OF THE FEDERAL ACQUISITION REGULATION (FAR) AND REQUIRED UNDER FAR SUBSECTION 15.403-4) SUBMITTED, EITHER ACTUALLY OR BY SPECIFIC IDENTIFICATION IN WRITING, TO THE CONTRACTING OFFICER OR TO THE CONTRACTING OFFICER'S REPRESENTATIVE IN SUPPORT OF _________* ARE ACCURATE, COMPLETE, AND CURRENT AS OF _________**. THIS CERTIFICATION INCLUDES THE COST OR PRICING DATA SUPPORTING ANY ADVANCE AGREEMENTS AND FORWARD PRICING RATE AGREEMENTS BETWEEN THE OFFEROR AND THE GOVERNMENT THAT ARE PART OF THE PROPOSAL.

FIRM ________________________________

SIGNATURE ___________________________

NAME _______________________________

TITLE _______________________________

DATE OF EXECUTION*** ________________

* Identify the proposal, request for price adjustment, or other submission involved, giving the appropriate identifying number (*e.g.*, RFP No.).

** Insert the day, month, and year when price negotiations were concluded and price agreement was reached or, if applicable, an earlier date agreed upon between the parties that is as close as practicable to the date of agreement on price.

*** Insert the day, month, and year of signing, which should be as close as practicable to the date when the price negotiations were concluded and the contract price was agreed to.

(END OF CERTIFICATE)

**Figure 6-6**

The submission requirement is met if all cost or pricing data reasonably available to the offeror are either submitted or identified in writing by the time of agreement on price. There is a clear distinction between submitting cost or pricing data and merely making available books, records, and other documents without identification. The latter does not constitute "submission" of cost or pricing data.

Contractors required to submit and certify cost or pricing data, are required to obtain like data from prospective or actual subcontractors. They will follow the same guidelines required for the prime contract. When requested by the contracting officer, a contractor may be required to submit with their proposals, certified cost or pricing data from the prospective subcontractors in compliance with FAR 15.403-4, *Requiring Certified Cost or Pricing Data*. The subcontractor certification may be considered necessary for adequately pricing the prime contract.

Contractors must submit, or cause to be submitted by subcontractors, certified cost or pricing data to the Government for subcontractors that are the lower of either: (1) $12,500,000 or more; or (2) both more than the pertinent certified cost or pricing data threshold and more than 10 percent of the prime contractor's proposed price, unless the contracting officer believes such submission is unnecessary (*FAR 15.404-4, Subcontract Pricing Considerations*).

Prime contractors must mitigate any liability to the Government for defective subcontractor cost or pricing data. The prime contractor should obtain indemnification from the subcontractor about such data. It must be remembered that the Government holds prime contractors responsible for all aspects of proposals they submit.

### Defective Certified Cost or Pricing Data (*FAR 15.407-1*)

As previously noted, cost or pricing data is factual information which can be verified. Furthermore, there is a distinction between fact and judgment. The contractor's certificate pertains to "cost or pricing data." The certification does not make representations about the accuracy of the contractor's judgment on the estimated portion of future costs or projections. It does, however, apply to the data upon which the contractor's judgment is based.

During negotiations and before agreeing upon price, a contracting officer may learn that cost or pricing data submitted are inaccurate, incomplete or non-current. When this happens, the matter will be brought to the attention of the offeror or contractor for resolution. It does not matter whether the defective data would increase or decrease the contract price, it would still be considered defective. The contracting officer will negotiate the proposal using any new data submitted or make allowance for the incorrect data. The facts and actions taken will be documented in the price negotiation memorandum (PNM) to be made a part of the contract file.

After contract award, the issue of defective pricing may be raised by the Government. Certified cost or pricing data found to be inaccurate, incomplete or non-current as of the date of final agreement on price, as given on the contractor's or subcontractor's Certificate of Current

Cost or Pricing Data, will entitle the Government to a price adjustment. Such adjustment will include profit or fee of any significant amount by which the price was increased because of the defective data.

To protect the Government's rights, each contract will contain one of the clauses prescribed in FAR 15.408, *Solicitation Provisions and Contract Clauses*, and set forth at FAR 52.215-10, *Price Reduction for Defective Certified Cost or Pricing Data*, and 52.215-11, *Price Reduction for Defective Certified Cost or Pricing Data – Modifications.* Those clauses give the Government the right to a price adjustment for defects in certified cost or pricing data submitted by a contractor, prospective subcontractor, or actual subcontractor. In addition to the price adjustment amount, the Government will be entitled to interest on any overpayment for supplies or services accepted by the Government.

In arriving at a price adjustment, contracting officers will take into consideration the following factors.

- The time by which the certified cost or pricing data became reasonably available to the contractor.
- The extent to which the Government relied upon the defective data.
- Any understated certified cost or pricing data submitted in support of price negotiations, up to the amount of the Government's claim for overstated price data arising out of the same pricing action. "Same pricing action" relates to the initial pricing of the same contract or the pricing of the same change order.

Such factors need not be in the same cost groupings (such as material, direct labor, or indirect costs).

After contract award, the contracting officer will request an audit if the CO either learns of or suspects that the data which had been provided for negotiation were not accurate, complete, or current. An audit may also be requested if the data were not adequately verified by the contractor as of the time of negotiation. The audit will be to test the accuracy, completeness and currency of that data. If the audit reveals that the data certified by the contractor were defective, the CO will then evaluate the profit-cost relationship. Repricing of the contract will not be made solely because the profit was greater than forecast or because some significant contingency did not materialize.

### Unit Pricing

Contractors may be required to identify in their proposals those items of supply which they will not manufacture or to which they will not contribute significant value. The government will use this information to determine whether the intrinsic value of an item has been distorted through application of overhead. The information will also aid in deciding whether such items should be considered for breakout from other line item prices.

The purpose of pricing all items of supplies and the distribution of those costs within contracts can ensure that unit prices are in proportion to the item's base cost. Base cost refers to manufacturing or acquisition costs. A pricing method that distributes costs equally among line items would not be acceptable unless there would be little or no variation in base cost. When the contracting officer determines that unit pricing is required, the clause at FAR 52.215-14, *Integrity of Unit Prices*, will be inserted in the solicitation and resulting contract.

## Contractor Cost Estimating System

The process by which a contractor prepares proposals for submission to its customers is called an estimating system. The consistent preparation of proposals using an acceptable estimating system will increase the accuracy and reliability of the proposals. This will benefit both the contractor and its customers. Under the direction of FAR 15.407-5, *Estimating Systems*, cognizant audit activities will establish and manage regular programs for reviewing selected contractors' estimating systems or methods.

The several goals of such reviews will be to reduce the number and scope of reviews to be performed on individual proposals. They are also designed to expedite the negotiation process, and increase the reliability of proposals. Significant deficiencies that are found but not corrected by a contractor will be considered in later proposal analyses and negotiations. The Department of Defense (DOD) has established a detailed and comprehensive treatment of estimating system policies and procedures. They are outlined in DFARS 215.407-5-70, *Disclosure, Maintenance, and Review Requirements*, and DFARS 252.215-7002, *Cost Estimating System Requirements*. The details of a cost estimating system must be disclosed in writing by certain large businesses. The requirement applies to companies that during the previous fiscal year received $50 million or more DOD prime or subcontracts for which cost or pricing data had been required. Other large businesses receiving only $10 million of DOD prime or subcontracts in a fiscal year may also be required to provide written disclosure of their estimating system. This lower requirement will be invoked when it is considered to be in the best interest of the Government.

Such a requirement could also be imposed if significant problems in estimating costs are believed to exist. Large businesses whose sales are predominately to the Federal Government are subject to frequent audits.

A cost estimating system consists of a contractor's policies, procedures, and practices for generating cost estimates that forecast costs based on information available at the time a proposal is being prepared. For an estimating system to be considered adequate it must be set up, maintained, reliable, and consistently applied. It must also produce verifiable, supportable and documented cost estimates. One of the more significant concerns the Government has had with contractor estimating practices are those that do not provide an adequate basis of estimate. The basis of estimate must provide the Government's negotiators with sufficient information to aid in establishing a fair and reasonable negotiation objective.

Administrative oversight of contractor cost estimating systems will be made by audit and contract administration activities which will make regular reviews of those systems. The reports resulting from the reviews will be furnished to the administrative contracting officer (ACO). That will permit a determination as to any impact there might be on current negotiations. The ACO may recommend a variety of actions to relieve the impact. They may allow additional time for correction of the estimating problems. The Government could proceed with negotiations using a different type of contract. One alternative would be the performance of additional cost analyses. The questionable areas of cost-reimbursable line items in the contract could be segregated. When all else fails the contracting officer could insert a clause in the contract which would provide for adjustment after award.

When estimating system deficiencies have been identified in a written report, the contractor must state its agreement in writing within 30 days. Then the contractor has sixty (60) days to correct the deficiencies or submit a corrective action plan. If the contractor disagrees with the report, it has 30 days to state its rationale for disagreeing. The ACO will evaluate the contractor's response and notify the contractor of the Government's determination concerning any remaining deficiencies and/or the adequacy of any proposed or completed corrective action.

If the contractor has neither corrected the deficiencies nor submitted the plan within the required time period, the ACO will issue a Notice of Disapproval of the system. That notice will be sent to the auditor and to each contracting office and contract administration office having substantial business with the contractor. The Notice of Disapproval will be withdrawn when the ACO determines the contractor has corrected the significant system deficiencies.

# CHAPTER 7

# SOURCE SELECTION PROCESS

## SOURCE SELECTION SEQUENCE

### Policy, Direction and Regulations

The policies and procedures for selection of a source or sources for award in competitive negotiated acquisitions are in FAR Subpart 15.3, *Source Selection*. They apply to source selection actions based on cost or price competition between proposals that meet the Government's minimum requirements stated in the solicitation. They also apply to competitions involving the evaluation and comparison of cost or price and other factors. However, they do not apply to sole-source awards or to purchases that do not exceed the simplified acquisition threshold.

Source selection procedures are designed to: (1) maximize competition; (2) minimize the complexity of the solicitation, evaluation, and selection decision; (3) ensure impartial and comprehensive evaluation of offerors' proposals; and (4) ensure selection of the source whose proposal has the highest degree of realism and whose performance is expected to best meet stated Government requirements.

The basic objective of source selection is to select the proposal that represents the best value to the Government. Agencies can obtain best value in negotiated acquisitions by using any one or a combination of source selection approaches. For example, the relative importance of cost or price may vary from one acquisition to another. It may be in the best interest of the Government to award a contract to other than the lowest bidder or other than the highest technically rated offer and a tradeoff must be made between cost and price and other evaluation factors and subfactors.

One of the best documents published by the Government on source selection is the *Army Source Selection Supplement* (AS3) to the Department of Defense Source Selection Procedures. It was designed for use by the entire acquisition workforce to promote a consistent understanding of best value and the various processes and techniques that can be used to achieve it.

### Tradeoff Process (*FAR 15.101-1*)

When it has been determined that a tradeoff may be appropriate for a particular procurement, the solicitation must contain certain information. All the evaluation factors and significant subfactors that will be used in making the award decision must be stated along with their relative importance. Also, the solicitation must state the relative importance of cost and pricing data to the other evaluation factors. The tradeoff process allows the Government to accept a proposal that is not the lowest priced one, if its other benefits are perceived to merit the higher price.

### Lowest Price Approach

Under the authority of FAR Subpart 15.101-2, *Lowest Price Technically Acceptable Source Selection Process*, agencies may specify in their solicitations "that award will be made on the basis of the lowest evaluated price of proposals meeting or exceeding the acceptability standards for non-cost factors." This approach is appropriate when best value is expected to result from selection of the technically acceptable proposal with the lowest evaluation price. One of the normal evaluation factors, contractor's past performance, may not always be a criterion for selection.

### Best Value Continuum (*FAR 15.101*)

"Best value" should be the goal of every acquisition, whether it is sealed bidding, simplified acquisition, commercial item acquisition, negotiated acquisition, or any other method or combination of methods. In the broadest sense, best value is the outcome of any acquisition that ensures the procuring agency meets it's customer's needs in the most effective, economical, and timely manner.

In a negotiated acquisition, best value may be obtained by using any one or a combination of source selection approaches. In addition to the approaches noted above, agencies should take into consideration the alternative methods (Chapter 4, *Contracting Methods*), types of contract (Chapter 5, *Contract Types*), and the potential risks in a specific approach (*Risk Management*, page 34).

### Responsibilities

Agency heads or their designees are responsible for all source selection activities within their agency. A cognizant technical official will be responsible for developing the technical and past performance requirements related to the source selection process. A contracting officer will be designated as the source selection authority (SSA), unless the agency head appoints another individual to perform that function for a particular acquisition or group of acquisitions. The SSA has responsibility for the contracting actions related to the source selection process. Those actions, described in FAR 15.303, *Responsibilities*, include the following basic functions.

- Establish the evaluation team.
- Approve the source selection strategy or acquisition plan.
- Ensure consistency among the source selection requirements.
- Ensure that proposals are evaluated based solely on the factors and subfactors contained in the solicitation.
- Consider the recommendations of advisory boards or panels (if any).
- Select the source or sources whose proposal is the best value to the Government.

### Formal Source Selection

In most competitive negotiated acquisitions a formal source selection process will be established. The process will involve a specific evaluation group structured to evaluate proposals and select the source for award. A Source Selection Plan will also be required. Since the plan is an internal agency guidance document, it establishes no legal rights to offerors or contractors. Therefore, they will not be in a position to protest if the agency does not follow its source selection plan as originally created.

The source selection organization in major acquisitions typically consists of an evaluation board, an advisory council, and a designated source selection authority at a management level above that of the contracting officer. This chapter will concentrate on that process.

### Informal Source Selection Process

Actually more contracts are awarded by the Government that do not go through the formal source selection process than those that do. This is because the largest volume of awards is made for other than large systems and major developments. While the latter are for larger dollar programs, they are outnumbered by the sheer numbers of smaller contracts.

The typical informal award process centers around the contracting officer. The CO collects from the ultimate user information needed to issue the solicitation. The CO must assure that any required publicizing is properly made. At the appropriate time the contracting officer will issue the solicitation, respond to inquiries from potential contractors and receive the bids or offers.

During the several stages of a procurement the CO calls on various persons of other disciplines for advice and assistance in gathering information and evaluating bids and offers. Based upon their inputs, it is the contracting officer that must make the final selection and award the contract.

## GOVERNMENT SOURCE SELECTION PROCESS

The selection of contractual sources is an iterative process, the major elements of which are outlined on the following pages. It involves the selection of the appropriate evaluation personnel, the development of an effective and thorough acquisition plan, and the implementation of that plan.

The titles given to the evaluation and groups discussed in this text are generic in nature. They may vary according to the different federal agencies that use source selection processes and procedures. The source selection team is usually a three level hierarchy. At the top is the individual with the final decision authority. That person is supported by a senior staff or council which oversees the activities of the larger base group called an evaluation board.

**Source Selection Authority**

The Source Selection Authority (SSA) is the official appointed to direct the source selection process. The SSA's functions involve the approval of the source selection plan, appointment of the chairperson and members of the Source Selection Advisory Council (SSAC). Most important will be selection of the source(s) for award and official announcement of the contract award. When other than the contracting officer, the SSA is usually a key official in the specific agency or department of the Government involved in the acquisition. In DOD it may be the Secretary of Defense, or the Secretary of the specific branch. The latter may delegate it to the Chief of Staff, who in turn may redelegate it, but not below the level of a division commander or equivalent. Other agencies have a similar restriction on the delegation authority.

**Source Selection Advisory Council**

The Source Selection Advisory Council (SSAC) is a group of senior Government personnel appointed to serve as the staff and advisors to the SSA during the source selection process. One of their important functions is to establish the evaluation criteria and weighing factors to be applied to the criteria. They will analyze, for the SSA, the results of the Source Selection Evaluation Board (SSEB) evaluations.

The SSAC prepares the analysis report which will be submitted to the SSA. The report contains the overall conclusions of the Council. It will contain such elements as: prices or costs; overall technical effectiveness; risk analysis; offeror's capabilities and past performance; negotiation results; and other appropriate factors.

**Source Selection Evaluation Board**

The Source Selection Evaluation Board (SSEB) is a group of military and/or civilian personnel, representing the various functional and technical areas involved in an acquisition. They are appointed by the Source Selection Advisory Council (SSAC). Their function is to direct, control and perform evaluations of proposals responsive to requirements. They also produce a summary of facts and findings required in the source selection process.

The SSEB evaluates and scores each proposal received from potential contractors against the technical and operational requirements set forth in the solicitation. They then prepare a narrative justification of the evaluation results, called the SSEB Evaluation Report. Evaluation is accomplished by reviewing and analyzing each offeror's proposal. The task is to determine if the offer meets the criteria standards. The evaluators must remember that they need not accept, without question, data presented in a proposal. They will use their expert knowledge and experience to determine the feasibility, logic and reasonableness of the offeror's response.

The SSEB is responsible for the analysis of each proposal as it relates to the evaluation criteria. The SSAC, utilizing the SSEB findings and reports, will evaluate each offeror against its competitors. Normally the SSAC will not recommend the winner in their report to the Source Selection Authority (SSA), unless requested to do so by the SSA.

**Acquisition Plan**

An acquisition plan is the key document for initiating and conducting the acquisition process. It provides guidance for the final selection of the source or sources from which the supplies or services will be acquired. Normally the plan will be prepared by a team consisting of all those who will be responsible for significant aspects of the acquisition, such as contracting, fiscal, legal and technical personnel. The requirement for an acquisition plan, as discussed in Chapter 3, *The Acquisition Process*, is required by FAR Part 7, *Acquisition Planning*.

When developing an acquisition plan the team must address their goals and their plan for reaching them. The written plan will be divided into two main sections, the background and objectives of the procurement and the plan of action.

The Acquisition Background and Objectives section of the plan will contain the following information (*FAR 7.105, Contents of Written Acquisition Plans*):

- A statement of need
- Applicable conditions affecting the acquisition
- Cost goals
- Capability or performance characteristics of the supplies or services
- Delivery or performance-period requirements
- Trade-offs already made
- Technical, cost and schedule risks
- Acquisition streamlining, if applicable

The Plan of Action section of the plan will contain the following information, when applicable:

- Prospective sources
- Competition plans
- Source selection procedures
- Contracting considerations
- Budgeting and funding
- Product description
- Use of priorities, allocations and allotments
- Contractor versus Government performance
- Management information requirements

- Make or buy programs
- Test and evaluation programs
- Logistics considerations
- Government-furnished property
- Government-furnished information
- Environmental and energy considerations
- Security considerations
- Contract administration
- Milestones for the acquisition cycle
- Identification of participants in the acquisition plan preparation

In addition to the competition plans cited above, the acquisition plan will address competition for subcontracting. The plan will describe how subcontract competition will be sought, promoted, and sustained throughout the course of the acquisition. This becomes especially important when effective subcontractor competition is considered to be both feasible and desirable.

The Source Selection Procedures portion of the acquisition plan is where the details of the source selection procedures to implement the requirements of FAR 15.3, *Source Selection*, are discussed. Those procedures are the significant processes that are concerns of this chapter.

**Oral Presentations (*FAR 15.102*)**

When the SSAC determines that oral presentations by offerors are required, they should be conducted before starting the evaluation process. The use of oral presentations as a substitute for portions of a proposal can be very effective in streamlining the source selection process. They may occur at any time during the acquisition process; however, they are subject to the same restrictions as written information, regarding timing and content. Oral presentations provide an opportunity for dialogue among the parties. Therefore, all members of the evaluation team should attend all oral presentations. This will aid them in maintaining an unbiased attitude for all competitors. When oral presentations are required, then all competitors still within the competitive range will make them.

**Evaluation Factors and Criteria**

The acquisition officials of an agency have broad discretion in the selection of evaluation factors and subfactors and their relative importance to be used in an acquisition. However, every source selection shall address evaluation factors for price or cost, past performance and quality associated with the non-cost evaluation factors. Any other relevant factors or subfactors, such as cost realism, may be included. The Government must always evaluate the quoted price of a proposal. The proposal cannot be eliminated from the competition solely on the basis of non-price factors.

Evaluation criteria set forth in the solicitation and used in the evaluation process should be tailored to the acquisition requirements. The criteria should address only those important and major aspects of the program which are pertinent to the source selection decision and considered essential to the success of the program.

Each evaluation criterion must be expressed in the simplest of terms, with clear lines of demarcation. It is important to eliminate any duplication and overlap in the evaluation process. The criteria need to be shredded-out to make the evaluation process easier. The following is an example of a simple shred-out.

- Area – Operations
  - Item – Maneuverability
    - Factor – Turn Radius
    - Factor – Excess Power
  - Item – Survivability
    - Factor – Subsystem Redundancy
    - Factor – Radar Cross Section
      - Subfactor – Front Quarter
      - Subfactor – Side View

Standards are prepared for each factor and subfactor to serve as positive indicators to offerors. Minimum performance or compliance standards must be identified. The offerors must know what is acceptable to meet the requirements of the request for proposal (RFP). The standards may be expressed in either qualitative or quantitative terms. They are also used as measurement guides for the evaluators to determine contractor responsiveness. Figure 7-1, *Evaluation Criteria*, on page 186 illustrates an example of qualitative criteria. In this example degrees of importance are placed upon the several items and the total score is calculated accordingly.

The evaluation criteria for all programs involving development should include an overall risk assessment for each proposal as a rated item or area in the evaluation process. The Government's risk is the issue at hand and logically related to any reliability evaluation factor in the solicitation. An example is when the risk analysis shows an offeror's product to be less reliable and have a prospective higher life cycle cost than other products. Projected "mean time between failure" conditions which would result in longer downtime and higher maintenance costs would be considered. Such factors could outweigh the advantage of an initial lower acquisition price.

## EVALUATION CRITERIA

| TECHNICAL FACTORS (650 Points) | | POINTS |
|---|---|---|
| MOST IMPORTANT | 1. Understanding of the system, program requirements and ability to meet RFP objectives. | 150 |
| | 2. Ability to foresee and identify problem and risk areas and have alternative means of meeting objectives. | 150 |
| VERY IMPORTANT | 3. Experience with similar efforts and application of background to the program. | 100 |
| | 4. Ability to meet schedules and interface with other participating agencies. | 100 |
| IMPORTANT | 5. Background of assigned personnel and applicability of experience. | 75 |
| | 6. Adequacy of proposed test program | 75 |

| MANAGEMENT AND COST FACTORS (350 Points) | | POINTS |
|---|---|---|
| MOST IMPORTANT | 1. Credibility of price and reasonableness of offering. | 150 |
| VERY IMPORTANT | 2. Proposed business operation including appropriateness of proposed organizational structures and cost control techniques. | 75 |
| | 3. Adequacy of subcontractor management program. | 75 |
| IMPORTANT | 4. Availability of site accommodations and site plans for proposed personnel utilization. | 50 |

**Figure 7-1**

Some items will have more impact than others on the source selection decision. Therefore, the use of numerical weights may be necessary to rank items as to their relative importance. Normally, the weight factors are not divulged to either the SSEB or to offerors in an effort at removing biased evaluations or biasing of the proposals by offerors.

Solicitations should be structured to provide for the selection of the source whose proposal offers the greatest value to the Government. They must clearly state the significant evaluation factors and their relative importance. Solicitations must inform offerors of minimum requirements that apply to particular evaluation factors and significant subfactors.

Furthermore, solicitations must state, as a minimum, whether all evaluation factors other than cost or price, when combined are: (1) significantly more important than cost or price; (2) approximately equal to cost or price; or (3) significantly less important than cost or price. Past performance must be an evaluation factor in all source selections for negotiated competitive acquisitions expected to exceed $150,000. Past performance need not be evaluated if the contracting officer makes the determination, and documents the reason, that past performance would not be appropriate for the specific acquisition (*FAR 15.304, Evaluation Factors and Significant Subfactors* and *DFARS 215.304, Evaluation Factors and Significant Subfactors*).

The usual method is for solicitations to divulge the relative degree of importance of the major elements of the evaluation criteria. These elements may be described in very broad terms. An example might be:

> "The technical proposal is twice as important as the management proposal, which is twice as important as the costs. Furthermore, within the cost area, cost realism is twice as important as absolute cost."

It may be fine-tuned within the technical and management areas, depending upon the nature and scope of the project. The use of a scoring or weighting system is not mandatory under the FAR, but is discretionary under agency policies and procedures.

When trying to graphically describe the evaluation factors being applied, use a chart such as Figure 7-2, *Proposal Evaluation Factors*, on page 188. With such a guide, the proposal team and the evaluators have a better understanding of where emphasis is being applied.

## Proposal Evaluation (*FAR 15.305*)

Proposal evaluation is an assessment of both the proposal and the offeror's ability to successfully accomplish the prospective contract. An agency will evaluate competitive proposals solely on the factors specified in the solicitation. Those factors will concentrate on the evaluation of cost or price, past performance and technical requirements.

Each offeror's proposal must undergo a verification process. The process involves a review of the proposed contractual documentation to be made a part of the proposed contract. Compliance with and responsiveness to all solicitation requirements, as well as consistency between the documents and the proposal, must be insured.

Agencies must evaluate competitive proposals and then assess their relative qualities solely on the factors and subfactors specified in the solicitation. The relative strengths, deficiencies, significant weaknesses, and risks supporting the individual proposal's evaluation must be documented in the contract file. The three major areas of proposal evaluation concern are: cost or pricing data, past performance, and technical capability.

Evaluation of the technical proposal will give the evaluation team a chance to review the past performance and technical capabilities of the offeror. It's an opportunity to verify that the organization understands the Government's technical requirements and also assess the risk of meeting the performance parameters established by the Government.

The Source Selection Authority may reject all proposals received in response to a solicitation, when doing so is in the best interests of the Government.

Quantitative ratings which indicate how well the offeror's proposal meets the minimum requirements are useful as an aid to the evaluation. The individual proposals are scored against stated standards. Scoring can be accomplished numerically, symbolically, or through the use of color codes, as indicated in Figure 7-3, *Scoring Examples*, on page 189.

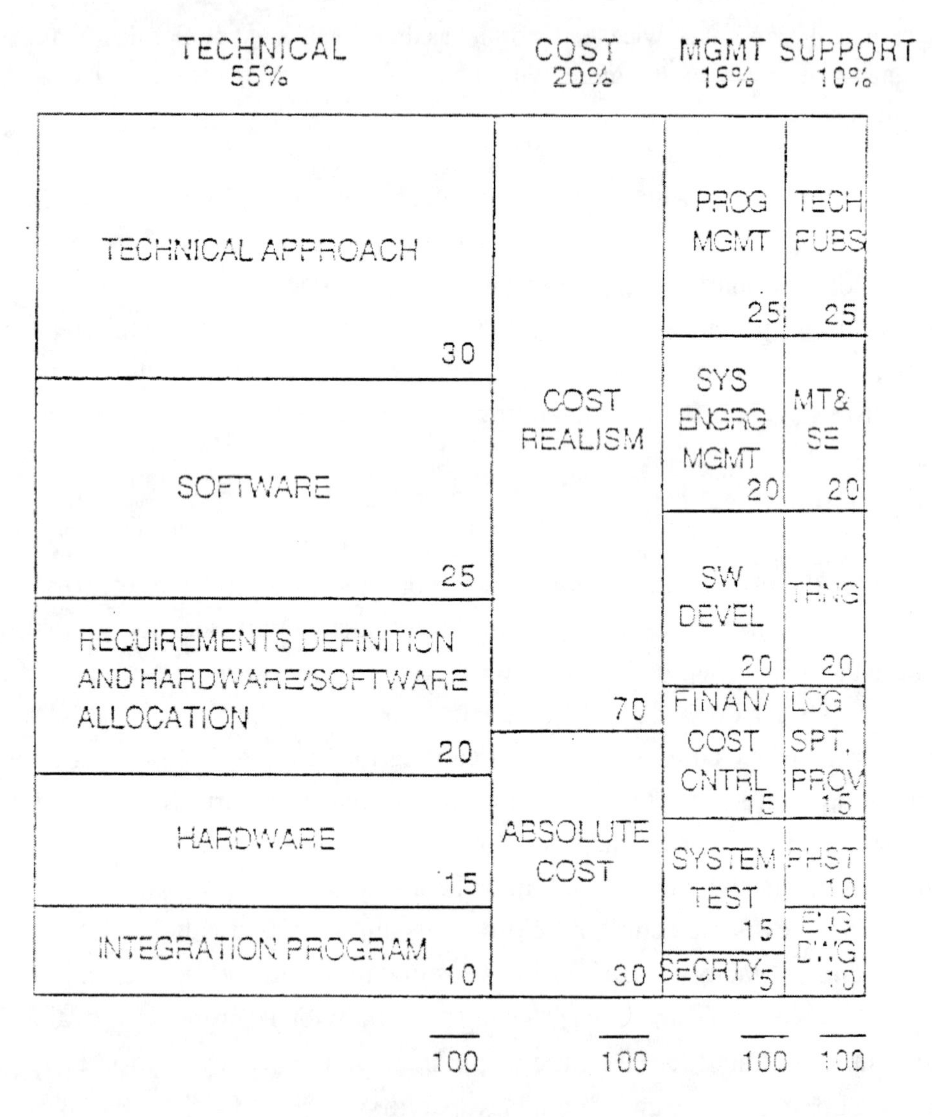


Figure 7-2

## SCORING EXAMPLES

| EVALUATION | NUMBERS | SYMBOLS | COLORS |
|---|---|---|---|
| **Exceptional** | 10<br>9<br>8 | X | Blue |
| **Acceptable** | 7<br>6<br>5 | √ | Green |
| **Marginal<br>to<br>Unacceptable** | 4<br>3<br>2<br>1<br>0 | — | Yellow<br><br>Red |

**Figure 7-3**

### Contractor Performance Information (*FAR 42.15*)

A contractor's past performance information (PPI) is a significant factor in assessing an offeror's ability to perform the contract successfully. The evaluation of an offeror's past performance must take into account such relevant factors as any predecessor companies, key personnel who have relevant experience, or subcontractors that will perform major or critical aspects of the program. The content and format of performance evaluations will be established in accordance with the individual agency's procedures. They should be tailored to the size, content and complexity of the contractual requirements (*FAR 42.1502, Policy*).

Government agencies make use of the Contractor Performance Assessment Reporting System (CPARS) for the collection of PPI. The PPI generated by the CPARS will be one of many tools used to communicate contractor strengths and weaknesses to source selection officials and contracting officers.

Over the past several years, there has been an increased emphasis by the federal Government in the use of past performance data in source selections. Past performance is considered a measure of performance risk. Thus it is viewed as a good indicator and predictor of a contractor's ability to deliver on future contracts. Contracting officers and evaluation boards are required to make use of available past performance information in all responsibility determinations and in award decisions on all new contracts over $150,000.

Federal departments and agencies must share past performance information with other departments and agencies when requested to support future award decisions. There is a three (3) year limit on the use of performance information from a completed contract in the source selection process. Organizations that have recently been created cannot be penalized for being new, regardless of whether an evaluation factor is obviously a past performance matter. Firms lacking relevant performance history may receive a neutral evaluation for past performance.

Since past performance has become an increasingly important data point in the evaluation process, so has the importance of the information's accuracy. Agencies are required to give offerors a chance to respond to any adverse past performance information that had been obtained from references, where the offeror has not had a previous opportunity to comment in rebuttal (*FAR 42.1503, Procedures*).

This subject is discussed further in Chapter 13, *Contract Performance*.

## Federal Awardee Performance and Integrity Information System (*FAR 9.104-6*)

A new database designed to provide comprehensive information about a prospective contractor's business ethics and quality of work has been implemented in the FAR. The *Federal Awardee Performance and Integrity Information System* (FAPIIS), FAR 9.104-6, is designed to collect information on a contractor's history of past performance, suspension and debarment, determination of non-responsibility, contract terminations, and prior criminal, civil, and administrative proceedings.

Contracting officers are required to review the FAPIIS information when awarding contracts valued above the simplified acquisition threshold. The CO also must document how the FAPIIS was used to make the responsibility determination. If FAPIIS contains information indicating there had been suspension or debarment action against the prospective contractor, before proceeding with the award, the contracting officer must contact the agency official that had initiated the action.

Offerors must be given the opportunity to defend such findings before any action is taken against them.

# EVALUATION OF COST PROPOSALS

## Responsibility for Evaluation

Prime responsibility for evaluation of contractor cost proposals rests with the contracting officers or their authorized representatives. The contracting officer must coordinate a team of experts, requesting advice from them, evaluating their counsel and utilizing those experts' skills. However, the contracting officer has the ultimate responsibility which cannot be transferred.

A concerted team effort is required to accomplish an effective evaluation. A typical proposal cost and price analysis team consists of the following individuals and disciplines:

- Price analyst
- Negotiator
- Buyer
- Project engineer
- Liaison auditor at the purchasing office
- On-all support from various functional disciplines for element evaluation

## Field Pricing Support

Frequently, contracting officers will request field pricing support to augment their in-house efforts in evaluating contracts and modifications. The estimated value and type of contract will be the determining factor for making such a request. The requests for field pricing support must be tailored to ask for minimum essential information. The goal is to assure that a fair and reasonable price is achieved.

FAR 15.404-2, *Data to Support Proposal Analysis*, recommends that contracting officers request field pricing assistance when the information available at the buying activity is inadequate to determine a fair and reasonable price.

The type of support information obtainable is quite varied. It may include audited cost information from current contracts and recently negotiated proposals. Data on an offeror's proposed subcontractors and their deliverables and prices of standard commercial items will frequently be needed. Of special importance will be current forward pricing advanced agreements and negotiated forward pricing rate agreements (FPRA).

Field pricing support will be obtained through agency or cross-servicing arrangements with other organizations.

- Defense Contract Management Command (DCMC) provides field pricing support for contractors within their assigned areas.
- Defense Contract Audit Agency (DCAA) assists contracting officers, plant representatives, and DCMC as requested.

The contract auditor is responsible for performing reviews and cost analyses where access to contractor's books and financial records is required. However, contracting officers, administrative contracting officers, or their authorized representatives, can request data from an offeror or review the offeror's records whenever necessary to discharge their responsibilities. Auditors are precluded from discussing their conclusions or recommendations on the offeror's estimated or projected costs with the offeror unless specifically requested to do so by the contracting officer.

**Proposal Analysis (*FAR 15.404*)**

The objective of proposal analysis is to ensure that the final agreed-to price is fair and reasonable. To reach that objective the contracting officer will perform or have performed some form of price or cost analysis, as directed by FAR 15.404-1, *Proposal Analysis Techniques*. Price analysis will be performed on those proposals when cost or pricing data are not required. It is also used to support or supplement cost analysis wherever appropriate.

Price analysis is the process of examining and evaluating a prospective price without evaluation of the separate cost elements and proposed profit. It does not require a determination of probable costs or the performance of cost analysis. Therefore, adequate price analysis may be had by a reasonable and good faith cost evaluation on the basis of the proposed target cost and exposure of the Government to cost growth.

Price analysis may be performed in a variety of ways. The following are some examples of price analysis actions:

- Comparison with other price quotations submitted.
- The comparison of prior quotations and contract prices with the current proposed prices for the same or similar end items. To provide a suitable basis for comparison, proper allowances must be made for differences in such factors as specifications, number of quantities ordered, time for delivery, Government-furnished materials and experienced trends of improvement in production efficiency. Such comparison may not detect an unreasonable current price. The reasonableness of the prior prices must first be established. Changes in the general level of business and prices must also be considered.
- The use of rough yardsticks, such as dollars per pound, dollars per horsepower, hours per unit or similar categories can be effective. They can point out apparent gross inconsistencies which should be subjected to greater pricing inquiry.
- The comparison of prices set forth in published price lists issued on a competitive basis, published market prices of commodities and similar indices, together with discount or rebate arrangements.
- Comparison of proposed prices with estimates of cost independently developed by personnel within the purchasing activity.
- Comparison of proposed prices with those for the same or similar items obtained through market research.

## Cost Analysis

Cost analysis is the fundamental evaluation technique for negotiated procurements. Cost analysis is the review and evaluation of a contractor's cost or pricing data and of the judgmental factors applied in projecting from the data to the estimated costs. An opinion can then be made on the degree to which the contractor's proposed costs represent what performance of the contract should cost, assuming reasonable economy and efficiency. FAR 15.404-1, *Proposal Analysis Techniques*, directs that cost analysis must be used when certified cost or pricing data are required, in order to evaluate the reasonableness of individual cost elements.

Cost analysis is used in the verification of cost data, evaluation of specific elements of cost and projection of these data. It is then used to determine the effect factors such as the following have on the quoted price.

- The necessity for, and reasonableness of, proposed costs including allowance for contingencies.
- The projection of the offeror's cost trends, on the basis of current and historical cost or pricing data.
- The reasonableness of estimates generated by appropriately calibrated and validated parametric models or cost-estimating relationships.
- The extent of uncertainties of contract performance and realism of any allowances for contingencies.

Cost analysis is used to verify that the cost elements submitted by a contractor are in accordance with FAR Part 31, *Contract Cost Principles and Procedures*. When evaluating subcontract costs an analysis of the prime contractor's make-or-buy performance record will be valuable.

One phase of cost analysis involves the comparison of a contractor's current proposed costs with the following cost data whenever they are available.

- Actual costs previously incurred by the contractor or offeror.
- Previous cost estimates from the offeror or from other offerors for the same or similar item.
- Current cost estimates from other sources.
- Forecasts or planned expenditures.
- Independent government estimates by technical personnel.

An adequate cost analysis must include an evaluation of trends and their effect on future costs. Therefore, trend analysis of basic labor and material costs is essential.

### Cost Realism and Should-Cost Analysis

Cost analysis is used in the absence of price competition to achieve what competition is presumed to supply. The assumption is that a pricing arrangement will be arrived at, which will likely result in payment of a fair and reasonable price. Cost analysis should uncover the facts needed to reach agreement on such an arrangement. For the arrangement to be realistic, it must be influenced strongly by the estimate of what it should cost to perform the work. Such a theory assumes the contractor operates with reasonable economy and efficiency. That theory may not be very realistic, and furthermore, the type of work being analyzed might not lend itself to hypothetical forecasting.

Cost realism analysis is made as a review of the costs proposed in an offeror's proposal. Cost realism means that the costs in an offeror's proposal are realistic for the work to be performed; reflect a clear understanding of the requirements; and are consistent with the various elements of the offeror's technical proposal.

Should-cost reviews are a specialized form of cost analysis. They differ from traditional evaluation methods because they do not assume that a contractor's historical costs reflect efficient and economical operation. Instead, these reviews evaluate the economy and efficiency of the contractor's existing work force, methods, materials, facilities, operating systems, and management.

FAR 15.407-4, *Should-Cost Review*, describes the basic concepts of should-cost analysis and the conditions under which it should be performed.

In the interest of maintaining adequate price competition and getting realistic prices, contracting officers will be on the alert for "buying-in" proposals by offerors. Buying-in, the practice of attempting to obtain a contract award by knowingly offering a price or cost estimate less than anticipated costs, is discussed in Chapter 1, *Contract Fundamentals*.

## EXCHANGES WITH OFFERORS

### Exchange Fundamentals

One very important element in the proposal evaluation process is conducting written or oral exchanges between the Government agency and offerors. This process will take place from the time proposals are received up to the time an award is made to the successful offeror.

The criteria in FAR 15.306, *Exchanges with Offerors after Receipt of Proposals*, give the contracting officer guidance for conducting discussions with offerors. Agencies are not required to hold discussions with every offeror that has responded to a request for proposals. In fact, when award without discussions is contemplated, it will be so noted in the solicitation. Then limited exchanges, referred to as clarifications, will allow offerors an opportunity to clarify certain aspects of their proposal or to resolve minor or clerical errors.

The Government may indicate to all offerors the cost or price that the Government's price analysis, market research, and other reviews have identified as reasonable. Along the same line, the contracting officer may inform an offeror that it's price is considered by the Government to be too high or too low, and reveal the results of the analysis supporting that conclusion.

When exchanges are contemplated they will be held both before and after the competitive range is established. FAR 15.306(b) discusses communications with offerors before establishment of the competitive range. The communications are exchanges between the Government agency and offerors leading to the establishment of the competitive range. These exchanges are limited only to offerors who fall into one of two categories: (1) offerors whose past performance information would be the determining factor preventing them from being placed within the competitive range; and (2) offerors whose exclusion from, or inclusion in, the competitive range is uncertain.

These exchanges will be conducted to enhance the Government's understanding of the proposals in question. They will not be held to cure any deficiencies or otherwise revise the proposal. The exchanges are for the purpose of addressing issues that must be explored to determine whether or not the proposal should be placed in the competitive range. When an agency has discussions with offerors that are in the competitive range, then it must have discussions with all offerors in the competitive range. However, if an agency wants to make clarifications with one offeror, it is not required to make clarifications with all offerors.

Once the competitive range has been established, the contracting officer will follow the directions in FAR 15.306(d), *Exchanges with Offerors after Establishment of the Competitive Range*. These exchanges are essentially negotiations which may include bargaining. The discussions are tailored to each offeror's proposal. The primary objective of the discussions/negotiations will be to maximize the Government's ability to obtain best value, based on the requirement and evaluation factors that had been set forth in the solicitation. At any time during the discussions, it may be determined that an offeror is no longer considered to be among those being considered for award of a contract. That offeror will be eliminated from the competitive range.

All offerors selected for discussions are advised of deficiencies in their proposals. They are given a reasonable opportunity to correct or resolve any such deficiencies. Contacts with offerors regarding the elimination of minor uncertainties or irregularities are not considered "discussions." However, the elimination of these could improve the offeror's scoring.

There are certain limitations placed upon Government personnel involved in the acquisition process. FAR 15.306(e), *Limits on Exchanges*, identifies several such situations. The personnel must not engage in conduct that favors one offeror over another. Nor can they reveal an offeror's technical or unique solutions to another offeror. The discussions must be handled so as not to result in transfusion of information between offerors. Furthermore, the discussions are not to involve auction techniques, which are prohibited. The FAR prohibits giving out any information concerning other offeror's prices or a price necessary for the proposal to have further consideration. It is permissible, however, for a contracting officer to tell an offeror that its price is too high or unrealistic.

Government negotiators and contracting officers are often faced with a dilemma in that they need to have meaningful discussions during a negotiation, but they do not want to have those discussions become "technical leveling." Disclosing deficiencies in an offeror's proposal must be distinguished from "technical leveling" or "technical transfusion." Technical leveling is helping an offeror bring its proposal up to the level of other proposals through successive rounds of discussions. An example would be pointing out weaknesses resulting from the offeror's lack of diligence, competence, or inventiveness in preparing the proposal. Transfusion relates to transferring one offeror's superior solution of the Government's problem to another offeror.

**Competitive Range**

Determination of which proposals are considered to be in the competitive range is largely left to the agency's discretion while the initial responsibility for that falls upon the contracting officer. The Government Accountability Office (GAO) will, however, question some competitive range determinations. They will usually pose that question when there has been a protest filed by an unsuccessful offeror.

FAR 15.306, *Exchanges with Offerors after Receipt of Proposals*, establishes the requirement for the determination of competitive range. It states in Subparagraph (c), *Competitive Range*, that agencies must evaluate all proposals in accordance with FAR 15.305(a) and, if discussions are to be conducted, they must establish the competitive range.

The competitive range must be determined on the basis of rating each proposal against all of the evaluation factors stated in the solicitation. Based on these ratings, the competitive range will be comprised of all of the most highly rated proposals. However, after evaluating all proposals, the contracting officer may determine that the number of the most highly rated proposals that otherwise would be included in the competitive range exceeds the number at which an efficient competition can be conducted. If the solicitation addressed this situation, the number of offerors may be trimmed to the greatest number that would permit an efficient competition among the offerors who are the most highly rated.

Broadly stated, for proposals to be within the competitive range, a proposal must at least address itself to all essential elements of the solicitation. It must show that the offeror understands those essential requirements. It also must be reasonably complete so a virtually new proposal will not be needed. The definition of this elusive property called "competitive range" is very vague, at best. The vagueness of the term stems from the fact that it can only be applied on the basis of expert judgment and the specific factors involved in each particular situation. The objective in its application is not to eliminate proposals from the source selection process. The true goal is to promote discussions and enhance proposal acceptability and competition.

One thing the agency must be careful about is possibly excluding one offeror from the competitive range and including another within the competitive range when there are no material differences in the weaknesses shown in each proposal. When the Government has discussions with offerors that are in the competitive range, they must be fair.

If a contracting officer determines that a proposal no longer has a reasonable chance of being selected for contract award it will be eliminated from further selection consideration. The unsuccessful offeror will be notified in writing or electronically at the earliest practicable time that its proposal is no longer eligible for award.

### Source Selection Conclusion

After all discussions have been held, organizations still within the competitive range will be given the opportunity to submit revisions to their proposals. A common cut-off date must be established with enough time to allow a reasonable opportunity for submission of any revisions. It is conceivable that some offerors will not wish to revise their proposal.

After receipt of the revised offers, the contracting officer will not reopen discussions unless it is clearly in the Government's interest to do so. If discussions must be reopened, then all offerors still within the competitive range will be so notified. The contracting officer must be careful that any further discussions do not give rise to claims that the Government is resorting to auctioneering, which could lead to a protest.

Following the final cut-off date and any further evaluations, selection will be made of the source whose offer is most advantageous to the Government. The contracting officer will award a contract to the successful offeror by furnishing the executed contract or other notice of the award to that offeror (*FAR 15.504, Award to Successful Offeror*).

One very important element of the whole process concerns how the contracting officer completes the source selection documentation. The agency must have adequate documentation in the acquisition file to support the decision leading to the final contract selection. Failure to create that adequate documentation will leave the door open for the agency to lose a protest filed by one or more of the losing competitors in the acquisition. Failure to provide that adequate documentation could easily have a source selection award to be re-evaluated and overturned. In this situation the protesting party could win its case and receive some relief.

## PROPOSAL DEBRIEFINGS AND STATUS ANALYSIS

### Debriefing of Offerors

While detailed debriefings are not always given automatically, any offeror may request a detailed debriefing. They are available to both the successful and the unsuccessful offerors in a negotiated procurement.

Offerors who have been excluded from the competitive range or otherwise excluded from the competition before an award has been made, may request a debriefing (*FAR 15.505, Preaward Debriefing of Offerors*). The offeror may submit a written request for a preaward debriefing or request a delay until after award. The contracting officer may also require that for compelling reasons a delay is necessary. The delayed debriefing must occur no later than when postaward debriefings are held.

FAR 15.506, *Postaward Debriefing of Offerors*, provides that, when a contract has been awarded on the basis of competitive proposals, an offeror, upon its written request for a debriefing, shall be debriefed and furnished the basis for the selection decision and contract award. Much of the debriefing process revolves around whether a debriefing is determined to be "required" or just an accommodation to an unsuccessful firm that had submitted a proposal. The debriefing becomes a "required" one only if the requester submits the request in writing to the agency within three days after receipt of notice of exclusion from the competitive range or within three days after receiving the notice of award.

To the maximum extent practicable, a "required debriefing" should occur within five days after receiving the written request. Delays in conducting a debriefing extend on a day by day basis the opportunity for the firm to file a protest and also delay contract performance. Once the required debriefing has been provided to the unsuccessful offeror, that organization has no more than ten (10) days to file a timely protest with the GAO (see page 99, Contract Award Protests).

Debriefings may be conducted orally, in writing, by electronic means, or any other method acceptable to the contracting officer. At a minimum, the debriefing information should include:

- The Government's evaluation of proposal weaknesses and deficiencies
- The overall evaluated cost or price and technical rating, if applicable, of the successful offeror and the debriefed offeror, and past performance information on the debriefed offeror
- Overall ranking of all offerors
- A summary of the rationale for award
- Reasonable responses to relevant questions of the debriefed offeror

The debriefing must not include point-by-point comparisons of the debriefed offeror's proposal with those of other offerors.

Under the Freedom of Information Act (FOIA) any person, whether a participant in the procurement activity or not, may request from the agency releasable records pertaining to the solicitation/procurement. Such a request by one of the competitors in the solicitation does not of itself constitute a request for a debriefing. A debriefing must not reveal any information exempt from release under the Freedom of Information Act, such as trade secrets and confidential financial information.

Losing contractors must be prepared for debriefing by first performing a self-critique. They should send objective observers to oral debriefings who will not be on the defensive, but go there to find out as much as they can as to why their company lost.

Debriefings provide losing contractors with areas where they can improve their proposal techniques and become more competitive in future acquisitions by the Government. Also, debriefings are often the last activity that either avoid or trigger a protest by a participant. During a debriefing, an agency will usually attempt to provide enough information that the requester will be satisfied the process was fairly conducted and its proposal was properly evaluated.

**Status Analysis by Losing Contractors**

To improve their chances of winning future contracts, losing contractors will need to learn the answers to questions such as the following:

- Why did we lose, and who or what caused it?
- How badly did we lose; what was our ranking in the competition?
- Can the deficiencies be corrected; and if so, what must be accomplished to prevent recurrence?

There are certain courses of action that the contractor may take after learning that they have lost a competition. The following five examples are typical of those choices:

- File a protest with the Government; demand a re-evaluation.
- Approach the winning contractor and bid for subcontracts.
- Hold back, but work like mad for the next phase.
- Keep current and work hard to improve existing capabilities; be "waiting in the wings" for similar programs.
- Look for new customers with needs employing the same technology or product line.

Losing a potential contract after expending considerable resources is not to be taken lightly. If there was a serious attempt to get the program, it is well worth the effort needed to find out why you were eliminated from the competitive range. This can be especially important if there have been several recent failures. If nothing else is done, someone should be tasked to critique the proposal and compare it to whatever feedback is obtained from the debriefing or other sources.

The basic answer to the whole affair is to communicate what has happened, correct the deficiencies or redirect the effort. The recommended actions coming from the critique could be as simple as making sure proposals are thoroughly proofread before release. It could be as serious as calling for a reorganization of the proposal organization and process. Most of all, you must turn the defeat of today into the "winning proposal" victories of tomorrow.

## Major Proposal Defects

There are many reasons why proposals are eliminated from the competitive range. The following list represents the major defects contracting officers have found in proposals submitted to the Government. Any of these has the potential of making a proposal become eliminated as being outside of the competitive range. When several of these conditions are found there is little doubt that the proposal will be eliminated.

- Failure to follow the RFP instructions
- Use of "boilerplate" material not closely related to the problem
- Poor personnel resumes
- Assuming the customer already knows a contractor's attributes
- "Buy-in" cost proposals
- Use of play-back techniques (don't parrot the RFP)
- Taking certain solicitation requirements too lightly
- Changing the customer's program
- Poor pricing rationale
- Lack of apparent corporate interest
- Non-responsiveness

# CHAPTER 8

# MANAGING CONTRACT RISK

## RISK MANAGEMENT – GENERAL

Risk is always a concern in the acquisition process. There is the risk that the contractor will not deliver on time, or that the product/service will not fulfill the need, or that the cost of performance will increase. Although risk is inherent in any acquisition, risk management ensures managers take measures to assess and handle risks.

Contracting is all about risk allocation and minimizing risk to include cost, schedule and performance. The more vague the contract work statement, the more risk that the Government assumes.

### Risk from Program Manager, Contracting and Investor's Perspective

Risk is a measure of the inability to achieve program objectives within defined cost and schedule constraints. Risk is associated with all aspects of the program, e.g., threat, cost, schedule, technology, design processes, work breakdown structure (WBS) elements, etc.

### Risk from a Lawyer's Standpoint

Does this contract adequately describe all essential work/expectations? Is there a schedule and is it enforceable? What are our remedies, if any?

Requiring activities and frequently contracting officers want to get an acquisition on contract as quickly as possible; sometimes too quickly. Thus, contracting officers and acquisition attorneys will frequently have to carefully review the overall acquisition to identify risks to cost, schedule and performance and recommend mitigation measures to decrease these risk areas.

### Risk from an Investor's Perspective

What is my expected payoff? The larger the expected payoff, the larger the associated risk, and vice versa. An investor, who is a shareholder in a contracting company, will seek to carefully balance the expected payoff with the associated risk, and he is incentivized to seek a large payoff, as long as the risk is acceptable. This perspective is unique in the sense that risk represents both opportunity and danger to the investor, while it only represents danger to the program manager and the lawyer. In other words, there is a misalignment in the perception of risk between the program manager, the lawyer, and the investor. It is ultimately the investor who owns the contracting company, and this misalignment will have an effect on the investor's behavior and the stock's performance.

## Types of Risk

Risks that could impact acquisition costs include increases in material prices, higher than anticipated labor rates, and other factors that can change current acquisition cost estimates. Risks that could impact acquisition schedule include late deliveries, political pressure, and changing requirements (user needs the system sooner or user adds requirements). Risks that could impact technical performance include use of new or exotic materials or processes, use of unproven technology, and use of new applications to meet demanding user requirements.

Risk should be measured in terms of the probability, or likelihood, of failing to achieve a particular outcome and the consequences, or impact, of failing to achieve that outcome.

Risk management is an integral part of acquisition management. It requires all team members to use a disciplined approach so that risk is reduced to an acceptable level. This is done by assessing and handling the risks associated with the design, manufacturing, technology, test, and support functions that are part of systems acquisition. A good risk management program can enhance acquisition management effectiveness and provide managers with an important tool for reducing a system's life cycle costs.

The application of risk management is particularly important during the early stages of an acquisition, however, the time and effort spent on risk management should be commensurate with the acquisition. Generally lower dollar or non-complex acquisitions require less risk management while higher dollar or complex acquisitions require more risk management.

Effective risk management requires collaboration between the government and the contractors. Characteristics of good government/contractor interaction include:

- Clear definition of risks and their assignment.
- Flexibility for assigning risk management responsibilities among the acquisition team, including collaborative government-contractor team.
- Strong emphasis on risk management best practices.

While there is much collaborative work on risk management between the Government and contractors, each party views risk from a different perspective.

Contractors typically divide risk into two basic types: Business Risk and Program Risk.

- Business risk involves the inherent chance of making a profit or incurring a loss on any given contract. As the definition suggests, business risk has both upside and downside potential for the contractor; however, risk for the Government is generally considered negative.
- Program risk includes uncertainties in technical requirements, design, cost, funding and scheduling. Although the Government does not dictate how the contractor should manage risk, some characteristics of good Government/contractor interaction include:

- Clear definition of risks and their assignment;
- Flexibility for assignment of risk and risk management responsibilities among the acquisition team;
- Strong emphasis on best management practices which, if followed, avoid unnecessary risk; and
- Conduct of systems engineering technical reviews

**Approaches to Risk Management**

Risk management in an acquisition management office may be either centralized or decentralized. In a centralized risk management approach, a dedicated group conducts risk management efforts. The acquisition manager establishes the team that is responsible for all aspects of risk management. The team writes the risk management plan, conducts assessments, evaluates risk-handling strategies, and monitors progress. Although this approach may be necessary early in an acquisition, it tends to minimize the concept that risk management is a responsibility shared by all members of the acquisition team.

In the decentralized risk management approach, assigned personnel conduct risk management as part of their normal engineering or management jobs within an acquisition team. The decentralized approach is recommended because it generally results in an efficient use of personnel resources.

The type of approach used will depend in large part on the nature and size of the acquisition and the desires of the acquisition manager. Regardless of which approach is used, the activities and responsibilities must be clearly stated and assigned to individuals.

One of the first steps a team can take to manage risk is develop a risk management plan. To initiate this plan, the team should:

- Conduct an initial meeting with the contractor to describe the acquisition.
- Train acquisition team members and members of the contractor's team.
- Review the acquisition's documentation requirements with the contractor.
- Work with the contractor to refine risk-monitoring plans and procedures.
- Establish program reporting requirements with the contractor.
- Work with the contractor to develop appropriate tracking measures.

## RISK MANAGEMENT PROCESS

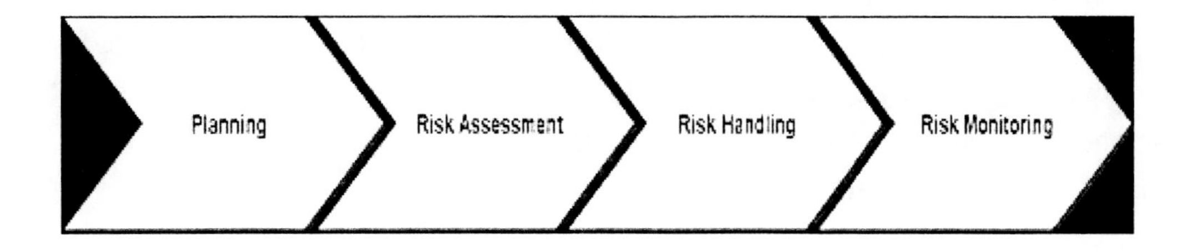

The risk planning phase is used to develop an organized, comprehensive strategy for identifying and tracking risk management activities. Risk planning involves developing an organized, comprehensive and interactive strategy and methods for identifying and tracking risk management activity. In order to do proper planning you must:

- Assign adequate resources to manage risk;
- Develop a risk management strategy and approach;
- Train personnel in risk management techniques; and
- Draft a risk management plan which provides a process to manage risk

The risk assessment phase is used to identify and analyze risk events. Risk assessment is one of the most important phases of the risk management process because the caliber and quality of assessments play a major role in determining the effectiveness of a risk management program. It is the problem definition stage of risk management that identifies, analyzes and prioritizes program risk events in terms of probability (likelihood) of occurrences and impacts (consequences) of those occurrences. The results form the basis for most risk handling actions. Techniques for risk assessment are discussed later in this chapter. The steps in this phase of the process are generally performed sequentially although there can be some concurrency involved (in practice the distinction between risk identification and risk analysis is often blurred, because some degree of risk analysis may occur during the risk identification stage).

Risk identification involves determining what risks might affect a program, and compiling a list of those risk events. They may be identified from experience of subject matter experts; historical data, such as lessons learned from similar programs; brainstorming; strengths, weaknesses, opportunities and threats (SWOT) analysis; checklists; and product and/or process decomposition.

Risk analysis is a technical and systematic process to examine identified risks, isolate causes, determine the relationship to other risks, express the risk rating (e.g., high, medium/moderate, and low) based on probability and consequences, and prioritize risks in a "watch" list. It usually begins with a detailed study of the risk events that have been identified to gather information for determining the probability of each event occurring, and the impact on cost, schedule, and performance if it does occur.

## RISK RATING

A risk rating may be qualitative or quantitative. Qualitative assessments are normally somewhat subjective and are based on detailed information that may come from such sources as comparisons with similar systems, lessons learned, experience, prototype and/or engineering model development, tests, experts/specialists, and modeling and simulation. Quantitative assessments use some form of numerical analysis, such as Monte Carlo simulations, decision analysis, and sensitivity analysis.

A simple method for representing risk ratings for risk events is a matrix similar to the one shown below. In this example, the probability or likelihood of the risk event occurring is shown on the "x" axis, and the impact or consequence of its occurrence is shown on the "y" axis. Consequences will be shown in terms of impacts to cost, schedule and performance as applicable.

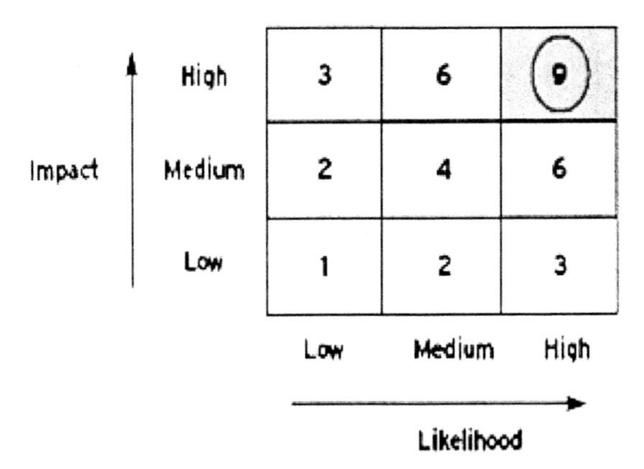


Assigning a risk rating to each event helps to determine the appropriate risk management strategy to use. The standard risk assessment techniques within the generic process described are listed below. Technique use is situational, and in some cases one or more techniques could be applied simultaneously. For example, we may want to look at both "process" and "product" risk using two techniques in assessing the risks.

**Process Risk Assessment**

This technique is used to assess (identify and analyze) the technical risks resulting from the contractor's processes. It is based on describing the risk areas contained in the various technical processes, e.g. design, test, production, etc., and specifying methods for reducing the risks in each area. Success of any risk reduction efforts associated with this technique will depend on the contractor's ability and willingness to make a concerted effort to replace any deficient engineering practices and procedures with best industrial practices.

One of the primary benefits of this technique is that it addresses pervasive and important sources of risk in most acquisition programs and uses fundamental engineering principles and proven procedures to reduce technical risks. The technique is accepted by many aerospace companies in normal business activities.

It should be used in preparation for major acquisition milestone decisions and source selection and may be used independently or in conjunction with other risk assessment techniques. Whenever feasible, a Government-industry evaluation team should be formed early in the acquisition to apply this technique.

This technique is sometimes referred to as the "Willoughby Template" method in honor of Mr. William Willoughby, who for many years served as the U.S. Navy's Top-Level Quality Chief.

## Program Documentation Evaluation Risk Identification

This technique provides a methodology for the comparison of key acquisition documents and plans to ensure that they are consistent and traceable to one another. If the content (activities, events, schedules, requirements, specifications, etc.) of a document or plan do not flow from or support the contents of those above, below, or adjacent to it, there is a strong chance that risk will be introduced into the acquisition, or that known risks will not be adequately addressed. This technique reduces those risks and improves the quality of the acquisition documentation.

The comparison of acquisition documentation and plans should be performed by a small team of experienced, knowledgeable personnel who are intimately familiar with the content of the total acquisition.

## Product (WBS) Risk Assessment

This technique identifies those risks associated with a given system concept and design. The difference between the process technique and this approach is simple: The process technique addresses the contractor's engineering and manufacturing processes while the product technique focuses on the resulting product. This technique is used to identify and analyze risks in the following critical risk areas: design and engineering, technology, logistics, concurrency and manufacturing.

The project work breakdown structure (WBS) serves as the starting point to describe contract work that will be done, and the resulting product, and determines the risk events in each critical risk area. The risk events – events that might have a detrimental impact on the system, subsystems, or components – are evaluated in terms of probability and consequence using a risk matrix chart (probability on "Y" axis, consequence/impact on "X" axis). From the chart, the risk event can be determined to be high, medium, or low risk.

This technique should be used shortly after the completion of the prime contractor's contract WBS. Thereafter, it should be used regularly up to the start of production. The technique can be used independently or in conjunction with other risk assessment techniques, such as the process risk assessment technique. It may also be used in establishing a performance measure baseline for the contract.

To apply this technique, program teams (joint Government-industry if possible) need to do the risk assessments and handling strategies for risks in their portion of the WBS. If necessary, complementary industry-only teams can be formed to take an in-depth look at selected areas at lower WBS levels – where the actual work is produced. At times it is desirable to include outside industry experts on the teams to aid in the examination of specific WBS elements or functional areas.

**Threat/Requirements Risk Assessment**

This technique describes an approach to assess risk associated with requirements and threats. It identifies those requirements and threat elements that are risk drivers. Because operational needs, environmental demands, and threats determine system performance requirements to a large degree, they are a major factor in driving the design of the system and can introduce risk in an acquisition. By using cost as an independent variable (CAIV), acquisition program managers can identify areas that are either not critical or not risky, and thus available for trade-offs to meet cost objectives.

The requirements assessment process focuses on: determining if operational requirements are properly established; ensuring that requirements are stable and achievable; the operating environment is adequately described; addressing logistics and suitability needs; and determining if requirements are too constrictive, thereby identifying a specific solution.

The threat assessment process addresses uncertainty in threat accuracy and stability, sensitivity of design and technology to threat, vulnerability of the system to threat countermeasures, and vulnerability of the program to intelligence penetration. Program managers should view requirements in the context of the threat and accurately reflect operational, environmental, suitability, etc. requirements in design documents. Gaining a complete understanding of the requirements and threat early in an acquisition precludes misunderstandings between the requirements and development communities, helps to identify risk areas, and allows early planning to handle risk. Consequently, the user should be actively involved in this process from the beginning.

**Cost Risk Assessment**

This technique provides an acquisition-level cost estimate at completion (EAC) that is a function of performance and schedule risks. It uses the results of prior risk assessments of low-level work breakdown structure (WBS) elements and their activities, and cost probability distributions developed for each of the elements' activities. These individual WBS activities are aggregated using a Monte Carlo simulation to obtain a probability distribution of the program-level cost EAC probability distribution function. These results are then analyzed to determine the actual risk of cost overruns and to identify the cost risk drivers.

The use of these lower level cost probability distributions as the basis for the acquisition-level cost estimate results in a more realistic EAC than the commonly used single point estimates for WBS elements, since they address both the probability of occurrence and consequences of potential risk events. Their use also eliminates a major cause of underestimating (use of point estimates) and permits the identification of technical performance or schedule causes of cost risk. Thus, this technique provides a sound basis for the determination of an "acceptable" level of cost risk.

This technique can be used in any of the acquisition phases. It should be used in conjunction with performance and schedule risk assessments, and may be performed by a small Government-industry team consisting of risk analysts, cost analysts, schedule analysts and technical experts that understand the significance of prior performance and schedule risk assessments. This technique requires close and continuous cooperation among cost analysts and knowledgeable technical personnel, and the support of the prime contractor's senior management to help get valid cost data.

**Quantified Schedule Risk Assessment**

This technique provides a means to determine acquisition-level schedule risk as a function of the technical performance and cost risk associated with the various activities that comprise the program. It estimates the acquisition-level schedule by developing probability distributions for each activity duration and aggregating these distributions using a Monte Carlo simulation or other analytical tools. The resulting acquisition-level schedule is then analyzed to determine the actual schedule risk and to identify the schedule risk drivers.

This technique expands the commonly used Critical Path Method (CPM) of developing an acquisition schedule to obtain a more realistic estimate of schedule risk. The basic approach CPM uses a single point estimates for the duration of the acquisition activities to develop the expected duration and schedule for the program. It invariably leads to underestimating the time required to complete the acquisition and schedule overruns, primarily because the point estimates do not adequately address the uncertainty inherent in the individual activities. The uncertainty can be caused by a number of factors and can be considered a reflection of the risk present in the activity.

The quantified schedule technique accounts for uncertainty by using a range of time that it will take to complete each activity instead of single point estimates. These ranges are then combined to determine the acquisition-level schedule estimate. This approach enables managers to estimate early in an acquisition if there is a significant likelihood of overrunning the schedule and by how much. It also identifies activities that are on the "highest risk path."

This technique can be used in any phase of the acquisition. The schedule probability distribution function for each key activity should be developed as soon as the activity is included in the master schedule. The distribution functions should be reviewed and revised periodically. The technique should be applied by a small Government-industry team consisting of schedule analysts and technical experts that understand the significance of prior risk performance assessments.

## Expert Interviews

A difficult part of the risk management process is the gathering of data. This technique provides a means for collecting relevant risk-related data from subject-matter experts and from personnel who are intimately involved with the various aspects of the acquisition. It relies on "expert" judgment to identify and analyze risk events, develop alternatives, and provide "analyzed" data. It is used almost exclusively in a support role to help develop technical data required by a primary risk assessment technique, e.g., product (WBS) risk assessment technique. It can address all the functional areas that make up the critical risk areas and processes, and it can be used in support of risk handling.

Expert judgment is a sound and practical way of obtaining necessary information that is not available from previous acquisitions or practical to develop using engineering or scientific techniques. However, interviewers should be aware that expert opinions may be biased because of over reliance on certain information and neglect of other information; unwarranted confidence; the tendency to recall most frequent and most recent events; a tendency to neglect rare events; and motivation. Results may have to be tempered because of bias.

## Analog/Comparison/Learned Studies

This technique uses lessons learned and historical information about the risk associated with similar acquisitions to identify the potential risks. It is normally used to support other primary risk assessment techniques, e.g., product (WBS) risk assessment, process risk assessment, etc. The technique is based upon the concept that "new" acquisitions are originated or evolved from existing acquisitions or simply represents a new combination of existing components or subsystems. A logical extension of this premise is that key insights can be gained concerning the various aspects of a current acquisition's risks by examining the successes, failures, problems and solutions of similar existing or past acquisitions. This technique addresses all the functional areas that make up the critical risk areas and processes.

## Risk Prioritization/Aggregation

These techniques provide a means to prioritize the risks present in an acquisition and to roll-up lower level risks into a meaningful value at the critical risk area and process level. The prioritized list of risks provides the basis for the development of risk handling plans, preparation of a risk handling task sequence list, and the allocation of risk handling resources. The aggregated risks – usually contained in a risk "watch" list – present a higher level view of risk that may be used by senior management to assess the acquisition's present and future status.

Both of these techniques require definitive criteria to evaluate the risks, such as, probability of failure (PF), consequence of failure (CF), along with any other factors considered appropriate.

The risks are evaluated using qualitative expert judgment and multi-voting methods to prioritize and aggregate risks. A qualitative approach using subject matter experts is generally preferred in this technique because of the tendency to rely on ordinal values/scales to describe both PF and CF, and the inherent inaccuracies that may result from using uncalibrated ordinal values.

**Risk Handling**

The risk handling phase is used to identify, evaluate, select, and implement strategies in order to set risk at acceptable levels; also referred to as risk mitigation.

There are four common strategies for handling acquisition risks: Risk Control; Risk Avoidance; Risk Assumption; and Risk Transfer. They can be used alone or in combination. When deciding which strategy to use, consider the following:

- Is the strategy feasible?
- Will it be effective?
- Is it affordable?
- Is there time to implement it?
- Is there a schedule impact?
- How does it affect the system's technical performance?

Controlling risk means lowering the chance that the event will occur by following some of the risk control actions below:

- Using multiple contractors;
- Conducting multiple tests;
- Reusing proven software versus developing new software;
- Parallel design and development of key sub-systems and components; and
- Incremental development

These actions may reduce the probability an event will occur and/or the impact to the program if it does occur.

Risk avoidance means changing the source (element or constraint) that is subjecting the acquisition to risk. Risk may be avoided by implementing some of the following avoidance techniques:

- Reducing the scope of performance objectives;
- Using more expensive materials or processes with proven track records; and
- Extending the schedule to increase the probability of success

Risk assumption with this strategy, you acknowledge the existence of a particular risk and then make a conscious decision to accept the level of risk associated with it, without identifying and applying any risk handling measures. All unknown or identified risks are assumed. Assuming risk means planning for the potential consequences by using some of the following techniques:

- Accepting the risk;
- Putting a monitoring process in place; and
- Taking action now (e.g., reserving funds, modifying schedules, etc.) that will support contingency actions if the risk materializes into an actual problem.

Risk transfer reallocates the risk from one part of the system to another, or redistributes risks between the government and the contractor, within government agencies, or between members of the contractor team. It means having someone else take accountability for the risk. Ways that risk can be transferred include: using firm-fixed price contracts and warranties to transfer cost risk to the contractor; and assigning the responsibility to the organization that is best suited to minimize the probability of a negative consequence.

**Risk Monitoring**

The risk monitoring phase is used to evaluate the performance of risk-handling options. Risk monitoring is used to systematically track and evaluate the performance of risk-handling actions against established metrics throughout the acquisition process. The results may also provide a basis for developing additional handling strategies and identifying new risks.

**Risk Documentation**

It is important to document all actions throughout the risk management process. The documentation will provide the basis for reporting risk and overall program information, both internally and externally. This information can be used on future acquisitions to help identify the appropriate types of risks and the most successful risk handling strategies.

There is always some risk associated with every acquisition, but remember the time and effort spent on risk management should be appropriate for the acquisition. It is important to identify the potential risks that could impact the acquisition early in the planning stages so that appropriate risk handling strategies can be implemented that will minimize the impact on the acquisition.

# RISK MANAGEMENT SUPPORTING PRE-ACQUISITION SOURCE SELECTION PLAN AND THE REQUEST FOR PROPOSAL

This section attempts to tie the risk management project process above to the risk assessment/management as used in early acquisition planning. In the risk assessment model, risks have three components:

- A future root cause (yet to happen), which, if eliminated or corrected, would prevent a potential consequence from occurring;
- A probability (or likelihood) assessed at the present time of that future root cause occurring; and
- The consequence (or effect) of that future occurrence

"Risks should not be confused with issues. The important difference between issue management and risk management is that issue management applies resources to address and resolve current issues or problems, while risk management applies resources to mitigate future potential root causes and their consequences."

The below chart identifies the probability on the left side and the consequences across the top. Low risk is in green, moderate risk is yellow, and high risk is depicted in red. The chart reveals only 1 high risk, 2 moderate risks, and the remainders are low risks.

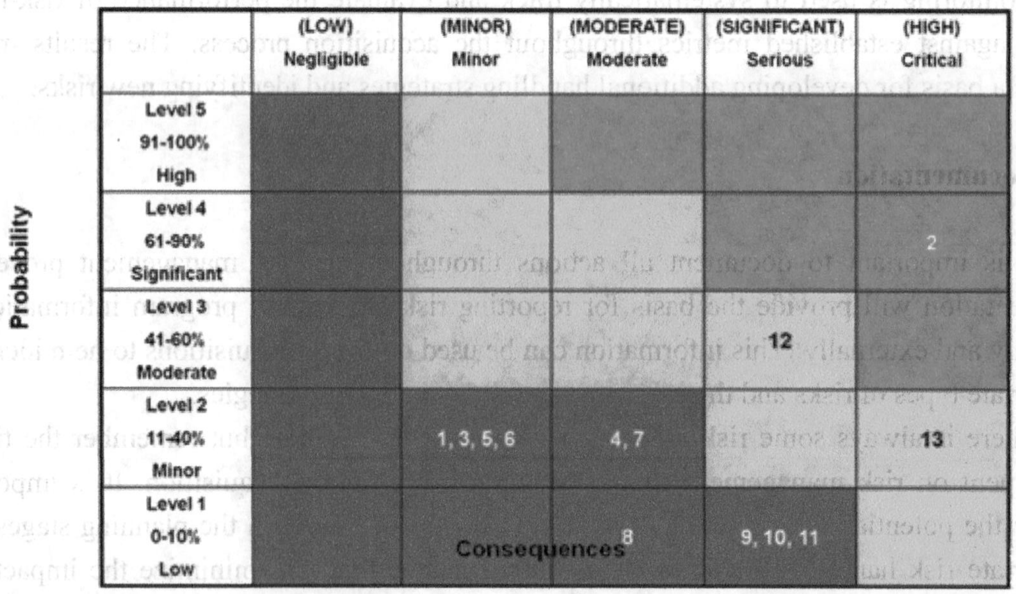

| Probability | (LOW) Negligible | (MINOR) Minor | (MODERATE) Moderate | (SIGNIFICANT) Serious | (HIGH) Critical |
|---|---|---|---|---|---|
| Level 5 91-100% High | | | | | |
| Level 4 61-90% Significant | | | | | 2 |
| Level 3 41-60% Moderate | | | | 12 | |
| Level 2 11-40% Minor | | 1, 3, 5, 6 | 4, 7 | | 13 |
| Level 1 0-10% Low | | | 8 | 9, 10, 11 | |

Consequences

The purpose of demonstrating the risk assessment process in an actual scenario is to show the relationship of the risk assessment as it becomes a critical element of the source selection plan and the RFP in the early acquisition planning.

**DOD's Risk Management Process**

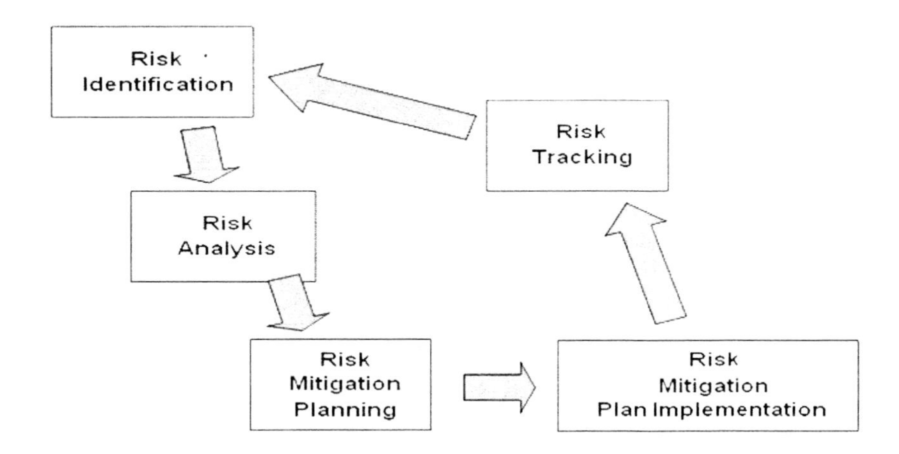


The above DOD risk management process answers five important questions:

- What can go wrong?
- How big is the risk?
- What is the program approach for addressing this potential unfavorable consequence?
- How can the planned risk mitigation be implemented?
- How are things going?

Start the process with risk identification. Risk identification answers the question "What can go wrong?" You can determine this by (1) looking at current and proposed staffing, process, design, supplier, operational employment, resources, dependencies, etc., (2) reviewing potential shortfalls against expectations, (3) monitoring test results especially test failures, and (4) analyzing negative trends.

Next comes risk analysis. Risk analysis answers the question "How big is the risk?" by (1) considering the likelihood of the root cause occurrence, (2) identifying the possible consequences in terms of performance, schedule and cost, and (3) identifying the risk level using a Risk Reporting Matrix.

Risk mitigation planning answers the question "What is the program approach for addressing this potential unfavorable consequence?" Some mitigations may be (1) avoiding the risk by eliminating the root cause and/or the consequence, (2) controlling the cause or consequence, (3) transferring the risk, and/or (4) assuming the level of risk and continuing on the current program plan (do nothing).

Risk mitigation plan implementation ensures successful risk mitigation occurs. It answers the question "How can the planned risk mitigation be implemented?"

Risk tracking also ensures successful risk mitigation by answering the question "How are things going?"

# CHAPTER 9

# TOTAL OWNERSHIP COSTS

## INTRODUCTION

The concept of total ownership costs is not new, it just has not been deemed as important in the past as it is now. With significant budget constraints federal agencies must take into consideration all of the costs incident to each and every program under consideration. Those costs start with the acquisition process of development, test and production, as appropriate, passing on to the operation and support phases and ultimately to the disposal phase.

## COST AS AN INDEPENDENT VARIABLE (CAIV)

In order to control the total ownership costs, agencies must set aggressive realistic cost objectives for acquiring and supporting their programs. Then they must actively manage them to achieve those objectives. Those objectives must be tailored to the specific circumstances associated with the program under consideration. Cost objectives must balance the agencies' needs and program requirements with the projected out-year fiscal resources. The agencies must take into account the state of requisite technologies and anticipated process improvements, both within the agency and the supporting businesses. This concept has become known as "cost as an independent variable" (CAIV). What CAIV means is, once the program or system performance and objective costs are decided, on the basis of cost-performance tradeoff, the acquisition process will make cost more of a constraint, and less of a variable in meeting the needs of the mission.

In order to achieve the objectives of cost as an independent variable, certain actions must be implemented. The agency must set realistic but aggressive cost objectives early on in each acquisition program. Then they must manage the risks to achieve cost, schedule and performance objectives. Early on they must devise appropriate metrics for tracking progress, both in setting and then achieving the cost objectives. Motivating both the Government and the business/industry managers to achieve the program objectives is essential. Then, in order to reduce operating and support costs, additional incentives for "fielded systems" should be put in place.

One important contributor to meeting the CAIV objectives under the total ownership costs concept is an active life-cycle cost (LCC) program. The best time to reduce life-cycle costs is early in the acquisition process. External parameters often change and program realities evolve. Cost-performance tradeoffs must occur throughout the acquisition cycle. Because of that, it is often advisable to incorporate a design-to-cost (DTC) process early in the program.

Life-cycle cost objectives, and when applicable, design-to-cost processes, should be incorporated in program requirement documents, the RFP, contract provisions and the source selection process. This chapter will further explore LCC and DTC as they apply to the concept of total ownership costs and cost as an independent variable.

## LIFE-CYCLE COSTS

### Definition of Life-Cycle Costs

Life-cycle cost (LCC) is defined as the estimation and analysis of the total cost of ownership of an item or system, over its total expected operational life. All costs, both direct and indirect, attributed to a particular system, are considered to be part of the life-cycle cost of that system. This will include development, acquisition, operating and support costs. For some products and systems, disposal costs will be a part of the total LCC.

The life-cycle cost program is designed to bring about reductions in system and equipment operating and support costs. This can be accomplished through increased consideration and analysis of the operating and support implications of design alternatives. Therefore, LCC is used as a management tool and decision criterion throughout the acquisition process of a system in support of the CAIV goals.

The best time to reduce life-cycle costs is early in the acquisition process. Cost/performance tradeoff analyses, conducted before an acquisition approach is finalized, will generate the most savings in life-cycle costs.

### Life-Cycle Cost Models

A life-cycle cost model comprises one or more mathematical relationships arranged in a systematic sequence. They are designed to formulate a cost methodology to get reliable cost estimates. The inputs to the formula will come from such sources as descriptions of equipment, organizational structures, processes and procedures. Life-cycle cost models always reflect later costs which are the direct result of the decision or action being contemplated, rather than merely the initial costs.

### Life-Cycle Costing Methods

The Department of Defense requires that for all Acquisition Category 1 and 1A programs, a life-cycle cost estimate must be prepared by the program office in support of program initiation (usually Milestone 1) and all subsequent milestone reviews. They also require that the component sponsoring the acquisition program must establish, as a basis for the life-cycle cost estimate, a description of the salient features of the acquisition program and the system itself. There are two basic techniques in making an LCC estimate, the Cost Estimating Relationship (CER) method and the Engineered Cost Estimate method.

The Cost Estimating Relationship method uses the statistical analysis of physical, performance and cost data from existing similar hardware systems. The CER method uses data which can be extrapolated and applied to the proposed new system. This method is frequently called parametric costing. This is when physical and performance measurements, called parameters, are used in the estimating equations. The CER method depends upon judgment that historical data reflects enough commonality with the proposed item to give a reasonable cost estimate.

In the Engineered Cost Estimate method the total system is anatomized into many elements. The elements are related through cost equations which reflect in detail the way they interact when the system is developed, produced, operated and supported. The engineered cost equations are compiled with estimates of the element values. The equation results are examined and revised based upon continued trade-off analyses or improved knowledge gained during the development and acquisition process.

The transition in costing methods from CERs to Engineered Cost Estimates is gradual rather than at a single changeover point. However, there should be enough knowledge of the system to analyze the costs in detail to prepare a good response to the RFP for the production contract.

Through continuous evaluation by the Government and contractors, the life-cycle cost estimates will be translated into design requirements after considering trade-offs between system effectiveness, cost and schedule.

## DESIGN-TO-COST

### Definition of Design-to-Cost

Design-to-cost is a concept that establishes cost elements as management goals to achieve the best balance between life-cycle cost, acceptable performance, and schedule. Under this concept, cost is a design constraint during the design and development phases and a management discipline throughout the acquisition and operation of the system or equipment (*FAR 2.101, Definitions*).

Cost as an independent variable (CAIV) and design-to-cost (DTC) have the same ultimate goal of a proper balance among design, development, test, production, operations and support costs. At the same time the mission needs must be met under an established schedule and within an affordable cost.

## Government Approach to DTC

Over the years DTC has been more related to program execution, emphasizing cost effective design and targeting an average unit procurement cost. It mostly concentrated on the contractor's activities in meeting the DTC requirements of the contract. Under the CAIV concept, the Government has changed the focus of DTC to consider cost objectives for the total life cycle of the program. Both the Government and the contractor must view CAIV with an understanding that it may be necessary to trade off performance to stay within cost objectives and constraints. Therefore, any contractual implementation of DTC must go beyond just encouraging the contractor to meet cost commitments, but to giving the contractor the incentive to seek out additional opportunities to reduce costs.

In order to effectively implement such goals, the Government program offices will need to provide cost visibility to design alternatives, advocate cost-driven solutions and provide a means of tracking the progress of meeting the cost objectives.

## Contractor Management Approach to DTC

Design-to-cost must be managed as any other element or system of the contract. Therefore, a systems management approach is essential in order for DTC to be set up, maintained, and tracked throughout the life of the contract.

Management must establish the DTC target if it is not already dictated by the RFP or contract. First a non-allocated reserve, to be controlled by management, will be set aside. The remainder is the budget to be distributed downward to the designated end items. The contractor must then pursue a vigorous program to achieve the DTC target. The initial efforts will take place in the design and development efforts. Parts selected must be easy to manufacture or inexpensive to purchase. The assembly, integration and test processes need to be as simple as possible to help meet or beat the end item targets. This is an example of where systems engineering can have a significant impact.

Design-to-cost adds an additional element to the task of program management, called "Design-to-Cost Impact Management." Every design decision and every change in design must be evaluated as to its impact on the DTC target. This will be in addition to the normal concerns for the impact on contract costs, schedule and performance, i.e., the total cost of ownership.

## DTC in the Contract

The mission of design-to-cost is to get contractors to design a product with a predetermined production or program cost. That cost may be set either as a requirement or as a target. When DTC is specified in a contract, it will have emphasis comparable to that of the contract performance requirements. The contract should contain a minimum number of performance specifications, those which are critical performance criteria. To be consistent with CAIV objectives, the specifications should identify trade-off flexibility in requirements and program baseline. It is during the design and development phases that the most significant impacts can be made on the DTC target. Therefore, DTC is attuned to development phases of a program or product rather than the production phase.

### Application of Design-to-Cost

Design-to-cost must be a key element of the mission for both the Government and contractor teams. Controlling cost should be addressed by all levels of both teams by challenging performance and schedule with cost estimating and analysis resources. Actually, the whole cost as an independent variable process, where design-to-cost and life-cycle cost targets are incorporated in a contract, requires that both the Government team and the contractor team work very closely together or there is a high probability that the CAIV objectives will not be achieved.

# CHAPTER 10

# CONTRACT COST AND PROFIT PRINCIPLES

## OVERVIEW

There are many differences between contracting with the Federal Government and contracting in the private sector. Perhaps one of the most significant of those differences deals with the treatment of cost incurred while performing contracts. The vast majority of contracts in the private sector are of a fixed-price nature. The government, on the other hand, expends a great deal of its appropriated funds on a cost reimbursement basis. Since government contracts involve spending public funds, the rules of the game are far different than if private or commercial funds are used. Even fixed-price government contracts have significant differences in this regard.

The laws and regulations that apply to government contracts and contractors are extremely complex. There is an ever increasing requirement for accounting and legal specialists to interpret and apply the rules properly. Any company that deals in both commercial and government contracting has an added burden. Their record keeping must satisfy their internal needs, the tax agencies and all the government agencies with which they contract. Therefore, they actually have to maintain multiple records. Improper records can raise the question of fraud in the eyes of government auditors. Contractors need to know the indicators of fraud. They must implement internal reviews and aggressive ethics programs to avoid claims and penalties. Government contracting is a complex process with the potential of expensive consequences for the uninformed contractor.

In this chapter we will explore the world of contract costs as seen by the Federal Government. The emphasis will be upon cost reimbursement type contracts. That is where the major issues arise between the government and its contractors and subcontractors.

## GOVERNMENT COST PRINCIPLES IN RETROSPECT

At the beginning of World War I, the government did not have a formalized program to control the costs or profits of munitions being procured. During the war, they tried to remedy that situation by the use of cost-plus-a-percentage-of-cost (CPPC) type contracting, by fixing prices and by imposing excess profits taxes. None of these approaches solved their problems. First of all the CPPC contracts had high total costs and excess profits. This was most likely because there were no incentives for the contractors to exercise cost control. On the other hand enormous profit margins were realized by low cost producers under the "fixed prices" concept. Lastly, the excess profits taxes gave no consideration to the nature and quality of a contractor's performance.

The first peacetime federal legislation to limit profits from munitions sales was the Vinson-Trammel Act of 1934 (V-TA). As originally written, it required contractors for certain naval vessels and aircraft to refund to the government any profits in excess of ten percent (10%) of the contract price. In 1940 the Act was extended to Army aircraft. In August 1940 the Treasury Department issued Treasury Decision 5000 (TD 5000) in support of V-TA. That document, TD 5000, gave illustrations of excess profits, established principles for determining the cost of performing a contract, defined the general composition of certain cost elements, provided guidelines on allowability of costs and considered the allocation of indirect costs to government contracts.

During World War II further progress was made. Many contracts included reference to and direct quotations from TD 5000 when defining reimbursable costs. Because of this, it became a standard statement of cost principles that were applicable to almost all military cost-type contracts. In December 1943 the War Department issued Technical Manual (TM) 14-1000, *Administrative Audit Procedures for Cost-Plus-a-Fixed Fee Supply Contracts*. Chapter 5 of TM 14-1000, subsequently issued in April 1944, added cost interpretation material intended to be consistent with the principles set forth in TD 5000. That manual became the basic guide for auditing military contracts.

After World War II, the government recognized the need for well-defined procurement regulations. Congress passed into law the Armed Services Procurement Act of 1947, to create the first completely organized set of regulations. Out of this Act came the Armed Services Procurement Regulations (ASPR). Section XV of ASPR, *Contract Cost Principles*, was published to be effective 1 March 1949 to provide a common set of cost principles applicable to cost-type contracts within the three military departments. The Federal Property and Administrative Services Act followed in July 1949. That Act created the Federal Procurement Regulations (FPR), which passed on to the non-DOD agencies and departments formal and standardized procurement procedures and cost principles patterned after ASPR.

In 1970 Congress passed Public Law 91-379 (50 U.S.C. App 2168). That Act created the Cost Accounting Standards Board (CASB) to implement the law by establishing standards, rules and regulations and the administration of the Cost Accounting Standards program. The Act required the CASB to develop Cost Accounting Standards (CAS) to be used in connection with negotiated national defense contracts and the disclosure of cost accounting practices to be used in such contracts. The law and CASB requirements were subsequently extended to contracts of non-DOD agencies and departments by a General Services Administration regulation that amended the Federal Procurement Regulations (FPR). Part 30 of the Federal Acquisition Regulation (FAR) now prescribes the policies and procedures for applying the CASB standards and regulations to negotiated government contracts and subcontracts.

# CONTRACT COSTS

## Cost Principles and Procedures

FAR Part 31, *Contract Cost Principles and Procedures*, contains the cost principles and procedures for pricing contracts and contract modifications wherever cost analysis is performed. This Part is also used for the determination, negotiation or allowance of costs when such action is required by a contract clause. Applicability of the FAR to the several kinds of contracts and contractors is described in the following subparts of FAR.

- *Fixed-Price Contracts* – FAR 31.102
- *Contracts with Commercial Organizations* – FAR 31.103
- *Contracts with Educational Institutions* – FAR 31.104
- *Construction and Architect-Engineer Contracts* – FAR 31.105
- *Contracts with State, Local, and Federally Recognized Indian Tribal Governments* – FAR 31.107
- *Contracts with Nonprofit Organizations* – FAR 31.108
- *Advance Agreements* – FAR 31.109
- *Indirect Cost Rate Certification and Penalties on Unallowable Costs* – FAR 31.110

FAR Part 31 lists selected items of cost and describes their condition of allowability. It is a representative listing designed to guide the government and contractors in dealing with the subject of allowability. Not all cost elements and costing situations are covered in Part 31. The cost principles for contracts with educational institutions, state, local and federally recognized Indian tribal governments and non-profit organizations are set forth in Office of Management and Budget (OMB) Circulars A-21, A-87 and A-122 respectively.

Part 31 is used in pricing fixed-price (FP) type contracts and modifications, whenever cost analysis is performed. However, there is no requirement to negotiate agreements on individual elements of cost, only an agreement on the total price.

FAR 31.2, *Contracts with Commercial Organizations*, sets forth the cost principles and procedures to be used in negotiated contracts and contract modifications with commercial organizations whenever cost analysis is used. The provisions of Subpart 31.2 are incorporated by reference in applicable contracts. They will be used as the basis for performing the following functions.

- Determination of reimbursable costs under cost reimbursement type contracts and subcontracts, and the cost reimbursement portion of time-and-material contracts.
- The negotiation of indirect cost rates applicable to government contracts.
- Proposing, negotiating or determining costs under terminated fixed-price or cost reimbursement contracts.

- The price revision of fixed-price incentive contracts.
- Price redetermination of fixed-price redeterminable contracts.
- Pricing changes and contract modifications for all types of contracts.

**Allowable Contract Costs**

A contractor will only be paid for the allowable costs incurred in performance of a government contract. When the contract is fixed-price, acceptable performance by the contractor is the basic criteria for payment. It is not so simple when the contract is a cost reimbursement type. To be allowable, a cost must be an element of the total cost of a cost reimbursement contract. The composition of total contract cost, as defined by FAR 31.201-1, *Composition of Total Cost*, is:

> "The total cost, including standard costs properly adjusted for applicable variances, of a contract is the sum of the direct and indirect costs allocable to the contract, incurred or to be incurred, plus any allocable cost of money pursuant to 31.205-10, less any allocable credits."

A cost will not be "allowable" if it cannot be "allocated" to a specific Government contract. Even when a cost is allocable, it is not necessarily allowable. The concept of allowability is addressed to the question of whether a particular item of cost should be recoverable as a matter of public policy.

There are several factors that affect the allowability of a cost. The five basic factors, as listed in FAR 31.201-2, *Determining Allowability*, are:

- Reasonableness
- Allocability
- Terms of the contract
- Limitations set forth in FAR Part 31
- Standards promulgated by the Cost Accounting Standards Board, if applicable, otherwise, generally accepted accounting principles and practices appropriate to the particular circumstances

The various elements of cost typically subject to allowability determinations are found in FAR 31.205, *Selected Costs*. However, it does not cover every possible cost element. Failure for any item of cost to be listed in FAR 31.205 does not imply that it is either allowable or unallowable. That determination will be based upon the principles and standards in all of FAR 31.2, *Contracts with Commercial Organizations*, and the treatment of similar or related selected cost items listed in FAR 31.205.

When more than one of the selected costs in Subpart 31.205 is relevant to a contractor's costs, the cost will be apportioned among the applicable subsections. Then determination of allowability will be based on guidance contained in those subsections. Similarly, when more than one of the selected costs is relevant, but apportionment is not practical or possible, determination of allowability will be based on guidance contained in the selected cost subsection that most specifically deals with, or best captures the essential nature of the cost at issue (*FAR 31.204, Application of Principles and Procedures*).

Some normal business expense items are not allowable under government contracts. While those costs would be included in the total price for a typical commercial product or service they may be unallowable as part of the costs paid by the government. Some examples of those costs are:

- *Public Relations and Advertising Costs* – FAR 31.205-1
- *Bad Debts* – FAR 31.205-3
- *Contributions or Donations* – FAR 31.205-8
- *Entertainment Costs* – FAR 31.205-14
- *Interest and Other Financial Costs* – FAR 31.205-20
- *Lobbying and Political Activity Costs* – FAR 31.205-22

**Reasonableness**

A cost is reasonable if, in its nature and amount, it does not exceed that which would be incurred by a prudent person in the conduct of competitive business (*FAR 31.201-3, Determining Reasonableness*). In the absence of effective competition restraints, the reasonableness of specific costs will be examined by the government. If a challenge of a specific cost is made, the burden of proof as to its reasonableness will be the contractor's responsibility. The incurrence of costs by a contractor or subcontractor is not of itself a measure or presumption of reasonableness. The reasonableness of a given cost is determined by a variety of considerations and circumstances. The following guidelines are traditionally applied to aid in the decision process:

- Is the cost necessary for the performance of a specific contract?
- Whether the cost is of a type generally recognized as being ordinary and necessary in the conduct of that contractor's business or in performance of the contract.
- The influence of such factors as generally accepted sound business practices, arm's length bargaining, federal and state laws and regulations, and contract terms and specifications.
- Action a prudent business person would take considering the responsibilities to the owners of the business, employees, customers, government and the public at large.
- Significant deviations from the established practices of the contractor which may unjustifiably increase the contract costs.

The principle related to compensation (*FAR 31.205-6, Compensation for Personal Services*), was revised to eliminate the need to evaluate the reasonableness of each element of compensation on an individual basis. In most cases it should be determined based on the *overall* level of compensation.

**Allocability**

A cost is allocable if it is assignable or chargeable to one or more cost objectives on the basis of relative benefits received or other equitable relationship (*FAR 31.201-4, Determining Allocability*). In *Boeing North America, Inc. v. Roche, U.S. Court of Appeals for the Federal Circuit No. 01-1011, March 15, 2002*, the court held that "the word 'benefits' as used in FAR 31.201-4 refers to an accounting concept and does not impose a separate requirement that the cost benefit the Government's interests for the cost to be allowable."

Subject to that definition, a cost is allocable to a contract if it is incurred specifically for the contract. It may also be allocable if it benefits both the contract and other work, and can be distributed to them in reasonable proportion to the benefits received by them. Another determination of allocability will be if it is necessary to the overall operation of the business, even though a direct relationship to any particular cost objective cannot be shown. In order for a cost to be allowable, it must be allocable. However, even if a cost is allocable, it may not be allowable (*FAR 31.205*).

**Contract Provisions**

The contract will contain a variety of terms and conditions that will affect cost allowability. First of all, it will cite the contract requirements and deliverables which will define the scope of the work to be performed. That scope is usually contained in the work statement, specifications and data requirement lists. Costs incurred in performance of the scope are direct allowable costs under normal circumstances.

Other contract clauses will address cost associated matters. Some of these are located in Part I, *The Schedule*, in the contract. There you will find clauses dealing with such topics as reimbursement for travel, relocation of personnel, precontract costs, and other advance agreements peculiar to that specific contract. Then in Part II, *Contract Clauses*, "boilerplate" type clauses are located. They deal with such topics as cost accounting standards, overtime premiums, limitation of costs and limitation of funds.

**Advance Agreements (*FAR 31.109*)**

Advance agreements on the allowability of certain peculiar costs are frequently entered into between the government and contractors. Such agreements are important and often necessary. The reasonableness and allocability of certain items of cost may be difficult to determine for an individual company or division. Therefore, advance agreements serve the purpose of avoiding possible disallowance or dispute issues during the life of the contract or after closure.

Advance agreements should be negotiated before the start of the contract and definitely before incurrence of the costs involved. All such agreements must be in writing, executed by both parties and incorporated into applicable contracts. Advance agreements may relate to a single contract or to several contracts with a commonality that the agreement addresses. Some advance agreements will be applicable to all contracts between a government agency and a company or one of its divisions.

The following are some examples of costs covered by advance agreements:

- Compensation for personnel services (e.g., off-site pay, incentive pay, location allowances, hardship pay and cost of living differential)
- Use charge for fully depreciated assets
- Deferred maintenance costs
- Precontract costs
- Independent research and development (IR&D) costs
- Royalties
- Selling and distribution costs
- Special travel costs
- Travel via contractor-owned, leased, or chartered aircraft
- Public relations and advertising
- Idle facilities and idle capacity
- Automatic data processing equipment
- Bid and proposal (B&P) costs
- Severance pay to employees on support service contracts
- Training and education costs

### Credits (*FAR 31.201-5*)

Whenever a contractor receives any income, rebate, allowance or other type of credit relating to any allowable cost, the applicable portion thereof must be credited to the government. The credit will be made either by a reduction of the contract price or by a cash refund.

### Accounting for Unallowable Costs (*FAR 31.201-6*)

Contractors are required to maintain their cost records in enough detail and depth to permit the government to perform its audits. During the audits the auditors will seek to identify unallowable costs, including directly associated costs, incurred in the performance of government contracts. This requirement is necessary because unallowable costs must be identified and excluded from any billing, claim or proposal applicable to a government contract. This applies to costs, including directly associated costs, that are expressly unallowable or mutually agreed to be unallowable.

A directly associated cost is one which is generated solely as a result of incurring another cost. It would not have been made had the other cost not been incurred. When an unallowable cost is incurred, its directly associated costs are also unallowable.

An unallowable cost is not necessarily one that can be avoided by a contractor. It is merely a cost that the government will not accept. Many unallowable costs are necessary expenditures for the conduct of a normal business. There is a definite conflict between operating a business and the government's cost principles.

**Direct Costs (*FAR 31.202*)**

A direct cost is one which can be identified specifically with a particular final cost objective. Costs identified specifically with a contract are direct costs of that contract and must be charged accordingly. Under certain circumstances, a direct cost of a minor dollar amount may be treated as an indirect cost, as long as it is consistently applied to all final cost objectives and produces substantially the same results as treating it as a direct cost.

**Indirect Costs (*FAR 31.203*)**

An indirect cost is one which is incurred for common or joint objectives and is not readily subject to treatment as a direct cost. Indirect costs are accumulated by logical cost groupings, such as manufacturing overhead, selling expenses, and general and administrative expenses.

The method of allocating indirect costs is based on the particular circumstances involved with the contract and the contractor. The method is normally in accordance with the Cost Accounting Standards promulgated by the Cost Accounting Standards Board. Where those Standards do not apply, the contractor's established practices are generally acceptable, providing they are in accordance with generally accepted accounting principles.

Indirect costs are allocated to a contract during the period in which they were incurred and accumulated. They will be distributed to the costs for direct contract work performed in that period. The method of allocating indirect costs is normally accomplished by applying approved indirect cost rates to the direct costs incurred in performing a contract. Those indirect or overhead rates are discussed later in this chapter.

Indirect costs are also divided into fixed and variable costs. Fixed indirect costs are those that normally are not affected by the volume of work being undertaken. They remain constant in total, regardless of changes in contract activity (i.e. rent, insurance, and taxes). On the other hand, variable indirect costs will change in direct relationship to the volume of work performed, either increasing or decreasing (i.e. payroll expenses, materials, and travel).

### Certificate of Indirect Costs (*FAR 42.703-2*)

In the majority of cost reimbursement contracts and certain fixed-price contracts, contractors are required to submit, upon completion of the contract, a proposal to establish the final indirect cost rates allowable for that contract. The proposal will not be accepted and no agreement will be reached in establishing those final indirect cost rates, unless the costs have been certified by the contractor (*10 U.S.C. 2324(h)* and *41 U.S.C. 256(h)*). The certificate used for this purpose is in FAR 52.242-4 (*Certification of Final Indirect Costs*).

An agency head, or designee, may waive the certification requirement when it is determined to be in the interest of the United States, and the reasons for such determination are put in writing and made available to the public.

If the contractor has not certified its proposal for final indirect cost rates and a waiver is not appropriate, the contracting officer may unilaterally establish the rates using audited historical or other data and set the rates low enough to ensure that unallowable costs will not be reimbursed.

Penalties may be assessed against contractors that include unallowable indirect costs in final indirect cost rate proposals submitted for the final statement of costs incurred or estimated to be incurred under a fixed-price incentive contract (*FAR 42.709, Scope*).

### Recurring and Nonrecurring Costs

The distinction between recurring and nonrecurring costs concerns the frequency with which such costs are incurred. Recurring costs are expected to be incurred in a repeating manner, such as the on-going management, engineering, production and operational efforts. Nonrecurring costs, on the other hand, are expected to be incurred only once or perhaps, only at certain intervals during the life of the contract. Examples of nonrecurring costs would include design and production of specialized test equipment, preparing for and attending the post-award conference.

Identifying and segregating these two types of cost is very important for both contracting parties. Their distinction is necessary in the development and analysis of cost proposals and then during the life of the contract.

### Facilities Capital Cost of Money

Facilities capital cost of money (FCCM) is an imputed cost. FCCM is determined by applying a cost-of-money rate to facilities capital employed in support of government contracts. A cost-of-money rate is derived from a common source and uniformly imputed to all contractors. Capital employed is determined without regard to whether its source is equity or borrowed capital. The resulting cost-of-money is not a form of interest on borrowings.

Facilities capital cost of money is allowable to contracts which meet the following criteria:

- The contractor's capital investment must be measured and allocated in accordance with the Cost Accounting Standards (CAS). The specific standard for FCCM is CAS 414, *Cost of Money as an Element of the Cost of Facilities Capital.*
- The contractor must maintain adequate records to demonstrate compliance with CAS 414.
- For FCCM to be allowable to a contract the estimated cost-of-money must be proposed by the contractor. The cost proposal relating to the contract under which the cost is being claimed must identify those costs the same as other cost elements.

The facilities capital cost of money need not be entered on the contractor's books of account. However, the contractor must make a memorandum entry of the cost. All relevant schedules, cost data and other data necessary to support the entry will be maintained in a manner that permits audit and verification.

For facilities capital cost of money to be allowable, it must be allocated and documented in accordance with the cost accounting standards. The allowable FCCM will be "incurred costs" for reimbursement purposes under applicable cost reimbursement contracts. This also applies for progress payment purposes under fixed-price contracts.

Some government agencies consider the cost-of-money to be equivalent to fee, not just an allowable cost. They will adjust the fee payable on their contracts by the amount of the allowable FCCM. This is compatible with the current weighted guidelines criteria.

## OVERHEAD RATES

### Categories of Rates

Audited overhead rates or negotiated overhead rates are the two resources available to negotiators in the settlement of government contracts. These rates are also used in the evaluation of billings and claims submitted by contractors. Most contractors use some combination of the following types of overhead rates in their estimating and accounting practices.

- Forward pricing/quoting rates – for proposal preparation
- Booking rates – for recording expenditures
- Billing rates – for invoicing purposes
- Reporting rates – for inputs to management, customers, governmental agencies, and stockholders
- Final reimbursement rates – for settlement of final expenditures and claims

## Forward Pricing Rate Agreements (*FAR 15.407-3*)

Forward pricing rate agreements (FPRAs) are written understandings negotiated between the government and contractors. Their purpose is to make certain rates are available for use in the pricing of contracts and contract modifications, during a specified period of time. The duration of an FPRA normally is no longer than one year and can be cancelled by either party prior to its expiration.

The standard practice is for FPRAs to be negotiated by the administrative contracting officer (ACO) having cognizance over the contractor's accounting system. The ACO will be actively supported by the appropriate government auditor. Rates specified in an FPRA are not binding. They are available for use by both parties. Failure to use them will just complicate the analysis and negotiation of a proposal.

## Billing Rates (*FAR 42.704*)

Billing rates are tentative overhead rates established for interim reimbursement purposes during the life of the contract. They may be negotiated rates or rates acceptable to the contracting officer. In order to prevent substantial overpayment or underpayment a contractor's billing rates may have to be revised, either prospectively or retroactively.

The elements of indirect cost and the base or bases used in computing billing rates shall not be construed as determined by the indirect costs to be distributed or of the bases of distribution to be used in final settlements. Payments received by contractors based upon billing rates are subject to appropriate adjustment when final indirect cost rates are established.

## Final Indirect Cost Rates (*FAR 42.705*)

Final indirect cost (overhead) rates can be stated in terms of a percentage or a dollar factor. They are used to express the mutually agreed upon ratio of direct-to-indirect expenses incurred by the contractor during a specified period. Depending upon each contractor's accounting system, the factor may be applied to costs incurred or labor hours expended. These rates are primarily authorized for use in cost reimbursement type contracts for R&D with commercial organizations and non-profit or educational institutions.

A significant purpose of final indirect cost rates is to effect uniformity of approach to multiple contracts with more than one government agency. They are also intended to effect economy in contract administration efforts. One of the most important purposes is to promote timely settlement of closed contracts and other claims for reimbursement.

A contracting officer of the agency having cognizance over a contractor's facility normally has the responsibility and authority to negotiate the contractor's final overhead rates. These rates will be used for all government contracts performed by that contractor or at that facility.

When more than one department or agency contemplates the use of final indirect cost rates with the same contractor, the agency having the preponderance of cost reimbursement type work will, generally, sponsor and conduct the negotiations. The Department of Defense (DOD) is a major exception to this arrangement. The Defense Contract Audit Agency (DCAA) has been given responsibility for determining final overhead rates to all commercial contractor locations where the DOD has predominant interest. The DCAA auditor's determination will be made in coordination with the administrative contracting officer for that contractor.

Settlement of final indirect cost rates is a lengthy process. The contractor will submit a proposed set of rates based upon its analysis of the allowable costs incurred during a given year. Negotiation of that year's rates will not be started until the previous year's rates are settled. Because of the severe time lag, both the contractor and the government may be willing to use early closure rates for certain contracts. That process will usually be limited to contracts where only a minimal amount of costs were incurred in the last year of their contract life.

## COST ACCOUNTING STANDARDS

### Cost Accounting Standards Board

The original Cost Accounting Standards Board (CASB) was established in 1970 under the authority of Public Law 91-379. The Board had five members and was chaired by the Comptroller General of the United States. During its ten year life span, the Board issued nineteen cost accounting standards. In 1980 the Board was disbanded when Congress failed to authorize further funds for its operation.

In 1989 the CASB was revived under the authority of Public Law 100-679, *Office of Federal Procurement Policy Act Amendments of 1988*, and placed under the Office of Federal Procurement Policy (OFPP). One provision of the legislation created an independent five member Cost Accounting Standards Board. It has the responsibility to make, promulgate, amend, rescind and maintain government-wide cost accounting standards. The CASB is chaired by the OFPP Administrator. The other four members are representatives from DOD, GSA, and two individuals from the private sector. One of the latter pair is from industry and the other is a cost accounting expert.

### Basic Concepts of Cost Accounting Standards

A Cost Accounting Standard (CAS) is a statement formally issued by the Cost Accounting Standards Board (CASB). It enunciates a principle or principles to be followed by contractors and establishes certain practices to be applied. A standard may also specify criteria to be employed in selecting from alternative principles and practices in estimating, accumulating and reporting costs of contracts subject to the rules.

The CASB has two primary goals. The first is to issue clearly stated standards to achieve an increased degree of uniformity in accounting practices among government contractors. The second goal is to achieve consistency in accounting treatment of costs by individual government contractors. The CASB has not sought to establish a single uniform accounting system or chart of accounts. Businesses engaged in government contract work are far too complex and diverse for that to be practical.

Increased uniformity and consistency in accounting are very desirable conditions to achieve. They improve understanding and communication, reduce the incidence of disputes and disagreements and facilitate equitable contract settlements.

**Uniformity**

Uniformity relates to the comparison of two or more accounting entities. The Board's objective here is to achieve "likeness under like circumstances." The Board recognizes the impossibility of defining or attaining absolute uniformity, largely because of the problems related to defining like circumstances. The Board, none-the-less, has sought ways to attain a practical degree of uniformity in cost accounting.

Uniformity is achieved when contractors with the same circumstances, with respect to a given subject, follow the practice appropriate for those circumstances. Any increase in uniformity will provide more comparability among contractors whose circumstances are similar.

**Consistency**

Consistency pertains primarily to one accounting entity over periods of time. Like uniformity, the attainment of absolute consistency can only be measured when like circumstances can be defined. The Board believes that consistency within an entity from one period to another can be improved, thereby enhancing the usefulness of comparisons between estimates and actuals. It will also improve the comparability of cost reports from one time period to another where there are like circumstances.

The concept of maintaining consistency includes the requirement that contractors inform the Government before making changes to their existing cost accounting practices. Such a notification will probably cause the Government to audit the contractor's cost accounting practices and the proposed changes to assure compliance with the standards. It might also require that the contractor file a cost impact proposal.

**Allocability of Costs**

The Cost Accounting Standards relate to the allocability of costs to government contracts. Allocability is an accounting concept affecting the attainment of contract cost. It results from a relationship between a cost and a cost objective, in such a manner that the cost objective appropriately bears all or a portion of the cost. To be charged with all or part of a cost, a cost objective should cause or be an intended beneficiary of the cost.

Cost Accounting Standards should result in the determination of costs which are allocable to contracts and other cost objectives. The use of the Standards has no direct bearing on the allowability of individual items of cost. As noted before, allowability decisions for contract costs are subject to limitations or exclusions set forth in the contract or are otherwise specified by the government or its procuring agency.

Contract costs, where Cost Accounting Standards are involved, are only one of several important factors which should be utilized in negotiating contracts. Therefore, the promulgated Standards, and the determination of contract costs by them, cannot be considered a substitute for effective contract negotiations. Where contract costs are required to be determined and Cost Accounting Standards are applicable, the Standards will determine which costs are allocable to contracts. It is a contracting agency's prerogative to negotiate the allowability of allocated costs, but not the allocation itself.

The Cost Accounting Standards are established to perform three functions. They are designed to measure the amount of costs which may be allocated to covered contracts. The standards determine the accounting period to which costs are allocable. Lastly, they determine the manner in which allocable costs can be allocated to covered contracts. The resulting cost measurement and allocation determinations become binding on both the contractor and the contracting agency.

**Procedures for Implementing CAS**

FAR Part 30, *Cost Accounting Standards Administration*, describes the policies and procedures for applying the Cost Accounting Standards Board (CASB) rules and regulations to negotiated contracts and subcontracts.

Copies of the CASB Standards and Regulations are printed in Title 48 of the Code of Federal Regulations, Chapter 99. They may be obtained from the Superintendent of Documents, U.S. Government Printing Office, Washington, DC 20402. Or visit their website: www.gpo.gov. The FAR contains the Appendix, *"Cost Accounting Standards Preambles and Regulations"* as a convenience to the users of the FAR. Subchapter B, *"Procurement Practices and Cost Accounting Standards,"* of the Appendix contains the detailed requirements and standards. Figure 10-1, *Cost Accounting Standards*, on page 235 lists the titles of the current standards.

The Appendix to the FAR also contains preambles published by the Cost Accounting Standards Board. While not regulatory, the preambles are intended to explain why the Standards and related Rules and Regulations were written, and to provide rationale for positions taken relative to issues that were raised at the time of their development.

# COST ACCOUNTING STANDARDS

The following list of standards was promulgated by the Cost Accounting Standards Board. A detailed description of each standard is contained in 48 CFR Chapter 99 (Appendix B, FAR loose-leaf edition).

CAS 401 – Consistency in Estimating, Accumulating and Reporting Costs

CAS 402 – Consistency in Allocating Costs Incurred for the Same Purpose

CAS 403 – Allocation of Home Office Expenses to Segments

CAS 404 – Capitalization of Tangible Assets

CAS 405 – Accounting for Unallowable Costs

CAS 406 – Cost Accounting Period

CAS 407 – Use of Standard Costs for Direct Material and Direct Labor

CAS 408 – Accounting for Costs of Compensated Personal Absence

CAS 409 – Depreciation of Tangible Capital Assets

CAS 410 – Allocation of Business Unit General and Administrative Expenses to Final Cost Objectives

CAS 411 – Accounting for Acquisition Costs of Material

CAS 412 – Composition and Measurement of Pension Cost

CAS 413 – Adjustment and Allocation of Pension Cost

CAS 414 – Cost of Money as an Element of the Cost of Facilities Capital

CAS 415 – Accounting for the Cost of Deferred Compensation

CAS 416 – Accounting for Insurance Costs

CAS 417 – Cost of Money as an Element of the Cost of Capital Assets Under Construction

CAS 418 – Allocation of Direct and Indirect Costs

CAS 420 – Accounting for Independent Research and Development Costs and Bid and Proposal Costs

**Figure 10-1**

The following are examples of contracts and subcontracts that are exempted from CAS requirements:

- Contracts and subcontracts for acquisition of commercial items that are firm-fixed-price or fixed-price with economic price adjustment exempt from CAS requirements
- Those where price is based on established catalog or market prices of commercial items sold in substantial quantities to the general public
- Those where price is set by law or regulation
- Contracts and subcontracts with small business concerns
- Sealed bid contracts
- Labor surplus area set-aside contracts
- Contracts with foreign governments

The procuring contracting officer (PCO) has the responsibility to determine when a proposed contract will require CAS coverage. The PCO will include the appropriate notice in the solicitation and ensure that each offeror has included the required solicitation certification in its proposal.

The modified application of the standards are mandatory for most negotiated contracts and subcontracts exceeding $700,000 but are under $50 million. Full coverage, that is compliance with all Cost Accounting Standards, is required for contractors that: (1) receive a single CAS-covered award of $50 million or more; or (2) received $50 million or more in net CAS-covered awards during their preceding cost accounting period. Contractors subject to modified coverage are required to comply with four standards: CAS 401, CAS 402, CAS 405 and CAS 406 (see Figure 10-1 on page 235).

Educational institutions, receiving negotiated contracts or subcontracts in excess of $700,000 are required to comply with CAS requirements and specified CASB rules. Federally Funded Research and Development Centers are exempt from this application of the CAS. Currently, the CASB rules specifically designed for covered educational institutions are:

- CAS 501 – Consistency in Estimating, Accumulating, and Reporting Costs
- CAS 502 – Consistency in Allocating Costs Incurred for the Same Purpose
- CAS 505 – Accounting for Unallowable Costs
- CAS 506 – Cost Accounting Period

Solicitations for proposed contracts subject to CAS will contain the FAR clause at 52.230-1, *Cost Accounting Standards Notices and Certification*. Each offeror must furnish with its offer, copies of its Disclosure Statement(s) or a certificate of exemption or previous submittal. Contract award cannot be made until an otherwise eligible offeror has submitted an adequate Disclosure

Statement. Adequacy of a Disclosure Statement is determined by the ACO assisted by the auditor. The main criterion of adequacy is that the statement must be current, accurate and complete.

The contracting officer will insert the clause at 52.230-2, *Cost Accounting Standards*, in negotiated contracts, unless the contract is exempt or is subject to modified coverage. For contracts over $700,000 but less than $50 million, and the offeror certifies it is eligible for and elects to use modified CAS coverage, the contracting officer will use the clause at 52.230-3, *Disclosure and Consistency of Cost Accounting Practices*. In addition to either of those two clauses, the contract will contain the clause at 52.230-6, *Administration of Cost Accounting Standards*.

Prime contractors must obtain Disclosure Statements from their subcontractors, and they from their lower-tiered subs. An exception occurs when a subcontractor has previously submitted its Disclosure Statement to the government. Most contractors and subcontractors consider that their Disclosure Statements contain privileged or proprietary information. Therefore, they have a real interest in keeping the information confidential and away from any competitors. Under those conditions, subcontractors may submit their statements directly to the Government rather than through a prime contractor.

Failure to comply with or follow any disclosed accounting practice can have serious consequences. Government approval of the Disclosure Statement may be withdrawn. That could result in the loss of new contracts. Payments for existing contracts could be withheld under certain circumstances. If the failure results in an increased cost paid by the government, the contract price or cost allowance is subject to adjustment.

## PROFIT PRINCIPLES

### Government Policy on Profit

The government recognizes that, in general, profit is the basic motive of a business enterprise. Therefore, from the government's point of view, profit has two important roles. One is to induce a company to undertake performance of a contract by offering prospects of a monetary reward. The other is to persuade the contractor to perform more effectively than it otherwise might, by affording the contractor the opportunity to earn even more profit.

The government's stated policy on profits is best summarized by the following statement released by the Office of Management and Budget's Office of Federal Procurement Policy.

a. It is in the government's interest to offer contractors profit opportunities sufficient to:
   (1) stimulate efficient contract performance,
   (2) attract the best capabilities of qualified large and small business concerns to government contracts, and
   (3) maintain a viable industrial base.

b. During contract performance, contractors may incur costs, such as interest, that the government does not recognize as allowable. In addition, actual cost may vary from estimated costs, particularly in high-technology, complex work. Therefore, earned profit may differ from negotiated profit or fee. In the long term, earned profit from government contracts must be compatible with return from other investment opportunities involving similar risks.
c. Both government and contractors should be concerned with profit as a motivator of efficient and effective contract performance. Negotiation of extremely low profits, use of historical averages, or automatic application of predetermined percentages to total estimated cost do not provide proper motivation for contract performance. Negotiations aimed merely at reducing prices by reducing profit, without proper recognition of the function of profit, are not in the government's best interest.
d. Structured approaches for determining profit or fee objectives provide a discipline for consideration of all relevant factors. They shall be used whenever practical to fit the profit or fee objectives to the circumstances of the particular contract.

### Industries Look at Profits

A prime goal of most commercial organizations is to perpetuate themselves through profitable operations. Due to the nature of doing business in a non-commercial world, many government contractors will optimize, not maximize, the profits on individual contracts.

There are many extra-contractual motivators that exist for industry. Contractors will consider them when determining the profit goal on any given procurement action. Those motivators may include one or more of the following considerations:

- The possible gain of future business.
- A way to increase profits on other contracts in operation at the same time. This can be done by providing a broader base for fixed overhead costs.
- Being able to retain and maintain an engineering or production capability that might otherwise be lost.
- The contribution to and improvement of the company's prestige and goodwill.
- Being able to contribute to and improve the nation's international reputation.

## PROFIT APPLICATIONS

### The Role of Profit

Price competition offers a reasonable assurance that the contract price will include a profit factor. The profit will normally provide an appropriate return to the contractor. The profit should reflect the financial risk assumed in taking on the contract at that price. In noncompetitive situations, the profit factor is keyed to other things. The contractor's efficiency in controlling costs and meeting desired standards of performance, reliability, quality and delivery will apply.

The parties should try to negotiate and use the type of contract which will stimulate outstanding performance. Both parties have the responsibility to ensure the successful completion of the contract. The proper contract type and a fair and reasonable profit are important factors that will assist the parties to reach that goal.

### Limitations on Profit and Fee

Certain limitations are set by statute (*10 U.S.C. 2306(d)* and *41 U.S.C. 254(b)*) on the fee for cost-plus-fixed-fee (CPFF) contracts (*FAR 15.404-4(c)(4)*).

Contracting officers may not negotiate a fee of more than fifteen percent (15%) of the estimated cost of a CPFF contract, for experimental, developmental or research work. That limitation is on the cost alone and not on the total price which will include the fee.

For architect-engineer service contracts for public works or utilities there are different limitations. The contract price for production and delivery of designs, plans, drawings and specifications cannot exceed six percent (6%) of the estimated cost of construction of the public work or utility, excluding fee.

The contracting officer may not negotiate a fee of more than ten percent (10%) of the estimated cost, excluding fee, of all other CPFF contracts.

Excluding the limitations on architect-engineer contracts, the limitations cited above also apply to the maximum fees allowable on CPIF and CPAF contracts. This is a regulatory limitation, not statutory as is the case with CPFF contracts. The agency head or designee may waive those limitations for a specific CPIF or CPAF contract. The same maximum fee limitations are also imposed upon cost-reimbursement subcontracts by FAR 44.203, *Consent Limitations*.

## PROFIT OBJECTIVES

### Contractor Objectives

Contractors determine their profit objective during the development of their price proposal. The profit will be included in the total price as an element of the price in the proposal. Contractors are not required to submit breakouts or supporting rationale for their profit or fee objectives. However, when that information has been submitted voluntarily, contracting officers may consider it along with the cost elements.

## Agency Responsibilities

The policies for establishing the profit or fee portion of the government's prenegotiation objectives are in FAR 15.404-4(b). Each government agency will normally develop a structured approach for determining the profit or fee portion of the prenegotiation objective. This is a mandatory requirement in acquisitions requiring cost analysis.

In determining the composition of its approach, an agency will consider its mission and the market environment from which it draws its sources of supplies and services. The agency's implementation of its approach may include specific exemptions for situations in which mandatory use would be clearly inappropriate. Instead of independently setting up its own procedures, one agency may adopt another agency's procedures.

The structured approach allows for tailoring of profit on individual contracts or modifications to fit the particular circumstances surrounding a contractual action. Contracting officers are not required to accept an overall profit or fee higher than that proposed by the contractor. This holds true regardless of the results achieved using a structured approach.

Agencies that recognize facilities capital cost of money as an allowable cost must be sure that their structured approach specifically takes this imputed cost into account when calculating a profit or fee objective.

## Contracting Officer Responsibilities (*FAR 15.404-4(c)*)

Contracting officers will develop their profit objectives before negotiation of a contract or contract modification. The process of determining prenegotiation objectives helps the contracting officer judge the overall reasonableness of proposed prices. It also allows the negotiation of a fair and reasonable price on cost and fee. In setting the prenegotiation objectives, the contracting officer will first analyze the offeror's proposal. The analysis will consider the field pricing report, the audit, and technical evaluations. Other pertinent data such as independent government cost estimates and price histories will be evaluated.

When a contract or modification involves price negotiation, the contracting officer will write a prenegotiation objectives memorandum. The scope and depth of the memorandum will relate directly to the dollar value, importance and complexity of the proposed contract or modification. Under a cost analysis situation, the prenegotiation memorandum will include such things as pertinent negotiation issues, maximum and minimum cost objectives and profit or fee objectives.

The government's cost objective and proposed pricing arrangement directly affects each profit or fee objective. Profit or fee is only one of several interrelated variables of a contract. Therefore, contracting officers will not agree on a profit or fee without concurrent agreement on cost and contract type. The negotiation process does not contemplate nor require total agreement on either the elements of the estimated cost or the profit elements.

### Contracts Priced Without Cost Analysis

On many contracts and subcontracts, good pricing does not require an in-depth examination of costs and profits. This would exist where adequate price competition exists, and in other situations not requiring cost analysis. As an example, award of a fully competitive fixed-price type contract can be made to the lowest responsible offeror without regard to the amount of its profits. Under these circumstances, the profit that is expected, or actually earned, should not be of concern to the government. In such cases, when a low offeror earns a large profit, it is considered the normal reward of efficiency in a competitive system. Efforts to reduce such profits are not in the best interests of the contracting parties.

### Structured Approach to Profit Analysis

FAR 15.404-4(b), *Policy*, requires agencies making noncompetitive contract awards over $100,000, totaling $50 million or more a year, to use a structured approach for determining the profit or fee objective in those acquisitions that require cost analysis. Structured approaches for determining profit or fee prenegotiation objectives provide a discipline for ensuring that all relevant factors are considered.

In FAR 15.404-4(d)(1), *Common Factors*, there are six factors that agencies will consider in developing their structured approach to profit analysis. The same factors are used by contracting officers in analyzing profit, whether or not using a structured approach. Those factors and related subfactors follow.

***Contractor Effort***. This is a measurement factor to assess the complexity of the work and the resources required of the contractor for effective contract performance. Contracts requiring a high degree of professional and managerial skill deserve greater profit opportunities. The same opportunities should go to contractors whose skill, facilities and technical assets will lead to effective contract performance. The following subfactors will be considered by the agencies in determining contractor effort.

- ***Material Acquisition***. The contracting officer will use this subfactor to measure the managerial and technical effort needed to obtain the required purchased parts and material, subcontracted items and special tooling. Consideration is given to the complexity of the items and the number of purchase orders and subcontracts to be awarded and administered. The contracting officer (CO) will consider whether existing sources are available or if the contractor must develop new or second sources. Lastly, the CO will consider if material will be obtained through routine purchase orders or through detailed specifications. Profit consideration should correspond to the managerial and technical effort involved.

- ***Direct Labor***. This subfactor is used to measure the contribution of direct engineering, manufacturing and other labor to convert the raw materials, data and subcontracted items into the contract end items. Consideration will include the diversity of engineering, scientific and manufacturing labor skills required and the contractor's ability to meet the precise requirements. The contracting officer will also consider the amount and quality of supervision and coordination necessary to perform the contract tasks.
- ***Indirect Costs***. This subfactor is a measurement of how much the indirect costs contribute to contract performance. The allocable labor elements get the profit consideration they would receive if treated as direct labor. The other elements of indirect cost are evaluated to determine whether they are routine expenses or are elements contributing significantly to the proposed contract. Routine expenses, such as utilities, maintenance and depreciation would merit lesser profit consideration.
- ***General Management***. This subfactor measures the contractor's other indirect costs and general and administrative (G&A) expense, their composition and how much they contribute to contract performance.

***Contract Cost Risk***. This factor is a measure of the degree of cost responsibility and associated risk that the contractor will assume. The risk will relate to the contract type contemplated and the reliability of the cost estimate in relation to the complexity of the contract tasks. There should be a close relationship between contract type and the risks involved in timely, cost-effective and efficient performance. This factor should compensate contractors for assuming greater cost risks.

The contractor assumes the greatest cost risk in a closely priced firm-fixed-price (FFP) contract. Under an FFP contract, the contractor agrees to perform the task correctly, on time and at a predetermined price. The contractor assumes the least risk in a cost-plus-fixed-fee (CPFF) contract. With a CPFF contract, the contractor agrees only to use its best efforts in performance of the tasks. For performing those tasks the contractor will get reimbursed for actual allowed costs.

***Federal Socioeconomic Programs***. This factor measures the degree of support given by the contractor to federal socioeconomic programs. These programs involve small business concerns, small business concerns owned and controlled by socially and economically disadvantaged individuals, women-owned small business concerns, veteran-owned, HUBZone, service-disabled veteran-owned small business concerns, handicapped sheltered workshops, and energy conservation.

***Capital Investments***. This factor measures the amount of contractor-financed investments in the facilities required for the contemplated contract. This may be either a negative or a positive consideration. Subfactors include consideration of the facilities' age, undepreciated value, cost-effectiveness, general or special purpose and remaining life compared with the length of the contemplated program. They will also take into consideration any special contract provisions that will affect the contractor's risk.

***Cost-Control and Other Past Accomplishments***. This factor allows additional profit opportunities to a contractor that has demonstrated improvements in productivity. It may also concern other cost-reduction accomplishments resulting in lower costs to the government. For example, the factor may be a special "productivity reward" to mitigate the loss of profit opportunity on follow-on contracts. It applies when costs on earlier contracts are reduced as a result of productivity gains or other cost-avoidance measures.

***Independent Development***. This factor rewards contractors that, without government financial assistance, develop items having potential government applications.

***Additional Factors***. In order to foster achievement of program objectives, each agency may include other factors in its structured approach or take them into account in the profit analysis of individual contracts (*FAR 15.404-4(d)(2)*).

## Weighted Guidelines Method

The best known and probably the most commonly used structured approach for the development of prenegotiation profit objectives is the weighted guidelines (WGL) method.

The weighted guidelines method, outlined in DFARS 215.404-71, *Weighted Guidelines Method*, provides contracting officers with a technique for setting profit objectives for use during negotiations. The WGL method insures consideration of the relative value of appropriate profit factors. It focuses on three profit factors: (1) performance risk; (2) contract type risk; and (3) facilities capital employed. WGL will also provide a basis for documentation of the profit objectives, including an explanation of any significant departure from them in reaching a final agreement. The contracting officer performs an analysis of the profit factors, based on information available before negotiations. Proposals, audit data, performance reports, preaward surveys and the like provide useful information for this purpose.

In all DOD contract actions requiring cost analysis, the contracting officer must use the weighted guidelines method to develop the prenegotiation objectives. The guidelines are also applicable to contract actions involving existing contracts. The DOD policy is to employ WGL to be sure that certain key factors are the main determinants of the contracting officer's profit objectives. They include things which motivate efficient contract performance and encourage facilities capital investment in the defense industrial base. The policy further directs the contracting officer to apply the weighted guidelines method or any alternate structured approach in a credible manner. They may not set arbitrary profit objectives or accomplish a profit analysis in an after-the-fact basis. When appropriate, the CO may use an alternative structured approach instead of weighted guidelines.

Alternate structured approaches, when approved for use, must consider contractor performance risk, contract type risk (including working capital), and facilities capital employed. The head of the contracting activity must approve in writing the use of an alternate structured approach. There is a variation used for an alternate structured approach where facilities capital cost of money (COM) is an allowable cost. The contracting officer will reduce the overall prenegotiation profit objective derived from that approach by one percent (1%) of total cost or the COM amount, whichever is less.

The following types of contract actions do not require use of the weighted guidelines method. However, an alternate structured approach will be applied.

- Architect-engineer contracts
- Construction contracts
- Contracts primarily requiring delivery of material supplied by subcontractors
- Termination settlements
- Cost-plus-award-fee contracts
- Contracts not expected to exceed $700,000
- Unusual pricing situations where the weighted guidelines method may not produce a reasonable overall prenegotiation profit objective

Contractors doing business with DOD frequently use the weighted guidelines method to develop their own profit objectives. While it is not mandatory, contractors often use WGL to arrive at their profit objectives when entering into negotiations with subcontractors.

The DD Form 1547, *Record of Weighted Guidelines Application* (Figure 10-2, page 245), is the document contracting officers use in performing the analysis necessary to develop their prenegotiation profit objectives. DFARS 215.404-70 requires the contracting officer to use and prepare the DD Form 1547, and ensure that it is accurately completed, whenever a structured approach to profit analysis is required by DFARS. After negotiations and contract award, the contracting officer will forward a copy of the form to an office designated for that particular agency. The form provides a summary record of the final results of the negotiation of fee or profit. It is also the principal source document for maintaining a DOD-wide management information system on profit and fee statistics.

### Profit Objective Calculations

In developing a weighted guidelines (WGL) profit objective, the contracting officer will consider the profit factors previously noted. Those factors include the contractor's degree of performance risk in producing the goods or services and the contract type risk assumed by the contractor. The level of working capital needed for contract performance and the nature of facilities capital employed by the contractor are also factors to consider.

# DD FORM 1547 – RECORD OF WEIGHTED GUIDELINES APPLICATION

| RECORD OF WEIGHTED GUIDELINES APPLICATION | | | | | | REPORT CONTROL SYMBOL DD-AT&L(Q)1751 | |
|---|---|---|---|---|---|---|---|
| 1. REPORT NO. | 2. BASIC PROCUREMENT INSTRUMENT IDENTIFICATION NO. | | | | 3. SPIIN | 4. DATE OF ACTION | |
| | a. PURCHASING OFFICE | b. FY | c. TYPE PROC INST CODE | d. PRISN | | a. YEAR | b. MONTH |

| | | ITEM | COST CATEGORY | OBJECTIVE |
|---|---|---|---|---|
| 5. CONTRACTING OFFICE CODE | | | | |
| 6. NAME OF CONTRACTOR | | 13. | MATERIAL | |
| | | 14. | SUBCONTRACTS | |
| 7. DUNS NUMBER | 8. FEDERAL SUPPLY CODE | 15. | DIRECT LABOR | |
| | | 16. | INDIRECT EXPENSES | |
| 9. DOD CLAIMANT PROGRAM | 10. CONTRACT TYPE CODE | 17. | OTHER DIRECT CHARGES | |
| | | 18. | SUBTOTAL COSTS *(13 thru 17)* | 0.00 |
| 11. TYPE EFFORT | 12. USE CODE | 19. | GENERAL AND ADMINISTRATIVE | |
| | | 20. | TOTAL COSTS *(18 + 19)* | 0.00 |

**WEIGHTED GUIDELINES PROFIT FACTORS**

| ITEM | CONTRACTOR RISK FACTORS | ASSIGNED WEIGHTING | ASSIGNED VALUE | BASE *(Item 20)* | PROFIT OBJECTIVE |
|---|---|---|---|---|---|
| 21. | TECHNICAL | % | | | |
| 22. | MANAGEMENT/COST CONTROL | % | | | |
| 23. | PERFORMANCE RISK (COMPOSITE) | | | 0.00 | |
| 24. | CONTRACT TYPE RISK | | | 0.00 | |
| 25. | WORKING CAPITAL | COSTS FINANCED | LENGTH FACTOR | INTEREST RATE | |
| | | | | % | |
| | CONTRACTOR FACILITIES CAPITAL EMPLOYED | | ASSIGNED VALUE | AMOUNT EMPLOYED | |
| 26. | LAND | | | | |
| 27. | BUILDINGS | | | | |
| 28. | EQUIPMENT | | | | |
| 29. | COST EFFICIENCY FACTOR | | ASSIGNED VALUE | BASE *(Item 20)* | |
| | | | % | 0.00 | |
| 30. | | | | TOTAL PROFIT OBJECTIVE | 0.00 |

**NEGOTIATED SUMMARY**

| | | PROPOSED | OBJECTIVE | NEGOTIATED |
|---|---|---|---|---|
| 31. | TOTAL COSTS | | | |
| 32. | FACILITIES CAPITAL COST OF MONEY *(DD Form 1861)* | | | |
| 33. | PROFIT | | | |
| 34. | TOTAL PRICE *(Line 31 + 32 + 33)* | 0.00 | 0.00 | 0.00 |
| 35. | MARKUP RATE *(Line 32 – 33 divided by 31)* | % | % | % |

**CONTRACTING OFFICER APPROVAL**

| 36. TYPED/PRINTED NAME OF CONTRACTING OFFICER *(Last, First, Middle Initial)* | 37. SIGNATURE OF CONTRACTING OFFICER | 38. TELEPHONE NO. | 39. DATE SUBMITTED *(YYYYMMDD)* |
|---|---|---|---|
| | | | |

**OPTIONAL USE**

| 96. | 97. | 98. | 99. |
|---|---|---|---|
| | | | |

DD FORM 1547, JUL 2002 PREVIOUS EDITION IS OBSOLETE. Adobe Professional 8.0

Figure 10-2

Contracting officers assign values to each profit factor. That value multiplied by the base results in the profit objective for that factor. Each profit factor has a normal value and a designated range of values. Normal value is representative of average conditions on the prospective contract when compared to all goods and services required by DOD. The designated range provides values based on above normal or below normal conditions. When compiling the price negotiation memorandum, the contracting officer need not explain any assignment of the normal value, but should address conditions that justified an assignment of the normal value. In addition, the CO should address the conditions that justified an assignment of other than the normal value. The following paragraphs summarize those factors.

Performance risk addresses the contractor's degree of risk in fulfilling the contract requirements to produce the goods and services purchased. DFARS 215.404-71-2, *Performance Risk*, details the criteria for developing these profit objectives. The factor is divided into two broad categories: technical and management/cost control. Each category has a standard designated range of 2% to 6% with a normal value of 4%. To compute the profit amount for performance risk the contracting officer multiplies the composite profit value for the two categories by total contract cost.

For WGL purposes, total contract cost excludes general and administrative (G&A) expenses, contractor independent research and development/bid and proposal (IR&D/B&P) expenses, and facilities capital cost of money (FCCM).

Technical consideration addresses such things as the technology applied or developed by the contractor, technical complexity, program maturity, performance specifications and tolerances, delivery schedules, and the extent of a warranty or guarantee. To assign a value above the normal value for a category, the contracting officer must determine there is a substantial technical risk, such as items being manufactured to specifications with stringent tolerance limits or the efforts requiring highly skilled personnel. Conversely, the contracting officer may assign a lower than normal value in those cases where the technical risk is low, such as acquisition of off-the-shelf items, routine services or production of simple items.

The contractor's management and internal control systems will be a significant element of the management consideration under the performance risk category. The contracting officer will be evaluating the degree of management effort necessary to ensure that contract requirements will be met. The contracting officer will also consider such factors as: management involvement expected on the prospective contract action; the cost mix indicating the types of resources applied and value added by the contractor; and the contractor's support of Federal socioeconomic programs (*DFARS 215.404-71-2(e), Evaluation Criteria for Management/Cost Control*).

The criterion for cost consideration under performance risk focuses on the contractor's efforts to reduce and control costs. Evaluation will concentrate on such areas as the expected reliability of cost estimates, cost reduction initiatives, and cost and schedule control management, and other factors affecting the contractor's ability to meet cost targets. The contracting officer may assign higher than normal values in those cases where the management effort in intense. Lower than normal values are appropriate when the management effort is minimal.

In contracts with R&D and service contractors with relatively low capital investment in buildings and equipment, the contracting officer may use an alternate to the standard performance risk values. The designated range for the alternate method is from 4% to 8% with a normal value of 6%. Under the alternate method, the contractor is not given any profit facilities capital employed.

When determining fee or profit to be applied to a contract, the contracting officer will apply the following designated ranges and normal values to contracts that do not provide for progress payments to the contractor.

| Contract Type | Designated Range | Normal Value |
|---|---|---|
| Firm-Fixed-Price | 4% to 6% | 5% |
| Fixed-Price-Incentive | 2% to 4% | 3% |
| Cost-Plus-Incentive-Fee | 0% to 2% | 1% |
| Cost-Plus-Fixed-Fee | 0% to 1% | .5% |

Contract type risk focuses on the degree of the cost responsibility accepted by the contractor under varying contract structures and incentive arrangements. The highest values go to the firm-fixed-price contracts with the lowest values going to cost-plus-fixed-fee contracts.

The amount of profit for contract type risk is computed the same as for performance risk. The value assigned by the contracting officer is multiplied by the total allowable costs. Those allowable costs will exclude expenses classified as: general and administrative (G&A), independent research and development (IR&D), bid and proposal (B&P), and facilities capital cost of money (FCCM).

Fixed-price contracts with progress payment provisions will have lower ranges and lower normal values than those shown above. However, the contracting officer will further adjust the values by adding an amount to recognize the contractor's investment in working capital. FFP contracts will have a 2% to 4% range and a 3% normal value. The range for fixed-price-incentive (FPI) contracts will be 0% to 2% with a 1% normal value.

A working capital adjustment factor is made by the contracting officer on all fixed-price type contracts. DFARS Subpart 215.404-71-4, *Facilities Capital Employed*, details the directions for relating facilities capital to the final profit objective. There is an upward adjustment limit of four percent (4%) for this factor. The purpose is to consider contractor working capital needs. This factor employs a formula approach that considers the amount of contract effort financed by the contractor, current interest rate and length of the contract. DFARS 215.404-71-3, *Contract Type Risk and Working Capital Adjustment*, provides the formula and ground rules for its application.

The facilities capital employed by the contractor in performance of the contract is recognized as a profit factor. The amount of recognition is differentiated among asset groups in proportion to the potential for productivity increases. The amount of profit is computed by multiplying the value assigned by the contracting officer times the net book value of facilities capital employed in each asset group. DD Form 1861, *Contract Facilities Capital Cost of Money* (Figure 10-3, page 249), is used to derive those values. The normal values of profit recognition, along with the designated range of minimum and maximum values for each asset category are as follows.

| Asset Type | Designated Range | Normal Value |
|---|---|---|
| Land | N/A | 0% |
| Buildings | 10% to 20% | 15% |
| Equipment | 20% to 50% | 35% |

# DD FORM 1861 – CONTRACT FACILITIES CAPITAL COST OF MONEY

| CONTRACT FACILITIES CAPITAL COST OF MONEY | OMB No. 0704-0267<br>OMB approval expires<br>Jul 31, 2007 |
|---|---|

The public reporting burden for this collection of information is estimated to average 10 hours per response, including the time for reviewing instructions, searching existing data sources, gathering and maintaining the data needed, and completing and reviewing the collection of information. Send comments regarding this burden estimate or any other aspect of this collection of information, including suggestions for reducing the burden, to the Department of Defense, Executive Services Directorate (0704-0267). Respondents should be aware that notwithstanding any other provision of law, no person shall be subject to any penalty for failing to comply with a collection of information if it does not display a currently valid OMB control number.

PLEASE DO NOT RETURN YOUR COMPLETED FORM TO THE ABOVE ORGANIZATION.
RETURN COMPLETED FORM TO YOUR CONTRACTING OFFICIAL.

| 1. CONTRACTOR NAME | 2. CONTRACTOR ADDRESS |
|---|---|
| 3. BUSINESS UNIT | |
| 4. RFP/CONTRACT PIIN NUMBER | 5. PERFORMANCE PERIOD |

6. DISTRIBUTION OF FACILITIES CAPITAL COST OF MONEY

| POOL a. | ALLOCATION BASE b. | FACILITIES CAPITAL COST OF MONEY c. | |
|---|---|---|---|
| | | FACTOR (1) | AMOUNT (2) |
| | | | |
| | | | |
| | | | |
| | | | |
| | | | |
| | | | |
| | | | |
| | | | |
| | | | |
| | | | |
| | | | |
| | | | |
| d. TOTAL | | | $0.00 |
| e. TREASURY RATE | | | % |
| f. FACILITIES CAPITAL EMPLOYED (TOTAL DIVIDED BY TREASURY RATE) | | | |

7. DISTRIBUTION OF FACILITIES CAPITAL EMPLOYED

| | PERCENTAGE a. | AMOUNT b. |
|---|---|---|
| (1) LAND | % | |
| (2) BUILDINGS | % | |
| (3) EQUIPMENT | % | |
| (4) FACILITIES CAPITAL EMPLOYED | 100% | $0.00 |

DD FORM 1861, AUG 2004 PREVIOUS EDITION MAY BE USED

Figure 10-3

# CHAPTER 11

# CONTRACT DOCUMENTATION

## OVERVIEW OF CONTRACTS

In the usual sense the term "Contract" means a mutually binding relationship. It is one that obligates the seller to furnish supplies or services, or otherwise perform some effort. In return the buyer must pay for the supplies or services received. A contract, as applied to the government acquisition process, means all types of agreements and orders for the procurement of supplies or services. Chapter 5, *Contract Types*, describes the various types and kinds of contracts the Federal Government uses in the acquisition process. Unilateral change orders under the Changes clause are not contracts. Supplemental agreements that formally modify existing contractual arrangements are contracts themselves. They establish a new contractual relationship between the parties. Just as with the original contract document, the supplemental agreement will be signed by both parties.

## CONTRACT FORMAT

### Contract Forms

The General Services Administration (GSA) issues several standard contract forms which are available for use by all government agencies. The two most common are Standard Form 26, *Award/Contract* (Figure 11-1, page 252) and Standard Form 33, *Solicitation, Offer and Award* (Figure 4-1, page 70). Contracting officers prepare contracts using the Uniform Contract Format, shown in Figure 11-2 on page 253, to the maximum practicable extent. This requirement is found in FAR 14.201-1, *Uniform Contract Format*, for sealed bidding and FAR 15.204-1, *Uniform Contract Format*, for contracting by negotiation. Note the difference between the formats in Figure 11-2 and Figure 4-3 on page 89. The latter one is used for solicitation of offers. Part IV of the solicitation, *Representations and Instructions*, normally is not retained in the definitized contract. However, it is common for the contract to incorporate by reference Section K of Part IV, *Representations, Certifications, and Other Statements of Offerors or Respondents*.

### Contract Execution

After the contracting officer (CO) drafts the contractual instrument, it is processed through the agency for concurrence in its terms and conditions. Approvals must be obtained from the program office, price and cost analysis group, legal office and procurement committee. For certain procurements, the head of the branch or division and even the Secretary of the Executive Department must approve the contract. After the CO obtains the necessary agency approvals, the unsigned document is transmitted to the contractor for signature.

# STANDARD FORM 26 – AWARD/CONTRACT

**AWARD/CONTRACT** | 1. THIS CONTRACT IS A RATED ORDER UNDER DPAS (15 CFR 700) ▶ RATING | PAGE OF PAGES

2. CONTRACT *(Proc. Inst. Ident.)* NO. | 3. EFFECTIVE DATE | 4. REQUISITION/PURCHASE REQUEST/PROJECT NO.

5. ISSUED BY CODE | 6. ADMINISTERED BY *(If other than Item 5)* CODE

7. NAME AND ADDRESS OF CONTRACTOR *(No., street, county, State and ZIP Code)*

8. DELIVERY
☐ FOB ORIGIN ☐ OTHER *(See below)*

9. DISCOUNT FOR PROMPT PAYMENT

10. SUBMIT INVOICES *(4 copies unless otherwise specified)* TO THE ADDRESS SHOWN IN ▶ ITEM

CODE | FACILITY CODE

11. SHIP TO/MARK FOR CODE | 12. PAYMENT WILL BE MADE BY CODE

13. AUTHORITY FOR USING OTHER THAN FULL AND OPEN COMPETITION
☐ 10 U.S.C. 2304(c)( ) ☐ 41 U.S.C. 253(c)( )

14. ACCOUNTING AND APPROPRIATION DATA

| 15A. ITEM NO. | 15B. SUPPLIES/SERVICES | 15C. QUANTITY | 15D. UNIT | 15E. UNIT PRICE | 15F. AMOUNT |
|---|---|---|---|---|---|
| | | | | | |

15G. TOTAL AMOUNT OF CONTRACT ▶ $

16. TABLE OF CONTENTS

| (X) | SEC. | DESCRIPTION | PAGE(S) | (X) | SEC. | DESCRIPTION | PAGE(S) |
|---|---|---|---|---|---|---|---|
| | | PART I - THE SCHEDULE | | | | PART II - CONTRACT CLAUSES | |
| | A | SOLICITATION/CONTRACT FORM | | | I | CONTRACT CLAUSES | |
| | B | SUPPLIES OR SERVICES AND PRICES/COSTS | | | | PART III - LIST OF DOCUMENTS, EXHIBITS AND OTHER ATTACH. | |
| | C | DESCRIPTION/SPECS./WORK STATEMENT | | | J | LIST OF ATTACHMENTS | |
| | D | PACKAGING AND MARKING | | | | PART IV - REPRESENTATIONS AND INSTRUCTIONS | |
| | E | INSPECTION AND ACCEPTANCE | | | K | REPRESENTATIONS, CERTIFICATIONS AND OTHER STATEMENTS OF OFFERORS | |
| | F | DELIVERIES OR PERFORMANCE | | | | | |
| | G | CONTRACT ADMINISTRATION DATA | | | L | INSTRS., CONDS., AND NOTICES TO OFFERORS | |
| | H | SPECIAL CONTRACT REQUIREMENTS | | | M | EVALUATION FACTORS FOR AWARD | |

*CONTRACTING OFFICER WILL COMPLETE ITEM 17 (SEALED-BID OR NEGOTIATED PROCUREMENT) OR 18 (SEALED-BID PROCUREMENT) AS APPLICABLE*

17. ☐ CONTRACTOR'S NEGOTIATED AGREEMENT *(Contractor is required to sign this document and return* __________ *copies to issuing office.)* Contractor agrees to furnish and deliver all items or perform all the services set forth or otherwise identified above and on any continuation sheets for the consideration stated herein. The rights and obligations of the parties to this contract shall be subject to and governed by the following documents: (a) this award/contract, (b) the solicitation, if any, and (c) such provisions, representations, certifications, and specifications, as are attached or incorporated by reference herein. *(Attachments are listed herein.)*

18. ☐ SEALED-BID AWARD *(Contractor is not required to sign this document.)* Your bid on Solicitation Number __________ including the additions or changes made by you which additions or changes are set forth in full above, is hereby accepted as to the terms listed above and on any continuation sheets. This award consummates the contract which consists of the following documents: (a) the Government's solicitation and your bid, and (b) this award/contract. No further contractual document is necessary. (Block 18 should be checked only when awarding a sealed-bid contract.)

19A. NAME AND TITLE OF SIGNER *(Type or Print)* | 20A. NAME OF CONTRACTING OFFICER

19B. NAME OF CONTRACTOR
BY ________________
*(Signature of person authorized to sign)*
| 19C. DATE SIGNED | 20B. UNITED STATES OF AMERICA
BY ________________
*(Signature of Contracting Officer)*
| 20C. DATE SIGNED

AUTHORIZED FOR LOCAL REPRODUCTION
Previous edition is NOT usable

**STANDARD FORM 26** (REV. 5/2011)
Prescribed by GSA - FAR (48 CFR) 53.214(a)

**Figure 11-1**

# UNIFORM CONTRACT FORMAT

(For use with Solicitation of Bids)

## Part I – The Schedule

| | |
|---|---|
| Section A | Solicitation/contract form |
| Section B | Supplies or services and prices |
| Section C | Description/specifications |
| Section D | Packaging and marking |
| Section E | Inspection and acceptance |
| Section F | Deliveries or performance |
| Section G | Contract administration data |
| Section H | Special contract requirements |

## Part II – Contract Clauses

| | |
|---|---|
| Section I | Contract clauses |

## Part III – List of Documents, Exhibits and Other Attachments

| | |
|---|---|
| Section J | List of documents, exhibits, and other attachments |

## Part IV – Representations and Instructions

| | |
|---|---|
| Section K | Representations, certifications, and other statements of bidders |
| Section L | Instructions, conditions, and notices to bidders |
| Section M | Evaluation factors for award |

**Figure 11-2**

The contractor's approval cycle is comparable to the Government's. If some element of the contract is not acceptable, it is necessary that the contractor's agent resolve the matter prior to signing the document. Once all issues are resolved the document is executed by the individual authorized to sign contracts for the contractor. The contractor returns the document to the contracting officer for execution on behalf of the United States of America.

**Contract Numbering System**

There is no standard government-wide method of assigning identification numbers to contractual documents. Each federal agency uses a contract numbering system peculiar to its own needs. The contract number will be one that permits the contract document to be readily identified, recorded and tracked.

The Department of Defense developed a system which makes use of a basic Procurement Instrument Identification (PII) number. The basic PII number consists of thirteen (13) alpha-numeric characters which remain unchanged for the life of the particular instrument. The arrangement is as follows.

- Positions 1 through 6 identify the contracting or purchasing office. The DOD Supplement to the FAR (DFARS) Subpart 204.7003, *Basic PII Number*, contains a listing of the DOD identifiers.
- Positions 7 and 8 are the last two (2) digits of the government's fiscal year in which the PII number was assigned.
- Position 9 is a capital letter designating the code for the type of instrument involved, as listed in DFARS 204.7003.
- Positions 10 through 13 identify the four (4) digit serial number of the instrument. A separate serial number may be used for each type of instrument. It is normal for the PII numbers for the same activity to commence with the number 0001 at the start of each fiscal year.

Supplementary numbers are used together with the basic PII numbers. They identify amendments to solicitation documents, modifications of contracts and agreements. Calls or orders under contracts, basic ordering agreements and blanket purchase agreements have their own sequential numbers.

**Defense Priorities and Allocations System**

Under Title I of the Defense Production Act of 1950, as amended (*50 U.S.C. App. 2061, et seq.*), the President of the United States is authorized to require that contracts in support of the national defense be accepted and performed on a preferential or priority basis over all other contracts.

That statute also specifies that allocation of materials and facilities are to be made in such a manner as to promote the national defense.

The Defense Priorities and Allocations System (DPAS) is a Department of Commerce (DOC) program. The DOC's Office of Industrial Resource Administration is responsible for administering and enforcing a system of priorities and allocations to carry out the dictates of Title I of the Act. DPAS was created to promote the timely availability of the necessary industrial resources to meet national defense requirements and to provide a framework to facilitate rapid industrial mobilization in case of national emergency. The DOC delegates to government agencies the authority to place priority ratings on contracts that support authorized programs. Briefly, the program assures the preferential treatment of national defense related orders and timely delivery in the acquisition of controlled materials. The preferential treatment relates to controlled materials of steel, copper, aluminum, nickel alloys in various shapes and forms.

There are two levels of priority for rated orders as established by the DPAS. They are identified by the rating symbols "DO" and "DX". Orders within each level have equal priority status. However, the order of precedence between levels is DX rated orders, DO rated orders and lastly unrated orders. The priority ratings are assigned to prime contractors who must extend the rating to their direct subcontractors, vendors and suppliers, which in turn must extend the rating to their suppliers.

The policies and procedures implementing DPAS are contained in FAR 11.6, *Priorities and Allocations*. When a contract will be awarded as a rated order, the solicitation will contain the clause at FAR 52.211-14, *Notice of Priority Rating for National Defense, Emergency Preparedness, and Energy Program Use*. The resulting contract will incorporate the clause at FAR 52.211-15, *Defense Priority and Allocations Requirements*. Contracts issued in support of programs authorized by the Federal Emergency Management Agency (FEMA) under Title I of the Act can participate in the DPAS.

Under the Defense Production Act, any willful violation by a contractor or lower-tier vendor of the Act, the DPAS, or any other official action taken by the Department of Commerce under the DPAS, is a crime punishable by a maximum fine of $10,000, one year in prison, or both.

## CONTRACT PROVISIONS

### Purpose of Contract Provisions

The provisions of a contract reflect the contractual requirements, conditions and obligations of the parties for that specific acquisition. Their purpose is to define all of the contractual requirements, not just a definition or description of the deliverable supplies or services. The deliverables are called Contract End Items (CEI). The provisions prescribe in varying detail how the contractor will produce and deliver the supplies or services.

Contract provisions prescribe certain aspects of how the contractor will conduct its business during the course of the contract. Many of the contract provisions will have a direct influence on the cost of doing business with the government. The contract provisions define the interface between the government and the contractor. Many first time contractors, especially small businesses, are not aware of or prepared to comply with the government's peculiar contract terms and conditions. Their inexperience frequently causes disputes and failures resulting in terminations.

The clauses in a contract remain in force until the contract is amended to make a change in the provisions. If the Government revises a clause for some reason, that revision will not affect contracts with earlier versions until they are amended to incorporate the newer version. Therefore, a contract must be interpreted by clauses in the contract, regardless of how many changes may have been made to some of those clauses, but not yet incorporated by a supplemental agreement endorsed by both the Government and the contractor.

On rare occasions, a contract clause that is required by the FAR, one that expresses ingrained Federal procurement policy, may have been inadvertently omitted from a contract. Such a clause is incorporated into the contract under what is known as the *Christian Doctrine*. That doctrine is named after a case entitled, *G. L. Christian and Associates v. The United States.*

## Types and Source of Contract Provisions

The provisions of a contract include the terms and conditions of the Uniform Contract Format specified in Part I, *The Schedule*, and in Part II, *Contract Clauses* (previously called the *General Provisions*). Documents attached to the contract document or incorporated by reference are identified in Part III, *List of Documents, Exhibits, and Other Attachments*.

Those contract clauses located in Part I, *The Schedule*, address the terms and conditions which are peculiar to that procurement. They cover such topics as the contract price, incentives, description of end items, funding, government property, delivery, and acceptance instructions. Reference data about Part II, Section I, *Contract Clauses*, are cited in Part I. Schedule clauses intended for use in a procurement appear in the invitation for bids (IFB) or request for proposals (RFP). They may be changed or augmented to reflect agreements reached during negotiations.

Part II, Section I, *Contract Clauses*, will contain the standard clauses designated by the FAR for that type of contract. Those clauses, in their complete text form, are published in FAR Part 52, *Solicitation Provisions and Contract Clauses*. Within each category or Subpart of FAR Part 52, there are three groups of clauses. There are those which are required in all contracts of a particular type. The second group includes clauses to be used when applicable for a specific contract. The third group includes "optional" clauses. The first group is mandatory clauses that may be excluded only after the contracting officer gets a special deviation. Absent such a special deviation, any mandatory clause inadvertently omitted from a Government contract will still be held to be in the contract in the event of a dispute. The other two groups of clauses may be negotiable, depending upon the circumstances of the procurement. Each clause derives its authority from other parts of the FAR or from a Public Law, Statute or Executive Order.

Additional provisions are contained in the attachments to the contract document and other documents incorporated by reference. Examples of these are:

- Statement of work (SOW)
- Contract data requirements list (CDRL)
- General systems specification (GSS) or design specification, as applicable
- Contract Security Classification Specification (DD Form 254) or Program Security Guide, as applicable
- Incentive or award fee plan
- A listing of government furnished supplies or services (GFE)

### Deviations from Standard FAR Clauses

The government encourages contracting officers toward the innovative development of new techniques or methods of procurement. However, such attempts may require deviations from the regulation. FAR 1.4, *Deviations from the FAR*, defines in detail what constitutes a deviation. It outlines the procedures for obtaining approval to deviate from prescribed regulations and clauses. The basic policy is that, unless prevented by law, executive order or regulation, deviations from the FAR may be granted. However, the change must be necessary to meet the specific needs and requirements of the agency.

## CONTRACT EXHIBITS

### The Statement of Work

Whether contained in the contract Schedule, made an attachment to the contract, or just incorporated by reference, the statement of work (SOW) is the primary contractual exhibit. The SOW, often referred to as the "work statement," defines or describes what is being procured and details tasks the contractor must perform. The SOW will reference the specifications, regulations or other documents with which the contractor must comply in providing the contractually deliverable supplies or services. Those deliverables are specified in the contract as Contract End Items (CEI). Therefore, the SOW defines "the Scope" of the contractual efforts and is part of the legal contract.

In addition to defining the scope of the contractual requirements, the SOW provides the basis for some very important functions. Offerors will use the SOW for estimating purposes in preparing cost proposals. A well written work statement allows opportunities for more organizations to compete. In writing the SOW it is important to set the tasks out in a logical and chronological order using a simple sentence structure. The work statement defines the contractor's tasks to be performed and all the deliverables clearly stated together with their acceptance criteria. The contracting agency's duties and obligations must also be clearly described.

The SOW will be a guide used by the Government in performing price or cost analysis of proposals received in response to their solicitation. Contract negotiations will center around the "scope" of the effort defined by the statement of work. The SOW is later used to determine "out-of-scope" changes to the contract. Pricing and price or cost analysis of those change proposals, either as a credit or debit, depend upon changes to the SOW. The work statement is the key document for determination of allowability of costs incurred by the contractor. Measurement of the contractor's performance over the life of the contract is made in comparison with SOW provisions.

From the government's viewpoint, a work statement is a controlling device. It should be definitive enough to protect the government's interests, yet broad enough not to stifle the contractor's creative efforts. SOWs should be considered "living documents" in that when either party to the contract becomes aware that a better and different approach is appropriate, they should bring it to the attention of the other party for a possible change in the document.

**Preparation and Format of Work Statements**

The preparation of a clear and complete statement of work (SOW) is essential to sound contracting. Each SOW is individually tailored by the procuring activity. The SOW must be consistent with the type of contract, the phase in the acquisition cycle and the type of contractor performance desired. Tailoring is especially important for contracts subject to acquisition streamlining procedures, as discussed in Chapter 3, *The Acquisition Process*. The SOW must provide enough flexibility for creativity by contractors, both in submitting their competitive proposals and in contract performance.

Work statements for fixed-price type contracts must be more definitive than those for cost-reimbursement types. The closer a procurement is to the production stage, the more definitive the SOW must be for the contracted effort.

There are two basic types of statements of work. The first describes a level-of-effort and is also called a Term SOW; the other is called a Task Completion work statement. The contracts will also be referred to in the same manner. Level-of-effort (LOE) work statements essentially require the contractor to furnish a definite amount of support to the Government over a specified period. Good examples of this are contracts for technical studies, management or technical support services, and maintenance and repair services. The usual deliverables under LOE contracts are study results, briefings and reports.

Task Completion SOWs require the performance of discrete tasks which are milestone oriented, such as the development and delivery of tangible end items. The following illustrates the significant differences between the two types of contracts. A contractor with a fixed-price LOE contract works up to the last day of the contract and does not proceed further without an extension of the contract. There is the assumption the contractor has been providing the level-of-effort prescribed in the SOW and in the contract. The same contractor with a fixed-price completion contract must complete all the tasks specified in the SOW, whether or not the end date of the contract is reached.

In contrast, the contractor with a cost-reimbursement contract works to the end of the funding limits or the end of the contract, whichever comes first. That applies whether the contractor is in either a completion or LOE mode. This is based on the theory that cost-reimbursement contracts are considered to be "best efforts" agreements.

There is no one standard format for statements of work. Each agency will use formats that correlate to their acquisition needs. There is a growing trend to structure the SOW to be compatible with the work breakdown structure (WBS) system. The WBS permits good correlation and traceability between the tasks and deliverables of a contract and their associated costs. It begins with the contractor's proposal and carries over into the cost accounting system.

Most work statements should include the following subject matter:

- A general description of the required objectives and desired results.
- Background information helpful for a clear understanding of the requirements and how they evolved.
- Technical considerations, such as any known specific phenomena or techniques.
- A detailed description of the technical requirements and subordinate tasks.
- A description of reporting requirements and any other deliverable items, such as data, experimental hardware, mock-ups, prototypes, etc.
- Any other special considerations that the contractor must follow during the contract.

An important aspect of a well-written work statement is its language. It is extremely important that statement of work writers never use terms that are either vague or ambiguous. Always use the simplest phrase possible to convey the intended meaning. Avoid long sentences and excessive punctuation. Be consistent in the use of terminology. It is very important to define acronyms and initials the first time they are used. Be sure to use mandatory language properly. The word "shall" is the accepted binding term in SOWs. Wherever the term "shall" appears, be advised that the referenced requirement is mandatory.

A checklist for work statement writers is contained in Figure 11-3, *Statement of Work Checklist*, on page 260 (*Source: MIL-HDBK-245D*).

Only the contracting officer may grant deviations from mandatory requirements. It is imperative that the terminology used in the contract and the statement of work reflect the real "intent" of the contracting parties. The SOW must pass the "third party test." That means that a third party could read the SOW and the entire contract as well, and understand what the contracting parties had intended.

# STATEMENT OF WORK CHECKLIST

- ✓ Is the SOW sufficiently specific to permit the writer and contractor to make a list of labor and other resources needed to accomplish it?

- ✓ Are specific duties of the contractor stated in such a way that it knows what is required? Can the contract administration office (CAO) representative who signs the acceptance report tell whether or not the contractor complied?

- ✓ Are sentences written so that there is no question whether the contractor is obligated to do the tasks? Does it state that "the contractor shall do this task?"

- ✓ Is the proper reference document shown? Is it really pertinent to the task? Is full or partial compliance required? Is it properly cited?

- ✓ Are any specifications or exhibits applicable? Are they a requirement or a guide? Is the latest issue cited?

- ✓ Is general information separated from direction? Is background information, suggested procedures and the like, clearly distinguishable from contractor responsibilities?

- ✓ Is there a date for each item the contractor is to deliver?

- ✓ Are proper quantities shown?

- ✓ Have headings been checked for format and grammatical usage? Are subheadings and text compatible with the titles?

- ✓ Have all requirements been reviewed to ensure compatibility with the data requirements? Are they properly cited?

- ✓ Can the SOW tasks be correlated to the work breakdown structure? Is the paragraph numbering system consistent?

- ✓ Have extraneous material and cross-references to contract clauses been expunged?

- ✓ Have all extraneous data requirements been expunged?

**Figure 11-3**

### Contract Data Requirements List (CDRL)

The second most important exhibit defining contract deliverables is the list of contractually required data. DD Form 1423, *Contract Data Requirements List* (Figure 11-4, page 262), defines the data to be delivered under a DOD contract. Except for the type of information discussed below, contractors are only required to prepare and submit data listed on the data requirements list.

Many contract clauses require data type information to be supplied under certain conditions or events. These are in addition to the "contractual deliverables" specified in the data requirements list. The following are several examples of such data and the circumstances that require their submission by the contractor.

- *Limitation of Funds*, 52.232-22 – Notice of cost variance and advance notice of funds exhaustion
- *Termination*, 52.249-xx – Submission of termination settlement proposal
- *Disputes*, 52.233-1 – Written appeal to a CO decision under dispute
- *Changes*, 52.243-xx – Submission of cost or pricing data for an equitable adjustment
- *Patent Rights*, 52.227-xx – Disclosure of inventions
- *Notice to the Government of Labor Disputes*, 52.222-1 – Notice to CO of labor disputes and potential strikes impacting contract
- *Disclosure and Consistency of Cost Accounting Practices*, 52.230-3 – Cost accounting disclosure statement

### Contract Security Classification Specifications

All classified Department of Defense contracts must contain a *Contract Security Classification Specification*, DD Form 254. This document is incorporated by reference. The specification will also be an attachment to the contract. It provides guidance to both government and contractor personnel for the disclosure, handling, storage and disposition of classified technical and contractual data on that particular contract.

Each RFP for a classified acquisition will contain a DD Form 254. After the contract is awarded, the DD Form 254 will be updated periodically by the government. A final issue is used at contract closure when retention of classified documents will be authorized.

# DD FORM 1423 – CONTRACT DATA REQUIREMENTS LIST

| CONTRACT DATA REQUIREMENTS LIST | *Form Approved* *OMB No. 0704-0188* |
|---|---|

The public reporting burden for this collection of information is estimated to average 440 hours per response, including the time for reviewing instructions, searching existing data sources, gathering and maintaining the data needed, and completing and reviewing the collection of information. Send comments regarding this burden estimate or any other aspect of this collection of information, including suggestions for reducing the burden, to the Department of Defense, Executive Services Directorate (0704-0188). Respondents should be aware that notwithstanding any other provision of law, no person shall be subject to any penalty for failing to comply with a collection of information if it does not display a currently valid OMB control number. Please do not return your form to the above organization. Send completed form to the Government Issuing Contracting Officer for the Contract/PR No. listed in Block E.

| A. CONTRACT LINE ITEM NO. | B. EXHIBIT | C. CATEGORY: TDP ____ TM ____ OTHER ____ |
|---|---|---|
| D. SYSTEM/ITEM | E. CONTRACT/PR NO. | F. CONTRACTOR |

| 1. DATA ITEM NO. | 2. TITLE OF DATA ITEM | | 3. SUBTITLE | 17. PRICE GROUP |
|---|---|---|---|---|
| 4. AUTHORITY *(Data Acquisition Document No.)* | | 5. CONTRACT REFERENCE | 6. REQUIRING OFFICE | 18. ESTIMATED TOTAL PRICE |
| 7. DD 250 REQ | 9. DIST STATEMENT REQUIRED | 10. FREQUENCY | 12. DATE OF FIRST SUBMISSION | 14. DISTRIBUTION |
| 8. APP CODE | | 11. AS OF DATE | 13. DATE OF SUBSEQUENT SUBMISSION | a. ADDRESSEE / b. COPIES: Draft, Final (Reg, Repro) |
| 16. REMARKS | | | | 15. TOTAL → 0 0 0 |

| 1. DATA ITEM NO. | 2. TITLE OF DATA ITEM | | 3. SUBTITLE | 17. PRICE GROUP |
|---|---|---|---|---|
| 4. AUTHORITY *(Data Acquisition Document No.)* | | 5. CONTRACT REFERENCE | 6. REQUIRING OFFICE | 18. ESTIMATED TOTAL PRICE |
| 7. DD 250 REQ | 9. DIST STATEMENT REQUIRED | 10. FREQUENCY | 12. DATE OF FIRST SUBMISSION | 14. DISTRIBUTION |
| 8. APP CODE | | 11. AS OF DATE | 13. DATE OF SUBSEQUENT SUBMISSION | a. ADDRESSEE / b. COPIES: Draft, Final (Reg, Repro) |
| 16. REMARKS | | | | 15. TOTAL → 0 0 0 |

| 1. DATA ITEM NO. | 2. TITLE OF DATA ITEM | | 3. SUBTITLE | 17. PRICE GROUP |
|---|---|---|---|---|
| 4. AUTHORITY *(Data Acquisition Document No.)* | | 5. CONTRACT REFERENCE | 6. REQUIRING OFFICE | 18. ESTIMATED TOTAL PRICE |
| 7. DD 250 REQ | 9. DIST STATEMENT REQUIRED | 10. FREQUENCY | 12. DATE OF FIRST SUBMISSION | 14. DISTRIBUTION |
| 8. APP CODE | | 11. AS OF DATE | 13. DATE OF SUBSEQUENT SUBMISSION | a. ADDRESSEE / b. COPIES: Draft, Final (Reg, Repro) |
| 16. REMARKS | | | | 15. TOTAL → 0 0 0 |

| 1. DATA ITEM NO. | 2. TITLE OF DATA ITEM | | 3. SUBTITLE | 17. PRICE GROUP |
|---|---|---|---|---|
| 4. AUTHORITY *(Data Acquisition Document No.)* | | 5. CONTRACT REFERENCE | 6. REQUIRING OFFICE | 18. ESTIMATED TOTAL PRICE |
| 7. DD 250 REQ | 9. DIST STATEMENT REQUIRED | 10. FREQUENCY | 12. DATE OF FIRST SUBMISSION | 14. DISTRIBUTION |
| 8. APP CODE | | 11. AS OF DATE | 13. DATE OF SUBSEQUENT SUBMISSION | a. ADDRESSEE / b. COPIES: Draft, Final (Reg, Repro) |
| 16. REMARKS | | | | 15. TOTAL → 0 0 0 |

| G. PREPARED BY | H. DATE | I. APPROVED BY | J. DATE |
|---|---|---|---|

DD FORM 1423, AUG 96 PREVIOUS EDITION MAY BE USED. Page ___ of ___ Pages

Adobe Professional 8.0

**Figure 11-4**

## Specification of Deliverables

The government uses some form of a product description for the acquisition and management of supplies and .services needed to perform its functions. Product descriptions include such documents as specifications, standards, voluntary standards, commercial item descriptions, or purchase descriptions.

The FAR policies and procedures for the development, management and use of specifications, standards and other product descriptions are in FAR Part 11, *Describing Agency Needs*.

A **specification** is a clear and accurate description of the technical requirements of a material, a product or a service. It will also include a procedure to determine that the contractor has met the requirements.

**Standards** are documents that establish engineering and technical limitations and applications of items, materials, processes, methods, designs, and engineering practices. They include any related criteria deemed essential to achieve the highest practical degree of uniformity in materials or products, or interchangeability of parts used in those products. Standards may be used in specifications, invitations for bids, proposals, and contracts.

**Voluntary standards** are standards established by a private sector body and available for public use. The term does not include private standards of individual firms. For further guidance, see OMB Circular No. A-119, *Federal Participation in the Development and Use of Voluntary Consensus Standards and in Conformity Assessment Activities*.

**Commercial item descriptions (CID)** are indexed, simplified product descriptions managed by the General Services Administration. They describe, by functional or performance characteristics, the available, acceptable commercial products that will satisfy the government's needs.

**Purchase description** means a description of the essential physical characteristics and functions required to meet the Government's minimum needs.

Plans, drawings, specifications, standards or purchase descriptions for acquisition are to state only the government's actual minimum needs. They must describe the supplies and services in a manner that will encourage maximum practicable competition. Specifications and standards are to be selectively applied and tailored in their application. This becomes especially important when a contract is subject to acquisition streamlining procedures, as discussed in Chapter 3, *The Acquisition Process*.

Government solicitations must cite by reference the applicable specification for items being procured. If no specification exists, then some form of a product or purchase description containing the necessary information will be substituted. Whatever document is cited, all amendments or revisions that apply to that acquisition must be identified. The proper date of the document is also important. These suggestions will help prevent any misconceptions or ambiguities about the real requirements.

In fulfilling the requirements of OMB Circular A-119, *Federal Participation in the Development and Use of Voluntary Consensus Standards and in Conformity Assessment Activities*, and FAR Part 12, *Acquisition of Commercial Items*, agencies must, to the maximum practicable extent, follow the following order of preference in their use of product descriptions:

- **Voluntary standards** are used in lieu of other product descriptions, or as part of other product descriptions;
- **Commercial item descriptions** are used in the acquisition of commercial or commercial type products whenever voluntary standards cannot be used;
- **Government specifications** that are stated in terms of functions to be performed or performance required, when voluntary standards or commercial item descriptions cannot be used; or
- **Government specifications** stated in terms of material, finish, schematics, tolerances, operating characteristics, component parts, or other design requirements only when no other form of product description can be used.

OMB Circular A-119 also removed the requirement for mandatory use of military specifications by DOD. The intent of the rule is to increase the use of voluntary standards and commercial item descriptions, which in turn will facilitate the use of commercial and other non-developmental items.

### Categories of Specifications

The government uses several classes or categories of specifications to describe its needs. The category selected for a contract depends upon the nature of the procurement. The three most common types are detailed specifications, functional specifications, and commercial item descriptions. In certain cases specialized specifications are developed because of the complex nature of the program.

### Detailed Specifications

Detailed specifications are also known as design specifications. These documents are the ones most commonly used in the sealed bidding process to describe the contract end items. They are also used for fixed-price production contracts in negotiated procurements. Detailed specifications are suitable for items developed by or for the government for items that can be exactly reproduced by any capable manufacturer without further development.

The detailed specification tells the prospective contractors precisely how the item should be made. In describing the item for production and delivery, the specification will contain complete detailed and precise information about measurements, tolerances, and materials. The specification will describe the required in-process and finished product tests, and quality control and inspection requirements. The document will contain any other information needed to assure compliance with the requirements.

### Functional Specifications

Functional specifications are also known as performance specifications. In contrast to a detailed specification, the precise measurements, tolerances and similar requirements may not exist. The use of functional specifications permits offerors and contractors to prepare alternative solutions to the government's needs.

These specifications are suitable for items of equipment or software available on the commercial market. Conversely, they are used where there are no suitable commercial items available, and where there is no standardized government design. A functional specification will state all performance characteristics desired for the item. It will also specify criteria for demonstrating compliance with the required performance parameters. In such specifications, the actual design, measurements, materials, etc., are not stated. They are not considered of prime importance as long as the contractor meets the performance requirements. With functional and performance specifications, the contractor accepts the general responsibility for design, engineering, manufacturing and achievement of those stated requirements.

### Commercial Item Description

A commercial item description is a document setting forth the essential physical and functional characteristics of required materials or services. It is used instead of detailed or functional specifications under certain conditions. When market research and analysis indicates that commercial or commercial-type products are available to meet the government's needs there is no need to draft a new specification. Such documents are frequently used for sealed bidding as well as small purchases.

### Specialized Procurement Specifications

Research, development, test and evaluation (RDT&E) programs normally make use of functional or performance specifications. Based upon the top program performance specification, a hierarchy of system segment, sub-system and component specifications are created. The top documents are frequently called Program System Specification or generically the General System Specification (GSS). This type of specification approach is frequently used in major system acquisitions and other large development programs.

## Government Warranty of Specifications

Solicitations issued for production contracts typically contain detail or design specifications. Bidders for contract award will submit bids that are responsive to the specification. After award, the contractor is responsible for full compliance with the specification. On occasion, some defect or flaw in the specification will prevent full compliance. When that happens, the contractor may seek and get some form of relief. Relief may be granted because of the implied warranty associated with government furnished specifications. However, the contractor must show that non-performance was a result of the defective specification. The following citation explains the principle of the implied warranty.

> The government's implied warranty of the adequacy of its specifications is based on its responsibility for the specifications rather than any presumed "superior knowledge" in the sense of greater expertise. When one of the parties to a contract undertakes to prepare the specifications, that party is responsible for the correctness, adequacy and feasibility of the specifications, and the other party is under no obligation to check and verify the work product of the party who assumed responsibility for the preparation of the specifications, even though he may be as much or more of an expert than the party who prepared the specifications. Courts have held many times that a bidder need not verify the correctness and adequacy of government specifications prior to bidding. *Harvey-Whipple, Inc. v. United States (10 CCP Para. 72,944) 169 Ct. 689 (1965), Ithaca Gun Co. v. United States (11 CCP Para. 80,493) 176 Ct. Cl. 447 (1966).*

The doctrine of implied warranty of specifications has been extended to government procurements where performance specifications are used. In *Consolidated Diesel Electric Corp. (ASBCA 10486, 67-2 BCA Para. 6669 (1967))*, the board found an implied warranty where the performance specification for an advertised contract called for the use of an existing engine governor and it was later found that no such governor was in existence.

## Other Exhibits and Applicable Documents

In addition to the above noted documents, it is routine for the contract and statement of work to incorporate other documents by reference. To properly incorporate documents into a contract by reference, the incorporation statement must be precise and explicit. A document that is merely attached to a contract and not expressly incorporated into the contract is not a part of the contract.

It is common for a system specification to cite lower tier specifications. Their purpose is to identify requirements for subsystems and components and processes for their fabrication and testing. Specific items like painting, heat treating and environmental constraints will also be there. Program plans and other documents supporting work statements will cover such topics as incentives, testing, production, subcontract management and quality programs.

**Order of Precedence**

Each solicitation and contract should contain an *Order of Precedence* clause in the Schedule or Contract Clauses. The clause, *Order of Precedence – Sealed Bidding*, at FAR 52.214-29, is applicable for all contract actions under sealed bidding procedures. *Order of Precedence – Uniform Contract Format*, at FAR 52.215-8, applies to all solicitations and contracts using the format in FAR 15.204, *Contract Format.*

The purpose of these clauses is to resolve any inconsistency that may exist between the various contractual provisions and documents. Inconsistencies are resolved by giving precedence in the following order. First comes the schedule, excluding the specifications. Following that are the representations and other instructions. Then come the contract clauses, and other documents, exhibits and attachments, whether incorporated by reference or otherwise. Lastly are the specifications which include drawings and the statement of work. If there is a conflict between the drawings and written specifications, the written specification will take precedence.

# CHAPTER 12

# FUNDAMENTALS OF NEGOTIATION

## NEGOTIATIONS AS A WAY OF LIFE

We are all negotiators and have been all our lives. It started very early, as early as babes in a crib, and it has continued throughout the years. We developed most of our basic negotiating skills long before we came into the business world. Our practice came during our dealings with parents, siblings, spouses, children, teachers and peers. Because of the varying degree of experience gained, some individuals have evolved into better negotiators than others.

With the shift from a manufacturing economy to a service economy the importance of negotiations has increased as a business tool, as buyers and sellers work in a more complex milieu of business arrangements. Negotiations are discussions between individuals or groups of individuals who have the same goals, that is, to harmoniously come to an agreement on a particular issue.

The principles and techniques of negotiating in business are sophisticated and structured approaches to those early practices. This chapter will address the subject of negotiations as it applies to the award of contracts and achieving at an equitable adjustment when the contract is modified.

## DEFINITION AND NATURE OF NEGOTIATIONS

### Definitions

The *American Heritage Dictionary of the English Language* defines negotiate this way:

> Negotiate. v. 1. To confer with another or others in order to come to terms. 2. To arrange by conferring; "negotiate a contract." (from Latin "negotium", business, lack of leisure.)

The *Armed Services Pricing Manual (ASPM)*), defined price negotiations as:

> The process of bargaining among buyers and sellers.

### Nature of Negotiations

Negotiation is the use of argumentation and persuasion, not to win an argument but to resolve issues. Procurement by negotiation is the art of arriving at a common understanding through bargaining on the essentials of a contract. Bargaining requires communications and lots of it. It also implies willingness between the parties to reach a mutually satisfactory agreement and settlement of a matter of common concern. Most negotiations involve a range of satisfactory outcomes for both parties.

Since it is the responsibility of both parties to ensure successful completion of the resulting contract, a cooperative negotiation is essential. Always remember a basic fundamental of successful negotiations; "arm's length negotiations" are productive, whereas "swords point" negotiations are destructive. Being ethical in negotiations is paramount.

The essentials or issues of the contract which are a matter of concern to the contracting parties and which need resolution are:

- Contract type
- Terms and conditions (primarily the clauses)
- Scope of effort (statement of work, specifications and data)
- Delivery and schedules
- Contract price (cost and profit or fee)
- Incentives

It is clear that negotiation requires effective communications. Without good communications issues are not resolved. The common concept of negotiations is a group of individuals gathered around the bargaining table. However, negotiations can be successfully concluded by other means as well. Communications are often conducted through written correspondence or electronically by telephone, e-mail, modem, TWX or FAX. Thanks to technological developments, negotiations can be conducted by closed circuit TV, or computer linkage.

Whatever method is available, the consensus holds that face-to-face negotiations are the most effective in resolving the issues. They are also the most rewarding to the individuals involved.

## NEGOTIATORS

### Negotiation Fundamentals

As a general rule in Government contracting, the Government cannot enter into a contract unless the Government official making the deal has the authority to bind the Government. This authority stems from the Constitution, Article 1 – Section 9, and is evidenced by the issuance of a Warrant to the official, usually a contracting officer.

**Authority of Government Agents**

Contracting officers, or their authorized representatives acting within the scope of their authority, are the exclusive agents of their respective departments or agencies. In this capacity, they enter into and administer contracts on behalf of the government under the regulations and departmental procedures (*FAR 1.602, Contracting Officers*).

The services of specialists are often used in the negotiation of contracts. The contracting officer (CO) will coordinate the team of experts, seek their advice, evaluate their counsel and make use of their skills. However, the CO will not transfer his responsibility to them. Therefore, determination of the suitability of the contract price to the government always remains the responsibility of the contracting officer (*FAR 15.405, Price Negotiation*).

The person negotiating on behalf of the government operates within the limited authority delegated to that individual. Government contracting officers have warrants which specify the extent of their authority. They may delegate a portion of that authority to another individual to physically conduct the negotiations. The CO should be present at that point in time when final offers are being exchanged and actually accept the final decisions with the traditional "Shaking of Hands."

**Authority of Contractor's Agents**

Company policies and procedures constrain contractor agents, similar to the constraints on Government agents. The authority granted an individual may range from limited authority for a specific contractual action, to unlimited authority for all such actions. An individual's authority is also dependent upon the person's status or position within the company organization.

The Government expects the contractor's agents to have authority to negotiate. However, it is recognized that both parties operate within certain limitations and constraints.

**Personal Abilities and Attributes of Negotiators**

The three primary attributes for a person to be an effective negotiator are knowledge, attitude and skill. Knowledge is, of course, the cornerstone upon which we must base our negotiations. An effective negotiator must understand the product and the legal and technical environment that surrounds the negotiation. The knowledge required covers the basic fields of engineering, finance, law and business administration. While individual specialists may effectively support a negotiation, these specialists can never take the place of an experienced individual. It must be a person who can understand and interpret the problems associated with the entire procurement. The individual must make the decisions necessary to orchestrate the negotiations effectively.

In addition, the negotiator must have the proper attitude and philosophy about the negotiation. This involves knowledge of his own psychology, the psychology of others and the interaction of groups. Successful negotiation skills are relevant throughout professional relationships between both customer and provider representatives. These skills require careful development. An effective negotiator must possess skill in identifying the issues involved in a negotiation. The person must also have the skill to plan the strategy and tactics to effectively resolve these issues. In addition, the negotiator should have the personal skills of communication, argument and persuasion which are necessary attributes of the actual negotiation.

Consideration must be given to the decision-making ability of any individual who is a candidate for a negotiator's assignment. Some persons are unable to make decisions, while others have no hesitancy whatsoever. Judging the individual's decision-making ability on two levels is a must. The first level is the ability to make decisions and the second is the degree of accuracy of the decisions made. Good negotiators must be capable of making decisions, and their decisions must be right about 99 percent of the time.

In summary, some of the skills considered important in a negotiator are:

- Planning: the ability to organize, to make both long-range and short-range plans and to execute them as planned.
- An ability to identify related issues and to make plans to resolve them.
- An ability to think clearly under stress.
- Verbal ability: an ability to communicate effectively with your own associates, as well as members of the other party.
- The habit of listening attentively to what others are saying.
- An ability to perceive and use power.

## Selection of Negotiation Representatives

There are two questions frequently raised by organizations regarding the size of their negotiation team. Should one person or a team of individuals be used for a specific negotiation? If we use a team approach, what should be its size? There are no easy answers since each negotiation is unique. What is right for one case will not be right for another. The size or dollar value is not always the deciding factor. One criterion that remains constant is the matter of issues. The number and complexity of issues to be resolved will normally dictate the composition of the negotiating team. Another factor too often overlooked in selecting negotiation team members, is avoiding persons who may be experts in their field but have a distinct fear of negotiating (i.e., having their expertise challenged).

## Use of a Single Negotiator

The use of a single negotiator has advantages, some of which are:

- It pointedly underlines the negotiator's responsibilities.
- It eliminates at-the-table disagreements on that side.
- It prevents the opponent's representatives from trying to split the team and thereby undercut its position.
- It allows the use of negotiators specialized in similar or specific areas or products.

Use of a single negotiator is appropriate when the procurement is simple. When the conditions are right, use of a single negotiator can serve as a good training device for the novice negotiator. Use of a single negotiator is not practical for major or complex procurements. That would require one person to be fully conversant with all aspects of the procurement. It is not possible for a single negotiator to have that much first-hand knowledge about all of the elements of a diversified technical program.

The negotiator must have full authority to settle all aspects of a procurement. Therefore, when contemplating the use of a single negotiator, it is advisable to select an individual who has a broad and diversified background. The more complex the proposal and program the more advisable it is to use a team approach to support the negotiator.

## Use of a Negotiation Team

While there may be many different factors favoring the use of the team approach the following are some of the most important:

- The psychological advantage of numbers.
- The increased effectiveness gained from simultaneous employment of specialized capabilities in prenegotiation planning.
- The presence at the table of experts able to counter the arguments presented by the opponent's representatives. They may also be able to expose any mistakes or misstatements the opponents may make.

Complex procurement actions demand the team approach. The nature of the procurement and the circumstances surrounding it will determine the team's membership.

The team leader and the negotiator should be one and the same person. Other team members may include another representative of the contracting function, legal counsel, technical and engineering personnel, auditors or price analysis personnel and field office representatives. When using the team approach it is imperative that all team members fully understand what their functions and roles will be during the negotiations. Team members accustomed to leading in their operating capabilities may find it quite difficult to play a secondary or supporting role at the negotiating table.

Members of the team must realize that the chief negotiator is the team leader. That person is the one, and only one, who actually negotiates with the other party. Others participate in the discussions only as planned. When asked a direct substantive question by one of the opponent's representatives, they should be extremely careful before giving a direct reply. The safest procedure is to seek the negotiator's assent in some way before answering. When this is not done, communications control can break down quickly, jeopardizing the team's position.

There are several risks in having too many members on the team. The other party's team may feel overwhelmed and make the negotiation more difficult. The larger the numbers there are on a team, the less chance there is for total unanimity. Communication control can be very difficult. A large team will mean that the team leader must exercise a greater amount of control. The logistics of arranging for a large group can be cumbersome and costly. With the current economic climate of keeping expenses down to the minimum, it is most probable that negotiation teams will be kept to the bare minimum.

The expensive cost of travel coupled with shrinking budgets will cause many companies, as well as the government, to give serious thought to using some form of electronic negotiations. A popular technique is the use of video cameras and screens by both parties.

## PRENEGOTIATION ACTIVITIES

### Preparation for Negotiation

Thorough preparation is an important prerequisite to effective negotiations. No amount of experience, skill or persuasion on the part of the negotiator can compensate for the lack of preparation. This is especially true for the buyer, since every seller begins negotiations knowing more about the proposal than the buyer. The seller's representatives at the table should know the assumptions underlying their estimates and the areas where contingencies were included. Most important, the seller probably knows the actual cost or price level at which they will be willing to accept the contract.

Only thorough preparation can help the buyer's negotiator balance that initial disadvantage. Preparation involves several important steps. It begins with selection of the negotiation representatives. That is followed by gathering facts and analyzing both the facts and the many intangibles that will affect later discussions. The buyer then establishes the negotiation objectives on the basis of the analysis. Finally, there must be planning on how to achieve these objectives at the negotiation table.

Prenegotiation planning is a three-dimensional concept; administrative, strategic and tactical. Administrative planning involves getting personnel and information where needed so the negotiation goes smoothly. Strategic planning is concerned with long-range goals and values. Tactical planning is concerned with maneuvers and techniques. Planning is needed to get the best results at the bargaining table to attain the organizational goals. The principal negotiator should establish a nondefensive game plan early in the process. The plan must outline the main objectives and prioritize the requirements.

The seller's negotiators are not immune from planning. They must become thoroughly familiar with the development of their proposal and know what technical and pricing analysis took place in its preparation. They must analyze and appraise the potential competition. Their negotiation team must be developed and its strengths and weaknesses must be compared to that of the buyer's team. The team must also objectively appraise the relative bargaining strength of the parties.

## Gathering the Facts

The customer's negotiator must amass a wealth of material to prepare for and ultimately enter into negotiations. The type of information needed is that which will relate to establishing the buyer's position and that which is useful in assessing a seller's position.

The most obvious source of information is the seller's proposal. Cost and price analysis is performed by the buyer's organization. Other agencies, such as plant representatives, DCAS and DCAA furnish support analysis and audit for the government negotiators. Visitation to the seller's facilities and fact-finding sessions will provide much more information than just the information in the proposal.

Another source is that information which will provide clues about the positions a seller may take. Most of this information is readily available to the public. Sources like those noted below can provide helpful information for the buyer. Much of this information comes from the seller's organization. Newspaper, magazine and trade journal articles also provide a wealth of information.

- The seller’s budgets and financial plans
- Publications and reports
- Press releases
- Instructional and educational material
- Advertising
- Speeches and public statements by offeror personnel
- Company biographies

## Analyzing the Facts, the Intangibles, the Issues

Issues, or different points of view, are what the negotiation is all about. The ingredients of each objective are the issues and facts. It is the issues upon which we must establish a position. A fact is considered information which both sides accept as true; therefore, negotiation is unnecessary. Issues are those elements upon which both sides disagree because of opposing interests and objectives.

To put it another way, a fact is an assertion known to be true and about which there is no disagreement. The difference between facts and issues are not always clear-cut. A fact may become an issue when someone challenges that fact and another defends it. There are times when information embodied in an assertion ought to become an issue. However, if no one takes sides, it is not an issue for the occasion. Information about which negotiators agree can be handled as fact for that negotiation. Therefore, no further inquiry is needed to verify it actually is a fact.

It is important to understand that issues contain the diverseness of the parties involved. Yet, it is through the issues that we can reach an agreement. Issues are vehicles for both clashing and resolution. The proper handling of issues is the key to successful negotiation.

Since the buyer's strategy is basically one of being on the offensive, the negotiator must organize the issues in preparation for the negotiations. Arrangement could be in order of importance, so the dominant issues will get immediate attention. An alternative would be to present the issues so when the seller makes a concession on one issue, the seller may find it necessary to make a concession on another to be consistent. Another approach is to arrange the issues in order of ease of agreement. The expectation is that the "snowballing" effect will lead to a rapid agreement of all issues.

## Establishing Negotiation Objectives

In contract negotiations, the primary objective is to reach an understanding and agreement on all the terms and conditions of the contract. That includes the work to be done, a fair and reasonable price paid for the work and a contract type that will sustain that price. When conducting a negotiated procurement, the contracting officers or buyers may have many objectives or just a few, based upon the particular situation. Some of the different objectives they may have are:

- Price objectives – planned for a definite dollar amount
- Contract-type objectives – related directly to the price objectives
- Future competition – this objective will require structuring the contract in a manner to foster competition downstream
- Incentive objectives – that fit in with the overall goal planning
- Technical objectives – these get special attention in R&D contracting

Objective planning should take place at a prenegotiation conference with all members of the negotiation team in attendance. Topics of discussion should include conduct of negotiations, establishment of positions, strategies and tactics, conduct and responsibilities of individual team members, and the negotiation objectives.

Price objectives should be set at the point where chances of the seller over-running the contract costs are as good as under-running. The overall price objective should include a minimum position, the real goal and the maximum position on each significant element of cost. The buyer assumes that the seller's maximum position is that presented in the proposal. What the buyer does not know are the seller's objective and minimum positions. The closeness of the opposing objectives makes for easy negotiations.

The ultimate objective will be an agreement that meets the interests of both parties, is lasting, is efficient and fosters a positive relationship between the parties.

## THE STAGES OF NEGOTIATION

### Fact-Finding

The fact-finding activity is the first formal group discussion of the seller's proposal. It should follow closely after completion of the initial technical and cost analyses.

Fact-finding sessions aid the buyer to set the negotiation plan and objectives. Information and knowledge gained will enhance the bargaining stage of the negotiations. Some of the actions the buyer will take during fact-finding are:

- Discuss seller's proposal and the results of cost/price analysis
- Obtain answers to questions raised during cost/price analysis
- Test realism of negotiation objectives
- Check inconsistencies between buyer and seller's cost information
    - Discuss for clarification such things as labor hours, rates, material lists, material prices, overhead, etc.
    - Probe for rationale behind the seller's basis of estimate for the various elements of the proposal
- Try to isolate the assumptions and judgments the seller used in developing the proposal
- Attempt to determine the range of the negotiation positions of each side
- Determine if both sides are ready for negotiations

During the fact-finding sessions, both the buyer and seller should avoid arguments about elements of the proposal. The buyer should not reveal any differences of opinion, or the negotiation position on any element. Therefore, the negotiator should not take a strong position with members of either team.

Whenever possible the fact-finding team should also be the negotiation team. This will provide the essential continuity from start to finish of the negotiation process. That continuity will be a real benefit towards attaining the set goals. An exception would be when a decision is made to switch to a single negotiator for the bargaining stage.

The buyer's strategy during fact-finding will be to ask detailed questions to get specific information required for further analysis efforts. In addition, the buyer may ask broad questions to bring out unsolicited but useful information. The underlying strategy is to question and listen.

Listening may be one of the more important "activities" both during fact-finding and also during the negotiation sessions. You must practice listening so as not to interrupt the other party before responding to their comments.

The seller's strategy during fact-finding will be to furnish as much information as possible that will lead to a successful negotiation. The seller must do this without divulging his/her objective or minimum positions. The strategy for responding to the buyer's questions should be threefold. Always answer direct questions with direct answers. Respond to broad questions with questions, to try and isolate the real question. Lastly, answer only questions asked and do not volunteer information. The seller must keep in mind that the person asking the questions has the initiative and, therefore, controls the discussions.

The length of the fact-finding sessions will depend upon the size of the proposal involved, questions needing answers and any inconsistencies involved. The interval between the fact-finding and later stages will be dependent upon several factors. Does the buyer require any additional data of the seller? Is any repricing required by the seller? Will the buyer require further evaluations? Are any necessary reviews, approvals or clearances required of higher authorities?

**Preliminary Negotiation Stage**

This is an interim and "sometimes" stage in the negotiation process. Its use is primarily to critique additional data or repriced inputs from the seller. Answers to new questions that have arisen since fact-finding dictate the need for another session.

Now is the time to narrow the negotiation range by resolving as many issues as possible. Both parties should try to determine the real objectives of the opposition. This is also the time when a negotiator will make changes or updates to his/her own negotiation objectives. If final negotiation objectives have not been determined, then it is obvious that the time for action has come. If both parties recognize there are no further open issues for resolution, then agreement is close at hand.

The preliminary stage may come and go without either party realizing that it had in fact occurred. Some negotiators consider this to be just another stage of the fact-finding process.

### Negotiation or Bargaining Stage

The last stage of the negotiation process is when the parties reach final agreement through the use of discussions, hard bargaining and compromise. If the parties fail to reach agreement on any of the major issues during the previous stages, then they must move into the bargaining stage. This is the point in time when both parties can identify the issues and one of the following conditions exists.

- They agree and thus need no further discussion
- They can reach a mutual position or compromise
- There are directly opposite interests or commitments

It is the latter group of issues that will receive the primary thrust during the final stage. No simple rule exists to determine what will be more effective. Is negotiation needed to resolve these issues or would hard bargaining or confrontation be more effective? Each issue and the environment in which it exists will dictate which approach the negotiators will need to take in order to reach resolution.

When reaching the final price of a negotiation, remember that a fair and reasonable price does not require that agreement be reached on every element of the contract costs (*FAR 15.405, Price Negotiation*).

During the bargaining stage, the negotiators are trying to get the most favorable terms possible for their organization. They will try to influence and control the opinions of each other, thus trying to induce the other party to accept their position. Negotiation becomes an art during the final stage.

## STRATEGY IN NEGOTIATIONS

### General Principles of Strategy

Negotiation strategy has been defined as the overall plan for conducting negotiations at the bargaining table.

When considering which strategies to employ, the first thing that must be done is to recognize that two types of strategies exist: strategic and tactical. When speaking of strategy being strategic in nature, the negotiator's concern is the long-range objectives of the organization. On the other hand, tactical strategies are those employed to achieve a victory in any given encounter. Any given tactical engagement, whether won or lost, normally will not affect the strategic position of the organization. However, a consistency in victories or defeats of tactical engagements may change or alter the organization's strategic position and objectives.

The buyer's tactics at the negotiation table must always be sensitive to the seller's approach. There is a danger in over-formulating strategy before the start of the discussions. It is not desirable to place too much reliance on a preconceived strategy. This could leave the negotiator unprepared if the seller says or does something completely different. Negotiators must formulate the strategy before actual negotiations, but only in the most general terms. They must avoid reliance on any detailed approaches and techniques that may backfire if the seller does the unexpected.

The best strategy is a flexible one. It provides for alternatives and for bargaining table options that allow the negotiator to take full advantage of what actually happens during the discussions. The negotiator can then adjust the buyer's position in the light of the seller's arguments, approaches and tactics. It cannot be over-stressed that this should be part of the negotiation planning.

**Strategic Planning**

The buyer's strategy or negotiation plan will be tailored to each negotiation. The plan may include the following determinations:

- The location of the negotiations.
- The substantive agenda for the bargaining session, including such things as: (1) the areas of major disagreement with the seller's offer; and (2) the order in which the buyer will address those issues.
- Whether to present a counteroffer and, if so, the timing of the initial counteroffer. Also the relation it bears to the maximum compromise that the buyer would accept, if forced to do so.
- The arguments that the buyer will raise in support of its position.
- The tactics that the buyer may use to deal with the individual personalities of the seller's representatives.
- Any other techniques that the buyer may use to improve its bargaining position; techniques intended to secure an agreement with the seller that represents the best overall arrangement.
- A definition of the roles and responsibilities of individual team members.

You cannot always conduct the negotiation conference in a step-by-step sequence. However, the buyer's strategy should permit the negotiator to adjust the initial approach as necessary, to better "sell" their position to the seller's representatives.

An agenda is a very useful tool for the negotiator to get the negotiations started on a favorable path. The negotiator should always set up an agenda of issues that the buyer wishes to consider with the seller in the conference. This helps the negotiator to confine the conference table discussions to important matters. The agenda is presented and discussed at the start of the conference. Any agenda should be in fairly general terms, since specifics may divulge the buyer's position on areas of disagreement.

## NEGOTIATION TACTICS AND TECHNIQUES

### Definition of Tactics

The *American Heritage Dictionary of the English Language* defines "tactics" as: "The technique or science of securing strategic objectives . . ." There is a distinction between strategy and tactics. Strategy deals with overall planning and direction, while tactics deals with the actual processes and maneuvers used to carry out the strategy.

### Principles of Tactics

In developing a tactical plan for negotiation, first look at the following nine principles and fundamentals of negotiation. Examine each of them and remember that they complement each other and are mutually dependent. In some situations they may actually conflict. Do not apply one principle to the neglect of the others. Sometimes the application of one or more principles may be partially sacrificed because of the circumstances existing at that time. A reasoned balance of these principles to best meet each specific situation is the aim of the successful negotiator.

### Principle of the Objective

The objective is the end you hope to attain by the employment of negotiations. Select the objective of each element of a negotiation to provide the maximum contribution towards reaching the final objective. The principle which controls all the others is the principle of the objective. Without an objective, and adherence to it, the other principles become meaningless. In a negotiation, there is always the danger of the goal becoming obscured. Therefore, each negotiator should consider every contemplated action in light of the objective.

### Principle of the Offensive

Throughout the negotiation, the negotiator must secure and maintain the initiative. That will permit the negotiator to preserve his freedom of action and impose his will on the opposition. The advantage of offensive action is that it normally enables the attacker to select the time, place and manner of engaging the opposition. There is a risk in constantly being on the offensive. The opposition could become adversarial and make the negotiations more difficult.

**Principle of Concentration**

This is the concentration of superior power at the decisive time and place to influence the outcome of the negotiation.

**Principle of the Whole**

This is the corollary principle to that of concentration. To achieve the concentration of superior power at the given time and place, one must reduce pressure elsewhere. This requires a careful evaluation, particularly where secondary efforts contribute significantly to the main effort.

**Principle of Flexibility**

Flexibility is the movement to dispose facts and assumptions in order to place yourself in a more advantageous position. Flexibility provides the necessary concentration at the proper time and place for attainment of the objective. Successful application of this principle often facilitates the attainment of surprise.

**Principle of Unity of Purpose**

Unity of purpose is the singleness of authority necessary to produce maximum effort. It provides for unity of effort and application of the maximum power directed towards attaining the objective.

**Principle of Security**

Security is protection from surprise. Through security we keep freedom of action. It not only prevents surprise, but is essential when surprising the opposition.

**Principle of Surprise**

Surprise means striking the opposition in a manner for which they are not prepared. You obtain surprise by being resourceful and daring.

**Principle of Simplicity**

A successful negotiation is largely dependent upon how well the team members understand and execute their assigned missions. The simpler the game plan and the role each person is to play, the easier it will be to attain your objective.

## Application of Tactics

Some examples of bargaining table tactics or "Games Negotiators Play" are illustrated at the end of this chapter in Figure 12-3, *Bargaining Table Tactics,* on page 290. Obviously, you cannot apply all of them in every negotiation, and as noted before, some of them are contradictory.

Negotiators must keep in mind the above listed principles when entering into negotiations. They are not out to destroy the opposition. The goal is a successful negotiation of a contractual arrangement that both parties will live with for some time to come. The following fundamentals of tactics, as they relate to negotiations, are worthy of serious consideration.

**Adjust your end to your means.** That may appear contrary to popular opinion, but it is not. The established negotiation objective must be realistic. It must be a goal that is supportable, desirable and one that can be utilized. The goal must also be financially sound and practicable.

**Always keep your objectives in mind.** This relates back to the first principle of negotiation tactics. Unless you know where you want to go, how will you know when you get there? Don't lose sight of your objective by becoming involved in subject matter that is either remotely or not related at all to your objective. If you do, the chances are you will fall short of the goal.

**Use a line or course of least resistance.** This requires a careful analysis of the opposition's weaknesses. The negotiator's position should be to attack at the weak points of the other party. These points may or may not represent your strongest points. Once you have attacked the course of least resistance, exploit it if possible.

**Take an approach which offers alternative objectives.** As pointed out in objective planning, three positions should be planned: maximum, minimum and the objective. Always strive for the goal, but be willing to accept one of the alternatives.

**Keep an open mind.** By having different options and not just one position, you're demanding, not negotiating.

**Be sure that your plan is flexible and adaptable to changing circumstances.** Do not develop a plan that leaves you limited freedom of action. As negotiations proceed, be prepared to take different courses of action.

**Do not put your weight behind an approach while your opponent in on guard.** Surprise is the key. Divert his or her attention from the main assault by secondary attacks on lesser issues. Lull your opponent into a sense of relaxation before making your main attack.

**Never renew an attack along the same line or in the same form after it has failed.** To do so, you violate the principle of surprise. Use maneuver and attack the opponent's position from a new and, if possible, unexpected avenue.

**Remember, silence is golden.** Silence can be a powerful negotiating weapon. Avoid the temptation to speak just to break the silence. After an offer has been made, it is often that the next person to speak will be the one making a concession.

**Provide your opponent with a ladder by which to "get off the limb."** It would be preferable to use a well calculated compromise which shows no sign of weakness on your part.

**Avoid working yourself into a corner.** It is important to leave yourself an open line to maneuver.

Remember that negotiating is a physical act directed by an intense mental process. The success of the negotiation hinges upon the negotiator coordinating those physical and mental aspects. The negotiator will be continually aware of the negotiation progress and the possible necessity to adjust or change tactics.

These are the fundamentals of negotiation tactics, employed within the scope of the principles discussed earlier. Negotiators must draw upon their own experience and exercise sound judgment in determining which, if any, of the various tactics or games to employ. A truly successful negotiation demands that the parties establish and maintain sound, cooperative and mutually respectful relationships.

**Control of the Bargaining Situation**

Control of the bargaining situation is normally the result of taking three actions. You can maintain control through the use of power, the application of specific procedures and customs, and through the flow of information, persuasion and discussion.

Power is the primary bargaining tool which both sides seek to use in controlling or counter-controlling the negotiation and its ultimate outcome. In the negotiation arena, power is the ability of a negotiator to influence the behavior of an opponent.

The following principles on the use and application of power affect negotiators who contemplate "exerting power" during a negotiation.

- Power is always relative; seldom if ever does a negotiator enjoy complete and continuous power.
- Power may be either real or apparent. The fact that logic, justice or force supports a position is not a guarantee of success. A seller may be in a preferred position, but if neither party perceives the advantage, there is none.
- Overt action is not always necessary for a negotiator to exert power. It may be unnecessary for you to take any action if your opponent believes that action against him is possible.
- Power is always limited. Its range depends upon the situation, government regulations, ethical standards and present or future competition.
- Power exists to the extent it is accepted.
- You cannot separate the ends of power from the means. One cannot hope to develop a loyal customer or contractor by using exploitative tactics.
- The exercise of power always entails cost and risk.
- Power relationships change over time. The balance of power moves as the balance of benefits and contributions from the parties change.

The second type of control or influence is the application of procedures and customs to the negotiation process. When negotiating a government contract, many external factors constrain the parties. Many of those factors or norms are beyond their control. Some of them are set by law and some just by custom. Most of these will add strength to the buyer's negotiation position, since the seller's bargaining power cannot affect them. Procedural norms are those which should put the two sides in a procedurally equal position. Examples of two procedural norms are: (1) an offer demands a counteroffer; and (2) a concession should always be met with a return concession. Underlying all genuine norms is the basic concept of fairness and reciprocity.

The flow of information, persuasion and discussion is an underlying factor in any negotiation. These are the basic elements of communications, without which there would be no negotiation. Normally, it is the buyer who is on the offensive. The buyer forms the questions, probing the seller's proposal and its basis of estimate. In the process the buyer seeks clarification and justification for the rationale used by the seller. Figure 12-1, *Words Used to Frame Questions*, on page 286, contains a group of probing words which will help the negotiator in controlling the bargaining session and also get the answers being sought.

**Factors That Influence Negotiations**

The negotiation or bargaining stage is normally the culmination of months and perhaps years of effort by both the buyer and seller organizations. For a new contract, the action starts somewhere along the acquisition cycle with a procurement plan.

Stemming from that procurement plan will be the issuance of a request for proposal (RFP) and the preparation and subsequent submission of responsive proposals by offerors. Then the buyer's team performs proposal evaluation leading to the source selection process. The buyer then proceeds with negotiation planning and fact-finding sessions. In the final stage the parties sit down to negotiate all the terms and conditions of the definitive contract.

Despite all their planning, the individual negotiators are not masters of their own fates. Much, if not all, of the planned strategy and tactics may be forced aside by circumstances beyond the negotiator's control. The following is a representative listing of factors that influence the process and outcome of most negotiations:

- The relative bargaining strength of the parties.
- The extent of cooperation and relationships existing between buyer and seller.
- The organizational level of the negotiators.
- The amount of prenegotiation preparation performed.
- The relative skills of the negotiators
- The strategy and tactics used by the parties.
- The size of the procurement and the risks involved.
- The intelligence that each side has of the other's values and objectives.
- The location of the negotiations.
- The agenda and sequence of the negotiations.
- The confidence that each negotiator has in the opponent.
- The interest each party has in desiring to reach a settlement.

# WORDS USED TO FRAME QUESTIONS

| | | |
|---|---|---|
| Classify | – | Demands the assembling, arranging and grouping of facts according to some common characteristics. |
| Compare | – | Requires the detection of resemblance and difference among facts. |
| Criticize | – | Exacts good judgment and a careful analysis of the subject. |
| Define | – | Requires the determination of definite boundaries or limits of a subject and the fixing of a clear meaning. |
| Describe | – | Calls for the selection and portrayal of the features or qualities which characterize a subject. |
| Discuss | – | Compels a minute examination of a subject presenting the pro and con considerations and adducing arguments or reasons in support of a position or attitude. |
| Explain | – | Makes necessary a clarification of any points which may obscure a subject and also makes a subject more intelligible. |
| Illustrate | – | Calls for examples that will explain or clear-up the subject under consideration. |
| Interpret | – | Necessitates bringing out the meaning of a subject in the light of an individual's belief or judgment. |
| Justify | – | Demands showing that something is reasonable or warrantable. |
| Outline | – | Makes necessary the sketching or showing of the main points in a discussion, argument or process. |
| Review | – | Compels going over a subject deliberately and giving it a critical examination. |
| Summarize | – | Asks for the presentation of a subject in a concise and compact manner. |
| Trace | – | Requires following in detail the development or progress of a subject. |
| Verify | – | Exacts proof that a thing is true. |

**Figure 12-1**

Figure 12-2, *Basic Rules of Negotiations*, on page 288, lists some of the basic rules negotiators should follow. The rules will have an influence upon the negotiations, depending upon how closely the negotiator adheres to their concepts.

Last, though perhaps most important, are those aspects of the negotiator's own demeanor and appearance that are within the control of the negotiator. The negotiator's personal neatness and grooming, punctual arrival at the conference, and bargaining table behavior and attitude are essential. Of course, attitudes may be altered to reflect changes in strategies and tactics.

The negotiator should always follow these precepts: be polite, while avoiding unnecessary interruptions; always use direct, clear and simple language; summarize the proceedings at appropriate points; and keep emotions in check at all times. The negotiator may, of course, want to display emotions as a tactic, but only for that purpose.

In summary, remember to conduct the negotiations in an atmosphere of cordiality, friendliness and mutual trust. A positive atmosphere will motivate both parties to reach agreement much more quickly. Furthermore, to repeat a point made earlier, a vital element of successful bargaining is communications control. That applies whether the organization is represented by a team or a single negotiator. Another point that bears repeating is a factor that each negotiator must keep in mind. Both sides have the responsibility to ensure the successful completion of a contract. The first step towards that goal is a negotiation which results in a mutually beneficial contract.

## CONCLUDING NEGOTIATIONS

### Timing the Closure

It is next to impossible to set a time for successfully closing a negotiation. This holds true even when some "higher authority" sets an artificial deadline. Any attempt to close negotiations prematurely can be as disastrous as closing too late. Once you reach the point where agreement is possible, cease all discussions of the issues and summarize all the understandings of the parties. The negotiator must be able to sense when the opponent is ready to accept a contemplated offer. This "sense of closure" is a difficult skill to acquire; yet it is a very important skill needed by a negotiator.

Active listening is the only way to grasp and understand the other party's position. Too many negotiations have been lost because of someone talking when they should have been listening. After reaching final agreement, if the parties have not observed the previous guidelines, the parties may be too exhausted to fully enjoy the fruits of their labors.

# BASIC RULES OF NEGOTIATIONS

1. Aim for a professional atmosphere, making allowances for differences of opinion which obviously will exist.
2. Strive for an equitable settlement of all contract elements.
3. Remember that both sides obviously have limited authority.
4. Be prepared for negotiations.
5. Don't dictate; you represent your organization (government or contractor), so you must be reasonable.
6. Never ridicule or insult.
7. Don't try to make anyone look bad or prove anyone wrong.
8. Don't push your opponent into a corner.
9. Plan an offensive retreat.
10. Throw your adversary a rope if he "falls in."
11. Don't be predictable in your approach.
12. Remember that for every action there must be a reaction.
13. Remember people are more creatures of emotion than logic.
14. Be discriminating – accept a good offer.
15. Fight hard on important points only.
16. Remember both parties are in a "near equal" negotiating position.
17. Guard against hoof and mouth disease. Know when to talk and when to sit and listen.
18. Stop talking when you have made your point, won your case, or reached an agreement.
19. Don't try to sell when someone else is selling.
20. Don't make a career out of a project/negotiation.
21. Keep cool; don't be terrorized.
22. Be professional, courteous and considerate.
23. **HAVE INTEGRITY!**

**Figure 12-2**

## Documenting the Agreement

It is the responsibility of each negotiator to be personally assured that all elements of the procurement are settled. Before terminating the bargaining session the buyer's negotiator has the primary responsibility to see to it that a mutual understanding has been reached. Misunderstandings at this stage may make further negotiations necessary.

Documenting the results of the negotiations is important. Always put the essential terms of the agreement into writing as a memorandum of understanding. Both parties should sign the memorandum before the conference ends. This is especially effective if the seller's negotiator dictates the memorandum, with the buyer's negotiator helping to complete the summary. This action becomes very important when there have been difficulties in reaching an understanding.

The seller should also submit a letter of confirmation to the buyer detailing all of the significant agreements. A *Certificate of Current Cost or Pricing Data,* Figure 6-6, on page 173, must be submitted when certified cost or pricing data has been required (*FAR 15.406-2, Certificate of Current Cost or Pricing Data*).

Upon receipt of the letter of confirmation, the contracting officer will prepare and release the contract or contract modification. Only when both parties have executed the document will the negotiation be fully closed.

After each negotiation, the government's negotiator will prepare a price negotiation memorandum (PNM). The PNM will summarize the actions and decision process used by the government's representatives in arriving at the final agreement. It will become an important part of the contract file (*FAR 15.406-3, Documenting the Negotiation*). Individual agencies determine their own PNM formats. The memorandum should contain enough detail to highlight any issues raised and resolved and any other topic that could possibly become a later issue. The Record of Weighted Guidelines Application (*DD Form 1547*), Figure 10-2 on page 245, will become a part of the PNM for certain DOD negotiations.

It is only logical that the contractor's agent should prepare a similar record for the company's contract file. These documents will provide an invaluable source for resolution of any disputes. Such topics as work scope, allowability of costs, and the rights and responsibilities of the contracting parties frequently become items of dispute. A good memorandum of negotiations provides an excellent resource to determine the real intent of the parties.

Part of the post-negotiation file should be an honest assessment of the negotiation team's activities and performance. The team should perform a "lessons learned" analysis as a "textbook" for future negotiations.

# BARGAINING TABLE TACTICS
# or
# "Games Negotiators Play"

| The Tactic | Example of Use and Countermeasures |
|---|---|
| 1. Make the other party appear unreasonable | ▪ Make concessions on minor issues and then ask for concessions on major issues in return. |
| Probe | ▪ "We've made concessions, now it's your turn." |
| Rebuttal | ▪ "Concessions! You've just become reasonable." |
| 2. Coercion or "Blackmail" | ▪ Threaten to go over the other party's head. |
| Probe | ▪ "If you don't want to settle, I'll call your boss." |
| Probe | ▪ "If you persist in being so unreasonable, we will contact your management." |
| Rebuttal | ▪ "That's OK with me. Here's the phone number." |
| 3. Place the other on the defensive | ▪ Ask a long series of questions. |
| Probe | ▪ Repeat a long series of questions on same topic. |
| Rebuttal | ▪ "You're not listening; pay attention, I just answered that." |
| 4. Show Indignation | ▪ Keep rejecting opponent's position as irrational. |
| Probe | ▪ "How can you justify THAT position? Right now it sounds totally unrealistic to me." |
| Rebuttal | ▪ "Once you understand it, you'll see that I've really offered a bargain." |
| 5. Throw the blame for inability to compromise on a third party. | ▪ Contractor's position:<br>▪ "Against company policy."<br>▪ "Management will not allow me to provide you with that information."<br><br>▪ Government's position:<br>▪ "Regulations won't allow it."<br>▪ "No funds available."<br>▪ "Contracting officer would never sign such an agreement." |

Figure 12-3

| The Tactic | Example of Use and Countermeasures |
|---|---|
| 6. That's Fine, BUT! | ▪ Keep looking for something closer to your objective |
| Probe | ▪ "I think we can do better than that . . . how about just settle . . .?" |
| Rebuttal | ▪ "That's an improvement, but what is your real position?" |
| 7. We are really of the same mind on this issue | ▪ Give the impression that both negotiators are on the same side. |
| Probe | ▪ "Justify that position so I can sell my higher authority on it." |
| Rebuttal | ▪ "I've already justified my position, you shouldn't have to go higher." |
| 8. White Hat v. Black Hat | ▪ One person takes an extreme position, while negotiator assumes the position that team really wants. The actual position appears good. (More moderate and conciliatory) |
| Rebuttal | ▪ Show how absurd the "extreme position" really is. |
| 9. Fishing Expedition | ▪ Look for mistakes in the proposal. |
| Probe | ▪ "We think you made a mistake in quoting . . .?" |
| Rebuttal | ▪ "You do? How do your figures compute?" |
| 10. Straw Issues | ▪ Contractor's position:<br>▪ Put items in the proposal to have them negotiated out (e.g. high overhead, excessive scrap or usage).<br>▪ Take a strong position on a relatively unimportant issue to use as a trade.<br><br>▪ Government's position:<br>▪ Use the same tactic in reverse.<br>▪ Make extremely low offer on individual issues.<br>▪ Take a strong position on those issues which the contractor least expects. |
| 11. Appeal to the Emotions | ▪ Appeal to the contractor's patriotism and desire to be liked. |
| Probe | ▪ "I don't think you realize how important this procurement is to the defense of our country!" |
| Rebuttal | ▪ "Yes I do! That is why I need enough to make a good product." |
| 12. The Walkout | ▪ The tactical use of walkouts is very difficult to perform properly. It should only be used when it can be backed up or the negotiator is skillful enough to "have a graceful change of mind." |
| Rebuttal | ▪ "Let us know when you're ready to negotiate." |

**Figure 12-3 (continued)**

| The Tactic | Example of Use and Countermeasures |
|---|---|
| 13. It's Time to Make-up | ▪ Attempt to bring an end to all agreements. |
| Probe | ▪ "I know I've been persistent in this, but I'm willing to give in if you'll only be a little more reasonable." |
| Rebuttal | ▪ "I don't mind being reasonable, but I can't give away the store." |
| 14. One More Time! | ▪ Keep the pressure on the opponent. |
| Probe | ▪ "I've told you before, that . . ." |
| Rebuttal | ▪ "What's the flip side of that recording?" |
| 15. The Recess or Caucus | ▪ A typical approach to restore control:<br>▪ When a team member gets out of line.<br>▪ When emotions get out of control<br>▪ When fatigue starts to take its toll.<br>▪ To get away from an area in which you are weak.<br>▪ To plan adjustments in negotiation strategy or tactics.<br>▪ To analyze progress of the bargaining session.<br>▪ When team communications seem to be out of hand.<br>▪ To analyze and reply to an offer. |
| 16. Agreement and Rebuttal | ▪ Appear to agree – to a point. |
| Probe | ▪ "Yes, of course . . . but . . ." "Yes, for that very reason we feel . . ." |
| Rebuttal | ▪ "If you understand that part, you shouldn't have further questions." |
| 17. Alternative Proposals | ▪ Make an offer in terms of alternative combinations of profit and contract types, alternative combinations of delivery terms, etc.<br>▪ Alternatives may not be any better. |
| 18. Change Team Members | ▪ Keep opponent off balance. |
| Rebuttal | ▪ Insist on detailed review of negotiations for new team. |
| 19. Pretend | ▪ Used when other side's statements are ambiguous, unclear or their thinking lacks organization.<br>▪ Forces opponents to clarify their statements and thinking.<br>▪ Gives negotiator time to organize own thinking. |
| 20. Deliberate | ▪ Attempt to get opponents rattled by misunderstanding their statements and cause them to repeat themselves.<br>▪ Forces other side to defend their point of view or discuss the subject further.<br>▪ Useful when other negotiator's meaning is not clear.<br>▪ May backfire by enabling opponent to better clarify arguments and thus strengthen position. |

**Figure 12-3 (continued)**

| The Tactic | Example of Use and Countermeasures |
|---|---|
| 21. Pro and Con Analysis | ▪ Attempt at correction of faulty thinking or obvious mistake without a flat contradiction. Also, to force an impartial consideration of the problem.<br>▪ List factors supporting or opposing an issue.<br>▪ Encourage other party to agree to all the facts presented, or provide more facts of their own.<br>▪ Be sure it will prove your position. |
| 22. It's a Precedent! | ▪ Justification based on previous negotiation.<br>▪ Restrictive in nature.<br>▪ May perpetrate an outmoded pattern.<br>▪ May cause the opponent to use the same rationale for another issue not to your advantage. |
| 23. Send in the Auditors | ▪ Threaten to send Government auditors to contractor's facility |
| Probe | ▪ Your supporting data is so messed up we might have to call in the auditors. |
| Rebuttal | ▪ "That's OK. Our books are open to inspection. Perhaps the auditors will help you understand how clear this really is." |
| 24. The "Nibble" | ▪ After agreement on an issue has been reached, an attempt is made to make a "minor change" in the terms. |
| Probe | ▪ "It's cleaner to work with whole numbers, so let's round out the $11,385 for the modification to an even $11,300." |
| Rebuttal | ▪ "I like whole numbers also. But, rounding to $11,400 makes more sense. Otherwise, forget it." |
| 25. It's late Friday and you have a plane to catch | ▪ Squeeze for a quick settlement because of time. |
| Probe | ▪ "Well here it is Friday afternoon. You have a plane to catch, why don't we just settle at . . .?" |
| Rebuttal | ▪ "Your offer is still not acceptable. But, I'm ready and willing to work all weekend to get this thing settled."<br>▪ Be sure you are ready to stay, they may call your bluff. |

**Figure 12-3 (continued)**

# PART 3

# THE POSTAWARD PHASE

# OF

# FEDERAL CONTRACTING

# CHAPTER 13

# CONTRACT PERFORMANCE

## CONTRACT ADMINISTRATION

Having gone through the lengthy process of solicitation, source selection, negotiation and contract formation, the Government and the contractor enter into the contract administration phase, This is where the proof of the pudding becomes reality. Now the contractor must perform as proposed.

Both parties have duties and responsibilities associated with their new role in performance of the contract. The Government, for its part, will act through its agent the contracting officer and perform certain functions. Basically those functions are direction, administration, surveillance, acceptance and payment. The degree of involvement depends upon the type and nature of the contract. For its part, the contractor is challenged to perform services and provide end items and related deliverables. The contractor must do all this in accordance with the terms and conditions of the contract. This chapter reviews some of the common contract administration functions designed to lead to the successful performance of Government contracts.

One very important element of the administration of a contract is management of changes to the contractual arrangement between the parties. The contracting officer and the contractor have dual responsibilities in this matter. It is only through mutual understanding of the contract requirements and the needs of the contracting parties that this aspect of the contract management will be properly implemented. Contract changes will be addressed later in this chapter.

## GOVERNMENT CONTRACT ADMINISTRATION AND CONTROLS

### Contracting Office Administration

FAR 42.2, *Contract Administration Services*, contains the policies and procedures for the several aspects of contract administration. It provides guidance for assigning, retaining or reassigning the contract administration responsibility. The provision defines the requirements for withholding normal functions or deleting additional functions when assigning contracts for administration. It also describes the process for requesting and performing supporting contract administration. Supporting contract administration means performance of specific contract administration functions by another contract administration office (CAO), as required, by either: (1) the CAO to which a contract has been assigned for administration; or (2) the contracting office retaining a contract for administration.

**Assignment of Contract Administration (*FAR 42.202*)**

Many federal agency contracting offices assign contracts for administration to a contract administration office (CAO). A CAO may be established by an agency to service contracts over a specific geographic area. The Department of Defense has the largest and most active network of contract administrative operations. Under the Defense Logistics Agency, DOD has established the Defense Contract Management Agency (DCMA) with the responsibility to provide all DOD agencies with contract administration support. DCMA has three different methods of providing that support. There is the residency support where single or limited contract administration functions are performed. The second system provides CAO activities on an itinerant basis. This latter support will be administered out of area offices throughout the three DCMA Regional Commands. Other CAO support is provided by the establishment of a Plant Representative Office resident in a contractor's facility. These offices perform multiple administrative functions.

When an agency requires field contract administration or audit services, and they do not have an established capability in an area needing such support, they are encouraged to use cross-servicing arrangements with existing contract administration and contract audit components of other agencies.

Except for any individual functions withheld by the contracting office, assignment of a contract to a CAO for administration automatically carries with it the authority to perform the functions applying to the contract. The designated administrative contracting office will be identified in the contract.

**Contract Administration Office**

Contract administration offices (CAO) are responsible for assuring compliance with the terms of their contracts in relation to the contract administration functions under their cognizance. They serve as a focal point for all inquiries regarding the status of deliverables and production, quality of material and other contract administration matters. The CAO has the responsibility of keeping the purchasing office and other interested activities advised of all pertinent matters relating to the contracts under their cognizance. When circumstances require it, the CAO will assign supporting contract administration functions to other offices.

The CAO will be staffed with the various disciplines that are necessary to perform the many functions that are assigned by their customers, the procuring agencies. Typically, in addition to the management and administrative staff personnel, the CAO will be comprised of administrative contracting officers (ACOs), cost and price analysts, quality control inspectors, Government property administrators, procurement system specialists, hardware and software engineers and other required specialists.

Of these specialists, the ACO has a key role. An ACO is the alter ego of the procuring contracting officer (PCO) or CO. The ACO acts on behalf of the CO in either performing or monitoring assigned contract administration functions. The ACO has a warrant just like the CO. The administrative contracting officer has the added responsibility of keeping the CO informed on the status of assigned contracts. Close cooperation and frequent communications between themselves and their contractors are key elements in successful contract administration.

### Supporting Contract Administration

Frequently, performance of specific functions will be performed at a location remote from the prime contractor's facilities. When that occurs, the contract administration office assigned responsibility for the prime contractor may request supporting contract administration from the CAO cognizant of the contractor's activities at that other site (*FAR 42.202, Assignment of Contract Administration*). The request will: (1) be in writing; (2) clearly state the specific functions to be performed; and (3) be accompanied by a copy of pertinent contractual and other necessary documents. A prime contractor is responsible for managing its subcontracts and subcontractors. Normally, the CAO's primary concern is with the prime contractor's management of its subcontractors. Therefore, supporting contract administrations will not be used for subcontracts unless: (1) the Government would otherwise incur undue costs; or (2) successful completion of the prime contract is threatened. For major system acquisitions (see Chapter 3, *The Acquisition Process)* the contracting officer may designate certain high-risk or critical elements of the program that would warrant the additional support.

### Contract Administration Functions (*FAR 42.302*)

Each contract assigned by a contracting office to a contract administration office (CAO) will contain or be accompanied by the procuring agency instructions or directives. When a contract is assigned, the functions and responsibilities listed in Appendix C to this text are the ones normally performed by that component. In addition, the memorandum of agreement between the two agencies will define the actual tasks that are delegated under the authority of FAR 42.3, *Contract Administration Office Functions.*

### Contracting Officer's Representatives

Some Government agencies provide additional support to the contracting officer in the person of a contracting officer's representative (COR). Some agencies use the term, contracting officer's technical representative (COTR). The CORs or COTRs for any given contract will vary in number. It may be a single individual who is also the program manager or project leader. The Government's contracting team could consist of as many as a dozen individuals: a CO and multiple CORs/COTRs. It will all depend upon the size and scope of the program and the various disciplines that need close attention. The CORs/COTRs will be designated by the contracting officer in a letter to the contractor. The letter will also delineate their authority. CORs/COTRs are frequently used by agencies that do not use contract administration services to the fullest extent.

The primary duty of a contracting officer's representative is to assist the contracting officer in insuring that a contractor's performance proceeds in accordance with the terms of the contract. CORs/COTRs provide technical advice and guidance regarding specifications, purchase descriptions and statements of work. Maintaining liaison and coordination between the contractor's representatives and the contracting officer is one of their key functions. They also perform inspections, acceptance and quality assurance functions. In addition, they provide other technical or administrative duties specified in the contracting officer's appointment letter.

Another important duty of the contracting officer's representative is to provide the contracting officer with current contract information. They must report to the CO any unusual circumstances involving the contract such as late delivery, security violations or questions, property matters, etc. Furthermore, the COR/COTR will ascertain if adequate (but not excessive) competent contractor personnel are assigned to the contract and are performing satisfactorily.

In the majority of contracts, CORs/COTRs have limited authority. Therefore, they must avoid any action which could be considered a constructive change. In those contracts, they do not carry the same authority as an administrative contracting officer (ACO). Therefore they must be careful in their discussions with contractor personnel. All changes involving unit cost, total contract price, quantity, quality, or delivery schedule must be accomplished by contractual direction from the contracting officer.

Contracting officer's representatives have been found to bind the Government even though the COR did not have the authority to do so. In one case, an implied-in-fact contract arose from the conduct of a COR. The Government was bound to an option even though the contracting officer never formally exercised the option (*Sociometrics, Inc*., ASBCA No. 51620, October 15, 1999).

## Management and Control Systems

A management system is a documented method for assisting managers in performing their various functions. Some of the functions which they must perform are applicable to contract management. Different systems are available to assist in many of these areas. The manager must define organizational policy, objectives and requirements. Two important tasks are the assigning of responsibility and controlling utilization of resources. A manager must periodically measure performance and compare that performance against stated objectives and requirements. Taking appropriate action, based upon information available, is another important task. A management system may encompass part or all of the foregoing areas and will require the information to be generated, prepared, maintained and disseminated by a contractor.

The responsibility for determining management systems requirements for a Government contract is vested in project offices, program managers, commodity managers or other requiring offices. Judicious application of management systems on all contracts is important. The regulations specify that appropriate management systems are to be contractually applied only if they are required by a standard FAR clause.

With the implementation of acquisition streamlining, as discussed in Chapter 3, *The Acquisition Process*, the Government's program manager and the contracting officer are required to be frugal in requiring management systems to assigned programs.

The following sections of this chapter address some of the most common areas of functional control that are of concern to the Government and its contractors.

## Total Quality Management

The discussion of contract management would not be complete without recognition of the concept known as total quality management (TQM). TQM is the application of quantitative methods and human resources to improve the materials and services supplied to an organization, all the processes within an organization, and the degree to which customer's needs are met. At the heart of every TQM principle is common sense.

Total quality management is applicable to Government agencies and contractors alike. TQM applies to all administrative, engineering and manufacturing processes within an organization. It is oriented to satisfying the needs of both internal and external customers. During the source selection process, TQM encourages competition based on quality and past history of exemplary performance. TQM also puts increased emphasis on overall cost by considering life cycle ownership costs as well as initial procurement costs. Total quality management affects the entire spectrum of acquisition and contracts management. Beginning with the initial procurement planning stages, TQM has application to all aspects of the procurement cycle right through final contract closure.

## Contractor Performance Information (*FAR 42.15*)

How contractors perform their contractual obligations during the life of a contract is growing more important all the time. As budgets grow tighter, agencies will strive to contract only with those contractors that have a good record of performance.

An evaluation of a contractor's performance will be undertaken by the procuring office under the guidance of the contracting officer. Generation of the performance data, referred to as past performance information (PPI), is required by FAR 42.1502, *Policy*. The PPI is to be created and compiled for all contracts and solicitations in excess of $150,000. Past performance may be evaluated in competitively negotiated acquisitions estimated at $150,000 or less at the discretion of the contracting officer.

The official past performance information (PPI) process begins at the time of contract completion. However, it is important that the procuring office begin gathering the necessary information early during the contract period of performance. Some of the PPI to be considered are the contractor's record in relation to the following:

- Conformance to contractual requirements and standards of good workmanship
- Record of forecasting and controlling costs
- Adherence to contract schedules
- History of reasonable and cooperative behavior and commitment to customer satisfaction
- The contractor's business-like concern for the interest of the customer

As soon as practicable after completion of the PPI report, the evaluated contractor is to be provided with a copy of the evaluation and allowed 30 days to respond. Any disagreements between the parties, not resolved at the CO level, will be submitted to a higher authority in the agency for review and the ultimate decision. These performance evaluations will become important factors in the selection of awardees in future solicitations by the procuring agency and other Government departments and agencies. The PPI may be retained and used for source selection purposes for three years after completion of contract performance (*FAR 42.1503, Procedures*). The issue of past performance was also discussed in Chapter 7, *Source Selection Process*.

## FINANCIAL ASPECTS OF CONTRACTING

### Contract Financing

The financing of Government contracts and contractors has a very limited application. Government financing is provided only to the extent actually needed for prompt and efficient performance, considering availability of private financing. Contract financing is administered as an aid to the acquisition process and is intended to be self-liquidating through contract performance. There are numerous types of Government financing available, depending on whether the acquisition is commercial or noncommercial. This section of the text will address the more significant aspects of financing. When deciding on which type of financing to implement, both the program manager and the contracting officer must weigh the pros and cons of each type and then tailor the appropriate type to their acquisition. Agencies will only use the methods for financing contractor working capital, not for the expansion of contractor-owned facilities or the acquisition of fixed assets.

Financing applies to only three situations. The Government guarantees loans made by public and private financial institutions to Government contractors performing contracts related to national defense. Advance payments are made to contractors prior to the initiation of actual effort on a contract. Lastly, contractors are provided with progress payments based on costs incurred.

FAR Part 32, *Contract Financing*, contains the policies and procedures for contract financing. The need for financing is not treated as a handicap in the source selection process. Contracts may be awarded using advance payments, progress payments or a guaranteed loan (with a reasonable percentage of guarantee) to qualified contractors deemed competent and capable of satisfactory performance. Unless agency regulations otherwise permit, contract financing will not be provided for purchases made under simplified acquisition procedures.

**Guaranteed Loans**

Government guaranteed loans are authorized under Title III of the *Defense Production Act of 1950.* Federal Reserve Banks act, on behalf of guaranteeing agencies, as fiscal agents of the United States in the making of loan guarantees for defense production. The only agencies designated as guaranteeing agencies are the Departments of Defense, Energy, Commerce, Interior and Agriculture, the General Services Administration and the National Aeronautics and Space Administration. FAR 32.3, *Loan Guarantees for Defense Production*, prescribes the policies and procedures for this method.

When a contractor or subcontractor working on a Government contract sees the need for financing operating expenses on a project, it can seek a loan from a private lending institution. The contractor requesting the loan can advise the lending institution that a Government loan guarantee can be arranged. The private lending institution would then apply to a Federal Reserve Bank in its district for the guarantee. Application forms and guidance are available at all Federal Reserve Banks.

If the Federal Reserve Bank gives approval of the Government guarantee, it will act as the agent of a guaranteeing agency referenced above. The private financial institution distributes the funds and administers the loan. The Federal Reserve Bank will make the loan guarantee agreements on behalf of the guaranteeing agency involved. The guaranteeing agency is responsible for certifying the contractor's eligibility for the guarantee and fixing the maximum dollar amount and maturity date for the loan. The borrower must also pay a fee to the Government for the privilege of the guarantee.

**Advance Payments**

The authority for making advance payments to contractors is derived from 10 U.S.C. 2307 and Public Law 85-804, 50 U.S.C. 1431-1435. The policies and procedures for making advance payments are contained in FAR 32.4, *Advance Payments for Non-Commercial Items*. Advance payments will be made to contractors when it is deemed to be in the best interests of the Government or to facilitate national defense.

These payments may be used with any type of contract; however, agencies are encouraged to use them sparingly. In fact, FAR 32.402, *General*, states that advance payments are the least preferred method of contract financing.

Advance payments are advances of money by the Government to a prime contractor prior to, in anticipation of, and for the purpose of complete performance under one or more contracts. They are liquidated from payments due to the contractor during performance of the contracts. Since they are not measured by performance, they differ from partial, progress, or other payments based on performance of a contract. When advance payments are authorized the contract will contain the clause at FAR 52.232-12, *Advance Payments*. Prime contractors may obtain advance payments for the purpose of making advances to subcontractors (*FAR 32.102(a)*).

## Progress Payments

Contractors receive progress payments as work progresses during the contract period. Progress payments based on costs are made for costs incurred by the contractor as work progresses under the contract (*FAR 32.102(b)*). They do not relate to the percentage or stage of contract completion accomplished, partial deliveries accepted by the Government, partial payments for a contract termination proposal or performance-based payments.

Progress payments based upon a percentage or stage of completion are authorized by the several statutes cited in FAR 32.101, *Authority*. Progress payments of this type may be used as a payment method under agency procedures. Those procedures must ensure that payments are commensurate with work accomplished, which meets the quality standards established under the contract (*FAR 32.102(e)*). Performance-based payments are contract financing payments made on the basis of: (1) performance measured by objective, quantifiable methods; (2) accomplishment of defined events; or (3) other quantifiable measures of results (*FAR 32.102(f)*).

Progress payments are appropriate for fixed-price type contracts. It is customary to apply a progress payment rate to the cost of performing the contract. The rate has ranged from 75 to 90 percent; however, for small business concerns the range has been from 80 to 95 percent. The contractor receives the remaining unpaid price upon successful completion of the contract. Flexible progress payments may be authorized to allow contractors to recover costs in excess of the customary progress payment rate.

The *Progress Payments* clause at FAR 52.232-16 allows the Government to reduce or suspend progress payments, or to increase the liquidation rate under specified conditions. To continue receiving progress payments a contractor must comply with all material requirements of the contract. That includes the requirement to maintain an efficient and reliable accounting system and controls, adequate for the proper administration of progress payments. If the contractor's system or controls are deemed to be inadequate, progress payments may be suspended until the necessary changes have been made. Payments may also be suspended if the contracting officer finds that contract performance is endangered by the contractor's financial condition or failure to make progress. If only a portion of the contractor's system is considered unacceptable, only the portion of the partial payments associated with that portion will be suspended. FAR 32.503-6, *Suspension or Reduction of Payments*, prescribes several other conditions that could result in progress payments being reduced or suspended.

## Performance-Based Payments (*FAR 32.10*)

Performance-based payments are contract financing payments that are not payment for accepted items. They are a preferred method of financing when the contracting officer finds them practical, and the contractor agrees to receive payment in that manner. In the event of default by the contractor, the payments are fully recoverable in the same manner as progress payments. But unlike progress payments, they are not subject to interest-penalty provisions because they are really classified as financing payments.

Performance-based payments may be applied in either of two methods, on a whole contract or on the basis of deliverable items. When on the whole contract basis, the payment will be applicable to the entire contract and not to specific deliverables. The other technique has the payments made for specific deliverable items or events. A deliverable item is a separate item with a distinct unit price. These payments may be made on performance measured by objective, quantifiable methods; accomplishment of defined events; or other quantifiable measures of results as described in FAR 32.1002, *Bases for Performance-Based Payments*. Any events so selected must be an integral and necessary part of the contractual performance requirements.

Performance-based payments may only be used under the following conditions: (1) the contracting officer and contractor are able to agree on the payment terms; (2) the contract will be a definitized fixed-price type contract; and (3) the contract does not provide for other methods of contract financing, except that advance payments (*FAR 32.4, Advance Payments for Non-Commercial Items*) or guaranteed loans (*FAR 32.3, Loan Guarantees for Defense Production*) may be used. FAR 32.1000, *Scope of Subpart*, details the several types of contracts where performance-based payments will not be used, such as, cost-reimbursement contracts and contracts awarded through sealed bid procedures.

Performance-based payments may be made either on a whole contract or on a deliverable item basis. A deliverable item, for these purposes, is a separate item with a distinct unit price. The events or items to be used as payment criteria must be clearly identified in the contract as well as the amount allocated to each criteria. Also, the contract must contain the clause at FAR 52.232-32, *Performance-Based Payments*.

## Partial Payments

Partial payments based upon the percentage or stage of completion accomplished are generally treated as a method of payment and not as a method of contract financing. The same applies for partial deliveries accepted by the Government. Using partial payments can assist contractors to participate in Government contracts without, or with minimal, contract financing. When appropriate, contract statements of work and pricing arrangements should be designed to permit acceptance and payment for discrete portions of the work, as soon as accepted by the Government (*FAR 32.102(d)*).

## Contract Funding

The second financial aspect of Government contracting is the process by which contracts and contractors are funded. Funding is accomplished by either of two methods; full funding at contract inception, or incremental funding throughout the life of the contract. Full funding is common in fixed-price contracts and relatively small cost-reimbursement contracts. Incremental funding is standard for contracts of either type when the period of performance extends beyond a single fiscal year. Funding depends upon each fiscal year's budget.

When using a cost-reimbursement type contract, the contracting officer must assure that sufficient funds are always available. The funds must cover the estimated costs to date, any fee incurred, and the potential termination liability (PTL) costs. The amount of funds allotted to a contract is stated on the face of the contract or in the schedule. With incremental funding, a notation is made of the estimated funds expiration date. Unfortunately all incremental funding does not occur in an orderly manner. Contractors get funded whenever the contracting officer receives funds from the program office.

Cost-reimbursement type contracts that are fully funded will contain the *Limitation of Cost* clause at FAR 52.232-20. Incrementally funded contracts will contain the *Limitation of Funds* clause at FAR 52.232-22.

These clauses require contractors to notify the contracting officer in writing when the allotted funds will not be enough to support the costs expected to be incurred within the next sixty (60) days. Accordingly, contractors must give a sixty (60) day notice to the contracting officer when they expect to expend seventy-five percent (75%) or more of the total funds allotted. These notice dates are designed to give the contracting officer adequate time to make some important decisions, such as, how to direct the expenditure of the remaining funds already under contract or to decide whether the contract limit will be increased. Failure to give the contracting officer adequate advance warning of funds exhaustion could result in disallowance of any overrun or even termination of the contract.

A good example of a contractor's failure to notify the Government of a probable overrun and the penalty experienced occurred in a Department of Transportation Board of Contract Appeals (DOTBCA) case, *PB Farradyne, Inc., DOTBCA No. 4063, December 14, 1999.* PB Farradyne discovered that its provisional overhead rate was 14 percent lower than what would be incurred, but it waited several years to notify the Government. Here, the overrun was clearly foreseeable, therefore, their claim for reimbursement was denied.

Contractors are admonished not to expend more than the funds allotted to the contract. This is critical because the Government is not obligated to reimburse contractors for more than the allotted funds. Therefore, contractors are not bound to continue performance under the contract or otherwise incur costs beyond the funding limit. However, if the contracting officer has issued notice of increased funding, the contractor may proceed on the good faith of that notice.

Under a cost-reimbursement contract, the contracting officer can take certain actions without immediately increasing the funds available. These actions are limited to issuing change orders, providing directions to replace or repair defective items of work, or sending termination notices. Change orders are not considered authorization to exceed the estimated cost of the contract, unless they contain a statement increasing the estimated cost. The contracting officer must be sure that funds are available for the directed actions. This relates to the fact that without enough funds the contractor is not required to keep working. The contracting officer may direct that any increase in the estimated cost or amount allotted be used for the sole purpose of funding termination or other specified expenses. Any Government personnel encouraging a contractor to continue work without funds will incur a violation of Revised Statutes Section 3679 (*31 U.S.C. 1341*). Such action may subject the violator to civil or criminal penalties (*FAR 32.704, Limitation of Cost or Funds*).

**Contractor Reimbursement**

There are certain criteria controlling the reimbursement of contractors for costs incurred in performance of Government contracts. Payments will depend upon the type of contract, its terms and conditions, and the allowability of those costs. Allowability criteria are specified in FAR Part 31, *Contract Cost Principles and Procedures* (see Chapter 10, *Contract Cost and Profit Principles*).

Actual reimbursement for authorized expenditures is made under the payments clause contained in the contract. Fixed-price type contracts normally contain the clause entitled *Payments* at FAR 52.232-1. Other clauses may be used for individual fixed-price contracts involving any financing. The appropriate clause for cost-reimbursement contracts is *Allowable Cost and Payment* at FAR 52.216-7. The clause is modified to indicate whether there is a fixed fee or an incentive fee.

Payments are made by the Government either by check or electronic funds transfer, at the option of the agency. Payment by electronic funds transfer (EFT) is required by 31 U.S.C. under certain situations. The payment office, not the contracting officer, will make the determination whether or not payment will be made by EFT. Payment by EFT is the preferred method of contract payment in normal contracting situations (*FAR 32.1101, Statutory Requirements*). The clause at FAR 52.232-33, *Payment by Electronic Funds Transfer Control – System for Award Management*, is used to authorize the electronic payment process.

The Department of Defense (DOD) has amended the Defense Federal Acquisition Regulation Supplement (DFARS) in clause 252-232-7003, *Electronic Submission of Payment Requests and Receiving Reports*, to **require** its contractors, with few exceptions, to submit payment requests and any supporting documentation electronically. When that clause is contained in a contract and the contractor fails to submit its invoice electronically, the invoice will be returned.

Where progress payments are not authorized, milestone billings (or partial payments) may be appropriate for fixed-price contracts. Milestone billings allow a contractor to be reimbursed for costs over the standard progress payment rate previously noted. Payment is made when the contractor demonstrates the occurrence of pre-established verifiable events. Typical examples are completion of a significant engineering task, like the preliminary design review (PDR) or final manufacture of a specific item of equipment. In return for getting milestone billings, the contractor must provide adequate consideration to the Government. Milestone billings are not used if the contract provides for flexible progress payments.

Flexible progress payment rates take into account a contractor's particular financing needs. To determine the proper rate the contracting officer feeds contractor furnished data into a DOD cash flow computer model. The data includes such factors as contract cost profile, delivery schedules, progress payments to subcontractors, liquidation rates, and payment and reimbursement cycles.

Any contractor wishing to use either milestone billings or flexible progress payments on a specific contract must first submit a request to the contracting officer. Final decision for milestone billing usage rests with the contracting agency.

Under cost-reimbursement type contracts, the normal procedure is to invoice the Government for allowable costs incurred as work progresses. Most agencies will not make payments more often than once every two (2) weeks. Reimbursements are made to contractors based upon actual expenditures and certain commitments. Payments will cover such expenses as the following:

- Actual payments made for items purchased directly for the contract
- Costs incurred but not necessarily paid for materials issued from inventory and used on the contract
- Actual cost for direct labor, direct travel, other direct in-house costs
- Properly allocable and allowable indirect costs
- Actual payments to subcontractors

If the Government overpays a contractor, and the overpayment was due to the contractor's submission of defective cost or pricing data, the contractor is liable for interest on the amount of overpayment. The contractor is also liable for an amount equal to the amount of the overpayment if the submission was a "knowing submission." These penalties apply to any overpayment made under contracts subject to 10 U.S.C. 2306(a), *Truth in Negotiations Act*. That statute requires the submission of cost or pricing data for contracts awarded using other than sealed bid procedures, certain subcontracts and changes or modifications expected to exceed $700,000.

Agency heads may reduce or suspend payments to a contractor in any case in which the Government finds substantial evidence that the contractor's request for advance, partial or progress payment is based on fraud (*10 U.S.C. 2307(f)*).

## Commercial Item Purchase Financing (*FAR 32.2*)

It is the responsibility of contractors and vendors to provide all resources needed to perform a contract. It is normally the contractor's responsibility to provide the financing when contracting with the Government for commercial items. However, in some markets the provision of financing by the buyer is a commercial practice. In these circumstances, the contracting officer may include appropriate financing terms in contracts for commercial purchases. In those cases the contract will contain the paragraph entitled "Payment" of the clause at FAR 52.212-4, *Contract Terms and Conditions – Commercial Items*.

There are three types of payments for commercial item purchases: commercial advance payment, commercial interim payment, and delivery payment. A commercial interim payment is given to the contractor after some work has been done, whereas a commercial advance payment is given to the contractor when no work has been done. Delivery payments are made for accepted supplies or services, including payments for accepted partial deliveries. All three of these payment methods are contract financing payments for prompt payment purposes.

## Prompt Payment Act

In 1982 Congress passed the *Prompt Payment Act (Pub. L. 97-177)* to require Government agencies to pay interest on contractor invoices not paid in a timely manner. The 100th Congress passed the *Prompt Payment Act Amendments of 1988 (Pub. L. 100-496)* to close several loopholes that allowed agencies to circumvent the 1982 Act. The following are some of the major features of the amended Act.

Under the Act, the Government must pay a proper invoice within thirty (30) days after its receipt. However that will be waived if a different payment schedule is in a contract. An interest penalty begins the day after the required payment date and ends on the date when payment is made. The interest is compounded at the Treasury Rate in effect at the time the payment became due. The Government is required to pay the interest automatically. An additional penalty is imposed if the Government fails to do so. If there is a problem with the invoice, the agency must notify the contractor within seven (7) days after the date it receives the invoice. That notice must explain any defects or improprieties found in the invoice.

The Act prohibits agencies from taking prompt payment discounts after the discount period has expired. So the burden of completing formal acceptance and making payments on time to qualify for the discount falls on the Government. Another feature provides that when funds are temporarily not available to make timely payments, that condition does not excuse the agency from obligations to pay interest penalties.

FAR 32.9, *Prompt Payment,* implements the provision of the Act. This subpart applies to all Government contracts (including contracts at or below the simplified acquisition threshold), except contracts with payment terms and late penalties established by other governmental authority. The provisions of this subpart apply to contract financing and invoice payments for commercial purchases in the same manner they apply to non-commercial purchases.

## Contract Budget Controls

The Department of Defense (DOD) has become the leader in establishing policies and management systems for the control and reporting on the expenditure of funds under Government contracts. This is due in part to the intense public interest in and the visibility of its programs and budgets. The basic DOD policy is to avoid imposing specific methods of management controls in the budget area. It encourages contractors to use management systems suited to their particular environment and specific management needs. However, it does require that the contractor's system of cost and schedule management meet certain acceptable standards.

A Cost/Schedule Control System Criteria (C/SCSC) Joint Implementation Guide was used for years by DOD to implement cost/schedule control system criteria. This has been replaced by ANSI/EIA Standard 748, *Earned Value Management Systems*. DOD guidance is contained in the DOD Earned Value Implementation Guide. The Office of Management and Budget is requiring all Federal agencies to implement earned value management on certain of their programs and projects.

## Financial and Schedule Reporting

Contractors must make regular status reports to the Government on all cost-reimbursement type contracts and incrementally funded fixed-price type contracts. The contract data requirements list or other contract terms will specify the actual deliverable reports. The main thrust of such status reports relates to the financial and schedule aspects of the contract. Typical reporting requirements address monthly funds status, cost performance, and program progress. Contract variance reports or proposals must be submitted whenever the cost to complete the contract will exceed the estimated cost of the contract. The more common term for this condition is "overrun." Variance proposals must explain in detail the reasons for and amount of the overrun. Otherwise, the contracting officer will not be able to increase the estimated cost and funding on the contract. The Government has the choice of funding the overrun, reducing the contractual effort or terminating the contract.

In addition to the typical financial reporting contractors make to the Government, there is an additional notification required in all types of contracts. FAR 52.242-13, *Bankruptcy*, will be inserted in all solicitations and contracts exceeding the simplified acquisition threshold. The clause requires contractors to notify the contracting office responsible for administering its contracts, by certified mail or electronic commerce method, within five (5) days of initiating proceedings relating to bankruptcy, whether voluntary or involuntary. The written notification must include, among other information, a listing of Government contract numbers and contracting offices for all Government contracts against which final payment has not been made. Upon receipt of such notification the cognizant contracting officer will take whatever actions are necessary to protect the Government's financial interests and safeguard Government property (*FAR 42.9, Bankruptcy*).

# AUDIT OF GOVERNMENT CONTRACTS AND CONTRACTORS

The statutes and regulations provide the Government with the right to examine and audit a contractor's books, records, documents and other evidence and accounting procedures and practices. The audits will be in enough detail to reflect properly all costs claimed by the contractor. The right of examination includes the right of inspection at all reasonable times of the contractor's plants engaged in performing Government contracts. This right begins with the start of a contract and continues until three years after final payment under the contract or final settlement of a contract termination. For certain records, shorter periods are specified in FAR 4.7, *Contractor Records Retention*. The audit rights may extend for longer periods as required by certain statutes or contract clauses.

The audit rights appear in 10 U.S.C. 2313(b) and (c), 41 U.S.C. 254(b) and (c), and 10 U.S.C. 2306(f). Those rights have been implemented by several FAR subparts and clauses. FAR 14.201-7, *Contract Clauses*, requires that the clause at FAR 52.214-26, *Audit and Records – Sealed Bidding*, will be inserted in all solicitations and contracts processed under sealed bidding procedures which are expected to exceed the threshold for submission of cost or pricing data. The threshold is currently $700,000. The clause also pertains to the pricing of modifications to those contracts.

The contracting officer will, when contracting by negotiation, insert the clause at FAR 52.215-2, *Audit and Records – Negotiation,* in solicitations and contracts. An exception here is for purchases not exceeding the simplified acquisition threshold or for utility services at rates not exceeding those applying to the general public. Prime contractors must "flow-down" that clause into all subcontracts that exceed the simplified acquisition threshold. Under the *Audit and Records – Negotiation* clause, the contracting officer, or duly authorized representative, will exercise the audit or inspection rights in covered contracts.

The Defense Contract Audit Agency (DCAA) has the charter to perform the functions under the auspice of the *Audit and Records – Negotiation* clause for all DOD components. In addition, the DCAA provides support audits for other agencies upon request. The DCAA usually performs support audits for agencies that have delegated contract administration functions to a contract administration office (CAO). The 1986 DOD Authorization Act, 10 U.S.C. 213, as amended, extends to the Director of DCAA certain subpoena powers. The authority of DCAA to subpoena materials gives it access to objective factual materials. Those materials include cost data useful in verifying the actual costs, including general and administrative (G&A) costs incurred in the performance of cost-type contracts. The amendment also provides for district court enforcement of subpoenas.

The Defense Contract Audit Agency also has the important function of reviewing and approving, for adequacy of description, the contractor's disclosure statement setting forth its accounting system as required by the Cost Accounting Standards regulations in FAR Part 30.

Auditors act as the contracting officer's principal financial advisor on contract costs. The auditor is responsible for expressing an opinion on the allowability, allocability, and reasonableness of contract costs claimed by contractors for reimbursement. The opinion will be the auditor's determination of the contractor's compliance with the pertinent public laws, procurement regulations and the cost accounting standards.

### Records Retention

In support of the Government's right to audit, contractors are obligated to retain certain documents in the manner prescribed by FAR 4.7, *Contractor Records Retention.* Federal contractors are required to "make available records, which includes books, documents, accounting procedures and practices, and other data, regardless of type and regardless of whether such items are in written form, in the form of computer data, or in any other form, and other supporting evidence to satisfy contract negotiation, administration, and audit requirements of the contracting agencies and the Comptroller General" (*FAR 4.703(a)*). The usual period of time contractors are required to make records available is three (3) years after final payment on the contract. However, there are certain records where longer periods are required, as described in FAR 4.703.

Contractors are not prevented from duplicating or storing original records in electronic form (*FAR 4.703(c)*). Contractors and subcontractors can provide photographic or electronic images of original records in audits.

Government agencies also have a requirement to retain contract files and records. FAR 4.8, *Government Contract Files*, prescribes the requirements for Government contract administration offices to establish, maintain and dispose of their contract files. Those agencies may retain their contract files "in any medium (paper, electronic, microfilm, etc.) or any combination of media," as long as they satisfy the FAR requirements (*FAR 4.802, Contract Files*).

## MANAGING CONTRACT CHANGES

### Contract Change Management

Effective administration of a contract depends heavily upon the management of events that may require the original contract to undergo changes. The *American Heritage Dictionary of the English Language* defines *Change* as "*(1) to be or to cause to be different, (2) to exchange for or replace by another.*" It is a rare contract that does not have some element changed during its period of performance. Such changes can be as minor as the change in the paying office, which will not impact any cost or performance factors. Other changes such as a revised schedule or redesign of the deliverable can have a significant impact upon many parts of the contract, in addition to costs.

How the contracting parties handle these contract change situations is important. A contracting officer can make changes in accordance with whichever of the *Changes* clauses at FAR 52.243-x is contained in the contract. While the Government has limited powers to make unilateral changes in a contract, the *Changes* clause in Government contracts gives the Government a great advantage. It can force contractors to perform beyond what they had originally agreed to do. These clauses are virtually unique to Government contracts and are rarely found in commercial contracts.

The *Changes* clause has definite limits, however. A contracting officer can, in a unilateral action, order a change only if it is within the scope of the contract. Any change beyond or outside the scope of the contract is deemed improper. Scope basically relates to the types of products and services defined in the contract schedule. "Out of scope" situations occur when there was a material difference between the modified contract and the original contract. Specifically, the changes in the type of work, performance period, and costs between the contract as awarded and as modified will be examined in detail. Any attempt to modify the contract performance with work that is out of scope is called a "cardinal change." Any such change must be incorporated into the contract by means of a supplemental agreement permitting the contractor to seek additional compensation.

Changes are permitted to be initiated by the contracting officer on a unilateral basis in one or more of the following situations:

- Drawings, designs or specifications
- Method of shipment or packing
- Place of inspection, delivery or acceptance
- Description of services to be performed
- Place of performance

The contractor has an equal responsibility in the management of changes. Timely submission of proposed changes is important. Timely responses to contracting officer inquiries and change notices are equally important. In addition, the elimination of changes that are not cost effective should be the goal of both parties. This is where configuration management and value engineering are aids in change management. Both of these are discussed later.

**Contract Modification Basics**

FAR Part 43, *Contract Modifications*, prescribes the policies and procedures for preparing and processing contract modifications for all types of contracts. Change usually means something has been altered, modified, varied, or somehow different than before.

"Contract modification" means any written alteration in the specification, delivery point, rate of delivery, contract period, price, quantity or other contract provisions of an existing contract. The alteration may be accomplished by unilateral action under a contract provision, or by mutual action of the contracting parties. The unilateral actions could be change orders, orders for provisioned items, administrative changes, notices of termination or notices of the exercise of a contract option. The bilateral actions are supplemental agreements signed by the contractor and the contracting officer.

There are four general types of contract modifications. The first are *administrative* changes which do not affect the substantive rights of the contracting parties and do not require the contractor's acceptance. An example would be a change in paying office or change in appropriation data. The other three – *change orders*, *supplemental agreements,* and *orders of provisioned items,* are discussed in more detail later.

Only contracting officers, acting within the scope of their authority, are empowered to execute modifications on behalf of the Government. Government personnel, other than contracting officers, are not authorized to execute modifications. They are admonished not to act in such a manner as to cause contractors to believe that they have authority to bind the Government. Neither are they to direct or encourage contractors to perform work which should be subject to a contract modification.

Modifications to contracts, including those issued unilaterally, are priced prior to their execution, if it can be done without adversely affecting the interest of the Government. When a modification could result in a significant cost increase, either a final price or a ceiling price must be negotiated. The contracting officer usually will do this before signing the document. Additionally, the contracting officer will get certification from the responsible organization that funds are available before executing a contract modification involving an increase in funds.

Contract modifications are normally issued on Standard Form 30, *Amendment of Solicitation/Modification of Contract*, Figure 13-1 on page 316.

## Initiating Contract Changes

A standard method of initiating changes in the technical requirements of a contract is through the use of an Engineering Change Proposal (ECP). Engineering changes may be proposed by either party to the contract.

MIL-STD-480, *Configuration Control – Engineering Changes, Deviations and Waivers*, cites the procedures and format for ECPs submitted by contractors for evaluation. The type of information listed below must accompany each ECP in enough detail to allow for effective evaluation.

- Identification of item or effort to be changed
- Technical description of proposed change
- Rationale for making the change
- Description of the effort involved in making the change, including time span, organizational and manpower changes

- Impact the change may have on delivery or other contractual schedules
- Impact the change may have on other contract items, performance estimates, mission capabilities, other contracts and contractors
- Detailed cost estimates (credit or debit)
- Identification of modification to statement of work, specifications, data requirements or other contract provisions

Non-technical changes may be initiated by a letter change proposal (LCP), containing much the same data as the ECP. Contracting officers must respond to all proposed changes (ECPs or LCPs) submitted by contractors.

**Change Orders**

Contracting officers follow the procedures of FAR Part 43, *Contract Modifications*, in their issuance and processing of unilateral change orders. The procedure applies to actions under the *Changes* clause of the contract, or other clauses of the contract invoking the *Changes* clause procedures. As noted before, all such changes must be within the general scope of the contract. Otherwise, the contracting officer must use some alternate procedure, such as a supplemental agreement. In some situations, the magnitude of the change may warrant a new procurement action.

Contracts cannot be modified solely for the benefit of a contractor. When a company submits an engineering change proposal it is imperative for them to show "loud and clear" how the Government will benefit by that action. Therefore, even with the showing of mutual consideration, there must be a strong showing of net benefit to the Government.

When the contractor has not already submitted a definitive price proposal, then such a proposal will be required for the change order. The *Changes* clauses require the contractor to assert its right to an equitable adjustment within thirty (30) days after receipt of a contracting officer's written order. The actual cost/impact proposal must be submitted within a reasonable period after authorized go-ahead. The *Changes* clauses also provide that the Government is not allowed to issue an equitable adjustment to a contractor who asserts a claim for such adjustment after final payment has been made on a contract.

Delays in submission of proposals can impact the ultimate negotiation, especially any profit or fee. Much will depend upon the amount of effort already completed by the time the proposal is submitted and negotiated. Contracting officers strive to complete negotiations before the contractor has performed over forty percent (40%) of the authorized efforts. When the actual expenditures exceed that percentage, there is a risk to both parties. The negotiated value could be considered a cost-plus-percentage of cost (CPPC) arrangement. CPPC contracts are illegal. Proposals for change orders are subject to the same analysis, negotiation and definitization process that proposals for basic contracts undergo. They are scaled to the magnitude of the change.

## STANDARD FORM 30

## AMENDMENT OF SOLICITATION/MODIFICATION OF CONTRACT

AMENDMENT OF SOLICITATION/MODIFICATION OF CONTRACT | 1. CONTRACT ID CODE | PAGE OF PAGES

2. AMENDMENT/MODIFICATION NO. | 3. EFFECTIVE DATE | 4. REQUISITION/PURCHASE REQ. NO. | 5. PROJECT NO. *(If applicable)*

6. ISSUED BY CODE | 7. ADMINISTERED BY *(If other than Item 6)* CODE

8. NAME AND ADDRESS OF CONTRACTOR *(No., street, county, State and ZIP Code)*

(X) 9A. AMENDMENT OF SOLICITATION NO.

9B. DATED *(SEE ITEM 11)*

10A. MODIFICATION OF CONTRACT/ORDER NO.

10B. DATED *(SEE ITEM 13)*

CODE | FACILITY CODE

**11. THIS ITEM ONLY APPLIES TO AMENDMENTS OF SOLICITATIONS**

☐ The above numbered solicitation is amended as set forth in Item 14. The hour and date specified for receipt of Offers ☐ is extended. ☐ is not extended.

Offers must acknowledge receipt of this amendment prior to the hour and date specified in the solicitation or as amended, by one of the following methods:
(a) By completing items 8 and 15, and returning ________ copies of the amendment; (b) By acknowledging receipt of this amendment on each copy of the offer submitted; or (c) By separate letter or telegram which includes a reference to the solicitation and amendment numbers. FAILURE OF YOUR ACKNOWLEDGMENT TO BE RECEIVED AT THE PLACE DESIGNATED FOR THE RECEIPT OF OFFERS PRIOR TO THE HOUR AND DATE SPECIFIED MAY RESULT IN REJECTION OF YOUR OFFER. If by virtue of this amendment your desire to change an offer already submitted, such change may be made by telegram or letter, provided each telegram or letter makes reference to the solicitation and this amendment, and is received prior to the opening hour and date specified.

12. ACCOUNTING AND APPROPRIATION DATA *(If required)*

**13. THIS ITEM ONLY APPLIES TO MODIFICATION OF CONTRACTS/ORDERS.**
**IT MODIFIES THE CONTRACT/ORDER NO. AS DESCRIBED IN ITEM 14.**

| CHECK ONE | |
|---|---|
| ☐ | A. THIS CHANGE ORDER IS ISSUED PURSUANT TO: *(Specify authority)* THE CHANGES SET FORTH IN ITEM 14 ARE MADE IN THE CONTRACT ORDER NO. IN ITEM 10A. |
| ☐ | B. THE ABOVE NUMBERED CONTRACT/ORDER IS MODIFIED TO REFLECT THE ADMINISTRATIVE CHANGES *(such as changes in paying office, appropriation date, etc.)* SET FORTH IN ITEM 14, PURSUANT TO THE AUTHORITY OF FAR 43.103(b). |
| ☐ | C. THIS SUPPLEMENTAL AGREEMENT IS ENTERED INTO PURSUANT TO AUTHORITY OF: |
| ☐ | D. OTHER *(Specify type of modification and authority)* |

**E. IMPORTANT:** Contractor ☐ is not, ☐ is required to sign this document and return ________ copies to the issuing office.

14. DESCRIPTION OF AMENDMENT/MODIFICATION *(Organized by UCF section headings, including solicitation/contract subject matter where feasible.)*

Except as provided herein, all terms and conditions of the document referenced in Item 9A or 10A, as heretofore changed, remains unchanged and in full force and effect.

| 15A. NAME AND TITLE OF SIGNER *(Type or print)* | | 16A. NAME AND TITLE OF CONTRACTING OFFICER *(Type or print)* | |
|---|---|---|---|
| 15B. CONTRACTOR/OFFEROR<br><br>*(Signature of person authorized to sign)* | 15C. DATE SIGNED | 16B. UNITED STATES OF AMERICA<br><br>*(Signature of Contracting Officer)* | 16C. DATE SIGNED |

NSN 7540-01-152-8070
Previous edition unusable

STANDARD FORM 30 (REV. 10-83)
Prescribed by GSA FAR (48 CFR) 53.243

**Figure 13-1**

A *Changes* clause action may cause an increase or decrease in the cost of, or the time required for performance of a contract. It may also affect other provisions of the contract. When this occurs an equitable adjustment will be made in the contract. The contract price, time of performance, or both, are subject to adjustment. Other contract provisions affected by the change will also be modified. The action will be definitized into the contract by a supplemental agreement.

### Acquisition of Replenishment Parts

The acquisition of replenishment parts (i.e., spare & repair parts) is accomplished by several methods. They may be acquired directly from the prime contractor concurrently with production of the end items, from a supplier to the prime contractor, or by full and open competition.

The Government orders spare and repair parts from the prime contractor by using Provisioned Item Orders (PIO). A contract clause will permit these orders to be issued unilaterally by the contracting officer. That will permit the timely manufacture or acquisition of the needed spares. The ideal situation is to place the orders during production of the contract parts. This is not always possible. PIOs are an administratively convenient way to order spares. Standard Form 30 (Figure 13-1, page 316) will be boldly marked as **PROVISIONED ITEMS ORDER**, when used for the ordering process. PIOs are frequently implemented as undefinitized contract actions (UCA) to expedite authority for concurrent production with contract end items. Like change orders, PIOs will generate a cost proposal to be negotiated and subsequently definitized by a supplemental agreement.

When the prime contract contains the clause *Restrictions on Subcontractor Sales to the Government*, FAR 52.203-6, spare parts may be acquired by contracting directly with the original supplier instead of going through the prime contractor. Full and open competition will be used when fully adequate drawings and any other needed data are available and the Government has the right to use them for acquisition purposes. Even when the Government does not have available data, there are several other avenues that can be explored. DFARS Subpart 217.75, *Acquisition of Replenishment Parts*, provides guidance on those methods.

### Supplemental Agreements

Supplemental agreements are bilateral documents which, when executed by the contracting officer and the contractor, create a new contractual relationship between the parties. Supplemental agreements are used in the following contract actions:

- They reflect the agreement reached in the negotiation of change orders.
- They are used in preference to a change order whenever possible, even though authority exists to accomplish a modification by change order.
- Supplemental agreements definitize letter contracts.
- Supplemental agreements definitize provisioned items ordered.
- They reflect other agreements of the parties modifying the terms of a contract.

## Undefinitized Contract Actions

As its name implies, an undefinitized contract action (UCA) is any contract action where agreement has not be reached for the contract terms, specifications or price before performance starts. Their primary purpose is to allow the contracting officer to issue a unilateral document permitting a contractor to start work immediately on a specific effort. A UCA may relate to either a contract or a contract modification. Methods of initiating a UCA include unpriced purchase orders, letter contracts, change orders, provisioning item orders, and unpriced orders under a basic ordering agreement. The *DOD Authorization Act of 1987, Pub.L. 99-661*, imposes limitations on the use of undefinitized contract actions by DOD agencies. Their use is limited to situations when a definitized contract or supplemental agreement cannot be issued in enough time to allow performance to begin promptly.

The UCA must include a not-to-exceed (NTE) price that will limit the Government's exposure. There must be a schedule calling for definitization of the UCA within one hundred and eighty (180) days. The Government intends that not more than fifty percent (50%) of the NTE estimate will be expended before definitization of the UCA. The profit allowed on the final negotiated price will reflect any reduced risk of the contractor for work already performed and future efforts.

## Constructive Changes

Constructive changes are also known as de facto changes. They occur because of some course of conduct or action taken by the contracting officer, or a specifically authorized representative. The action may cause the contractor to perform additional or different effort from that required by the terms and conditions of the contract. The conduct may be an affirmative act by the Government agent or even a failure to act. It may be either in writing or oral, and need not be specific in direction or order.

Conditions giving rise to constructive changes include the following situations:

- Furnishing the contractor with a defective government specification
- Requiring adherence to delivery schedules when a contractor is entitled to a time extension
- Denying a contractor the opportunity to employ a permissible method or sequence of work
- Erroneously requiring a contractor to perform contrary to its correct interpretation of the contract requirements
- Unwarranted rejection of supplies following inspection
- Changes in inspection requirements
- Causing or requiring accelerated performance by a contractor

Whenever a contractor considers that some conduct by the Government has affected or may affect the contract terms and conditions, prompt action is required. This is especially urgent when the change has not been identified as such in writing by the contracting officer. The contractor must notify the Government in writing as soon as possible. A delay in the notification could jeopardize any claim the contractor may have.

Upon receipt of a notice or claim of a constructive change, the contracting officer must immediately investigate the circumstances of the alleged change. Based upon the evaluation, the contracting officer should promptly advise the contractor regarding the Government's position on the claim. The contracting officer may confirm the alleged Government conduct as a legitimate change. The contractor will proceed with the effort as directed. At that point the contracting officer will issue the appropriate written direction to validate the action. Contractors prefer this response because it will probably lead to an equitable adjustment to the contract.

In contrast, the contracting officer may countermand the alleged action as an improper and unwanted change. The contractor runs the risk that costs incurred for that effort may be disallowed. Lastly, the contracting officer may advise the contractor that no change was effected by the alleged action. That position holds that the action was "in-scope of the contract" and not subject to a contract change. When the contractor disagrees with the contracting officer's response, the dispute procedures are available for possible relief.

The contracting officer may insert the *Notification of Changes* clause at FAR 52.243-7 in negotiated research and development or supply contracts for the acquisition of major weapon systems or principal subsystems. If the contract amount is expected to be less than $1,000,000, the clause will probably not be used, unless the contracting officer anticipates that situations will arise that may result in a contractor alleging that the Government has effected changes other than those identified as such in writing and signed by the contracting officer. The clause sets forth the agreed-to procedures for the contractor and Government in handling those potential constructive changes.

**Equitable Adjustments**

The term "equitable adjustment" is used in the *Changes* clause and other procurement documentation. It specifically relates to an increase or decrease in contract price resulting from a change or delay in the contract work. Under Government contracts equitable adjustments are obtained in a variety of ways. They cover the entire span from undocumented agreements to the formal settlements of disputes by Boards of Contract Appeals or Courts of Claims. The most common application relates to the means of arriving at a price adjustment for a contract modified by a change order or other contractual direction. There is no formal definition of the term, however, in *Bruce Construction Corporation v. United States (163 Ct. Cl. 197, 100, 324 F. 2nd 516, 518 (1963)),* the court held that:

> equitable adjustments...are simply corrective measures utilized to keep a contractor whole when the Government modifies a contract. Since the purpose underlying such adjustments is to safeguard the contractor against increased costs engendered by the modification, it appears patent that the measure of damages cannot be the value received by the Government, but must be more closely related and contingent upon the altered position in which the contractor finds himself by reason of the modification.

While a request for an equitable adjustment by a contractor, of itself, may not be a claim, a claim is really a request for an equitable adjustment. As noted above, a request for an equitable adjustment is filed under the *Changes* clause. Also, if a contractor files a request for an equitable adjustment and the contracting officer agrees with the issue raised, then the whole claim process will be avoided. All contractor personnel are responsible for recognizing situations where a request for equitable adjustment (REA) situation exists. Those involved in a contract's performance must be able to recognize when a deviation from the contractual SOW, terms of the contract, and period of performance has occurred, thus calling for a REA.

The FAR Council issued Federal Acquisition Circular (FAC) 2001-08 which clarifies that the distinction between claims "arising under a contract" and those "relating to a contract" is that claims "arising under" can be resolved under a contract clause while claims "relating to" cannot. Therefore, successful "relating to" claims must be resolved by incorporation into the contract by means of a supplemental agreement.

To be successful in pursuing a claim for an equitable adjustment, contractors must take the following steps. First, you must preserve your right to file a claim. This is done by following the specific procedures and time frames under the clause in the contract for giving notice and presenting claims to the Government. The two main types of changes are change orders and constructive changes. You must also document all changes and delays, so good record keeping is essential. Lastly, you must choose the right method for calculating the costs resulting from changes or delays. The most appropriate method will depend upon the facts of your individual claim and the degree to which you segregate the actual costs of the impact from the other contract costs.

The Defense Federal Acquisition Regulation Supplement (DFARS) addresses the issue of contractor claims by use of a request for equitable adjustment. DFARS 243.205-71, *Requests for Equitable Adjustment,* states, "Use the clause at 252.243-7002, *Requests for Equitable Adjustment*, in solicitations and contracts estimated to exceed the simplified acquisition threshold." DFARS 252.243-7002 states:

> The amount of any request for equitable adjustment to contract terms shall accurately reflect the contract adjustment for which the Contractor believes the Government is liable. The request shall include only costs for performing the change, and shall not include any costs that already have been reimbursed or that have been separately claimed. All indirect costs included in the request shall be properly allocable to the change in accordance with applicable acquisition regulations.

Contractors must certify that requests for equitable adjustment exceeding the simplified acquisition threshold are made in good faith and that the supporting data are accurate and complete. In developing the cost estimate for a contract change, it is proper to use the same principles and procedures discussed in Chapter 6, *Developing Competitive Proposals*, on the preparation of cost proposals. The efforts will be scaled to the overall scope of the change.

## Options

Another technique by which the Government may modify a contract is by the use of options. An option is a unilateral right incorporated into a contract by the mutual agreement of the contracting parties. During a period specified in the contract, the Government may choose to procure additional supplies or services. Options are also used to extend the term of the contract. Unlike a typical change order, options are anticipatory. During the contract planning stage, the Government may recognize the chance such action could be required. The acquisition plan will define the requirement and process for exercising the option. FAR 17.2, *Options*, prescribes the policies and procedures for the use of options in solicitations and contracts.

In a contract providing for the exercise of options, the solicitation will include all the appropriate provisions and clauses related to the option. The solicitation will state the basis upon which the option(s) will be evaluated. Any limitation on the price of the option will also be noted. In addition, the solicitation will state if an option may be exercised at time of award. When there are multiple option periods identified in the solicitation, the first option period is frequently exercised simultaneously with the initial contract award.

Offerors must be mindful that, should they win the contract award, the value of the option is what they propose. Therefore, pricing the option is just as important as pricing the main effort. Normally, they will not have another chance to negotiate the price. One specific exception will be a change in contract value under a fixed-price contract with economic price adjustment (FPEPA) provisions.

The contract, when awarded, will specify limits on the purchase of additional supplies or services. It will also specify limits on the overall duration of the contract term, including any extensions. Under most circumstances, the total of the basic and option periods will not exceed five (5) years. The contract will also state the period within which the contracting officer may exercise the option(s). The period must be set so as to provide the contractor adequate lead time to ensure continuous production.

When exercising an option, the contracting officer must provide written notice to the contractor within the period(s) specified in the contract. Furthermore, one of the cardinal rules to follow when exercising an option is that it must be exercised exactly as required by the contract. Failure to follow the rules precisely can put the Government in a difficult position. Among other required actions, the contracting officer must determine that all funds are available and the need for the option still exists.

An important decision by the Government is the determination that exercising the option is the best method of fulfilling the need, price and other factors considered. The contracting officer will document the file with a written determination that all administrative and regulatory requirements were met. The contract will then be modified to incorporate the option, citing the appropriate contract clause as the authority.

An interesting factor relating to options deals with a contractor's financial status. A provision of the Bankruptcy Reform Act prohibits the Government from failing to exercise an option to renew a contract simply because the contractor has filed for bankruptcy. While bankruptcy can influence the ability of a contractor to execute its contractual obligations, it alone does not prevent successful prosecution of a contract.

Contractors are not guaranteed that the option will be exercised by the Government. The standard language in option clauses give the Government the discretion to pick up or not pick up the option. Some contractors who are awarded contracts with options mistakenly think that the Government is guaranteeing them to work in the option years. When the Government does not pick up the option, they sometimes try to contest it. Unless they can prove bad faith on the part of the Government, they will not have much luck.

## ENGINEERING MANAGEMENT

### Systems Engineering Management

Systems engineering is the function by which a contractor manages the engineering efforts required to meet the contractual requirements. Those engineering efforts are defined in the statement of work and the general systems specification (GSS) or systems performance specification. The basic function of systems engineering is to plan and execute an integrated effort to achieve those requirements.

Many DOD development programs require contractors to comply with EIA-632, *Processes for Engineering a System*, IEEE 1220, *Standard for Application and Management of the Systems Engineering Process*, and ISO 15288, *Systems and Software Engineering – System Life Cycle Processes*. These documents set forth the concepts of an acceptable systems engineering operation. There is usually a data requirement for the preparation and maintenance of a system engineering plan (SEP). The plan shows the authoritative relationships and functional responsibilities of the organizational elements of the prime contractor and subcontractors. It describes the systems engineering, technical program planning and control, and the technical integration elements of the planned efforts.

## Configuration Management

Configuration management is a discipline that imposes controls on contractor and customer alike. It prevents both parties from making arbitrary changes in the technical requirements. One of its important functions is to provide traceability to the engineering decision process and related documentation.

The current national standard on configuration management practices for systems is EIA-649, *National Consensus Standard for Configuration Management*. Also see MIL-HDBK-61A, *Configuration Management Guidance*.

Both standards define configuration management as: "A management process for establishing and maintaining consistency of a product's performance, functional, and physical attributes with its requirements, design and operational information throughout its life."

The key elements of configuration management as applied to a contract are:

- Configuration management plan
- Configuration identification
- Interface control
- Configuration audits
- Engineering release control
- Control of engineering changes
- Configuration management reports and records

## Value Engineering (*FAR Part 48*)

Value engineering (VE) deals with the elimination or modification of any nonessential element of a Government contract that contributes to the overall cost of that contract. VE constitutes an organized effort that systematically analyzes the functions of systems, equipments, facilities, services and supplies. The purpose of the analyses is to achieve the essential functions at the lowest life cycle cost, consistent with the contractually required performance, reliability, quality and safety.

Value engineering is equally related to Government agencies and to their contractors. In FAR 48.102, *Policies*, it states, "agencies shall establish and maintain cost-effective value engineering procedures and processes." OMB Circular A-131, *Value Engineering*, paragraph 7, *Policy*, states that:

> Federal agencies shall use VE as a management tool, where appropriate, to ensure realistic budgets, identify and remove nonessential capital and operating costs, and improve and maintain optimum quality of program and acquisition functions.

The Government's basic policy on value engineering is to provide contractors with a substantive financial incentive to undertake value engineering in a contract on the premise that both parties will benefit (*FAR 48.102, Policies*). Subcontractor participation is provided and encouraged through the extension of prime contractor VE incentive provisions to appropriate subcontractors. VE incentive payments do not constitute profit or fee subject to the limitations imposed by 10 U.S.C. 2306(d) and 41 U.S.C. 254(b), noted in Chapter 10, *Contract Cost and Profit Principles*.

There are two approaches to value engineering taken in Government contracts. The first is an incentive arrangement, implemented by the *Value Engineering Incentive (VEI)* clause. Contractor participation is voluntary and the contractor uses its own resources to develop and submit any value engineering change proposals (VECPs). This voluntary approach to value engineering should not in itself increase costs to the Government. The contract provides for sharing of savings and for payment of the contractor's allowable development and implementation costs only if a VECP is accepted by the Government.

Development and implementation costs are those the contractor incurs on a VECP specifically in developing, testing, preparing and submitting the VECP. They also include the cost the contractor incurs to make the contractual changes required when the Government accepts the VECP.

The second approach is implemented by the *Value Engineering Program Requirement (VEPR)* clause. This clause requires a specific value engineering program effort within a contract. The contractor must comply with the scope and level of effort specified in the contract. The VE program requirement appears as a separately priced line item of work in the contract schedule. The objective of the value engineering program requirement is to ensure that the contractor's value engineering effort is applied to areas of the contract that offer opportunities for considerable savings consistent with the functional requirements of the end item of the contract.

The VE savings are shared by the Government and contractors. The sharing is based upon the type of VE program, the type of contract and whether it is "acquisition savings" or "collateral savings." Acquisition savings result from application of a VECP to contracts awarded by the same contracting office for essentially the same unit. The savings may apply to the instant contract or a concurrent or future contract. Collateral savings are those measurable net reductions resulting from the VECP in the agency's overall projected collateral costs, whether or not the acquisition costs change. The projected collateral costs are exclusive of the acquisition savings.

No-cost settlements of VECPs are permitted when the contracting officer determines that the balance of the administrative costs of negotiating a settlement against those anticipated would be cost effective and in the Government's best interest (*FAR 48.104-4, Sharing Alternative – No-Cost Settlement Method*).

VECPs can be implemented before an equitable adjustment has been negotiated in order to realize any cost savings as soon as possible. However, there are two barriers to value engineering implementation: (1) the time required for pricing changes; and (2) procurement policies that prevent implementation before pricing is complete. It should be noted that neither the FAR nor the DFARS restrict the implementation of a VECP before an equitable adjustment has been negotiated.

In June 2012, OFPP sought comments on revisions to OMB Circular A-131. As a result of public comments, and discussions with other agencies, OMB revised A-131 to provide:

- Establishing a definition of "value engineering study" to recognize that VE may be tailored and scaled based on factors such as project cost or complexity, stage in the project life cycle, and project schedule.
- Clarifying that the VE process generally is performed in a workshop environment by a multidisciplinary team of contractor and/or agency personnel, facilitated by experienced, trained, and/or certified agency or contractor staff.
- Directing agencies subject to the Chief Financial Officers (CFO) Act to identify a senior accountable official responsible for ensuring the appropriate consideration and use of VE.
- Requiring CFO Act agencies to maintain guidelines and procedures for identifying programs and projects with the most potential to yield savings from VE studies.
- For new projects and programs, increasing the threshold for considering VE from $1 million to $5 million.
- For existing projects and programs, granting agencies discretion to determine the extent to which VE is applied, but requiring them to establish criteria to help managers determine when VE may be suitable.
- Clarifying that documentation must be maintained to explain the basis of waivers and, where VE studies are conducted, the reason for not implementing recommendations made in the studies.
- Emphasizing that VE can be used with acquisition management techniques such as strategic sourcing and modular development.

The complete text for the final revised circular is available on the OMB website.

The *Value Engineering* clause at FAR 52.248-1, with the proper alternate, will be in all supply or service contracts of $150,000 or more. The policies and procedures for value engineering are prescribed in FAR Part 48, *Value Engineering*.

## GOVERNMENT PROPERTY

### Government Property Basics

The management of property owned by the Federal Government, if not done properly, can cause as many problems as any other aspect of contract administration. Due to the hundreds of billions of dollars used to procure and manage the vast amount of Government property in existence, the magnitude of the problem is immeasurable. Both the Government and its contractors have a great responsibility regarding the proper care and handling of all forms of Government property paid for with public funds.

Government property means all property owned by, leased to, or acquired by the Government under the terms of a contract. Government property includes both real and personal property and it may also be tangible or intangible. Tangible property is divided into five separate categories. Those groupings are material, facilities, special tooling, special test equipment and agency-peculiar or personal property. The intangible property must be in some form of data or information supplied under the terms of a contract.

There are two additional ways of classifying Government property. The first is *Government-Furnished Property* in the possession of or acquired directly by the Government. This property is eventually delivered or otherwise made available to a contractor. The second group, *Contractor-Acquired Property*, applies to items procured or otherwise provided by a contractor in performance of a contract, acquired with the use of Government funds. Title to these latter properties also becomes vested in the Government.

Managing Government property is not an easy task. Managing item unique identification descriptions (IUID) and the subject of who has title to property in use by contractors is frequently the cause for a dispute between the Government and its contractors. The source of the funding used in the acquisition is usually the foundation of the dispute. FAR Part 45, *Government Property*, and the clauses at FAR 52.245-1 and 52.245-2, contain the policies and procedures for the use and management of Government property.

Advantages to consider in using Government property may include a reduction in contract costs and the possibility of moving Government equipment from one contractor to another, which would allow multiple contractors to participate in an acquisition, and thus avoid a sole source situation. Contract cost/expense can be reduced, by shifting investment risk from the contractor to the Government. Cost savings can be attributed to the use of items that exist in Government inventory for current and follow-on contracts. Also, in some cases, the Government may be in a better position to purchase production materials at better market prices than a contractor.

The value of IUID in improving asset visibility, maintenance management and financial accountability is becoming increasingly clear. The key to achieving these substantial benefits leading to enhanced support to the warfighter begins with including IUID requirements in contracts in a manner that adheres to standard contract construction policy. This communicates clearly and without ambiguity to both contractor and Government representatives what is required with respect to IUID.

The importance of creating acquisition contracts that are clear, unambiguous, and comprehensive in their IUID requirements cannot be overstated. Individual contract sections should not only clearly communicate IUID requirements respective of their section's content and format, but be written in a manner that provides an improved overall understanding of IUID requirements when all sections are taken together.

## Facilities

Except for specified limited situations, contractors are required to furnish all facilities required for performing Government contracts. The Government will not furnish contractors with new facilities unless existing Government-owned facilities are either inadequate or cannot be furnished economically. A primary example of this is when the facilities are for use in a Government-owned contractor-operated (GOCO) plant, operated on a cost-plus-fee basis. Another exception is for GOCO plants operated in support of industrial preparedness programs.

Government-owned facilities are provided to a contractor or subcontractor only under a facilities contract.

## Material

Material are those items of manufacture consumed during contract performance. Normally contractors are responsible for furnishing all material required in the performance of the contract. Material is furnished to a contractor only when determined to be in the best interest of the Government. That is usually done to effect economy, standardization, expediting production or other appropriate circumstances.

## Special Tooling

The Government policy on special tooling is for contractors to provide it at their own expense. When performing defense contracts, the intent is for contractors to retain title to such special tooling. Special tooling may be provided if it will not disrupt programs of equal or higher priority or if advantageous to the Government.

FAR 2.101 provides the following definition of special tooling:

> "Special tooling" means jigs, dies, fixtures, molds, patterns, taps, gauges, and all components of these items including foundations and similar improvements necessary for installing special tooling, and which are of such a specialized nature that without substantial modification or alteration their use is limited to the development or production of particular supplies or parts thereof or to the performance of particular services. Special tooling does not include material, special test equipment, real property, equipment, machine tools, or similar capital items.

The Government acquires title to special tooling under all cost-reimbursement contracts. Contracting officers have to consider many different criteria before deciding to acquire title to special tooling under fixed-price contracts. The most critical criteria deal with cost of acquisition and cost of ownership once the special tooling is acquired.

When adequate price competition is not present, the Government will usually pay the full cost of special tooling. Title or rights to these items belong to the Government. Contracts authorizing the use of existing special tooling will contain a description of the special tooling and the terms and conditions for its use.

**Special Test Equipment**

It is the policy of the Government to offer existing Government-owned special test equipment to contractors when advantageous to the Government. The same terms and conditions for special tooling apply to special test equipment.

FAR 2.101 provides the following definition for special test equipment:

> "Special test equipment" means either single or multipurpose integrated test units engineered, designed, fabricated, or modified to accomplish special purpose testing in performing a contract. It consists of items or assemblies of equipment including foundations and similar improvements necessary for installing special test equipment, and standard or general purpose items or components that are interconnected and interdependent so as to become a new functional entity for special testing purposes. Special test equipment does not include material, special tooling, real property, and equipment items used for general testing purposes or property that with relatively minor expense can be made suitable for general purpose use.

A contractor desiring to procure additional special test equipment must first notify the contracting officer of the intent to acquire or fabricate items of special test equipment. Within thirty (30) days after receipt of the notice, the contracting officer must take certain actions. Either the CO or the ACO will review the proposed special test equipment items as to their necessity and classification as "special." An agency-wide search is made for existing Government-owned special test equipment available for use on the contract. Finally, the CO will notify the contractor of the Government's approval or disapproval of the proposed acquisition or fabrication. The notification will specifically state when the Government will furnish the equipment, if that is the decision.

**Government Property Provided "As Is"**

At times the Government makes Government owned production and research property available for contractor use on an "as is" basis. This is normally limited to fixed-price, time-and-material and labor-hour contracts, and occasionally to facility contracts. Offerors are advised to carefully inspect the property before submitting their cost proposals. The successful offeror will bear the cost of transporting, installing, modifying, repairing, or otherwise making the property suitable for use.

## Financing Government Property

One provision of the *1987 DOD Appropriations Act (Pub. L. 99-500)* requires contractor participation in financing certain Government property. DOD contractors may be required to finance up to fifty percent (50%) of the cost of special tooling and special test equipment they acquire. This requirement applies to certain negotiated cost-reimbursement production contracts. It applies to production contracts "where the purchase of additional quantities of like items is contemplated in subsequent years." In these contracts the items are designated production special tooling (PST) and production special test equipment (PSTE) when they are to support production rates and quantities. The contractor would not be able to charge more than fifty percent (50%) of the full acquisition cost of the PST or PSTE as a direct cost to the current contract. The remaining costs are amortized over the life of the program. When the financing condition is imposed, the contracting officer will have the discretion to include an indemnification provision in the contract. The provision outlines the amortization schedule for the remaining costs of the PST/PSTE if the contract is terminated for reasons other than the fault of the contractor. In addition, the contracting officer will have the discretion to include a provision in those contracts allowing DOD to take title to the PST and PSTE.

## Consideration for the Use of Government Property

The Government has a firm policy on the usage of Government production and research property in the possession of contractors and subcontractors. That policy is to put such property to the greatest possible use in the performance of Government contracts or subcontracts. However, such use must not confer a competitive advantage on the contractor or subcontractor.

When authorized under the following conditions by the contracting officer, a contractor or subcontractor may use Government production and research property without charge.

- The contract specifically authorizes use without charge;
- The contracting officer having cognizance of the prime contract determines that the Government will receive adequate consideration for the use of the property, either through reduced costs for the supplies or services or some other value; and
- Concurrence is received in the proposed use of any property under the cognizance of another contracting officer.

When rent-free use is not authorized, contractors are charged rent for the use of Government property. Rent is computed in accordance with the *Use and Charges* clause at FAR 52.245-9. When an agency head determines it to be in the Government's interest, rent for certain classes of production and research property (other than plant equipment) may be charged on the basis of use rather than the rental period. In such cases the *Use and Charges* clause would be appropriately modified. The contracting officer with cognizance of the Government property ensures the collection of any rent due the Government.

Contracting officers try to eliminate any competitive advantage afforded contractors by the acquisition or use of Government property. The Government will either charge rent or use rental equivalents in evaluating bids and proposals when a contractor has requested rent free use. However, when certain costs or savings accrue to the Government that would affect the evaluation, the contracting officer may waive the requirement.

### Management of Government Property

Property management is the joint responsibility of the Government agencies and contractors. FAR 45.5, *Support Government Property Administration*, prescribes requirements for establishing and maintaining control over Government property in the possession of and under the control of contractors. Contracts providing for the use or acquisition of Government property, will contain one of the clauses at FAR 52.245-1, *Government Property*, or FAR 52.245-2, *Government Property Installation Operation Services*. FAR 45.107, *Contract Clauses* provides the details for their use.

### Contractor Responsibility

Contractors are responsible for all Government property in their possession or under their control. This includes property provided under their prime contract but actually in the possession or control of a subcontractor. The actual terms and conditions of the prime contract define those responsibilities and obligations. The requirements cited in the prime contract are passed on to subcontractors as appropriate.

Contractors must establish and maintain a property administration system acceptable to the Government. They must maintain records of accountability. DOD contractors use DD Form 1149, *Requisition and Invoice/Shipping Document*, to transfer and show accountability. All Government property must be identified, marked and physically separated from contractor-owned property. The Government and the contractor conduct periodic physical inventories of the property. Any reporting requirements are specified in the contract.

Contractors and subcontractors accept responsibility for the proper care, maintenance and use of Government property in their possession or control. The obligation begins when they take possession of the property. They remain at risk until properly relieved of responsibility under the terms of their contract.

The contractor may be liable for shortages of Government property, or for lost, damaged or destroyed property. Liabilities may occur when there is evidence of unreasonable use or consumption of Government property. Allowances provided for by the terms of the contract, the bill of material or other appropriate criteria are used to measure the scope of that liability. Without Government permission, contractors may not install or construct special tooling or special test equipment on land not owned by the Government in such a manner as to be non-severable.

**Government Responsibility**

The Government is responsible to deliver the property described as Government Property in the contract Schedule. This includes related data and information required for the intended use of such property. The Government warrants that the property will be delivered to the contractor by the dates stated in the Schedule. Even if no dates are stated, delivery must be in time to enable the contractor to meet its contractual delivery or performance dates. The warranty implies that the property will be suitable for use by the contractor for its intended purposes. There is an exception for property furnished on an "as is" basis.

Several things may occur when the Government does not fulfill its obligations. The contracting officer will, when requested by the contractor, adjust the contract for any recognized delay when the property is not delivered or is delivered late.

There are times when a contractor receives property which is not suitable for its intended use. When that happens the contractor must immediately notify the contracting officer. The CO will advise the contractor to return or otherwise dispose of the property at Government expense. When practical, they will authorize the contractor to make repairs or modifications to the property. The contracting officer will then make an equitable adjustment to the contract under the authority of the *Changes* clause.

**Acquisition of Information Technology (*FAR Part 39)***

Acquisition policies and procedures for use in acquiring information technology, including financial management systems, consistent with other parts of the FAR, OMB Circular No. A-127, *Financial Management Systems*, and OMB Circular No. A-130, *Management of Federal Information Resources*, are prescribed in FAR Part 39, *Acquisition of Information Technology.* FAR Part 39 applies to the acquisition of information technology (IT) by or for the use of agencies except for use in the national security systems. Acquisition of IT for those systems must be conducted in accordance with 40 U.S.C. 1412 with regard to requirements for performance and results-based management, the role of the agency Chief Information Officer, in acquisitions and accountability. These requirements are addressed in OMB Circular No. A-130.

In 1996 Congress passed the *Information Technology Management Reform Act (ITMRA), Public Law 104-106, Division E,* which is also known as The Clinger-Cohen Act. The Act established new factors against which federal agencies must review and approve their information technology programs. Those factors include such things as investment considerations, time limits and risk analysis. The Clinger-Cohen Act prompted OMB to revise Circular A-130 to its present state and also the revision of FAR Part 39. The Act requires federal agencies to manage their IT programs as if they were a capital investment.

When acquiring information technology, agencies must identify their requirements giving consideration to security of resources, protection of privacy, national security and emergency preparedness, accommodations for individuals with disabilities, and energy efficiency. When the contracting officers are developing an acquisition strategy they need to consider the rapidly changing nature of IT. That will be accomplished through market research and the application of technology refreshment techniques (*FAR 39.101, Policy*). Because IT changes so rapidly, the Clinger-Cohen Act specifies that any IT contract should be awarded within six months of the solicitation or the competition should be canceled.

Prior to entering into a contract for IT, an agency must analyze the probable risks, benefits, and cost. Types of risk may include situations associated with schedules, technical obsolescence, cost, contract type, technical feasibility, funding and program management. To manage and mitigate risk during the acquisition of IT, the Government must apply techniques such as the use of prudent project management, the use of modular contracting, thorough acquisition planning, continuous "risk management" and prototyping prior to implementation. Contracting, finance and program office officials are jointly responsible for assessing, monitoring and controlling risk when selecting projects for investment and during program implementation (*FAR 39.102, Management of Risk*).

Modular contracting is recommended to be used, to the maximum extent practicable, in the acquisition of major IT systems. Modular contracting is intended to reduce program risk and to incentivize contractor performance while meeting the Government's need for timely access to rapidly changing technology. When using modular contracting, an acquisition of a system of information technology may be divided into several smaller acquisition increments. The characteristics of an increment may vary depending upon the type of IT being acquired and the nature of the system being developed. For each increment, contracting officers must choose an appropriate contracting technique that facilitates the acquisition of subsequent increments (*FAR 39.103, Modular Contracting*).

# QUALITY ASSURANCE

## Contract Quality Control Requirements

The policies and procedures to ensure that supplies and services acquired under a Government contract conform to the contract's quality and quantity requirements are prescribed in FAR Part 46, *Quality Assurance.* Those requirements include the functions of inspection, acceptance, warranty and other measures associated with quality requirements. All Government contracts will have a clause or clauses relating to quality control. The terms quality control and quality assurance are interchangeable.

There are three (3) basic categories of contract coverage for assuring conformance of products and services to contract requirements: *Contractor Inspection, Standard Inspection,* and *Higher-Level Contract Quality Requirements.* The category selected by the contracting officer will depend upon the extent of quality assurance needed by the Government for the acquisition involved.

## Contractor Inspection

The first category, *Contractor Inspection,* will be applied when the Government relies upon the contractor to accomplish all required inspection and testing. This approach is typical of small purchase actions. In those cases the contractor has the responsibility to be sure the deliverable supplies conform to contract quality requirements. In addition, the contractor performs all inspection actions before tendering the items to the Government for acceptance.

The clause, *Contractor Inspection Requirements*, at FAR 52.246-1, normally is used in solicitations and contracts for supplies and services when the contract amount is expected to be at or below the simplified acquisition threshold. Inspection by the contractor will not be relied upon for all small purchases. A different level of inspection is levied if the Government desires to test the supplies in advance of their tender for acceptance. That would also apply when the Government desires to pass upon the adequacy of the contractor's internal work processes (*FAR 46.202-2, Government Reliance on Inspection by Contractor*).

When contracting for commercial items, the Government usually relies on the contractor's existing quality assurance system rather than the Government's inspection and testing before tender by the supplier. If customary market practices for a commercial item being acquired include in-process inspection, the in-process inspection will be conducted in a manner consistent with commercial practice (*FAR 46.202-1, Contracts for Commercial Items*).

Contracting officers consider several factors when determining if contractor inspection requirements adequately protect the Government's interests for a particular contract. The contracting officer will analyze the nature of the supplies and services and their intended use when making a purchase. Another consideration would be the potential losses in event of default and the likelihood of uncontested replacement or correction of defective work. An all important factor is the added cost of performing detailed Government inspections.

### Standard Inspection

Under the second category, *Standard Inspection Requirements*, at FAR 46.202-3, the contractor must provide and maintain an inspection system acceptable to the Government. In addition, the Government gets the right to make inspections and perform tests while work is in process. The contractor must keep complete records of its inspection work and make them available to the Government.

Under the authority of FAR 46.304, *Fixed-Price Service Contracts,* contracting officers will insert the clause at 52.246-4, *Inspection of Services – Fixed-Price,* in solicitations and contracts for services, or supplies that involve the furnishing of services, when a fixed-price contract is contemplated and the contract amount is expected to exceed the simplified acquisition threshold. The contracting officer may insert the clause in such solicitations and contracts when the contract amount is expected to be at or below the simplified acquisition threshold and inclusion is in the Government's interest. When the Government performs inspections or tests on the premises of the contractor or a subcontractor, the contractor must furnish, and require subcontractors to furnish without additional charge, all reasonable facilities and assistance for the safe and convenient performance of those functions.

Standard inspection requirements are used when, for practical reasons, it is desirable to have assurance a contractor's inspection system functions properly. All cost-reimbursement contracts and fixed-price contracts exceeding $10,000 include the standard inspection requirements.

Standard inspection requirements for the various types of contracts are contained in the clauses prescribed in FAR 46.302 through 46.308. Actual clause selection depends upon the type of contract involved and in the product or service specifications and contracts themselves.

### Higher-Level Requirements

The third category is *Higher-Level Contract Quality Requirements,* FAR 46.202-4. Because of particular complex or critical technical requirements, the Government may require that higher-level quality controls be maintained. Those requirements may require "control of such things as work operations, in-process controls, and inspection; or attention to such factors as organization, planning, work instructions, documentation control, and advance metrology." In those cases the standard inspection provisions do not provide enough coverage. The contracting officer will consult technical personnel before establishing these requirements in the contract.

Government specifications have been replaced with references to commercial quality standards as examples of higher-level contract quality requirements. FAR 52.246-11, *Higher-Level Contract Quality Requirement,* contains the details for this level of quality control.

Choice of quality requirements are usually based upon the classification of the contract item (supply or service) as determined by its technical description, its complexity and the criticality of its application. FAR 46.203, *Criteria for Use of Contract Quality Requirements,* describes those criteria which are used on the guide and explained here.

"Technical description" means the items may be technically classified as commercial or military-federal.

The term "complex items" relates to items that have quality characteristics, not wholly visible in the end item, which require progressive contractual conformance. Such conformance may require precise measurements, tests and controls applied during purchasing, manufacturing, performance, assembly and functional operation. They apply those functions either to an individual item or in conjunction with other items. Noncomplex items have quality characteristics for which simple measurement and test of the end item are enough to determine conformance to the contract requirements.

A "critical application" of an item is one in which the failure of the item could injure personnel or jeopardize a vital agency mission. A critical item may be either *peculiar*, meaning it has only one application, or *common*, meaning it has multiple applications. Failure of a "noncritical application" normally would not cause injury to personnel or jeopardize vital missions. Noncritical items may also be either peculiar or common.

**Responsibilities of Contracting Parties**

Contractors are responsible for carrying out their obligations as set forth in the terms and conditions of the contracts and the applicable specifications. They are responsible for controlling product quality and offering to the Government for acceptance, only those supplies or services that conform to contract requirements. When required, a contractor must maintain and furnish substantiating evidence of conformance (*FAR 46.105, Contractor Responsibilities*).

The following list, found in FAR 46.105, are some of the many areas where quality actions and functions apply:

- Manufacturing processes, to ensure that the product is produced to, and meets, the contract's technical requirements.
- Drawings, specifications, and engineering changes, to ensure that manufacturing methods and operations meet the contract's technical requirements.
- Testing and examination, to ensure that practices and equipment provide the means for optimum evaluation of the characteristics subject to inspection.
- Reliability and maintainability assessment (life, endurance, and continued readiness).
- Fabrication and delivery of products, to ensure that only conforming products are tendered to the Government.
- Technical documentation, including drawings, specifications, handbooks, manuals, and other technical publications.

- Preservation, packaging, packing, and marking.
- Procedures and processes for services to ensure that services meet contract performance requirements.

The Government determines the type and extent of Government procurement quality assurance actions to be required on each acquisition. The following are some of the quality assurance actions they may include in a procurement:

- Inspection of supplies and services.
- Review of the contractor's inspection system, quality program, or of any other means employed by the contractor to control quality and comply with contract requirements.
- Maintenance of Government records to reflect actions, deficiencies and corrective measures.
- Review and evaluation of quality information, including reports from the user, to initiate required corrective actions or to adjust Government procurement quality assurance actions.
- Assist the contract administration office (CAO) for the prime contract to determine the prime contractor is ensuring conformance of subcontracted supplies or services with prime contract requirements.
- Perform specialized inspections of supplies before the contractor submits them to the Government for acceptance.

The Government must perform all inspections and tests in a manner that will not unduly delay the work being performed by the contractor. However, the inspector is neither required to inspect the product until it is ready, nor work at the contractor's convenience. If the Government fails to conduct inspections or tests, the contractor is still responsible for furnishing supplies as specified by the contract.

The Government divides the responsibility for quality assurance functions among several activities:

- The technical activity prescribes inspection, testing, or other contract quality requirements essential to a procurement. This is the same group that established the other technical requirements, such as specifications, drawings and standards.
- The purchasing office translates the requirements, prescribed by the technical activity, into contractual requirements. This office also issues Government inspection instructions to the cognizant contract administration office (CAO).
- The CAO performs the Government procurement quality assurance actions assigned by the purchasing office.

Each contract will state the place or places where the Government reserves the right to perform its quality assurance actions. Those are the actions considered necessary to determine that supplies or services conform to contract requirements. FAR 46.4, *Government Contract Quality Assurance*, defines the circumstances or situations that determine where functions are performed. The government normally performs these actions at the source when the contract requires the contractor to establish and maintain an inspection system or a quality program. Normally Government quality actions performed at the destination are limited to inspection of supplies.

**Acceptance of Supplies and Services (*FAR 46.5*)**

The purchasing office assigns the responsibility for acceptance of supplies and services to the activity that also provides the other quality assurance functions for a supplier. Normally that would be the contract administration office (CAO). When an agency uses the inspection and acceptance services of another Government activity or department they will be bound by that organization's decisions.

Acceptance constitutes acknowledgment that the supplies or services conform with applicable contract quality and quantity requirements. Supplies or services will ordinarily be accepted before completion of Government contract quality assurance actions.

Depending upon the provisions of the contract, acceptance may be effected prior to, at the time of, or after delivery. Each contract will specify the place of acceptance for the supplies or services. Contracts that provide for Government contract quality assurance at source ordinarily will also provide for acceptance at source. A contract that provides for quality assurance at destination will ordinarily provide for acceptance at destination. Once supplies are accepted at a point other than destination, reinspection at destination is only for acceptance purposes. However, the receiving agency will examine the supplies for identity, damage in transit, quantity and possible substitution and fraud. Ordinarily acceptance is evidenced by execution of an acceptance certificate or letter. Each agency uses their own form or procedure. Three forms typically used for inspection and receiving are:

- DD Form 250, *Material Inspection and Receiving Report* (Figure 13-2, page 338)
- DD Form 1155, *Order for Supplies or Services*
- Standard Form 44, *Purchase Order-Invoice-Voucher*

In certain instances where the Government may incur small losses from defects in supplies, the contract may be written to include a *Certificate of Conformance* clause at FAR 52.246-15. In those contracts the certificate becomes the sole basis of acceptance. However, this would not prejudice the Government's right to inspect supplies under the inspection provisions of the contract. This technique is also appropriate where knowledge of the contractor's reputation or past performance provides assurance of supply replacement without contest.

# DD FORM 250 – MATERIAL INSPECTION AND RECEIVING REPORT

MATERIAL INSPECTION AND RECEIVING REPORT

*Form Approved*
*OMB No. 0704-0248*

The public reporting burden for this collection of information is estimated to average 20 minutes per response, including the time for reviewing instructions, searching existing data sources, gathering and maintaining the data needed, and completing and reviewing the collection of information. Send comments regarding this burden estimate or any other aspect of this collection of information, including suggestions for reducing the burden, to the Department of Defense, Executive Services and Communications Directorate (0704-0248). Respondents should be aware that notwithstanding any other provision of law, no person shall be subject to any penalty for failing to comply with a collection of information if it does not display a currently valid OMB control number.

PLEASE DO NOT RETURN YOUR COMPLETED FORM TO THE ABOVE ORGANIZATION.
SEND THIS FORM IN ACCORDANCE WITH THE INSTRUCTIONS CONTAINED IN THE DFARS, APPENDIX F-401.

| 1. PROCUREMENT INSTRUMENT IDENTIFICATION (CONTRACT) NO. | ORDER NO | 6. INVOICE NO./DATE | 7. PAGE | OF | 8. ACCEPTANCE POINT |
|---|---|---|---|---|---|
| | | | | | |

| 2. SHIPMENT NO. | 3. DATE SHIPPED | 4. B/L<br><br>TCN | 5. DISCOUNT TERMS |
|---|---|---|---|
| | | | |

| 9. PRIME CONTRACTOR CODE | 10. ADMINISTERED BY CODE |
|---|---|
| 11. SHIPPED FROM *(If other than 9)* CODE FOB: | 12. PAYMENT WILL BE MADE BY CODE |
| 13. SHIPPED TO CODE | 14. MARKED FOR CODE |

| 15. ITEM NO. | 16. STOCK/PART NO. DESCRIPTION *(Indicate number of shipping containers - type of container - container number.)* | 17. QUANTITY SHIP/REC'D* | 18. UNIT | 19. UNIT PRICE | 20. AMOUNT |
|---|---|---|---|---|---|
| | | | | | |

**21. CONTRACT QUALITY ASSURANCE**

**a. ORIGIN**

☐ CQA ☐ ACCEPTANCE of listed items has been made by me or under my supervision and they conform to contract, except as noted herein or on supporting documents.

DATE — SIGNATURE OF AUTHORIZED GOVERNMENT REPRESENTATIVE

TYPED NAME:

TITLE:

MAILING ADDRESS:

COMMERCIAL TELEPHONE NUMBER:

**b. DESTINATION**

☐ CQA ☐ ACCEPTANCE of listed items has been made by me or under my supervision and they conform to contract, except as noted herein or on supporting documents.

DATE — SIGNATURE OF AUTHORIZED GOVERNMENT REPRESENTATIVE

TYPED NAME:

TITLE:

MAILING ADDRESS:

COMMERCIAL TELEPHONE NUMBER:

**22. RECEIVER'S USE**

Quantities shown in column 17 were received in apparent good condition except as noted.

DATE RECEIVED — SIGNATURE OF AUTHORIZED GOVERNMENT REPRESENTATIVE

TYPED NAME:

TITLE:

MAILING ADDRESS:

COMMERCIAL TELEPHONE NUMBER:

* *If quantity received by the Government is the same as quantity shipped, indicate by (X) mark; if different, enter actual quantity received below quantity shipped and encircle.*

**23. CONTRACTOR USE ONLY**

**DD FORM 250, AUG 2000** PREVIOUS EDITION IS OBSOLETE Adobe Professional 8.0

**Figure 13-2**

## Nonconforming Supplies or Services (*FAR 46.407*)

The Government policy is to reject supplies and services not conforming in all aspects to the contract requirements. Normally, rejection will occur when the failure to conform will adversely affect one or more of the following:

- Performance
- Durability
- Reliability
- Interchangeability of parts and assemblies
- Effective use or operations
- Weight or appearance (when they are a factor)
- Health or safety

Whenever practicable within the required delivery schedule, contractors ordinarily will be given the opportunity to correct or replace nonconforming supplies or services, without additional cost to the Government. Such corrections are performed under the terms of the contract and the applicable "Inspection" clause. In some instances, the Government may have the right to charge the contractor for the cost of Government reinspection and retest.

Acceptance by the Government of nonconforming supplies or services is in fact a deviation or waiver from the contractual requirements. The contracting officer may grant a waiver only when it is in the best interest of the Government. Except in cases of minor nonconformance, the contracting officer will modify the contract when accepting nonconforming supplies or services. The modification will provide for an equitable price reduction or other consideration accruing to the Government.

## Title, Risk of Loss and Liability

Title to supplies furnished under a Government contract passes to the Government upon formal acceptance by the Government's agent. An exception to this occurs when a contract clause specifically provides for earlier passage of title. Title will pass regardless of when or where the Government takes possession (*FAR 46.505, Transfer of Title and Risk of Loss*).

Risk of loss or damage to supplies furnished under a Government contract remains with the contractor until one of the following conditions happens. At that time the risk will pass to the Government. Unless some contract clause provides otherwise, title will pass to the Government upon:

- Delivery of the supplies to a carrier, when transportation is f.o.b. origin.

- Acceptance by the Government or delivery of the supplies to the Government at the destination specified in the contract, whichever is later, when the contract designates that transportation is f.o.b. destination.

Contractors are not liable for loss or damage caused by the negligence of officers, agents or employees of the Government acting within the scope of their employment. The Government normally acts as a self-insurer for the loss of or damage to Government property under certain conditions. That applies when loss or damage occurs after acceptance of the supplies delivered to the Government or performance of services for the Government. It also applies when the loss of or damage to property results from any defects or deficiencies in such supplies or services (*FAR 46.803, Policy*).

The above stated policy does not apply, in supply contracts, to the loss of or damage to the contract end item itself. Contractors may be relieved of liability in contracts for high-value items, except when contractor liability can be preserved without increasing the contract price. Another controlling factor is when a clause authorized by the regulations expressly provides for contractor liability.

Except as noted above, or for the procurement of high-value items, the basic *Limitation of Liability* clause at FAR 52.246-23 is inserted in all contracts when the contract amount is expected to be in excess of the simplified acquisition threshold. In contracts requiring the performance of services the clause *Limitation of Liability – Services*, at FAR 52.246-25, will be utilized. These clauses relieve the contractor from liability for loss or damage to Government property, except end items delivered under the contract. The contracting officer, in response to a contractor's specific request, may insert one of these *Limitation of Liability* clauses in a contract at or below the simplified acquisition threshold and obtain any price reduction that is appropriate.

In the procurement of high-value items, the Government normally relieves contractors from liability for loss of or damage to a major item occurring after acceptance. High-value items normally exceed $100,000 in unit cost. They include major items like missiles, aircraft, tanks, ships, aircraft engines and navigational or communication systems. In these cases the *Limitation of Liability – High-Value Items* clause at FAR 52.246-24 is incorporated in the contract. These clauses do not limit the Government's rights otherwise arising under the contract.

In a contract providing for the acquisition of both high-value items and other contract end items, the contracting officer will incorporate both the basic clause at FAR 52.246-23, and *Alternate I* of the clause at FAR 52.246-24.

### Warranties (*FAR 46.7*)

A warranty is a promise or affirmation given by the seller to a purchaser regarding the nature, usefulness or condition of the supplies furnished or services performed. In Government contracts the principal use of warranties is to delineate the rights and obligations of the contractor and the Government for defective items and services. The real goal of a warranty is to foster quality performance (*FAR 46.702, General*).

Warranties normally survive final acceptance of the contract end items. They last for the time or use stated in the contract, or until the occurrence of a specified event. Such warranties take precedence over other contractual provisions concerning acceptance by the Government. They afford the Government additional time in which to assert its right not to receive defective items and services.

Individual agency procedures control the use and approval process for warranties. In deciding whether or not to use a warranty in a specific contract for either supplies or technical data, the contracting officer will consider the following factors:

- The nature of the item and its use.
- The potential benefits expected compared to the cost of the warranty.
- The existence of an adequate administrative reporting system for defective items.
- Customary warranties of the product in the trade.

Typical hardware warranties are not in cost-reimbursement type contracts. There are certain "implied warranties" contained in the *Inspection of Supplies – Cost-Reimbursement* clause at FAR 52.246-3, and the *Inspection of Research and Development – Cost-Reimbursement* clause at FAR 52.246-8. A warranty clause will not limit any rights the Government has under provisions of an inspection clause. This especially applies to rights relating to latent defects, fraud or gross mistakes that amount to fraud.

As far as possible, the warranty clause of a contract should express all the warranties contemplated. During contract formation, ensure that the warranty clause is consistent with all other warranty provisions in the contract. Sometimes there are warranties contained within the specifications.

Warranty clauses for use in contracts for commercial items may require modification or specific detailing to satisfy the peculiar needs of the procurement. In contracts for the repair and replacement of commercial items, contracting officers are advised to take advantage of a contractor's offer of commercial warranties, including extended warranties, where appropriate and in the Government's best interest (*FAR 46.709, Warranties of Commercial Items*). The Government may adopt the contractor's standard commercial warranty. The contracting officer must be sure the provisions are consistent with the rights afforded the Government under the standard warranty clauses or other provisions of the contract.

Warranties must clearly set forth the exact nature of the item, its components, and characteristics that the contractor warrants. The warranty clause must define the extent of the contractor's warranty. The clause must include all of the contractor's obligations to the Government for any breach of the warranty (*FAR 46.706, Warranty Terms and Conditions*). In preparation of the warranty provisions, the contracting officer must consider all of the following guidelines:

- The extent of the contractor's obligations.
- The remedies that are available to the Government.
- The time or duration that the warranty will be in effect.
- The period during which the Government must notify the contractor about the discovery of defective items.
- The requirement for the contractor to stamp or mark items which are under warranty.
- Ensure that the warranty clause and any other warranty provisions in the contract (e.g., in the specifications or an inspection clause) are consistent.

## PROCUREMENT SYSTEMS

One contract management activity that gets considerable attention by the Government is contractor procurement systems. The primary reason these systems receive so much attention is that great sums of federal funds flow through prime contractors to their vendors and subcontractors. Consequently, the Government spends considerable efforts in monitoring the procurement actions of their prime contractors. In this section we will explore three of the most common procurement functions, make-or-buy programs, subcontract management and contractor purchasing system reviews. There is also a discussion of small business subcontracting and teaming arrangements by contractors.

### Make-or-Buy Programs (*FAR 15.407-2*)

Make-or-buy (MOB) programs are important elements of any company's operations. They identify major subsystems, assemblies, subassemblies and components to be manufactured, developed or assembled in the prime contractor's facilities. These are classified as "make" items. A make item is any item produced, or work performed, by the prime contractor or its affiliates, subsidiaries or divisions. The MOB efforts will also identify items that will be acquired by subcontract from other sources. These are classified as "buy" items.

Negotiated procurements may require information concerning prospective contractor make-or-buy programs. When the estimated value of a new program will be $12.5 million or more for a negotiated acquisition requiring certified cost or pricing data, contracting officers may require prospective contractors to submit a make-or-buy program plan.

An exception will be when the proposed contract is for research or development and, if prototypes or hardware are involved, no significant follow-on production is anticipated. When the estimated value will be under $12.5 million, the contracting officer may require a make-or-buy program plan only when it has been determined that the information is necessary and the file is documented with the reasons for that decision (*FAR 15.407-2, Make-or-Buy Programs*).

Information about make-or-buy programs will be confined to items which normally would require company management review of the make-or-buy decision. Those reviews are made because of complexity factors, large quantities, high costs, or the requirement for additional production facilities. As a general guideline, the MOB program should not include items or work effort costing less than one percent (1%) of the total estimated contract price or a minimum dollar amount set by the agency, whichever is less. Normally, MOB plans do not include raw materials, commercial items and off-the-shelf items.

**Make-or-Buy Procedures**

Solicitations must state when contractors are required to submit make-or-buy (MOB) information with their proposals. The request for proposal (RFP) should identify any special MOB factors to be used in evaluating the program. It will also state whether or not the MOB plan will become a contractual requirement.

When formulating a make-or-buy plan, the contractor must take into consideration many factors. Of primary concern is the company's capability to perform the tasks. If capability is not an issue then the next concern is the current plant capacity. In addition, a series of questions need answers. What is the availability of small business concerns as subcontract sources? Should they establish new facilities, and if so, where? What are the current contract schedules and will this project interfere? Does their company have any proprietary processes which will dictate the source? Is there any technical superiority or exclusiveness that should be considered? Finally, what are the technical risks involved?

The contractor's make-or-buy committee or similar group will evaluate the information compiled regarding those factors. Their decisions will be cited in the proposed make-or-buy plan. The plan will identify work that the company considers it or its affiliates, subsidiaries or divisions:

- Must perform as "must make"
- Must subcontract as "must buy"
- Can either perform in-house or acquire by subcontract as "can either make or buy"

The prospective contractor will state the reasons for its recommendations of "must make" or "must buy." Enough detail is provided so the contracting officer can determine that sound business and technical judgment were applied to each major element of the program. The contractor must include the following information about its proposed make-or-buy program.

- A description identifying each major item or work effort.
- A recommendation to make or to buy each item or to defer the decision.
- A recommendation to make or to buy for any "can either make or buy" item.

- Reasons for categorizing items and work efforts as "must make" or "must buy."
- The proposed subcontractors, if known, including location and size classification.
- Designation of the plants or division in which the contractor proposes to make the item, stating whether the existing or proposed new facility is in or near a labor surplus area.
- Sufficient information to permit the contracting officer to evaluate the proposed program.

The Government buys management from the prime contractor along with goods and services. It places responsibility on the contractor to manage programs to the best of its ability. That includes placing and administering subcontracts as necessary to assure performance at the lowest overall cost and technical risk to the Government. Although the Government does not expect to participate in every management decision, it may reserve the right to review the contractor's management efforts, including the proposed make-or-buy program. Part of the MOB review deals with proposed new contractor facilities. The prime contractor will be encouraged to set up any new facility in or near labor surplus areas.

All of the proposed make-or-buy programs should be evaluated and negotiated as soon as practical after receipt of the contractors' proposals. In any event it should be done before contract award or definitization of unpriced actions.

In reviewing and evaluating a proposed make-or-buy program, the contracting officer must assure the plan includes all appropriate items. At the same time the contracting officer should delete inappropriate items. In conducting the review, the contracting officer will seek the advice of personnel whose knowledge would contribute to the adequacy of the review. That support will come from technical and program management personnel, as well as small business specialists.

The review gives primary consideration to the effect the proposed MOB program will have on technical, manufacturing or financial risks. The reviewers give a close look at price, quality, delivery, performance and contemplated types of subcontracts. The contractor has the basic responsibility for the make-or-buy decisions. The contractor's recommendations are usually accepted unless they adversely affect the Government's interests or are inconsistent with Government policy. The evaluation of "must make" and "must buy" items is normally confined to assuring that the items are properly categorized.

Proposed "make" items normally will not be agreed to by the contracting officer when the contractor is not a regular manufacturer or supplier of the products or services under consideration. Such non-concurrence usually occurs when the items are available – quality, quantity, delivery and other essential factors considered – from any other firm at prices no higher than if the contractor should make or provide the products or services. Non-concurrence may also occur when a contractor regularly manufactures or provides the items, but they are available – quality, quantity, delivery and other essential factors considered – from other firms at lower prices. However, concurrence in the make decision may be made if the contracting officer determines that the overall cost of the contract or program to the Government will increase if the item were bought.

**Incorporation of the Make-or-Buy Program into Contracts**

When the solicitation requests make-or-buy (MOB) information, the contract will incorporate the MOB program in negotiated contracts for major systems or their subsystems or components, regardless of contract type. Frequently contracting officers determine that technical or cost risks justify Government review and approval of changes or additions to the MOB program. MOB programs are also incorporated in contracts for other supplies and services. The MOB program can apply to a cost-reimbursement contract, or a cost-sharing contract in which the contractor's share of the cost is less than twenty-five percent (25%). The FAR clause at 52.215-9, *Changes or Additions to Make-or-Buy Program*, is included in all contracts with a MOB program requirement.

Under certain circumstances the Government may approve an item of significant value as "buy" when it would usually be more economical to have it "made" or vice versa. This action only happens when it is in the best interests of the Government. When this occurs in any FPI or CPIF contract, the contract will specifically address those items in the Contract Schedule as either a "make" item or a "buy" item. The clause will specify that such items are subject to the price adjustment provision of the clause if the make-or-buy designation is changed.

**Subcontract Management**

In Government contracting the term "subcontracts" includes purchase orders and the term "subcontractors" includes vendors and suppliers. The Government requires its contractors to carry on the same "buyer-seller" relationship with their subcontractors in the same manner as the Government does with its prime contractors. Prime contractors will:

- Prepare and distribute solicitations to prospective subcontractors;
- Perform source selection and evaluations;
- Make purchase awards or negotiate and award subcontracts; and
- Perform subcontract administration and management.

Prime contractors are responsible for managing their subcontract programs. The government's contract administration office (CAO) normally limits its actions to evaluating the effectiveness of the prime contractor's program management. The contracting officer may call for special treatment of certain high risk or critical subsystems or components under a major system acquisition. Those contracts will require application of special management surveillance in addition to the normal administrative attention and support.

Solicitations for major system acquisitions and other large programs normally require prime contractors to develop Subcontract Management Plans. The plans will describe the working relationship between the contractor's procurement system and the program. Critical or key subcontracts are identified along with specific methods of administrating those subcontracts. Key personnel like subcontract managers, responsible equipment engineers, resident representatives and their respective functions and responsibilities are identified. The Subcontract Management Plan may be a key element in the source selection process. The plan will probably become a contractual requirement, incorporated into the prime contract by reference.

In 2008 a new regulation regarding business ethics for both the prime contractors and their subcontractors was issued. FAR 52.203-13(d) was issued to deal with subcontracts. Contractors are now required to include that clause in all solicitations and subcontracts that have a value in excess of $5,000,000 and have a performance period of performance of more than 120 days. The only exceptions are for the acquisition of commercial items and where performance will be entirely outside the United States.

Under certain circumstances contractors must notify the contracting officer before awarding subcontracts. Prior consent from the contracting officer may also be required before placing certain other subcontracts. Contractors that have an approved purchasing system can be exempted from the prior consent requirement, except when specific contracts requiring consent are identified by the contracting officer. Fixed-price incentive and fixed-price redeterminable contracts are also exempt, as are time-and-material, labor hour and letter contracts under the simplified acquisition threshold. FAR 44.2, *Consent to Subcontracts*, outlines the notification and consent requirements. The appropriate "Subcontract" clauses are found at FAR 52.244-2 and 52.244-4. The clause *Competition in Subcontracting* at FAR 52.244-5 will be included in solicitations and contracts for negotiation over the simplified acquisition threshold, unless the contracting officer contemplates one of the following: (1) a firm-fixed-price contract, awarded on the basis of adequate price competition or whose prices are set by law or regulation; or (2) a time-and-material, labor hour or architect-engineer contract.

The Government is not assuming added responsibility when it consents to a subcontract, or granting relief from the requirement for obtaining consent. Such actions are not a determination by the Government of the acceptability of the subcontract price. To be allowable, costs incurred by the subcontractor will also have to meet the same standards as the prime contract. Furthermore, consent to a subcontract does not constitute approval by the Government of the subcontract terms and conditions.

Even though the Government requires all of the reviews, approvals and other checks, it is still just dealing with the prime contractor. As noted before, the Government does not have a contractual relationship with the subcontractors and vendors. The accepted terminology for this situation is "privity of contract." The buying agency has privity of contract with the prime contractor, but not with that contractor's suppliers. Under some unusual circumstances the Government may become involved directly with the subcontractors and vendors. However, that is a rare occurrence.

With passage of the *1991 Defense Authorization Act (Pub. L. 101-510)*, prime contractors must require each subcontractor to whom they award a contract, in excess of the small purchase limitation, to disclose to the contractor whether the subcontractor is or is not, as of the date of subcontract award, debarred or suspended by the Federal Government from Government contracting or subcontracting. The requirement is being applied government-wide in an attempt to keep debarment and suspension rules and procedures uniform to the extent practicable.

Federal Acquisition Circular 2001-02 amended FAR 44.202-2, *Considerations*, by adding a new preference for the award of subcontracts under service contracts to nonprofit workshops designated by the Committee for Purchase from People Who are Blind or Severely Disabled (*Javits-Wagner-O'Day Act*). The requirement applies to all service contracts and states that: (1) contractors providing services to the federal government who subcontract for those services must give preference in awarding those subcontracts to nonprofit workshops, if those services are listed by the Committee for Purchase from People Who are Blind or Severely Disabled; and (2) contracting officers must consider that preference when reviewing a subcontract for services subject to FAR 44.2, *Consent to Subcontracts*.

**Contractor Purchasing System Reviews**

The Government conducts reviews of contractor purchasing systems under the procedures stated in FAR 44.3, *Contractors' Purchasing Systems Reviews*. The initial review will be performed when sales to the Government are expected to exceed $25,000,000 during the next twelve (12) months. This limitation applies when using other than sealed bid procedures and sales of commercial items pursuant to FAR Part 12, *Acquisition of Commercial Items*. Follow-up reviews of approved systems are conducted as necessary, based on the determination of the contracting officer, but at least every three (3) years.

A contractor purchasing system review (CPSR) will help the Government determine if a contractor's systems and practices provide maximum protection to the Government. The Government seeks to determine if the system conforms to public laws, prime contract clauses and requirements and has sound industrial purchasing practices. A typical review will include an analysis of the company's history and its purchasing organization. It will also cover purchasing policies and procedures, source selection practices, cost or price analysis methods, and the system of subcontract award and administration. Subcontract clauses, terms and conditions are reviewed for compliance with regulations and prime contracts.

The reviews are usually conducted by a team of purchasing systems analysts (PSA). As their title implies, they are specialists in the field. Other Government personnel provide support when needed. They come from such disciplines as contracts administration, small business administration, transportation, property, auditing, production, quality control, packaging, price analysis and legal counsel.

Administrative contracting officers (ACO) may initiate special reviews of approved systems when weaknesses are revealed. Follow-up reviews are made on systems where approval has been withheld or withdrawn. They will be held as soon as evidence is received from the contractor that factors leading to such action have been corrected.

There are several objectives for conducting a CPSR. They provide a means for evaluating the efficiency and effectiveness with which the contractor spends Government funds. They help check on contractor compliance with the Government policies. CPSRs also provide the basis for an ACO to grant, withhold or withdraw approval of the contractor's purchasing system.

The CPSR also provides reliable information to the contracting officer (CO) on the contractor's purchasing system for use in source selection. It is an aid in determining the appropriate type of contract and in establishing profit and fee objectives. The CPSR provides an independent review of the contractor's purchasing system to optimize its effectiveness in following Government policy. In performing a CPSR in accordance with the requirements of FAR 44.303, *Extent of Review*, the following information gets special attention by the analysts.

- The degree of price competition obtained
- Pricing policies and techniques, including methods of obtaining accurate, complete and current certified cost and pricing data, and certifications as required
- The methods of evaluating subcontractors' responsibility
- The treatment accorded affiliates and other concerns having close working arrangements with the contractor
- The extent to which assurance is obtained that the principal subcontractors apply sound pricing practices and a satisfactory purchasing system in dealing with lower tier subcontractors
- The appropriateness of types of subcontracts used
- Practices pertaining to small business concerns, including small disadvantaged, women-owned, veteran-owned, HUBZone, and service-disabled veteran-owned small business concerns
- The management of major subcontract programs
- Compliance with the Cost Accounting Standards in awarding subcontracts
- The evaluation of make-or-buy programs

The cognizant ACO is responsible for granting, continuing, withholding or withdrawing approval of a contractor's purchasing system. The ACO also maintains surveillance of the contractor's system to assure it warrants continued approval.

An approved purchasing system has other advantages to a contractor than just the benefit of having a more effective and efficient operation. In some cases, the contractor receives a waiver of the requirement for advance *written consent* for the *placement* of certain subcontracts and purchase orders. In other cases, the approval may waive the requirement for *advance notification* of the *intent to place* certain subcontracts and purchase orders. An approved purchasing system should be a positive factor in establishing profit or fee objectives.

**Commercial Item Subcontracts**

Contractors and subcontractors at all tiers are required, to the maximum extent practicable, to incorporate commercial items or nondevelopmental items as components of items delivered to the Government. Because of this requirement prime contractors do not need to flow-down all of the procurement related FAR clauses in the prime contract, when procuring such commercial items from its suppliers. FAR 44.4, *Subcontracts for Commercial Items and Commercial Components*, prescribes the policies limiting the contract clauses a prime contractor may be required to apply to any subcontractors that are furnishing commercial items or commercial components.

The clause, *Subcontracts for Commercial Items*, at FAR 52.244-6 will be inserted in solicitations and contracts for supplies and services other than commercial items. Prime contractors will include the terms of that clause in all of their subcontracts. In accordance with that clause, a contractor is not required to include any FAR provision or clause, other than those noted below to the extent they are applicable and may be required to establish the reasonableness of prices, in a subcontract at any tier for commercial items or commercial components.

- 52.203-13, *Contractor Code of Business Ethics and Conduct*
- 52.203-15, *Whistleblower Protections Under the American Recovery and Reinvestment Act of 2009*
- 52.219-8, *Utilization of Small Business Concerns*
- 52.222-26, *Equal Opportunity*
- 52.222-35, *Equal Opportunity for Veterans*
- 52.222-36, *Affirmative Action for Workers with Disabilities*
- 52.222-40, *Notification of Employee Rights Under the National Labor Relations Act*
- 52.222-50, *Combating Trafficking in Persons*
- 52.225-26, *Contractors Performing Private Security Functions Outside the United States*
- 52.232-40, *Providing Accelerated Payments to Small Business Subcontractors*
- 52.247-64, *Preference for Privately Owned U.S.-Flag Commercial Vessels*

**The Small Business Subcontracting Program (*FAR 19.7*)**

It is the Government's policy to place a fair proportion of its acquisitions with small business concerns and small disadvantaged business concerns. It is also the policy that those concerns have the maximum practicable opportunity to participate as subcontractors in the contracts awarded by any executive agency. All of this must be consistent with efficient contract performance. The Small Business Administration (SBA) counsels and assists small business concerns. They also help contracting personnel ensure placement of a fair proportion of contracts for supplies and services with small businesses. FAR 19.7, *The Small Business Subcontracting Program*, contains the requirements for subcontracting within the framework of this policy.

Any contractor that receives a contract for more than the simplified acquisition threshold is agreeing to support the Government's small business goals. The contractor agrees that small business, veteran-owned small business, service-disabled veteran-owned small business, HUBZone small business, small disadvantaged business, and women-owned small business concerns will have the maximum practicable opportunity to participate in performance of the contract. All of this must be consistent with efficient contract performance (*FAR 19.702, Statutory Requirements*).

To be eligible for award of a Government contract exceeding $650,000 with subcontracting possibilities an offeror/bidder must submit a subcontracting plan acceptable to the contracting officer. The threshold for construction contracts is $1,500,000. Subcontracting plans are not required: (1) from small business concerns; (2) for personal service contracts; (3) for contracts or contract modifications to be performed entirely outside the U.S. and its outlying areas; or (4) for modifications to contracts that do not contain the clause 52.219-8, *Utilization of Small Business Concerns*.

Plans are required in contracts containing the clause at FAR 52.219-9, *Small Business Subcontracting Plan* or its *Alternate I.* One significant element of the plan will be the small business, veteran-owned small business, service-disabled veteran-owned small business, HUBZone small business, small disadvantaged business, and women-owned small business goals proposed by the contractor. The prime contractor/offeror's plan must include all subcontracts that contribute to contract performance. The goals are expressed as dollar volume or a percentage of the total anticipated subcontracting efforts. They must be realistic because they could become contractual requirements. After award, any contract modification of the same magnitude noted above will require the contractor to submit an updated subcontracting plan. The clause at 52.219-8, *Utilization of Small Business Concerns*, will be inserted in all contracts falling within the requirements of the regulation. Any contractor or subcontractor failing to comply in good faith with the requirements of its approved subcontracting plan will be in material breach of its contract.

Contracting officers may encourage the development of increased subcontracting opportunities in a negotiated acquisition by providing monetary incentives to the contractor. The inclusion of the clause, *Incentive Subcontracting Program*, at FAR 52.219-10 will be inserted in the contract to authorize the action. Any such incentive provision based upon rewarding the contractor monetarily for exceeding goals in the subcontracting plan must ensure the plan's goals are realistic and the rewards are commensurate with the efforts the contractor would not have otherwise expended. Incentive provisions should be negotiated after full agreement on the subcontracting plan has been reached.

The importance of the small business/small disadvantaged business plan and its goals was increased by *The Business Opportunity Development Reform Act of 1988, Pub.L. 100-656*. The Act requires the payment of liquidated damages to the Government by contractors who, through a lack of good faith, fail to meet the small business plan goals contained in their contracts. "Failure to make a good faith effort to comply with the subcontracting plan" means, "willful or intentional failure to perform in accordance with the requirements of the subcontracting plan, or willful or intentional action to frustrate the plan." (*FAR 19.701, Definitions*)

Liquidated damages are imposed only where a failure of good faith efforts are found. Damages are not imposed for failure to meet the goals. The measure of liquidated damages is the difference between the contract goal and the amount of the subcontracting actually achieved. Any unfavorable decision by the contracting officer is appealable under the *Contracts Disputes Act*. When a solicitation or contract contains FAR clause 52.219-9 noted above, the contracting officer will also insert the clause at 52.219-16, *Liquidated Damages – Subcontracting Plan*.

**Teaming Agreements**

When two or more organizations choose to work closely together in pursuit of a federal program they frequently form teams. To seal their commitments to each other they will execute quasi-contractual documents called teaming agreements. The agreements will designate which organization will act as the prime contractor and which will be first tier subcontractors. Other matters addressed in the agreements include the division of work, resources each party will contribute, and the effective period of the agreement. In technology projects the agreement will describe procedures for protecting each other's proprietary information.

Teaming agreements offer numerous potential benefits both to the Government and to contractors. From the Government's standpoint, teaming by contractors can reduce the total cost of a procurement by increasing the competitive strength of the proposals it receives in response to solicitations. From the contractor's standpoint, teaming offers three principal potential benefits. It permits contractors to pool their technical resources, which will enhance their competitive position. Teaming may enable a contractor to compete and perform on procurements where otherwise they might not have been eligible. A teaming arrangement may provide an opportunity for a contractor to develop expertise and products that will help it secure a market niche in future procurements.

Normally, teaming agreements expire upon award of a subcontract by the prime contractor. The superseding subcontract reflects the program requirements as awarded by the Government and the efforts divided among the team members.

Teaming agreements are not the same as joint ventures. Joint venture partners normally establish a business organization that has a limited life, such as the length of the programs they are pursuing. Their relationship is more formal and will address all aspects of their business arrangement, including the sharing of profits and losses.

# CHAPTER 14

# DATA, PATENTS AND COPYRIGHTS

## OVERVIEW

Three of the most misunderstood and disputed aspects of federal contracting are the rights contracting parties have to data, patents and copyrights conceived and developed under a Government contract. In this chapter we will address the issues of data management, data rights, data retention, proprietary data, patents, copyrights and royalties.

There has been much debate on the subjects of data, patents and copyrights and how they are to be addressed in federal procurements. The eternal question is, "Who should have the rights to them and to what extent?" This chapter will not try to resolve the issue; only provide a discussion of the current requirements. Resolution of that knotty problem will be left to the governing bodies.

## DATA MANAGEMENT

### Data Requirements

Data means recorded information, regardless of form, or the media on which it may be recorded, and includes technical data and computer software. The terms, as they relate to the Government's rights in data, do not include information incidental to contract administration. The latter includes data like contract cost analyses or financial, business and management information. However that type of data often is deliverable under the contract *(FAR 27.401, Definitions)*. The Federal Acquisition Regulation (FAR) and Defense Federal Acquisition Regulation Supplement (DFARS) have basically the same definitions for "technical data."

Some provision of the contract must specify the technical data or computer software a contractor will deliver to the Government. Deliverable data requirements are found in a contract data requirements list (CDRL), a line item in the contract or in the statement of work. The method used depends upon the individual federal agency.

In addition to the contractually deliverable data, many contract clauses require contractors to furnish the Government with administrative type information. What data is required and its delivery date depend upon the nature of the contract, federal socioeconomic policies or specific events that occur during the life of the contract. Chapter 11, *Contract Documentation*, shows examples of such data.

Use of a data requirements list, such as the DD Form 1423 (Figure 11-4, page 262) or the NASA "Data Procurement Document," helps Government agencies achieve their data acquisition goals. Some of the more important objectives are as follows:

- To acquire most economically the minimum amount of data needed to procure and support systems, material and services.
- To assure the acquisition of required data on time to serve its intended purpose.
- To establish data requirements on the basis of needs in an agency's management, engineering and logistics functions and to fulfill these needs on the basis of cost-effectiveness analyses.
- To specify data requirements in solicitations with enough detail to provide for full, clear and firm understanding between the contracting parties of the total data requirements at the time the contract is placed. This requirement may be satisfied by a contractual provision for the right to defer the selection, ordering or delivery of technical data specified in the contract.
- To provide competent administration of contracts requiring the furnishing of data, and assure that all contract provisions regarding data are fully satisfied.
- To maintain quality assurance procedures in the acquisition of data to assure the adequacy of the data for its intended purpose.
- To provide for the continued currency of acquired data in consonance with requirements.
- To prevent the acquisition of duplicate or overlapping data pertaining to material, systems or services and avoid data which would serve the same end, has been or is being acquired by the Government from the same or other contractors.

It is not always possible to define the total data requirements before a contract begins. This is especially the case with technical data and computer software in development programs pursuing the state-of-the-art. Therefore, in certain defense contracts the contracting officer (CO) will use deferred ordering and deferred delivery provisions in those contracts (*DFARS 227.7103-8, Deferred Delivery and Deferred Ordering of Technical Data*).

Deferred ordering is the situation where the Government may require technical data or computer software, but the precise need has not been determined. To reserve this option, the contracting officer will incorporate the *Deferred Ordering of Technical Data or Computer Software* clause at DFARS 252.227-7027 in the solicitation and resulting contract. In addition to technical data and computer software ordered under other provisions, the clause permits contracting officers to order data from time to time during contract performance or within three (3) years after acceptance of all deliverable items, except technical data or computer software. When the data or computer software is ordered, the parties will negotiate the delivery dates. Also, the Government will compensate the contractor for converting the technical data or software into the prescribed form. Compensation will not include the cost of the information which has already been paid for by the Government. Subcontractor obligations under this requirement expire three (3) years after the date the prime contractor accepts the last item under the subcontract.

Deferred delivery situations occur when the Government can identify needed technical data in a defense contract but not the time of its delivery. The clause *Deferred Delivery of Technical Data or Computer Software* at DFARS 252.227-7026 will be contained in the solicitation and resulting contract. The contracting officer may request delivery of the previously identified technical data from time to time during performance of the contract. In addition, the request can be made at any time within two (2) years after acceptance by the Government of all items under the contract, other than technical data or computer software. Subcontractor and supplier delivery requirements are the same as the prime contractor. A contract must specify which technical data or computer software is subject to deferred delivery. Contracting officers must provide sufficient notice to permit timely delivery of the data or software. The total contract value includes the price for these items. Therefore, the contractor will not receive any additional compensation.

There is no restriction on changing the contract deliverable data requirements during the life of the contract. Such changes are possible as long as the parties can arrive at an equitable adjustment to the contract.

## RIGHTS IN DATA

Both the Government and industry have specific and valid interests in data. The Government has extensive needs for many kinds of technical data. It exerts its authority to acquire data and the rights to that data in nearly all of its contracts. Its needs may well exceed those of private commercial contractors. Contractors have a valid economic interest in data pertaining to items, components or processes which they have developed at their own expense. They resist disclosure of information to competitors that would jeopardize their competitive advantage. Therefore, each contractual arrangement should contain provisions for balancing the Government's requirements for data against the contractor's interest in protecting data considered to be proprietary.

### Terminology and Definitions

There are three levels of data rights that the Government has at its disposal to protect its interests. The three are *unlimited, limited* and *restricted* rights. The following paragraphs provide explanations of those rights and their applications to Government contracts. FAR 27.401, *Definitions*, provides the basic definitions for the various terms used to describe data and data rights.

- *Unlimited rights* means "the rights of the Government to use, disclose, reproduce, prepare derivative works, distribute copies to the public, and perform publicly and display publicly, in any manner and for any purpose, and to have or permit others to do so.
- *Limited rights* means "the rights of the Government in limited rights data as set forth in a Limited Rights Notice.

- *Limited rights data* means "data, other than computer software, that embody trade secrets or are commercial or financial and confidential or privileged, to the extent that such data pertain to items, components, or processes developed at private expense, including minor modifications.
- *Restricted rights* means "the rights of the Government in restricted computer software as set forth in a Restricted Rights Notice.
- *Restricted computer software* means "computer software developed at private expense and that is a trade secret, is commercial or financial and confidential or privileged, or is copyrighted computer software, including minor modifications of the computer software.

Data which has been developed at "private expense" has not been paid for in whole or part by the Government. Likewise, neither was the effort performed in connection with the development of an item, component, or process relating to the data. Furthermore, such development was not a requirement of a Government contract or subcontract, and was not necessary for performance of a Government contract or subcontract.

The Government considers independent research and development and bid and proposal costs contractor expenditures. Therefore, contractor efforts using those funds are "at contractor expense" and booked in accordance with the contractor's accepted accounting practices.

**Intellectual Property**

A great deal of attention is being focused on the form of data categorized as "intellectual property." Intellectual property is primarily some form of technical data, such as copyrights, trademarks, trade secrets, computer software and of course the patents related to inventions. This chapter addresses the significant policies relating to data of all types, including intellectual property.

**Government Policy on Data Rights**

The Government's basic policy is to acquire only such technical data and data rights essential to meet its needs in carrying out its missions and programs. FAR 27.4, *Rights in Data and Copyrights,* specifies the policies, procedures and instructions regarding rights in data and copyrights. The subpart also addresses the acquisition of data for all civilian agencies and NASA. Department of Defense policies, procedures and instructions for those subjects are cited in Defense Federal Acquisition Regulation Supplement (DFARS) Subpart 227.4, *Rights in Data and Copyrights*. The Department of Defense has taken the position that it's contracting officers have the authority, through DFARS 227.7102-1, *Policy*, to buy additional technical data for form, fit, and function, technical data for repair and maintenance, and data to support commercial item or process modifications at Government expense. This is an exception to the general FAR prohibition for such action. Under FAR 27.4, *Rights in Data and Copyrights*, contracting officers are limited to using only the data that has been publicly released by their contractors, such as advertising, when purchasing commercial items.

It is important to keep in mind that the rights-in-data clauses help the Government and not the contractors. Contractors must continue to be alert, throughout the life of their contracts and even afterward, to protect the data already developed at their own private expense, to prevent disclosure of that data to their competitors.

The source of funds used in developing data dictates the type of data rights clause to be used in a contract. When the Government funds the entire development of an item, component or process, the Government is entitled to and will normally obtain unlimited rights in the technical data. The situation is different for data used in performance of a contract but developed by a contractor or subcontractor exclusively at private expense. Then the Government is entitled to limited rights to that data. When the Government only partially funds that development, it may still have entitlement to unlimited rights in the technical data. However, if the contracting officer determines that unlimited rights are not required and the contractor contributes to the development costs, then the Government obtains Government Purpose License Rights. This is accomplished by tailoring the Government's rights to the technical data by negotiation with the contractor. The negotiation results are specified in the contract. The same rights are obtained if the contractor is a small business firm or nonprofit organization that agrees to commercialize the technology.

The Government usually has **unlimited rights** to data it acquires in the following situations:

- Data resulting directly from performance of experimental, developmental or research work specified as an element of performance in a Government contract or subcontract.
- Data necessary to enable others to manufacture end-items, components and make modifications. An exception applies to data for items, components or processes developed at private expense.
- Data prepared or deliverable under any Government contract or subcontract and constituting corrections or changes to government-furnished data.
- Data about end-items, components or processes, prepared or deliverable under any Government contract or subcontract, to identifying sources, size, configuration, mating and attachment characteristics and performance requirements. This is known as "form, fit and function" data. This class of data includes items like specifications, control drawings, catalog sheets, and envelope drawings.
- Manuals or instructional materials prepared or deliverable under a Government contract or subcontract for installation, operation, maintenance or training purposes.
- Data which is in the public domain. Data that has been or is normally released or disclosed by the contractor or subcontractor without restriction or further disclosure.

The Government obtains **limited rights** to data so specified in the Schedule of the contract. That listing is based upon a mutual agreement of the parties prior to contract award. These limited rights apply to unpublished data about items, components or processes developed at private expense. Limited rights also apply to computer software documentation related to computer software acquired with restricted rights.

The limited rights protection will be effective only if the data, to which limited rights are asserted, are suitably identified and marked by the contractor. To properly mark the data use the notice specified in either the clause at FAR 52.227-14, *Rights in Data – General*, or DFARS 252.227-7013, *Rights in Technical Data – Noncommercial Items*.

The Department of Defense (DOD) has more extensive regulations in the DFARS on rights in technical data and computer software than the FAR. DOD's regulations cover both commercial and non-commercial items. In addition, the DFARS contains an additional category on data rights – *Government Purpose Rights, DFARS 227.7103-5(b)*.

The Government obtains restricted rights in computer software. The contract may list the restricted computer software or reference a license or agreement identifying data with restricted rights. In addition, the contractor must mark the software with the notice specified for such restricted rights in the above cited clause.

Whenever possible, but ideally before contract award, the offeror should identify data it intends to deliver with limited rights. If the Government is willing to accept such data with limited rights, the contract will contain information defining the arrangement. This procedure is referred to as predetermination of rights in data. Solicitations normally permit offerors to identify in advance those data items that they intend to deliver with limited rights. The Government may desire to acquire unlimited rights in such limited rights data. One way of doing that is by negotiation with an individual contractor or subcontractor. Another way is by stating unlimited rights are required during a competition among several contractors or subcontractors. However, data delivery requirements should not normally require that a contractor provide the Government, as a condition of the procurement, unlimited rights in data that qualify as limited rights data or restricted computer software. However, form, fit or function data may be furnished with unlimited rights in lieu of the qualifying data. When greater rights are needed such need must be clearly set forth in the solicitation and the contractor fairly compensated for those greater rights.

Department of Defense contractors must satisfy their contractual obligations to the Government while ensuring that the rights afforded subcontractors are recognized and protected. To meet these obligations, prime contractors will include the DFARS clauses 252.227-7013, *Rights in Technical Data – Noncommercial Items*, and 252.227-7037, *Validation of Restrictive Markings on Technical Data*. A subcontractor with the right to furnish technical data with limited rights may furnish such data directly to the Government rather than through the prime contractor. Prime contractors and higher-tier subcontractors cannot use their power to award subcontracts as economic leverage to acquire rights for themselves of their subcontractor's data.

**Protection of Proprietary Data**

The Government and its employees have the responsibility to protect data acquired with limited rights or of a similarly proprietary nature. The terms of the contract must recognize the acquisition of data with limited rights. However, the data must be clearly and adequately marked as proprietary to gain the proper protection. Government employees are subject to criminal liability under 18 U.S.C. 1905 (1964) for the unlawful disclosure of proprietary information:

> Whoever, being an officer or employee of the United States or of any department or agency thereof, publishes, divulges, discloses, or makes known in any manner or to any extent not authorized by law any information coming to him in the course of his employment or official duties or by reason of any examination or investigation made by, or return, report or record made to or filed with, such department or agency or officer or employee thereof, which information concerns or relates to the trade secrets, processes, operations, style of work, or apparatus, or to the identity, confidential statistical data, amount or source of any income return or copy thereof or any book containing any abstract or particulars thereof to be seen or examined by any person except as provided by law; shall be fined not more than $1,000, or imprisoned not more than one year, or both; and shall be removed from office or employment. (62 Stat.791).

As the technical complexity of the Government's programs escalate it is becoming increasingly common for many contractors to work together in teaming arrangements or joint ventures on a single project. In other programs they would still be competitors. When this occurs, it may be necessary for them to execute a written agreement that they will protect each other's proprietary data as if it were their own. They will further agree not to use such data except in performance of that contract or project. The Government may become an "interested third party" to such an arrangement by virtue of a contract with one of the companies. It may require the contractor to submit a copy of the agreement to the contracting officer for inclusion in the contract file. This is frequently the case when a contractor will be performing the role of a systems engineering, integration and technical direction contractor.

**Data Retention**

Contractors and subcontractors must retain and make available to the Government certain books, records, documents and other supporting evidence of a technical or management nature. The terms and conditions of each contract contain its peculiar data retention requirements. FAR 4.7, *Contractor Records Retention*, provides the policies and procedures for retention of records by contractors to meet the Government's records review requirements. The Code of Federal Regulations, Volume 33, Number 42 of the *Federal Registe*r contains a *Guide to Record Retention Requirements Title 1, Appendix A*. This is a ready reference of the retention requirements for the various Governmental agencies.

Under the deferred ordering requirements in DFARS 252.227-7027, *Deferred Ordering of Technical Data or Computer Software*, contractors must retain data for three (3) years after Government acceptance of all deliverable items, except technical data and computer software delivered under the contract. Compliance with the deferred delivery requirements in DFARS 252.227-7026, *Deferred Delivery of Technical Data or Computer Software*, requires the retention of that data for a two (2) year period.

As a minimum, contractors must retain their management records until the expiration of three (3) years after final payment under a contract. Financial, cost accounting, payroll, acquisition and supply records must be retained for at least four (4) years after the completion of the contract, unless contract performance is the subject of enforcement action (*FAR 4.705-2, Pay Administration Records*). Data about warranties, limitations of liabilities and indemnification for hazardous risks, also require longer retention periods. Each such requirement will be identified in a contract clause. If the required information is maintained on a computer, contractors must retain the computer data on a reliable medium for the time periods prescribed in the FAR and DFARS.

Government contractors must make their records available for audit and examination by authorized Government agents in order to comply with one of the following FAR clauses:

- 52.214-26, *Audit and Records – Sealed Bidding*
- 52.215-2, *Audit and Records – Negotiation*

## PATENTS, COPYRIGHTS AND ROYALTIES

### Principles of Proprietary Rights

One basic standard of a free society such as ours is the right of protection for proprietary property and information. The proprietary rights are those an owner of property has by virtue of his or her ownership. To claim ownership and seek the proper protection, the owner of the property must take certain actions. There are four basic methods of protecting proprietary property. The first three – patents, copyrights and trademarks – require overt public action on the part of the owner. The fourth – trade secrets – requires the owner to avoid any public disclosure for protection.

### Patents

A patent is an agreement between an inventor and the Government in which the inventor agrees to disclose the invention to the public. In exchange, the Government agrees to give the inventor the right to exclude all others from using the invention for twenty (20) years.

The right to patent inventions has its origin in the U.S. Constitution, Article I, Section 8, which gives Congress the power:

> to promote the progress of science and the useful art by securing, for a limited time, to authors and inventors the exclusive rights to their respective writings and discoveries.

Based upon that Constitutional article, the U.S. Patent Law was created. Title 35, Section 1101 of that law states that: "Whoever invents or discovers any new and useful process, machine, manufacture, or composition of any matter, or any new and useful improvements thereof, may obtain a patent therefore..."

The statute implementing the constitutional authority is 34 U.S.C. 101. That statute defines six classes of inventions that can be patented, which are:

- Processes (methods)
- Apparatus (machines, electrical devices or circuits)
- Articles of manufacture
- Composition of matter (chemical)
- Ornamental designs
- Plants

**Trade Secrets**

Black's Law Dictionary defines a trade secret as:

> A plan or process, tool, mechanism, or compound known only to its owner and those of his employees to whom it is necessary to confide.

Another definition is found in the *Uniform Trade Secrets Act, 14 U.L.A. 437 (1990)*:

> A "trade secret" is information that derives independent economic value from not being generally known to, and not readily ascertainable by, other persons who can obtain economic value from its disclosure or use and which is subject to efforts that are reasonable under circumstances to maintain secrecy.

The nature of legal protection given trade secrets is substantially different from that afforded patents. To start with, the basis for the legal protection of a trade secret is the common law rather than statutes or the Constitution.

A trade secret loses it legal protection through disclosure of the information by public communication. It may also be lost by release of a product on the market whereby someone can find out the secret. Therefore, secrecy must be maintained to preserve legal rights in the trade secret.

The Government may be held accountable for the improper disclosure of a trade secret by a Government employee. Action may be brought in a federal court under the authority of the *Federal Torts Claims Act, 28 U.S.C. 1346.*

Information typically classified as a trade secret includes customer lists, marketing and sales plans, cost and pricing data, inventions, new products under development, and source codes of proprietary software.

**Copyrights**

A copyright is the right to prevent others from copying the "form of expression" used by the creator of certain types of work. Material subject to copyrighting includes written works such as books, poems, and magazine articles, works of art, musical compositions, photographs and motion pictures. A copyright exists at the time of creation, whether or not registered with the Copyright Office.

The basic copyright statute was created by the *Copyright Act of 1976.* It provides the owner of a copyright with the following five exclusive rights: (1) reproduction of copyrighted work; (2) preparation of derivative works based on the original; (3) distribution of the work; (4) performance of the work publicly; and (5) displaying the work in public.

In 1978 the U.S. copyright law extended the term of a copyright for the life of the creator plus fifty years. The law lists factors which are considered in determining what constitutes "fair use" of the work. It considers the purpose and character of the use, the nature of the copyrighted work, the amount of copying and the effect of the use upon the potential market for the copyrighted work.

**Trademarks**

The term "trademark" refers to a distinctive word, form of words, motto, device, emblem, mark or symbol. Trademarks are used to identify a source of goods or services that distinguish them from those of others. They include marks affixed to goods, service marks, collective or organizational marks and certification marks. Organizations wishing to retain the exclusive right to use their trademark must register it as soon as possible. First use of such a mark can have a significant impact on who has that right.

The original statute on this matter was the *Trademarks Registration Act of 1875*. That Act provided for the establishment of a register of trademarks in the Patents Office. It further provided for the registration of trademarks as belonging to particular classes of goods.

## Patent Policy

The *Presidential Memorandum on Government Patent Policy to the Heads of Executive Departments and Agencies,* dated February 18, 1983, set the Government's basic patent policy. FAR 27.3, *Patent Rights under Government Contracts*, is the regulation that carries out the policy.

The Federal Government's stated patent objectives are:

- To use the patent system to promote the use of inventions arising from federally supported research and development;
- Encourage maximum participation of industry in federally supported research and development efforts;
- Ensure that these inventions are used in a manner to promote free competition and enterprise without unduly encumbering future research and discovery;
- Promote the commercialization and public availability of the inventions made in the United States by United States industry and labor;
- Ensure that the Government obtains sufficient rights in federally supported inventions to meet the needs of the Government and protect the public against nonuse or unreasonable use of inventions; and
- Minimize the costs of administering patent policies.

A contractor may, after disclosure to the Government, choose to retain title to any invention made in the course of or in the performance of work under a contract. This is permissible unless otherwise prevented by a provision in the contract. In most cases the Government will have a nonexclusive, nontransferable, irrevocable, paid-up license to practice the invention throughout the world. The right also permits the Government to have the invention practiced for or on behalf of the United States by a third party. These rights exist even when a contractor elects retention rights. In addition, if provided in the contract, the Government may have the right to sub-license the invention to any foreign Government or international organization pursuant to a treaty or agreement.

After the determination that one or more of the following conditions exists, the Government may receive the right to any inventions conceived during a contract.

- The contract is for operation of a government-owned research or production facility;
- An exceptional circumstance exists which will promote the policy and objectives of the Presidential Memorandum;
- It is essential to protect the security of foreign intelligence or counterintelligence activities;
- The contractor has not disclosed the invention within the time specified in the contract; or
- The contractor has relinquished or failed to pursue its rights in any country.

When a proposed effort is for experimental, developmental or research work, and will be performed in the United States or its possessions, the contract will include the following clause: *Patent Rights – Ownership by the Contractor* at FAR 52.227-11. It is also used in contracts where the public interest in the availability of inventions is best served by permitting the contractor to acquire greater rights than a nonexclusive license.

When those conditions do not exist, the contracting officer will insert into the contract the clause, *Patent Rights – Ownership by the Government* at FAR 52.227-13.

The above noted clauses require contractors to provide the Government with a written disclosure of each invention. The patent clause requires notice from the contractor within two (2) months after the inventor discloses it in writing to the company. As an alternative the notice may be given within six (6) months after the contractor becomes aware that a subject invention had been made. Also interim annual reports must be submitted listing all inventions not previously reported. The contractor will submit a final report before final settlement of the contract. The final report lists all inventions whether or not previously reported.

The interim and final reports are submitted on DD Form 882, *Report of Inventions and Subcontracts.* A follow-up system is maintained by the Government to assure identification of inventions to establish and protect its rights.

**Copyright Assignment**

Engineers and scientists frequently write scientific and technical articles based on the work performed under Government contracts. Those articles then get published in academic or technical journals. Normally, contractors who employ the writers of those articles have the right to establish claim to copyright the article under FAR 52.227-14, *Rights in Data – General.* However, their contract may specify certain limitations on release and use which could supersede that right. Contractors must obtain approval to establish the claim to copyright. Approval may require the work be submitted for agency review before publishing the work.

Copyrighted material must not be incorporated in deliverable contract data, unless first produced under the contract. The contracting officer may grant exceptions if the contractor requests permission. Exceptions are also authorized when the contractor grants the Government unlimited rights to the data.

In certain contracts the Government may acquire the right to obtain assignment of copyright from the contractor. FAR 27.404-3, *Copyrighted Works*, and FAR 27.404-4, *Contractor's Release, Publication, and Use of Data*, provide the specific details on how copyrighted data assignments will be made on Government contracts.

## Royalties

Patent holders receive royalties for granting others the authority and privilege of using the subject matter of the patent. The requirement to pay a royalty imposes added obligations on Government contractors. In negotiated procurements, contractors must provide royalty information and reports to the Government. Royalty information is not required in sealed bid contracts unless the need for such information is approved at a level above that of the contracting officer as being necessary for proper protection of the Government's interests. The Government agencies use the information received to determine whether royalties anticipated or actually paid are excessive, improper or inconsistent. They compare the royalties with rights which the Government may already have in particular inventions, patents or patent applications (*FAR 27.202-1, Reporting of Royalties*).

In certain situations it may be questionable whether or not the contractor or its subcontractors will have to pay substantial amounts of royalties. When negotiating a fixed-price contract under those conditions the target or contract price may include the royalties. However, if the royalties are not paid, a provision in the contract will require reimbursement to the Government of the unpaid amount. Contractors must furnish to the contracting officer, before final payment under their contract, a statement of royalties paid or required to be paid in connection with performing the contract and its subcontracts. After complying with the royalty statement requirement, the contractor will be compensated for royalties reported, to the extent that the royalties were included in the contract price. Furthermore, the contracting officer must determine that they were properly chargeable to the Government and allowable under the contract (*FAR 27.202-4, Refund of Royalties*).

Contracting officers (CO) will take prompt action when there is reason to believe that any royalties are inconsistent with Government rights, excessive or otherwise improper. The CO will report the facts to the office having cognizance of patent matters for the procuring activity concerned. In coordination with the contracting officer that office will take prompt action to protect the Government. A major concern is the possible payment of royalties on supplies or services where the Government has royalty-free license. There is also protection against royalties that are at a rate more than the Government's license rate, or royalties that are, either in whole or in part, an improper charge.

When appropriate, an agency may get a refund or enter into negotiation for a reduction of the contract value applicable to the unpaid royalties. The authority for this action is found in the *Refund of Royalties* clause at FAR 52.227-9.

# PATENT INFRINGEMENT

Infringement of patents held by other parties is a civil offense. The normal recourse in the commercial world is for the patent holder to seek an injunction against the offending party from further use of the patented item. In addition to the injunction the patent holder will file suit and seek damages from the infringing party. These legal proceedings will all be processed through the civil court system.

In the world of Government contracts the matter of patent infringement is significantly different from the commercial environment. Under 28 U.S.C. 1498, any infringement of a United States patent that occurs in connection with a federal contract falls under a completely different set of rules. The statute covers those cases where the Government has authorized or consented to the manufacture or use of a patented invention. The patent holder will bring an infringement claim only against the Government. The claim must be based on the manufacture or use by or for the United States of an invention described in and covered by a patent of the United States. The claim is filed in the U.S. Claims Court against the Federal Government and not against either the contractor or subcontractor (*FAR 27.201, Patent and Copyright Infringement Liability*).

## Authorization and Consent

In support of 28 U.S.C. 1498, contracts for supplies and services will contain the *Authorization and Consent* clause at FAR 52.227-1. Contracts for experimental, developmental or research work, or where that is the primary purpose of the contract will include Alternate I to FAR 52.227-1. The purpose of these clauses is for the Government to give its authorization and consent to its contractors and their subcontractors for the use and manufacture of any invention described in or covered by a U.S. patent in the performance of the contract or any subcontract at any tier.

There is a very logical and important reason for the Government's use of authorization and consent provisions. The Government wants to insure that contractor or subcontractor performance is not stopped by reason of a patent infringement claim. Such actions could easily impede the progress of the contractual effort in the same manner as may occur to a commercial contractor under similar circumstances. Since the infringement claim is brought against the Government and not the contractor or subcontractor, who otherwise would be enjoined from further action, work on the contract can proceed.

## Infringement Claims

Any individual or organization claiming an infringement of a patent by a Government contractor must file its claim under 10 U.S.C. 1498:

> Whenever an invention described in and covered by a patent of the United States is used or manufactured by or for the United States without license of the owner thereof or lawful right to use or manufacture the same, the owner's remedy shall be by action against the United States in the Court of Claims for the recovery of his reasonable and entire compensation for such use and manufacture.

The necessity for the Government's consent to use of a patented article so action for infringement can be brought against the Government, was emphasized in *Wood v. Atlantic Gulf and Pacific Co., 296F. 718 (5th Cir. 1924)*, when the court said:

> When the Government knows and obliges the contractor to use the patented article, of course the Government should be willing to pay; but it will be going entirely too far to say that, because an independent contractor for his own convenience saw fit to use the patented article in doing Government work, the Government should pay for such use by him, when they did not know he was using it.

The Government's liability for damages in a patent infringement suit may ultimately be borne by the infringing contractor or subcontractor. Individual agency policies and procedures for processing claims vary to some degree. However, they all comply with directives in FAR Part 27, *Patents, Data and Copyrights*.

One of the key elements in patent rights claims centers around whether or not the item has "been reduced to practice," and if so, when. Many court cases have argued this point. In *RCA v. International Standard Electric*, the court made the following decision:

> We think it is clear that reduction to practice does not mean that whatever is being worked upon has to be in shape to be commercially marketable. On the other hand, it must be a demonstration that the inventor's idea works, not that he has thought the matter out and devised something that ought to work and may work but actually something that will work to accomplish its intended purpose. *Radio Corp. of America v. International Standard Electric Corp., 232 F. 726, 730 (3d. Cir. 1956).*

**Patent Indemnification**

The Government has a method of getting reimbursed for its liability resulting from patent infringements by contractors and subcontractors. Construction contracts or contracts for supplies or services normally on sale to the general public may contain one of the Patent Indemnity clauses at FAR 52.227-3, *Patent Indemnity*, or FAR 52.227-4, *Patent Indemnity – Construction Contracts*, and appropriate alternates thereto.

The same contract may contain both a patent indemnity clause and an authorization and consent clause. However, the Government does not use patent indemnity clauses under any of the following conditions:

- When the Authorization and Consent clause, FAR 52.227-1, with its Alternate I, is included in the contract;
- When the supplies or services clearly are not for sale in the commercial open market;
- When performance or delivery is outside the U.S.;
- When contracts are awarded using simplified acquisition procedures; and
- Architect and engineer contracts.

Contractors must notify the contracting officer if they receive a notice or claim of patent or copyright infringement. They must also aid the Government in any resulting suit or claim. To ensure compliance the CO will incorporate FAR 52.227-2, *Notice and Assistance Regarding Patent and Copyright Infringement*, in contracts containing the Authorization and Consent clause.

# CHAPTER 15

# CONTRACT TERMINATION AND CLOSEOUT

## OVERVIEW

Every business contract must come to an end at some time. The original contract period of performance may get extended from time to time. However, a federal contract normally will not be extended beyond a total of five years. Of course, there are exceptions to that rule.

Basically there are three ways that a Government contract comes to an end. The first and most dramatic is when some serious situation is discovered and the contract is voided. This could occur because it is determined that the Government lacked authority to enter into the contract. That would mean that neither an *Authorization Act* nor an *Appropriation Act* containing provision for the procurement had been passed by Congress. Another situation could occur when it is found that the contract was obtained by fraudulent means.

The next most dramatic situation is when the Government must terminate the contract before the total period of performance has occurred. Timing action by the contracting officer is very important. While the Government does not want the contractor to continue spending funds needlessly, it must be certain that termination is the proper action to be taken. The several types of termination actions are discussed in the following parts of this chapter.

The last way of ending a contract happens when the period of performance has expired and there are no further extensions. At this point the contract goes into the closure process. The contract closeout process is covered starting on page 384 and a listing of closeout problems is shown on Figure 15-2, page 389.

## TERMINATIONS

### The Scope of Terminations

Governmental authority to terminate contracts prior to the expiration of the period of performance is well founded. The right to terminate for default, or for breach of contract, stems from the common law. Under common law, any aggrieved party to a contract has the right to terminate a contract for breach thereof, and seek damages. If challenged for a termination for default, the Government must prove the default or breach in a court of law.

However, unlike a private party, the Government, through the courts, has limited the Government's liability for what turns out to be an erroneous termination for default, by a judge turning the termination for default into a termination for convenience. This provides for an equitable adjustment and eliminates the possibility of a judgment against the Government for damages (see *Constructive Termination* on page 376)

Governmental authority to terminate a contract for its convenience is based on its sovereign powers to safeguard public funds and protect the best interests of the Government. Convenience terminations are almost unique to governmental bodies. However, some very large corporations have imposed them on their subcontractors for non-government contracts.

Under the *Armed Services Procurement Act of 1947*, the Department of Defense received the authority to publish policies and regulations necessary to carry out its procurement activities. The termination clauses and related regulations and procedures were developed and promulgated under authority of the Act. They document the Government's authority to terminate its contracts. The clauses and procedures carried over into the Federal Procurement Regulations and subsequently into the Federal Acquisition Regulation (FAR).

FAR Part 49, *Termination of Contracts*, cites the policies and procedures concerning the termination of contracts, covering complete or partial terminations, either for the convenience of the Government or for default. It prescribes the appropriate contract clauses relating to terminations and excusable delays. FAR Part 49 also includes instructions for using termination and settlement forms.

As long as it follows the prescribed procedures, the Government may terminate any of its contracts. Termination will be for one of the following reasons:

- Default of the contractor;
- Breach of contract by the contractor; or
- For the convenience of the Government

The Government may terminate its contracts, either completely or partially, as its needs dictate. The contractual authority for a termination comes from a terminations clause, other contract clauses or the Federal statutes. A default is considered to be a claim by the Government, not by the contractor. The term "termination for default" means the exercise by the Government of its contractual right to completely or partially terminate a contract because of the contractor's actual or anticipated failure to perform its contractual obligations. Contractors will seek to convert the Government's "claim" in a default termination to a claim for convenience termination.

A partial termination means one that is for part but not all of the work that has not been completed and accepted under a contract. Partial terminations also can result in a contractor's claim for an equitable adjustment, based upon impact the termination has made upon the continuing contractual efforts. FAR 49.304, *Procedure for Partial Termination*, provides instructions for the termination contracting officer on dealing with partial terminations.

**Termination for Default (FAR 49.4)**

The bases for termination for default are two legal rights of the Government. First, it is the exercise of a basic legal right of the Government to terminate a contract, in whole or in part. In addition, it has the contractual right to terminate, by reason of the contractor's failure to perform its obligations under the contract. The regulations authorize a termination action for either actual or anticipatory failure.

A default termination is a drastic sanction of a contractor that requires the Government to be held accountable for its actions. It is the Government that bears the burden of proof that its actions were proper, legal and performed in accordance with the regulations. The presence of a default termination clause in a contract does not require the Government to terminate on a finding of default. The clause gives a contracting officer the discretion to decide whether to take that action or seek an alternative solution to the problem. There are numerous alternatives to take into consideration.

The Government may exercise its right to terminate for default if the contractor:

- Fails to make delivery of supplies or to perform the services within the time specified in the contract;
- Fails to perform any other provision in the contract; or
- Fails to make progress, endangering performance of the contract.

Showing proof that a contractor has failed to make delivery or perform services as contractually required usually will be an easy task. Were the schedule dates met or not? Is there evidence that a service was performed? If the answers are negative, what is the severity and impact of the failures? Based upon those answers the contracting officer will make the appropriate termination decision.

Failing to comply with other contractual provisions, such as violation of security provisions, not maintaining required manning levels, submitting false certifications and the like, can be cause for a default termination.

A contractor's failure to make progress toward completion of performance, despite the fact the final period of performance had not been reached, can trigger a default termination. A Court of Federal Claims decision stated that termination for failure to make progress can be evaluated on two different bases: (1) whether the contractor has fallen so far behind schedule that timely completion is unlikely; or (2) whether the contractor's work is so defective that it is unlikely that compliant work could be performed in a timely manner (*Hannon Electric Co. v. U.S. Fed. Cl. 135, 143 (1994)*). In that first *"failure to make progress"* category *(i.e., fallen behind)* the contracting officer tries to establish that failure to make progress exists by comparing the amount of work done with the amount of work left to be accomplished. The Government has the burden of proving that the contractor could not complete the required tasks and that a termination is proper.

The FAR clause 52.249-9, *Default (Fixed-Price Research and Development)*, provides in part:

(a) (1) The Government may, subject to paragraphs (c) and (d) of this clause, by written Notice of Default to the Contractor, terminate this contract in whole or in part if the Contractor fails to –

(i) Perform the work under the contract within the time specified in this contract or any extension;

(ii) Prosecute the work so as to endanger performance of this contract (but see paragraph (a)(2) of this clause); or

(iii) Perform any of the other provisions of this contract (but see paragraph (a)(2) of this clause).

(2) The Government's right to terminate this contract under subdivisions (a)(1)(ii) and (iii) of this clause may be exercised if the Contractor does not cure such failure within 10 days (or more, if authorized in writing by the Contracting Officer) after receipt of the notice from the Contracting Officer specifying the failure.

The effect of a default termination can be very traumatic on a contractor. The Government is not liable for the contractor's expenditures on undelivered work. Furthermore, the Government is entitled to reimbursement of any advance payments and any progress payments applicable to the undelivered work.

A default termination may require the contractor to transfer title and deliver completed supplies and manufactured materials to the Government. The Government will then pay the contractor the contract price for completed supplies it is willing to accept. The contracting officer and the contractor will negotiate the value for any residual manufacturing materials accepted by the Government.

The greatest impact on the contractor will be liability to the Government for reprocurement costs, liquidated and other damages. These matters will be discussed later in this chapter.

Contractors usually make a concerted effort to have a termination for default rescinded, or at least converted to a termination for convenience of the Government. This may be possible if the contractor can establish that failure to perform arose out of causes beyond its control and without its fault or negligence. The following are some of the other major defenses and claims raised by contractors for such conversion, and perhaps even compensation:

- Excusable and other delays
- Suspensions of work and stop work orders received
- Changes beyond the scope of the contract
- Defective specifications
- Late or defective Government furnished property
- Acts of God or of the Public Enemy
- Acts of the Government in either its sovereign or contractual capacity

The contracting officer will use one of the clauses at FAR 52.249-x to protect the Government's right to terminate a contract for default. The basic clauses are:

- *Termination (Cost-Reimbursement)* at FAR 52.249-6
- *Default (Fixed-Price Supply and Service)* at FAR 52.249-8
- *Default (Fixed-Price Research and Development)* at FAR 52.249-9

If, through some error on the part of the individuals drafting a contract, the termination for convenience clauses are missing, the clauses will be held to be present via the *Christian Doctrine* (*G. L. Christian Assoc. v. United States, 312 F2d. 418 (Ct. Cl. 1963)*). Under the *Christian Doctrine*, if a significant clause is required to be included in a Government contract, the contract will be read to include it even though the clause does not actually appear in the document.

**Termination for Breach of Contract**

For contracts that do not contain a defaults type clause, which would be rare, the Government still retains the right to terminate a contractor for breach of contract.

When a contractor fails to perform its contractual obligations, the contracting officer will investigate the causes of the delinquency. When the investigation indicates that the contractor has breached the contract, the contracting officer will evaluate the severity of the situation. Significant breaches call for termination actions. After approval of legal counsel, the CO will send the contractor a breach notice. That notice will be sent by telegram or registered mail with return receipt requested, or hand delivered with a written acknowledgment from the contractor. The standard format for that notice is:

> You are hereby notified that your failure to perform Contract No.__ as required by the terms thereof constitutes a Breach of Contract. The Government will no longer accept delivery thereunder and at its option may procure the undelivered supplies from another source. The Government will hold you liable for any and all damages resulting from your Breach of Contract.

It is not just the failure to perform the contractual tasks that can bring on a default termination. Failure to comply with Schedule and Contract Clauses and also the Federal Statutes may be grounds for termination. The following are several examples of this condition.

- The *Equal Opportunity* clause at FAR 52.222-26, incorporated in most contracts, imposes the following condition on all contractors/applicants for such assistance:

> If the Office of Federal Contract Compliance Programs (OFCCP) determines that the Contractor is not in compliance with this clause or any rule, regulation, or order of the

Secretary of Labor, this contract may be canceled, terminated, or suspended in whole or in part and the Contractor may be declared ineligible for further Government contracts, under the procedures authorized in Executive Order 11246, as amended. In addition, sanctions may be imposed and remedies invoked against the Contractor as provided in Executive Order 11246, as amended; in the rules, regulations, and orders of the Secretary of Labor, or otherwise provided by law.

- In the *Covenant Against Contingent Fees* clause at FAR 52.203-5, there is another example:

The Contractor warrants that no person or agency has been employed or retained to solicit or obtain this contract upon an agreement or understanding for a contingent fee, except a bona fide employee or agency. For breach or violation of this warranty, the Government shall have the right to annul this contract without liability or, in its discretion, to deduct from the contract price or consideration, or otherwise recover, the full amount of the contingent fee.

- The courts have held that contracts may be cancelled on the grounds of public policy. The following court decisions are examples of this situation:

(1) In *United States v. Mississippi Valley Generating Co.*, 364 U.S. 520 (1961), the court held that a contract that was tainted with a conflict of interest was void as being opposed to public policy and that the contractor could receive nothing for the work performed on the contract.

(2) In a case involving a violation of the anti-kickback statute (*41 U.S.C. 51-54, (1964)*), which forbids any subcontractor from making a gift to a prime contractor or his employee as an inducement for the award of a subcontract, the Supreme Court held that contract cancellation was a proper remedy for a violation of that statute although the statute does not provide for such remedy. They made the ruling on the basis of public policy. (*U.S. v. Acme Process Equipment Co.*, 348 U.S. 917 (1966))

Under the Tucker Act, the Government permits contractors to sue the Government for breach of contract. The *Government Delay of Work* clause, FAR 52.242-17, required in all fixed-price supply contracts for other than commercial or modified-commercial supplies, provides for such actions. An essential element in a breach of contract claim by a contractor is the existence of actual damages. Without showing proof of such damages, the contractor will not be successful in a breach of contract suit against the Government.

The following three elements are necessary to support a claim of breach of contract by the Government:

- The Government breached the contract
- The contractor suffered specific damages
- The damages were the result of the breach

## Termination for the Convenience of the Government

The Government has the right to terminate a contract whenever it is in the best interest of the Government. Action of this nature constitutes a "Termination for the Convenience of the Government." Termination may be for the entire contract, or just part of it. Partial terminations can actually occur several times during the life of a contract. The contracting officer has the authority to make those decisions.

The termination of a contract, either for default or convenience, is the prerogative of the Government and action is not available to contractors. If by chance a termination clause has been left out of a contract, a *Termination for Convenience* clause is read into the contract as a matter of law. As noted on page 373 this is known as the *Christian Doctrine*.

Under the termination clause, after a partial termination, a contractor may request an equitable adjustment in the price or prices of the continued portion of a fixed-price contract. When a contract is partially terminated for convenience, there are four common results that may require an equitable adjustment: (1) increased material costs; (2) increased labor costs; (3) unabsorbed fixed direct costs; and (4) unabsorbed overhead. Unless delegated to a termination contracting officer (TCO), the contracting officer will be responsible for negotiation of the contractor's proposal for price adjustment and issuance of any resulting supplemental agreement. Both the CO and the TCO must ensure that no portion of the costs included in the equitable adjustment is included in the termination settlement. Termination contracting officer duties and functions are covered, starting on page 377, *Termination Procedures*.

Most fixed-price type contracts contain the clause at FAR 52.249-1, *Termination for Convenience of the Government (Fixed-Price) (Short Form)* or FAR 52.249-2, *Termination for Convenience of the Government (Fixed-Price).* Cost-reimbursement contracts will have the clause at FAR 52.249-6, *Termination (Cost-Reimbursement).*

The following are typical cases when a contracting officer could exercise a termination for convenience:

- The requirement for an item or service no longer exists;
- There has been a change in regulations;
- The Government has adopted a new type of item;
- A change in requirements is so significant that it amounts to a *cardinal* change, thereby creating a modification outside the scope of the original contract;
- The contractor's failure to perform or make progress in performance of its contract is due to causes beyond its control and without its fault or negligence; and
- A contract has been terminated for default and it is later found that the contractor was not at fault.

When the price of the undelivered balance of a contract is less than $5,000, the contract should not normally be terminated for convenience but should be permitted to run to completion (*FAR 49.101, Authorities and Responsibilities*).

### Constructive Termination

Constructive termination for convenience is a judge-made doctrine that allows for retroactive termination of a contract. The concept is appropriate when the Government has stopped a contractor's performance for reasons that later turn out to be questionable or invalid. Under a U.S. Supreme Court ruling, a party may justify terminating a contract by showing there was adequate cause at the time, even though that cause did not become known until a later date. (*College Point Boat Corp. v. U.S.*, 267 U.S. 12 (1925)).

A constructive termination judgment provides the Government with a defense in a breach of contract action. The defense limits damages to the costs provided for in the Termination for Convenience clause. "Constructively, the clause can justify the Government's actions, avoid breach, and limit liability." (*G.C. Casebolt Co. v. U.S.,* 421 F.2d 710 (1970)).

### Reprocurement and Other Damages

When the supplies or services are still required after a default termination, the contracting officer will repurchase the same or similar supplies or services against the contractor's account as soon as practicable. The contracting officer will repurchase at as reasonable a price as practicable, considering the quality and delivery requirements. The contracting officer may repurchase a quantity in excess of the undelivered quantity terminated for default when the excess quantity is needed, but excess cost may not be charged against the defaulting contractor for more than the undelivered quantity terminated for default (including variations in quantity permitted by the terminated contract). Generally, the contracting officer will make a decision whether or not to repurchase before issuing the termination notice.

If the repurchase is for a quantity not over the undelivered quantity terminated for default, the *Default* clause authorizes the contracting officer to use any terms and acquisition method deemed appropriate for the repurchase. However, the contracting officer must obtain competition to the maximum extent practicable for the repurchase. If the repurchase is for a quantity over the undelivered quantity terminated for default, the contracting officer will treat the entire quantity as a new acquisition, with a new RFP and contract.

If repurchase is made at a price over the price of the supplies or services terminated, the contracting officer will, after completion and final payment of the repurchase contract, make a written demand on the original contractor for the total amount of the excess, giving consideration to any increases or decreases in other costs such as transportation, discounts, etc. If the contractor fails to make payment, the contracting officer will follow the procedures in FAR 32.6, *Contract Debts*, for collecting contract debts due the Government.

When a contract is terminated for default or if a course of action in lieu of termination for default is followed, the contracting officer will promptly ascertain and make demand for any liquidated damages to which the Government is entitled under the contract. Under the contract clauses for liquidated damages at FAR 52.211-11, *Liquidated Damages – Supplies, Services, or Research and Development*, these damages are in addition to any excess repurchase costs. If the Government has suffered any other ascertainable damages, including administrative costs, as a result of the contractor's default, the contracting officer will, on the basis of legal advice take appropriate action as prescribed in FAR 32.6, *Contract Debts*, to assert the Government's demand for the damages.

Direction and guidance for recovering damages and other claims by the Government are contained in FAR 49.402-6, *Repurchase Against Contractor's Account*, and FAR 49.402-7, *Other Damages*.

## Termination Procedures

Some Government agencies have contracting officers who specialize in the processing of contract terminations. Those individuals are designated as termination contracting officers (TCO). The two titles (CO & TCO) are used interchangeably in this discussion.

The termination contracting officer must follow the uniform policies and procedures on contract terminations in FAR Part 49, *Termination of Contracts*. Failure to apply properly the termination procedures will be to the Government's disadvantage in the ultimate settlement process. Such failures are frequently adequate reason to convert a default termination into one for the convenience of the Government.

When the contractual delivery date has passed, the Government may lose the authority to retroactively terminate a contract for default due to a contractor's failure to meet a scheduled delivery date; especially when the Government permits the contractor to continue performance. When the Government fails to act in a timely manner the consequences could be both the creation of a constructive change in the contractor's favor and also the contractor may avoid the stigma and consequences of a default termination.

Terminations are time consuming and expensive for both the Government and the contractor. Therefore, the contracting officer will seek an alternate approach to resolve the situation. Rather than issuing a notice of termination, the contracting officer will try to enter into a no-cost agreement with the contractor. That can be done when the following conditions exist:

- The contractor will accept a no-cost settlement;
- No government property was furnished to the contractor; and
- There are no outstanding payments, claims or other contractor obligations.

The contracting officer must consider many factors in determining whether to terminate a contract for default. The very first action must be a review of the provisions of the contract and applicable laws and regulations. Then, the specific failure(s) of the contractor are assessed. Unless time does not permit, the contractor's excuses for the failure(s) will be reviewed. If the Government still requires the supplies or services, their availability from other sources must be determined. The CO will review any urgency in the need for the supplies or services and the time required to get them from other sources. The agency will compare that information with the delinquent contractor's revised delivery schedule. All of this activity will have a direct impact upon the termination and repurchase decisions.

In addition, the contracting officer must assess how essential the contractor is to the Government procurement program and the effect a termination for default will have upon the contractor's capability as a supplier under other contracts. Also to be considered is the effect a default termination will have on the ability of the contractor to liquidate guaranteed loans, progress payments or advanced payments. The CO must take into account any other pertinent facts and circumstances available for review.

Contracting officers can take several courses of action in lieu of terminating a contract for default. As with most actions, they will act in the best interest of the Government. The following are some of the alternatives available. They may permit the contractor, surety, or guarantor to continue performance of the contract under a revised delivery schedule. As an alternative, they may permit the contractor to continue performance of the effort under a subcontract or other business arrangement with an acceptable third party. This choice is available only if they adequately preserve the rights of the Government. The contracting officer can exercise the option to execute a no-cost termination settlement agreement. This alternative is available if the requirement for the supplies or services specified in the contract no longer exists. Also, the contractor cannot be liable to the Government for damages.

There is no such thing as an oral termination. Contracts can only be terminated, either for convenience or default, by a written notice to the contractor. FAR 49.601-2, *Letter Notice*, provides a letter format suggested for use if a contract for supplies is being terminated for convenience. The contracting officer should make appropriate modifications to that letter when terminating contracts for other than supplies and in terminating subcontracts. Contracting officers are directed to send these notices by certified mail, return receipt requested. If the initial termination notice is sent by telegram, a confirming letter is required to be sent.

The termination notice must be timely, clear and unambiguous. It must state that the termination is either for the convenience of the Government or for default. It will cite the contract provisions authorizing such a termination. The notice must specify the effective date of the termination and the extent of termination, whether it is total or partial. When it is only a partial termination, the notice must identify the portion of the contract effort the contractor must continue performing. The notice must also contain recommended actions the contractor must take to minimize the impact on personnel. This is a major concern if the termination, together with all other outstanding terminations, will result in a significant reduction in the contractor's work force. In addition, the notice will detail any special instructions considered essential to aid the termination process. FAR 49.102, *Notice of Termination*, provides the details for notifications.

After compliance with the regulations and procedures governing terminations, the contracting officer may determine that termination for default is proper. If the contractual delivery date has not been reached a "Cure Notice" must be issued, provided there is still time for the "cure" to be accomplished. FAR 49.607, *Delinquency Notices*, provides the formats for "Cure Notices" and "Show Cause Notices."

The cure notice must specify the nature of the failure. It must provide the contractor ten (10) days to cure the failure. The TCO may authorize a longer period. When time is critical the TCO will use this notice in lieu of the show cause notice. After the authorized period (10 or more days) the TCO normally will issue a notice of termination for default. The TCO will postpone or discontinue that action if the contractor cures the source of failure or has provided convincing evidence that a convenience termination would be more proper.

A contractor must take receipt of a cure notice very seriously and provide the contracting officer with a detailed and timely response. That response must address the Government's assertions that the contract could not be completed in a timely manner. It should also include a description of whatever excusable delays may have occurred that would justify an extension to the period of performance. Furthermore, the contractor must ensure that the response provides the CO with a completion schedule that demonstrates, with as much precision as possible, how it intends to complete the contract within the time remaining. Failure to respond to a cure notice will give justification to the Government's conclusion that timely completion is highly unlikely. A response without a reasonable plan for completion will likely result in termination.

If the time remaining in the contract delivery schedule is not sufficient to permit a realistic "cure" period of ten (10) days or more the "Cure Notice" will not be used. Instead, a "Show Cause Notice" may be used to alert the contractor of the situation. The notice should be sent immediately upon the expiration of the delivery period if not sent earlier. The notice calls the contractor's attention to its contractual liabilities if the contract is terminated for default. The letter will request an explanation of the contractor's failure to perform the contract. It may further state that the Government may take failure of the contractor to present an explanation as an admission that no valid explanation exists. It is usually appropriate for the letter to invite the contractor to discuss the matter at a conference.

The written notice of termination for default must be unequivocally clear so there are no ambiguities, and must comply with FAR 49.402-3, *Procedure for Default*. The notice must at least provide the information listed below:

- The contract number and date;
- Describe the acts or omissions constituting the default;
- State that the contractor's right to proceed further with performance of the contract (or a specified portion of the contract in a partial termination) is thereby terminated;

- State that supplies or services terminated are subject to procurement against the contractor's account, and that the contractor is liable for any excess costs;
- If the contracting officer has determined that the contractor's failure to perform is not excusable, the notice must state that it constitutes such a decision, and that the contractor has the right to appeal such a decision under the Disputes clause.
- State that the Government reserves all rights and remedies provided by law or under the contract, in addition to charging excess costs; and
- State that the notice constitutes the contracting officer's formal decision that the contractor is in default as specified, and that the contractor has the right to appeal in accordance with the procedures stated in the Disputes clause.

Except as otherwise directed by the Termination Contracting Officer (TCO), the contractor must comply with the notice of termination and the termination clause of the contract. FAR 49.104, *Duties of Prime Contractor after Receipt of Notice of Termination*, provides guidance for terminated contractors. Among other things, the contractor must take the following actions:

- Stop work immediately on the terminated portion of the contract and discontinue placing subcontracts thereunder.
- After receipt of a termination notice, establish charge numbers to document any costs incurred regarding the termination.
- Terminate all subcontracts related to the terminated portion of the prime contract.
- Immediately advise the TCO of any special circumstances preventing the stoppage of work.
- If the termination is partial, perform the continued portion of the contract. Promptly submit any request for an equitable adjustment of price relating to the continued portion of the contract. Provide supporting evidence of any increase in costs.
- Take any necessary action to protect and preserve Government property in the possession of the contractor. Dispose of the Government property as directed by the TCO.
- Promptly notify the TCO in writing of any legal proceedings against the contractor growing out of any subcontract or other commitment related to the terminated portion of the contract.
- Settle all outstanding liabilities and all claims arising out of termination of subcontracts, obtaining any approvals or ratifications required by the TCO.
- Promptly submit the contractor's own settlement proposal, supported by appropriate schedules. The standard requirement is that the contractor must submit its settlement proposal within one year from the effective date of the termination, unless the contracting officer approves a later date.
- Dispose of any termination inventory, as directed or authorized by the TCO.

One important function of the termination contracting officer is directing the actions of the prime contractor. That includes execution of a no-cost settlement agreement when appropriate. The notice of termination provides the initial direction. Any later directions are also made in writing. The termination contracting officer will follow the directions of the termination clause in the contract (*FAR 49.105, Duties of Termination Contracting Officer after Issuance of Notice of Termination*).

The TCO will convene a conference with the contractor as promptly as possible after sending the notice of termination. During the conference they will develop a definite program for effecting the settlement.

Another important TCO function is examination of the prime contractor's settlement proposal, and when appropriate, examination of subcontractor settlement proposals. It is in the best interest of the Government for the TCO to negotiate the proposal promptly and enter into a settlement agreement with the contractor. If unable to negotiate a settlement after due and diligent effort, the TCO must promptly settle the contractor's claim by determination.

When advised that settlement has been reached on the termination, the contracting officer is responsible for the release of excess funds resulting from the termination unless that responsibility was specifically delegated to the TCO (*FAR 49.101(f)*).

**Settlement of Subcontract Claims**

Since there is no privity of contract between subcontractors and the Government, subcontractors have no contractual rights against the Government upon the termination of a prime contract. However, a subcontractor may have rights against the prime contractor or intermediate subcontractor with whom it has contracted. Upon termination of a prime contract, the prime contractor and each subcontractor are responsible for the prompt conclusion of the settlement proposals of their immediate subcontractors. Prime contractors must promptly terminate all subcontracts issued under the prime contract. In partial terminations, only the affected subcontracts are terminated.

Termination contracting officers examine subcontract settlements to protect the Government's interests. They need to satisfy themselves that the subcontract termination was caused by the partial termination of the prime. They want assurance that the settlement is a reasonable amount arrived at in good faith, and is allocable to the terminated portion of the prime contract (*FAR 49.108, Settlement of Subcontract Settlement Proposals*). Any settlement with the subcontractor must be related to the terminated contract. Settlement cost will be paid to the prime contractor only if they were incurred on the subcontract for work to be delivered under the prime contract.

The TCO, upon written request, may give authorization to the prime contractor to conclude settlements of subcontracts terminated in whole or part without approval or ratification when the amount of settlement is $100,000 or less. That amount may be increased. It may also be limited to specific subcontracts or classes of subcontracts. The prime contractor and the contracting officer may proceed with their actions and set aside the subcontract portion of the claim. This is a common practice when settlement of a subcontractor's claim would delay the submission and settlement of the prime contractor's claim. This is not to the prime contractor's detriment because no fee will be payable to the prime contractor under that portion of the claim anyway.

In unusual cases, the TCO may determine that it is in the best interest of the Government to offer assistance to the prime contractor in settling a particular subcontract.

**Termination Settlement Agreements (*FAR 49.109*)**

Terminated contracts are settled either by a negotiated agreement, upon a determination by the termination contracting officer, costing-out by vouchers for cost-reimbursement contracts, or a combination of these methods. If the TCO suspects fraud or other criminal conduct related to the settlement of a terminated contract, the TCO will discontinue negotiations and report the facts under agency procedures.

Negotiation is the preferred method of settling termination claims. When a termination settlement has been negotiated and all required reviews have been obtained by the parties, the contractor and the TCO will execute a settlement agreement on Standard Form 30, *Amendment of Solicitation/Modification of Contract* (Figure 13-1, page 316). The settlement will cover any set-offs and counterclaims which the Government may have against the contractor. TCOs apply the set-offs against the terminated contract. The final settlement includes subcontractor claims. However, the parties may exclude some subcontractor claims from the agreement and reserve them for separate settlement.

There will be times when the parties cannot reach an agreement on the settlement proposal. If that impasse occurs under a termination for convenience situation, the contractor may have its proposal converted into a "claim." A typical example of an impasse happens when the Government does not make a response to a contractor's settlement proposal.

The Government uses settlement by determination when the parties cannot reach agreement on the termination claim. In addition, the TCO can make a determination when the contractor does not submit the claim within the period required by the termination clause. At that point the TCO sends the contractor a statement outlining the Government's position. That statement is the contracting officer's determination of the amount due; it also constitutes the final decision for dispute purposes.

In formulating the determination, the TCO gets guidance from the termination clause in the contract and any cost principles incorporated therein by reference. Before issuing a determination of the amount due the contractor, the TCO will give the contractor at least fifteen (15) days' notice to submit written evidence substantiating the amount previously proposed. The contractor has the burden of establishing, by proof satisfactory to the TCO, the amount proposed.

The cost principles and procedures in FAR Part 31, *Contract Cost Principles and Procedures*, apply to the settlement of termination claims. FAR Part 31 provides the guidelines for claiming, negotiating or determining cost relevant to the termination. It applies to settlements under fixed-price and cost-reimbursement type contracts with other than educational institutions. FAR Part 31 serves as a guide for the negotiation of settlements for R&D work with educational institutions.

The TCO may execute a no-cost settlement agreement if: (1) the contractor has not incurred costs for the terminated portion of the contract; or (2) the contractor is willing to waive the costs incurred; and (3) no amounts are due to the Government under the contract.

## Contractor Appeals

The Disputes clause permits defaulted contractors to file appeals to reverse or offset a default termination or contest the assessment of excess costs under a determination settlement. There are two basic reasons contractors will appeal a default termination. The first and most obvious is the "default" aspect and all the negative factors associated therewith. The other reason is contractors may be dissatisfied with the financial impact of a default termination. The settlement negotiations could have been very severe or the contracting officer could have made a unilateral determination of the settlement amount. However, contractors lose the right to appeal a settlement by determination when it fails to submit its settlement proposal within the allotted time. To protect against this, contractors must request an extension of the authorized submission date when it is obvious that the due date will not be met. Such extensions are not always granted.

Appeals of a default termination are made to the appropriate board of contract appeals or to the Court of Federal Claims (formerly the U.S. Claims Court). The disputes process is discussed in detail in the next chapter. However, it is important to remember that the claims court will not hear an appeal where there is not some monetary claim included. The courts have held that they do not have jurisdiction over a case contesting only the propriety of a default termination which presents no claim for money (*Overall Roofing & Construction, Inc. v. U.S., 929 F.2d 687 (Fed. Cir. 1991)*). Therefore, contractors must be aware that a challenge to a default termination unaccompanied by a monetary claim must be brought to the appropriate board and that such an appeal is therefore subject to the shorter limitations period for submitting the claim. The time starts running whenever the contractor receives a final decision from the contracting officer regarding its appeal of the termination itself or the settlement determination.

Supplemental agreements will be prepared by the TCO in order to modify the contract to document Contract Appeals Board or Court of Federal Claims decisions favorable to a contractor's appeal.

### Interest on Termination Settlements

On the day a contractor submits a properly certified proposal for settlement of termination costs, interest begins to accrue on the amount found due for such costs. The Boards of Contract Appeals have found that termination cost settlement proposals are claims under the Contract Disputes Act. That has been the finding irrespective of whether the Government disputed the amount proposed. This interest is not a penalty against the Government. It is the Government's payment to the contractor for the continued use of money, from the time that it became due following a convenience termination until actual payment.

### Reinstatement of Terminated Contracts

The purchasing office may reinstate the terminated portion of a contract, either in whole or part, by an amendment to the notice of termination. The TCO must fully document the decision to reinstate a contract. That document will be permanently retained in the contract file. Before reinstatement of a contract, all of the following situations must exist:

- Circumstances clearly indicate a continued requirement for the terminated items;
- The TCO has the written consent of the contractor to the reinstatement; and
- Reinstatement is advantageous to the Government

## CONTRACT CLOSEOUT

### Definition of Closeout

Contract closeout is the action that occurs upon the physical completion of a contract. Its purpose is to insure that the contractor has complied with all the contractual requirements and that the Government has also fulfilled its obligations.

A contract is physically complete when both contracting parties agree to the following:

- The contractor has completed the required deliveries of supplies and they have been inspected and accepted by the Government;
- The contractor has performed all services and the Government has accepted them;
- Any option has expired, in those contracts with option provisions; or
- The Government has given the contractor a notice of complete termination.

Facilities contracts and rental, use and storage agreements are physically complete when a notice of complete termination has been issued or the contract period has expired (*FAR 4.804-4, Physically Completed Contracts*).

Except for small purchases getting limited administration, contracts are fully closed when they are both physically and administratively complete. However, a completed contract is not fully closed while in litigation, pending an appeal before a Board of Contract Appeals, or awaiting final completion of any termination actions.

**Closeout Schedule**

The Government has established the following standard times for contract closure actions. Their purpose is to promote the timely closeout of its contracts *(FAR 4.804-1, Closeout by the Office Administering the Contract*).

- Files for contracts using simplified acquisition procedures should be considered closed when the contracting officer receives evidence of receipt of property and final payment, unless otherwise specified by agency regulations.
- Files for firm-fixed-price contracts, other than those using simplified acquisition procedures, should be closed within 6 months after the date on which the contracting officer receives evidence of physical completion.
- Files for contracts requiring settlement of indirect cost rates should be closed within 36 months of the month in which the contracting officer receives evidence of physical completion.
- Files for all other contracts should be closed within 20 months of the month in which the contracting officer receives evidence of physical completion.

A contract file shall not be closed if: (1) the contract is in litigation or under appeal; or (2) in the case of a termination, all termination actions have not been completed.

DOD gets the contractor to assist in maintaining the closeout schedule. They insert the following or similar clause in its contracts. They also make use of the *Contract Closeout Check-List, DD Form 1597* (Figure 15-1, page 386), and an applicable status report on closeout progress deliverables.

Contract Closeout Schedule

> Within 120 days following the ending date set forth in Part II of the Schedule, the Contractor shall submit a plan for final closeout of this contract. The closeout plan and status reports thereon shall be submitted in accordance with the instructions set forth in Exhibit _ _ *(CDRL, DD Form 1423)*.

When setting the schedule and while working toward its successful and timely completion, both parties must remember the five year limitation that may be imposed on the availability of the appropriated funds. This could seriously affect some of the actions the parties may take during the closeout process.

# DD FORM 1597 – CONTRACT CLOSEOUT CHECK-LIST

CONTRACT CLOSEOUT CHECK-LIST
*(Use a separate page to attach any comments.)*

1. CONTRACT NUMBER

2. CONTRACT MODIFICATION NUMBERS *(If applicable)*

3. NAME OF CONTRACTOR

4. DATE OF PHYSICAL COMPLETION *(YYYYMMDD)*

| 5. ACTION ITEMS | | 6. MILESTONES/CALENDAR MONTHS AFTER PHYSICAL COMPLETION *(FAR 4.804-1)* | | | 7. FORECAST COMPLETION DATE *(YYYYMMDD)* | 8. DATE ACTION COMPLETED *(YYYYMMDD)* *(NA if not applicable)* |
|---|---|---|---|---|---|---|
| | | Category 2 | Category 3 | Category 4 | | |
| a. DISPOSITION OF CLASSIFIED MATERIAL COMPLETED | | | | | | |
| b. FINAL PATENT REPORT SUBMITTED *(Inventions Disclosures)* | DD 882 | | | | | |
| c. FINAL ROYALTY REPORT SUBMITTED | | | | | | |
| d. FINAL PATENT REPORT CLEARED *(Inventions Disclosures)* | | | | | | |
| e. FINAL ROYALTY REPORT CLEARED | | | | | | |
| f. ISSUANCE OF REPORT OF CONTRACT COMPLETION | | | | | | |
| g. NO OUTSTANDING VALUE ENGINEERING CHANGE PROPOSAL *(VECP)* | | | | | | |
| h. PLANT CLEARANCE REPORT RECEIVED | DD 1593 | | | | | |
| i. PROPERTY CLEARANCE RECEIVED | DD 1593 | | | | | |
| j. SETTLEMENT OF ALL INTERIM OR DISALLOWED COSTS *(DCAA Form 1)* | | | | | | |
| k. PRICE REVISION COMPLETED | | | | | | |
| l. SETTLEMENT OF SUBCONTRACTS BY THE PRIME CONTRACTOR | | | | | | |
| m. PRIOR YEAR OVERHEAD RATES COMPLETED | | | | | | |
| n. CONTRACTOR'S CLOSING STATEMENT RECEIVED | | | | | | |
| o. FINAL SUBCONTRACTING PLAN REPORT SUBMITTED | | | | | | |
| p. TERMINATION DOCKET COMPLETED | DD 1593 | | | | | |
| q. CONTRACT AUDIT COMPLETED | | | | | | |
| r. CONTRACTOR'S CLOSING STATEMENT COMPLETED | | | | | | |
| s. FINAL VOUCHER SUBMITTED | SF 1034 | | | | | |
| t. FINAL PAID VOUCHER RECEIVED | SF 1034 | | | | | |
| u. FINAL REMOVAL OF EXCESS FUNDS RECOMMENDED | | | | | | |
| v. ISSUANCE OF CONTRACT COMPLETION STATEMENT *(Or MILSCAP Format Identifier PK9)* | | 6 | 36 | 20 | | |
| w. OTHER REQUIREMENTS COMPLETED *(Specify)* | | | | | | |

9. RESPONSIBLE OFFICIAL

| a. TYPED NAME *(Last, First, Middle Initial)* | b. TITLE |
|---|---|
| c. SIGNATURE *(Sign only upon completion of all actions)* | d. DATE SIGNED *(YYYYMMDD)* |

DD FORM 1597, APR 2000 PREVIOUS EDITION MAY BE USED. Adobe Professional 8.0

**Figure 15-1**

## Government Closeout Process

Usually the Contract Administration Office (CAO) is responsible for insuring completion of all contract administration actions and for initiating closeout action after receiving evidence of a contract's physical completion. The primary exception is when the procuring office retains the contract administration functions.

The administrative contracting officer (ACO), or designated representative, obtains statements from other organizational elements certifying completion of actions required by their group. The ACO makes the determination that completion is successful. Then the ACO certifies to the fact and forwards the certificate to the contracting officer (CO). At that time all organizations can retire their contract files following agency procedures.

## Contractor Closeout Actions

Just as the contracting officer directs the Government's closure actions, the contract administrator must do the same for the contractor. Of a high priority, the administrator must determine that the contractor has complied with all of the contractual requirements. To perform this task, the contract administrator should take the following actions:

- First, obtain a statement from the program manager certifying completion of all contractual requirements.
- Second, secure evidence that all data was delivered.
- Third, obtain a statement from Product Assurance that all deliveries were made and there is evidence of Government acceptance for each item.
- Fourth, check with Finance and Legal to be sure there are not any claims or litigation actions operative or pending.

It is imperative that the contract administrator perform a personal audit of the contract file as a double check. The use of some form of a checklist will aid the closure process. The list prescribes all the items needed to verify each closeout action. Figure 15-2, *Potential Closure Problems*, on page 389 identifies a series of situations which could jeopardize the orderly closure of a contract. Some of them may be appropriate for the recommended checklist.

Figure 15-2 notes two conditions that need careful checking. The first is whether or not any efforts were expended beyond the period of performance. The other is whether costs incurred exceed the amount of contractual funding. If either of these conditions exist, it is important that the contract administrator act promptly to obtain a contract modification. Such a modification is needed to extend the period of performance and possibly increase the funding. Without a modification, costs incurred under those conditions are subject to disallowance.

In some closure actions a contract modification may not be necessary. A letter written to the CO can serve the purpose in many cases. The contractor certifies to the completion of all contractual requirements. The letter should contain a request that the contracting officer issue a letter of concurrence. A DD Form 250, *Material Inspection and Receiving Report* (Figure 13-2, page 338), may also serve this purpose.

Administrative closure actions on the part of the contractor include:

- Closing out of all work orders;
- Assuring that all terms and conditions, change orders and supplemental agreements were incorporated into the contract;
- Disposition of residual Government property, special tooling and special test equipment;
- Implement appropriate closure actions for all subcontracts, purchase orders, etc.;
- Verify full funding on the contract for all work performed;
- Disposition of classified documents in accordance with the final DD Form 254;
- Submission of the final patent, new technology and royalty reports;
- Submission of a final price proposal on FPI contracts;
- Submission of final overhead rates proposal for cost-reimbursement (if not done on a company-wide basis); and
- Submission of final invoice upon incorporation of final overhead rates.

Upon receipt of final payment on the contract, the administrator should send a letter to the contracting officer. The letter should state that all administrative actions have been completed and the contractor considers the contract completely closed. At this point both parties will proceed with the disposition of their contract files. The contracting officer will follow the requirements set forth in FAR 4.8, *Government Contract Files*. The contractor will use its own policies and procedures for data disposition. Those procedures must be compatible with the contractual data retention requirements. In addition, the contractor must retain data for tax and other audit purposes. This is the time when the contracting parties can consider the contract is administratively closed as they have finished all contractual efforts.

The three most significant exceptions to having "complete closure" in a contract, which were discussed in previous chapters of the text, are:

- Any data retention requirements;
- The expiration of any contractual warranties; and
- The disclosure of any possible latent defect situations.

# POTENTIAL CLOSURE PROBLEMS

- In a cost reimbursement contract, has the performance of work exceeded the contract end date?

- A variance (overrun) on the contract developed as a result of circumstances which prevented proper notification as required by the Limitation of Cost clause or other terms of the contract.

- There was direction to perform work on the contract (i.e., constructive change) and there is an unresolved claim outstanding.

- There were changes of direction for submission of documentation, but not reflected in the contract data requirements list.

- Delinquent reports or other data are still to be submitted.

- Disposition of government-furnished documents or property yet to be accomplished.

- Litigation or dispute still pending, either with the Government or a subcontractor.

**Figure 15-2**

# CHAPTER 16

# CONTRACTUAL CHALLENGES

## OVERVIEW

The objective of the federal acquisition process is to obtain the supplies, equipment and services needed to support governmental operations and programs on time and at reasonable prices. As we all know from experience, most goals are not reached one hundred percent of the time. The world of Government contracts is not immune. All too frequently something arises that creates a challenging situation for the contracting parties. The situation may do nothing more than cause a short delay in the contractual process. On the other hand, the impact could be catastrophic. It could result in unpleasant conditions, such as disputes, litigation or termination of the contract.

The natural reaction of contracting parties, when these challenges occur, is to discuss how to resolve the problem. The outcome of the discussions varies due to the many factors involved. Some of those influencing factors are well within the control of the concerned parties. However, neither party can influence or control many things that impact programs and contracts. Resolution is usually enhanced when both parties approach the problem with a positive and cooperative attitude.

This chapter discusses some of the situations which present a challenge to the contracting parties. We will look at issues like delays, disputes, mistakes in contracts and requests for extraordinary relief. We will also address how the Government and contractors deal with those situations.

## CONTRACTUAL DELAYS

It is not uncommon for the original schedule, milestones and delivery dates, as envisioned by the contracting parties, to undergo changes during the contract period of performance. The factors which bring about the change have a direct bearing upon the contract and the contractor. The contractor's degree of responsibility in causing missed schedules will have a significant influence upon whatever relief may be forthcoming. The consequence of such missed schedules ranges from the onus of having the contract terminated for default to the positive relief of receiving an equitable adjustment to the contract. Depending upon the factors involved, the contractual adjustment may or may not include compensation for the contractor. Contract terminations and their impact on both the Government and the contractor were discussed in the previous chapter. The following four sections will address the major types of contractual delays, their ramifications and remedies.

## Excusable Delays

Contractors are not always held in default for failure to perform under the terms of the contract. Relief from a default termination may include, but are not limited to the following situations (*FAR 52.249-14, Excusable Delays*):

- Acts of the Government in either its sovereign or contractual capacity
- Acts of God or of the public enemy
- Fires, floods, and unusually severe weather
- Epidemics and quarantine restrictions
- Strikes and freight embargoes

Occurrence of such situations creates an excusable delay condition. Normal relief to contractors for an excusable delay, when recognized as such by the contracting officer, will be a revision of the delivery schedule. Financial relief is not available, unless it can be shown that the Government assumed the risk. When the Government grants financial relief, they will cite some other provision of the contract as authority for the action, not *Excusable Delay*. Even without compensation by some form of an equitable adjustment, there may be financial relief in an incentive contract. Computation of "total allowable cost," under Subparagraph (e)(4)(i) of the *Incentive Fee* clause at FAR 52.216-10, excludes costs arising from an excusable delay for the purpose of fee adjustments.

Failure of a subcontractor to perform or make progress is the prime contractor's responsibility. However, the prime may not be in default if the failure arises out of causes beyond the control of both the contractor and subcontractor and without the fault or negligence of either. Even this condition may not hold true if the following conditions apply.

- The supplies or services to be furnished by the subcontractor were obtainable by the prime contractor from other sources;
- The contracting officer had ordered the contractor in writing to procure such supplies or services from those other sources; and
- The contractor failed to comply reasonably with that order.

An act of the Government that delays a contractor, does not automatically entitle the contractor to an excusable delay. It must be shown that the Government in some way interfered with the contractor's prosecution of the contractual effort (*Royal Electric, Inc.,* ASBCA 3481, 1962 BCA 3552). Even though a contractor can establish that an event or occurrence was unforeseeable, beyond its control and occurred without its fault or negligence, the contractor may not be entitled to an excusable delay. The contractor must prove that it was actually delayed in the performance of the work (*Fuller, Webb & Hardeman,* ASBCA 9590, 1964 BCA, 4396). A constructive acceleration occurs when there is no formal acceleration but the project is speeded up another way. To prove a constructive acceleration, a contractor must prove an excusable delay giving rise to an acceleration order and extra costs.

There can be no delay, however, without a deadline to miss. So the contract schedule must state a specific delivery date. The Government has a responsibility to not interfere with a contractor's work. On one occasion where the Government did interfere, a remedy was made available to the contractor. In *Minority Enterprises, Inc.*, ASBCA No. 38927, 1994, the board converted the termination for default to a termination for convenience, thus allowing the contractor the possibility of financial relief.

**Compensable Delays**

There is specific language in most contracts which permits the Government to make compensation for delays caused to contractors. The several *Changes* clauses at FAR 52.243 provide for an equitable adjustment to a contract, including schedule, cost and fee/profit. These clauses are the most common authority used to provide such relief. Other clauses that can provide for an equitable contract adjustment include: *Government Property* at FAR 52.245-1; *Suspension of Work* at FAR 52.242-14; and *Stop-Work Order* at FAR 52.242-15.

Without specific contract language, Government involvement may enable a contractor to recover delay costs, as the examples cited below demonstrate:

- If the delay is caused by the Government's negligence or failure to exercise reasonable diligence, the Government will be held liable (*Ben C. Gerwick, Inc. v. United States*, 151 Ct. Cl. 69, 285 F.2d 432 (1961));
- Unreasonable delays in testing and accepting supplies under the contract will also be considered breaches by the Government (*Continental Illinois National Bank v. United States*, 126 Ct. Cl. 631, 115 F. Supp. 892 (1953));
- Liability may result from delays caused by the issuance of changes beyond the scope of the contract (*P.L. Saddler v. United States*, 152 Ct. Cl. 557, 287 F.2d 411 (1961));
- The contractor may find relief for delays caused by other contractors (*L.L. Hall Construction Co. v. United States*, 177 Ct. Cl. 870, 379 F.2d 559 (1966)); or
- The Government may be liable for delays resulting from its failure to divulge material information to the contractor (*Helene Curtis Industries, Inc. v. United States*, 160 Ct. Cl. 437, 312 F.2d 774 (1963)).

## Government Delay of Work

The *Government Delay of Work* clause at FAR 52.242-17 will be inserted in solicitations and contracts when a fixed-price contract is contemplated for supplies and services other than commercial or modified-commercial items. The clause is optional for fixed-price contract for supplies that are commercial or modified-commercial items. The clause provides a means for the expeditious administrative settlement of claims for certain delays and interruptions of the contract work. It applies to acts, or failures to act, of the contracting officer where the contract does not otherwise specifically provide for an equitable adjustment for such delays or interruptions. Examples of clauses that do have that provision are the *Government Property* and *Changes* clauses. The *Government Delay of Work* clause permits an adjustment in the cost of performance (excluding profit), delivery or performance dates and any other term or condition affected by the delay or interruption.

The *Government Delay of Work* clause does not authorize the contracting officer to order a suspension, delay or interruption of the work. Neither is its use authorized as the basis for or justification of such an order.

## Suspension of Work

Contracting officers may select from two suspension of work type clauses to order a contractor to stop or suspend effort on a contract. The *Suspension of Work* clause at FAR 52.242-14 is for use in solicitations and contracts when a fixed-price construction or architect-engineer contract is contemplated. Under this clause the contracting officer may order the contractor to suspend, delay or interrupt all or any part of the contract work. Any order to suspend work must be in writing and signed by the contracting officer. The suspension may be for any period of time that the contracting officer determines to be appropriate for the convenience of the Government. If the suspension is for an unreasonable period, an adjustment may be made by increasing the cost of performance of the contract. No additional profit is added to the contract value.

The second option for the contracting officer (CO) is the *Stop-Work Order* clause at FAR 52.242-15. This clause is for use in solicitations and contracts for supplies, services or research and development. Under this clause the contracting officer may order the contractor to stop all, or any part, of the contract work. These orders must also be in writing and signed by the contracting officer. The order can be for ninety (90) days or any further period to which the parties may agree.

Upon receipt of a stop-work order, the contractor must immediately comply with its terms and take all reasonable steps to minimize incurring any costs allocable to the work covered by the order during the period of work stoppage. All suspensions are temporary; therefore, within the ninety days, or any extension, the contracting officer must take positive action.

First of all, the contracting officer can cancel the stop-work order and permit the contractor to resume the efforts. This could occur for several reasons, such as: (1) new material evidence has been discovered; (2) there has been a change in management or ownership; (3) the reason for the suspension has been eliminated; or (4) other appropriate reasons. After resumption of work, the contract will be subject to an equitable adjustment and modification. The alternative action available is to terminate the work covered by the stop order. Based upon the circumstances that initially prompted issuance of the Stop-Work Order, the CO will issue a termination for "Default" or "Convenience" of the Government.

The right to order suspension actions is not available to the Government if the contract does not contain either of these suspension type clauses. In those cases, contracting officers must use the termination provisions of the contract if it was essential that work on the contract be interrupted.

## LEGAL AND PARALEGAL ACTIONS

### Contract Disputes Act of 1978

The Contract Disputes Act of 1978, as amended (*Public Law 95-563, 41 U.S.C. 601-613*), established procedures and requirements for asserting and resolving claims subject to the Act. In addition, the Act provides for: (1) the payment of interest on successful contractor claims; (2) certification by contractors of claims submitted; and (3) a civil penalty for contractor claims that are determined to be fraudulent or based on a misrepresentation of facts.

FAR Part 33, *Protests, Disputes, and Appeals*, prescribes the policies and procedures for filing protests and for processing contract disputes and appeals. With the possible exception of foreign Governments and agencies, FAR Part 33 and the *Disputes* clause at FAR 52.233-1 apply to all Government contracts, either expressed or implied, covered by the Federal Acquisition Regulation. *Alternate I* of the clause also applies if, under agency procedures, unusual circumstances make continued performance vital. Under the *Disputes* clause a contractor must continue performance of the contract, pending resolution of a dispute. Performance will be in accordance with the contracting officer's decision and other directions.

However, if the dispute arises outside of the contract, or in breach of the contract, there is no obligation to continue work. In unusual circumstances, the performance of some contracts may be vital to the national security or to the public health and welfare. So that performance must be guaranteed under any form of dispute or breach of contract. In those unusual cases, procuring agencies may provide for a change to the *Disputes* clause or use *Alternate I* to assure a continuation of the work.

## Claims, Disputes and Appeals

Contractors submit claims to the Government because they believe that they have not received a fair decision from a contracting officer on some matter. The U.S. Court of Appeals for the Federal Circuit held that a claim need meet only the three basic requirements of FAR 2.101, *Definitions*: (1) be a written demand, (2) seeking as a matter of right, (3) the payment of money in a certain sum (*Reflectone, Inc. v. Dalton,* 60 F.3d, 1572, 1575 (Fed. Cir. (1995)). The Court did not address the lesser elements of the definition, regarding "the adjustment or interpretation of contract terms or other relief arising under or relating to the contract." Cost proposals submitted in response to a change or delay in the contract work are not of themselves a claim. Neither are payment requests for work performed or supplies delivered. It is only when the parties cannot agree on the nature or magnitude of the matter that a claim may come into being.

The Government policy, consistent with the Contracts Disputes Act, is to try and resolve all claims by mutual agreement at the contracting officer's level. The policy is to avoid litigation if at all possible. Reasonable efforts will be made to resolve controversies prior to the contractor submitting a claim. Agencies are encouraged to use alternative dispute resolution (ADR) procedures to the maximum extent practicable. (ADRs are discussed in detail starting on page 401.) Success of that policy depends on keeping an open mind on the matter in dispute. It will also depend upon the adequacy of the information provided in support of the claim by both the contractor and the Government.

One type of claim by contractors received considerable attention in 2010 concerning past performance evaluations in source selection activities. The U. S. Court of Federal Claims found that negative past performance evaluations could be the basis for a claim within the court's jurisdiction. In that case the judges concluded "that a past performance evaluation could be a claim." They denied the government's motion to dismiss the claim, and allowed the contractor to prove his claim was valid. (*BLR Group of America, Inc. v. United States,* U.S. Court of Federal Claims No. 07-579C, August 16, 2010)

Before issuing a contracting officer's decision on a claim, informal discussions between the parties could aid in the resolution of differences by mutual agreement. This is the time for both parties to fall back, before proceeding further, and follow the old adage that states "When all else fails . . . Read the Contract." Too many disputes could be resolved by the parties sitting down and reading that part of the contact which has created the misunderstanding. Another possibility is to involve individuals who have not participated substantially in the subject under dispute. This option is discussed later in the section on alternative dispute resolution procedures. Poor record keeping by the contractor will have a direct negative impact on chances of winning a claim.

When a contractor and the contracting officer cannot resolve their differences on a contractual issue through discussions, then a dispute situation is probable. At this point the contractor must request the contracting officer to issue a formal decision on the matter.

Before making a final decision, the contracting officer will review the available facts pertinent to the matter. When there is any doubt that the issue is subject to the disputes procedure, the CO will make a decision under the *Disputes* clause. The disputes procedure will not be used where a disagreement is clearly not subject to the procedure. Before rendering a decision, the contracting officer will obtain advice and assistance from legal and other advisors. However, it is the contracting officer's responsibility to make the final decision.

Submission of a formal claim presupposes that the contracting parties are in dispute. If a contractor has not challenged a situation and asked for the contracting officer's decision by submitting a formal claim, a dispute does not exist. Therefore, the contracting officer is not able to issue a "formal decision." The Department of Transportation Board of Contract Appeals concluded that a contracting officer had to await "a failure of negotiations after affording the contractor time to comment on the Government's position and pending claim." (*World Computer Systems, Inc.,* DOT BCA No. 2802 (1995)).

The final decision must be furnished to the contractor in writing. It should include a statement of facts in enough detail to enable the contractor to understand both the decision and the basis thereof (*FAR 33.211, Contracting Officer's Decision*). To be a valid final decision, it must be the personal and independent decision of the contracting officer. A more detailed discussion of this requirement starts on page 101 in Chapter 4, *Contracting Methods*.

The contracting officer will send a copy of the decision to the contractor, by certified mail, return receipt requested, or any other method that provides evidence of receipt. As a minimum, the decision statement must include the following information:

- A description of the claim or dispute;
- A reference to pertinent contract provisions;
- A statement of the factual areas of agreement or disagreement;
- A statement of the contracting officer's decision, with supporting rationale; and
- Paragraphs substantially as follows:

> "This is the final decision of the Contracting Officer. You may appeal this decision to the agency board of contract appeals. If you decide to appeal, you must, within 90 days from the date you receive this decision, mail or otherwise furnish written notice to the agency board of contract appeals and provide a copy to the Contracting Officer from whose decision the appeal is taken. The notice shall indicate that an appeal is intended, reference this decision, and identify the contract by number.
>
> With regard to appeals to the agency board of contract appeals, you may, solely at your election, proceed under the board's: (1) small claim procedure for claims of $50,000 or less or, in the case of a small business concern (as defined in the Small Business Act and regulations under that Act), $150,000 or less; or (2) accelerated procedure for claims of $100,000 or less.

> Instead of appealing to the board of contract appeals, you may bring an action directly in the United States Court of Federal Claims (except as provided in the Contract Disputes Act of 1978, 41 U.S.C. 603, regarding Maritime Contracts) within 12 months of the date you receive this decision."

The contracting officer must issue a decision on any claim less than $100,000 within sixty (60) days from receipt of a written request for that decision within that time period. On claims for more than $100,000, either a decision must be issued in 60 days after receiving a certified claim or the contractor given specific notice of the time when it will be issued (*FAR 33.211, Contracting Officer's Decision*).

When a contractor gets into a dispute with the Government, the contractor generally must continue to work while the dispute goes on. The contractor typically does not have the option of resolving the dispute before resuming work on the contract. This is referred to as the "duty to proceed." The standard disputes clause obligates the contractor to proceed while the dispute is pending. There are very few exceptions to this duty to proceed. A decision by the Armed Services Board of Contract Appeals found a contractor was justified in not proceeding with work while a dispute continued because the Government failed to give the contractor proper instructions (*Marine Construction and Dredging, Inc.,* ASBCA Nos. 38412 et al. (1994)).

When dissatisfied with the contracting officer's decision, the contractor may appeal to the appropriate Board of Contract Appeals. Prior to filing an appeal, the contractor should carefully consider the efforts, costs and time that will have to be expended. Successful contract appeals are reached in less that 50 percent of the cases, most cases last over four (4) years and when factoring in attorney fees and other costs of litigation, an appeal may not make good economic sense.

When a contractor decides to go ahead, it must file the appeal within ninety (90) days from receipt of the contracting officer's decision. The 90 day deadline in which to appeal to a board is ironclad, it's a statutory requirement and cannot be waived. When contesting the receipt of an appeal within the 90 day deadline, the Government has the burden of establishing the date that the contracting officer's final decision was received by the contractor. Therefore, the use of certified mail, return receipt requested, is the ideal method of sending the final decision.

Even after an appeal is filed, the contracting parties are encouraged to continue efforts at seeking an agreement to settle the controversy. Any such efforts to resolve a controversy will not result in a suspension of the appeal process. Sometimes the discussions will result in the parties coming to an equitable agreement wherein the claimant withdraws or "releases" its claim. It is essential that such release truly reflect a meeting of the minds of both parties in order that the release be effective. In all situations the Board of Contract Appeals will have jurisdiction over the claim and may order or authorize a suspension of the appeal.

After receiving the contracting officer's decision, the contractor has one other possible action available. The contractor can submit any additional information which it believes the contracting officer did not use when making the final decision. When submitting this type of information it must be done in a formal request for reconsideration. Further review by the contracting officer suspends the finality of the decision until a decision is reached on the reconsideration.

The Boards of Contract Appeals have authority to grant any relief that would be available to a litigant asserting a contract claim in the Court of Federal Claims (formerly the U.S. Claims Court). Therefore, they may hear appeals involving "questions of fact," breach of contract or mistakes. In performing their functions, the boards can issue subpoenas enforceable by the U.S. District Courts. They can also seek related facts and data through the discovery process and take depositions as necessary.

Dispositions of cases before the appeals boards, including opinions and decisions, are always issued in writing. The boards dispose of their cases in one of the following manners:

- They may issue a formal written decision and opinion on the case, determining all the issues.
- They may remand the case to the contracting officer for further proceedings. In so doing, the Board will cite specific directions to the CO.
- The Board may dismiss the appeal with prejudice against the appellant.
- The Board may dismiss the appeal without prejudice against either party.
- They may approve a stipulation of the parties agreeing to a settlement arrived at “out of court.”
- Finally, they may permit the withdrawal of an appeal.

The disputes process dictates that the contracting officer promptly carries out the board decisions favorable to the appellant. In some cases only the question of entitlement is decided by the board. The question of amount is remanded to the parties for negotiation. If the parties do not reach agreement, the appellant may request a prompt decision from the contracting officer and can then appeal.

Either the contractor or the Government may appeal Board decisions. Appellants have 120 days to file an appeal with the U.S. Court of Appeals for the Federal Circuit. Contractors may assert appeals directly to the court. However, the contracting officer must first obtain concurrence of the agency head and the Department of Justice before initiating an appeal on behalf of the Government. If either party desires to appeal the decision of the court of appeals, they will file an appeal with the U.S. Supreme Court. They have 60 days after the appeals court ruling to file with the Supreme Court. There are no time limits imposed upon the Supreme Court as to when they must reach their decision.

The contractor may choose to appeal the contracting officer's final decision directly to the Court of Federal Claims (COFC) instead of filing with a Board of Contract Appeals. In this case the appeal must be filed within one year after receiving the CO's final decision. As noted in Chapter 15, *Contract Termination and Closeout*, the claims court will not hear an appeal of a default termination from a contractor without a monetary claim being involved. There are no time limits on the court to render a decision. Either party may appeal the decision of the COFC to the Court of Appeals for the Federal Circuit, but they only have 60 days to assert an appeal. As before, there are only 60 days to file with the U.S. Supreme Court an appeal of the Court of Appeals decision.

The Contract Disputes Act (CDA) dictates that contractor claims must be submitted in writing to the contracting officer for a decision within six (6) years after accrual of a claim. However, the contracting parties may agree to a shorter time. In the same manner, the contracting officer must issue a written decision on any Government claim initiated against a contractor within six (6) years after accrual of the claim, unless the contracting parties agree to a shorter time period (*FAR 33.206, Initiation of a Claim*).

**Certification of Claims**

Contractors must certify to any claim in excess of $100,000 regardless of the amount when using arbitration or any other ADR technique. The exact wording of the certificate is set out in FAR 33.207, *Contractor Certification*. The certificate will state as follows:

> I certify that the claim is made in good faith; that the supporting data are accurate and complete to the best of my knowledge and belief; that the amount requested accurately reflects the contract adjustment for which the contractor believes the Government is liable; and that I am duly authorized to certify the claim on behalf of the contractor.

The regulations require that the certification may be executed by any person duly authorized to bind the contractor with respect to the claim.

A recurring problem in claims litigation centers on the language that contractors use to certify their claims. Contractors are advised to follow the exact statutory and regulatory language of the certification verbatim rather than risking any deviation, however slight or well-intended. When contractors do not use the exact words of the statute the Government could be left wondering whether the partially correct certification is valid. Deviations and variations from the language will be scrutinized by the boards to see whether the language used had the effect of diluting the strength of the certification. If there is any doubt by the boards, the claim may be rejected and held to be insufficient.

Contracting officers expect a contractor's total claim to be submitted at one time with all the information required by law that is needed to make a decision. The question arises as to the legality of a claim when the contractor submits several pieces of paper over a long period of time, sometimes changing amounts and changing rationales for the claim. Few such claims are as fortunate as the case in which the court concluded that "a contractor's prior submissions, taken together with the so-called claim letter, adequately stated a claim even though the submissions were not a model of clarity or form." (*Al Munford, Inc. dba Munford Construction Co. v. The United States,* U. S. Court of Federal Claims No. 93-177C, (1993)).

The Contract Disputes Act also provides that if certifying contractors fail to prevail on the claim before the board they stand to lose more than their case. The Government may later find there was misrepresentation of fact or fraud on the part of the contractor. If that is the reason for not winning their case, the Government will have a claim against the contractor. The contractor may be liable to the Government for an amount equal to the unsupported claim. In addition, the contractor must pay for all costs the Government incurred in reviewing that portion of the claim.

The Act provides that interest is payable on successful contractor claims, when found due and unpaid. The interest will run from the date the contracting officer received the claim from the contractor. If a contractor claim has been rejected for having a defective certification, and the contractor is able to provide a proper certificate correcting a defective certificate, interest will be paid from the date of receipt of the proper certificate.

### Alternative Dispute Resolution (*FAR 33.214*)

Alternative dispute resolution (ADR) means any procedure or combination of procedures voluntarily used to resolve issues in controversy without the need to resort to litigation. The ADR procedures may include, but are not limited to, assisted settlement negotiations, mediation, facilitation, conciliation, fact-finding, ombudsman, mini-trials and arbitration. Most of these procedures may be tailored to meet the needs of the parties involved in the dispute.

The objective of using alternative dispute resolution procedures is to increase the opportunity for relatively inexpensive and expeditious resolution of issues in controversy. Essential elements in the use of ADR are: (1) the existence of an issue in controversy; (2) the voluntary election by both parties to participate in the ADR process; (3) an agreement by the parties on alternative procedures and terms to be used in lieu of formal litigation; and (4) participation in the process by officials of both parties who have the authority to resolve the issue in controversy (*FAR 33.214(a)*). Under FAR 52.233-1, *Disputes*, if the parties do enter into ADR proceedings, it is likewise necessary that the contractor certify the claim if it is above $100,000.

While the statute may allow either party of a dispute to decline participation in the alternative disputes resolution process, there are definite constraints. If the contracting officer rejects a contractor's request for ADR proceedings, the CO must provide the contractor with a written explanation citing one or more of the conditions from the statute (*5 U.S.C. 572(b)*) or some other specific reason why ADR would not be appropriate. If the contractor rejects an agency request to use ADR proceedings, the contractor must provide a written explanation of the specific reasons for rejecting the request (*FAR 33.214(b)*).

Mediation is one of the more popular ADR techniques for resolving disputes. It is an informal process that includes any voluntary, non-adjudicatory dispute resolution process involving a third party. Under mediation the parties maintain a high level of control over the process, which is especially important when performance is continuing and maintaining a good working relationship is critical. The mediation process makes use of the neutral third party to hear the issues from both parties and work with them to discover their mutual interests. Hopefully, the mediator will be able to define the best and worse alternatives to an agreement by the parties. The mediator will then work with them to reach a negotiated settlement.

The mediation process involves the least risk of any of the ADR techniques and is much less costly than arbitration. Since it is voluntary, either party may withdraw at any time. Unless both parties agree, mediation is non-binding. It does encourage the parties to settle at a much earlier point in time than most other dispute procedures.

In one type of mediation, called ***facilitation***, presentations are made to a neutral third party who facilitates the discussions with the aim of having the parties arrive at their own agreement.

The ***conciliation*** type of mediation also uses a neutral third party in the role of an evaluator. The evaluator hears the parties' presentations and then forms a recommendation as to what the claim is worth and how it should be resolved. While pressure may be exerted on the parties, the recommendation is non-binding.

The ***ombudsman*** type of neutral third-party mediation process is significantly different from the others. The ombudsman makes his or her non-binding recommendation to the senior management of the disputing parties as to how the dispute should be resolved.

When none of those procedures appear applicable to a particular situation, there are other non-arbitration ADR procedures available within the board's jurisdiction. Those ADR procedures include settlement judges, mini-trials and summary trials with binding decisions.

- A settlement judge is a member of a board of contract appeals. The judge is appointed by the board to facilitate a settlement. Even though the judge has no decision making authority, the parties gain the benefit of a judicial review of the strengths and weaknesses of their positions without jeopardizing their ability to obtain an impartial Board hearing if they fail to reach a settlement. The settlement judge's recommendations are not binding.
- Mini-trials are very flexible review procedures. Each party presents an abbreviated version of its case to a Board appointed neutral advisor. The advisor's role is to assist the parties in negotiating a settlement. The neutral advisor's recommendations are not binding.
- A summary trial is different from the other two in several ways. The appeal is tried informally before an administrative judge or a panel of judges. All decisions under the summary trial procedure are final. The contractor cannot appeal the decision, nor may it be set aside, except in cases of fraud.

Alternative dispute resolution efforts were given a real boost by the passage of Pub. L. 101-552, *Administrative Dispute Resolution Act*. The Act required each agency to adapt a policy addressing the use of alternative dispute resolution (ADR) proceedings. The agencies are also authorized the use of arbitration in resolving disputes. From an agency's standpoint, binding arbitration, as an ADR procedure, may be agreed to only as specified in that agency's guidelines. Those guidelines will provide advice on the appropriate use of binding arbitration.

Arbitration proceedings are the most formal and costly of the ADR methods. However, arbitration has long been the mainstay of the ADR process. Together with mediation, arbitration has served as an effective means of avoiding some of litigation's pitfalls, most of all the excessive time and expenses incurred in litigation. The time element alone can last for several years.

A settlement by arbitration may be binding or non-binding upon the parties, based primarily upon the nature of the dispute and the agreements of the parties when entering into the process. Arbitration is a relatively formal process where presentations are made to either a single arbitrator or a panel of arbitrators. The arbitrators perform in the role of a judge whereby they ask questions and cross-examine witnesses.

A binding arbitration is adjudicative in its process, while a non-binding arbitration is a technique to help the parties realistically evaluate their respective cases and ultimately settle their differences. In a non-binding situation, when the presentations are concluded, the arbitrators will deliver their decision for the parties to use in their settlement negotiation. While a final binding arbitration award is enforceable under the Act, it cannot serve as an estoppel in any related proceeding. Furthermore, the award may not be used as precedent or otherwise considered in any factually related proceedings.

While the use of such ADR procedures is encouraged, they should not be used if any of the following conditions exist:

- A definitive or authoritative resolution is required for precedent setting value, and the ADR proceedings are not likely to be accepted generally as an authoritative precedent;
- The matter involves significant policy questions that require additional procedures before final resolution may be made, and the ADR proceedings would not likely serve to develop a recommended policy for the agency;
- When maintaining established policies is of special importance, so that variations among individual decisions are not increased and the ADR proceedings would not likely reach consistent results among individual decisions;
- When the matter significantly affects persons and organizations that are not parties to the ADR proceedings;
- In cases where a full public record of the proceedings is important; or
- When it is important for the agency to maintain continuing jurisdiction over the matter. Have the authority to alter the disposition of the matter in light of changed conditions or circumstances, and the ADR would interfere with the agency's ability to fulfill that requirement.

The Administrative Dispute Resolution Act also amended the Contract Disputes Act (CDA) to specifically authorize the use of ADR proceedings for resolving claims. Even though ADR proceedings are used, contractors will still be required to certify their claims under the requirements of the CDA. ADR awards are still subject to judicial review.

The Armed Services Board of Contract Appeals (ASBCA) is a strong advocate of alternative dispute resolution techniques. The Board has successfully conducted abbreviated dispute proceedings over the telephone. That has saved the parties considerable time and expense. The Board's Fiscal Year 1988 report said the following regarding the use of ADR:

> The parties should consider using ADR options more frequently. Too often, parties litigate because of habit. While there are many disputes for which litigation is the only means of reaching a resolution, more appeals should be resolved by responsible management decision makers. Litigation is the last resort, not a negotiation position. We need ADR in Government contracting because there is too much litigation. ADR serves its purposes best in reminding the contracting parties that the negotiating table, not the courtroom, is the forum of choice in a healthy and productive business relationship.

## Subcontractor Claim and Appeal Rights

Subcontractors do not have the same claim and appeal rights available to prime contractors. This is because there is no "privity of contract" between the Government and the subcontractor. Prime contractors cannot include clauses in their subcontracts which give the subcontractor the right of a direct decision of the contracting officer. Contracting officers must not consent to subcontracts obligating the CO to deal directly with the subcontractor or subcontracts that make results of arbitration, judicial determination or voluntary settlement between the prime contractor and subcontractor binding on the Government (*FAR 44.203, Consent Limitations*).

Under the Contract Disputes Act subcontractor remedies against the Government are limited to claims sponsored by the prime contractor in either the U.S. Claims Court or the appropriate board of contract appeals. To allow subcontractors to proceed in district courts would expose the Government to multiple subcontractor suits. One rare exception to this principle is seen in a decision by the Corps of Engineers Board of Contract Appeals. The board allowed the subcontractor to sue because the contract between the agency and prime contractor expressly allowed the subcontractor to sue the Government (*John M. Cockerham and Associates, Inc.,* EBCA No. C-930917, (1995)).

As opposed to the right of direct action, subcontractors affected by a dispute arising under a prime contract may have the right of indirect appeal to an appeals board or the courts. This indirect appeal process, a "pass-through action," permits a subcontractor's claim to be taken forward to the Government in either of the following ways:

- The prime contractor may include the subcontractor's claim as a part of its own claim.
- The prime contractor may file the appeal on behalf of the subcontractor.

In either case the contractor is acting as the agent for the subcontractor. The contracting officer's decision is passed down to the subcontractor. The subcontractor will repay the prime contractor for expenses incurred on behalf of the subcontractor.

In what is known as the *Severin Doctrine,* a prime contractor is precluded from maintaining a suit on behalf of its subcontractor only when a clause or release completely exonerates the prime contractor from liability to its subcontractor. The subcontractor release must expressly negate any liability of the prime contractor to the subcontractor. Furthermore, the "prime" may maintain an action even if its liability to the "sub" is extinguished merely by prosecuting the "sub's" claims against the Government or paying over to the "sub" any recovery obtained from the Government.

Contracting officers do not participate in disputes between a prime contractor and its subcontractors. The normal avenue for resolution of a dispute between the two is through the civil court system in the state having jurisdiction over the contract. Prime contractors prefer adjudication of any legal action under the laws of their home state or country. In many cases it is more logical to use the laws of the subcontractor's home state. Legal jurisdiction belongs where the work is actually performed. There is a significant exception to having these cases in the civil court system. Any case involving national security must be held in the federal court system. On federal contract matters having to do with national security, state law is totally displaced by federal common law.

Only on very rare occasions has a Board of Contract Appeals heard and acted upon a dispute emanating from a subcontractor. These will be situations far different than the preceding exception. On these occasions some very extenuating circumstances permitted the Government to ignore the fact that no privity of contract existed. Certain events must have happened before a board will assume jurisdiction of a subcontractor's claim under the Contracts Disputes Act. First, the subcontractor must have filed a claim through the prime contractor. A contracting officer, board or court must have denied the claim. Lastly, the subcontractor must have filed an appeal of the denial.

## False Claims and Fraud

Multiple situations exist where a contractor may be charged with making a false claim against the Government. In doing that the contractor is susceptible to an investigation and possible litigation for fraud. The following are some of the situations where a fraudulent condition may be found:

- Claims filed under the disputes procedures
- Certified cost or pricing data
- Invoices for reimbursement
- Product substitution
- Falsified time cards and accounting records
- Frivolous lawsuits that are tantamount to fraud

Fraud is defined in Black's Law Dictionary as:

> A false representation of a matter of fact, whether by words or by conduct, by false or misleading allegations, or by concealment of that which should have been disclosed, which deceives and is intended to deceive another so that he shall act upon it to his legal injury.

The Civil False Claims Act (*31 U.S.C. 3729*), as amended, defines a "knowing" false claim as one in which the defendant (i.e., contractor) had actual knowledge, or acted in deliberate ignorance of the truth, or acted in reckless disregard of the truth or falsity of information. It goes on to state that no proof of specific intent to defraud is required. The Act states that the Government may establish the existence of a civil false claim when the preponderance of evidence supports such facts. If a contractor is unable to support any part of its claim and there is evidence that the inability is attributed to misrepresentation of fact or to fraud on the part of the contractor, the contracting officer will refer the matter to the agency official responsible for investigating fraud.

In 2009, the False Claims Act was again amended to reverse court decisions that had limited the Government's rights under the act. In part the amendment went beyond fraud by Government contractors to include persons and entities that use Government funds (i.e., Amtrak or government grantees). The amendment also addressed: (1) contractors and individuals who fail to return Government property in their possession; and (2) failures by contractors to return overpayments they may have received during the life of a contact.

Subcontractors can be subject to the False Claims Act the same as the prime contractor. A false claim can arise from an invoice in which a Government contractor or subcontractor certifies adherence to the program's requirements, when in fact a subcontractor had actually violated program requirements. A more common situation of a false claim would occur when federal funds are flowing through the prime contractor to a subcontractor's invoices with inaccurate certifications of compliance.

Contractors must be aware that every defective pricing case or other false claim allegation may be a potential candidate for fraud prosecution. They should also be aware that any ruling of fraud in part of a contract can condemn the entire contract. Therefore, any subsequent claim submitted will probably be denied because of a previous finding of fraud by the contractor for some other matter.

**Contractual Mistakes**

Contractors frequently claim there is a mistake in their contract. To correct or mitigate the effect of a mistake, they will seek rescission or reformation of the contract. Requests for relief under Public Law 85-804 are not claims under the Contracts Disputes Act or the Disputes clause but are processed under FAR Part 50, *Extraordinary Contractual Actions and the Safety Act.*

However, relief formerly available only under Public Law 85-804; i.e., legal entitlement to rescission or reformation for mutual mistake, is now available within the authority of the contracting officer under the Contract Disputes Act and the Disputes clause (*FAR 33.205, Relationship of the Act to Pub. L. 85-804*).

While reformation is the most difficult to substantiate, it is the remedy contractors most frequently seek. Reformation requires a demonstration of what the parties would have agreed to originally. This was confirmed in a decision by the General Services Board of Contract Appeals. The board said it could reform a contract on the basis of mutual mistake only where "the mistaken belief constituted a basic assumption underlying the contract and the mistake had a material effect on the bargain" (*Jay P. Altmayer et al. v. General Services Administration*, GSBCA No. 12720, 1994). Reformation is normally sought when the contractor has already begun work on the contract prior to discovery of the mistake. Under most circumstances the remedy of rescission at that time would not benefit either party.

The time a mistake is discovered can have an important impact on the contractor's ability to obtain relief. In numerous rulings, the Comptroller General has held that in most cases the contractor waives the right to have a mistake corrected if any of the following events have occurred:

- The contractor completes performance of the contract before claiming the mistake.
- The contractor executes the contract having knowledge of the mistake.
- The contractor confirms its bid with the mistake before contract award.

When deciding cases involving contract mistakes, the courts have generally followed the established common law rules that the mistake must be "mutual." That basically means that both parties acknowledge and accept the mistake. Mistakes may also be remedied under the authority of Public Law 85-804, as discussed in the next section.

**Extraordinary Contractual Adjustments**

Public Law 85-804 (*Act of 28 August 1958), 72 Stat. 972; 50 U.S.C. 1431-1435*, bestows certain unusual powers on the President of the United States. The Act empowers the President to authorize departments and agencies to exercise certain specific functions in connection with the national defense. When authorized under the P.L. 85-804, the agencies may enter into contracts, amend or modify contracts and make advance payments, without regard to other provisions of law relating to the making, performance, amendment or modification of contracts. The President will consider such action if it would facilitate the national defense.

Many departments and agencies have Contract Adjustment Boards to carry out the process. The boards have the delegated authority to administer requests for contractual adjustments under the Act. The following limitations restrict the level to which the agencies may delegate the authority (*FAR 50.102-1, Delegation of Authority*):

- Authority delegated shall be to a level high enough to ensure uniformity of action.
- Authority to approve requests to obligate the Government in excess of $65,000 may not be delegated below the secretarial level.
- Regardless of dollar amount, authority to approve any amendment without consideration that increases the contract price or unit price may not be delegated below the secretarial level, except in extraordinary cases or classes of cases when the agency head finds that special circumstances clearly justify such delegation.
- Regardless of dollar amount, authority to indemnify against unusually hazardous or nuclear risks, including extension of such indemnification to subcontracts, shall be exercised only by the Secretary or Administrator of the agency concerned.

Losses occurred under a contract are not, by themselves, a sufficient basis for the Government agent to exercise the authority conferred by the Act. The proper authority must make sound judgments in each case to determine the appropriate action. They must be sure that an amendment without consideration, correction of a mistake or ambiguity in a contract or formalization of an informal commitment, will facilitate the national defense. The government may adjust the contract where an actual or threatened loss under a defense contract, however caused, will impair the productive ability of a contractor. Continued performance and operation by the contractor as a source of supply must be essential to the national defense. A contract adjustment, without consideration, will only be to the extent necessary to avoid such impairment to the contractor's productive ability. When loss is the result of Government action, the character of that action will generally determine whether or not to make an adjustment and to what extent (*FAR 50.103-2(a), Amendments Without Consideration*).

Contracts may be amended or modified to correct or mitigate the effect of a mistake, including the following examples:

- A mistake or ambiguity which consists of the failure to express, or to express clearly, in a written contract, the agreement as both parties understood it.
- A mistake on the part of the contractor which is so obvious that it was or should have been apparent to the contracting officer.
- A mutual mistake as to a material fact.

Amending contracts to correct mistakes with the least possible delay normally will facilitate the national defense by expediting the contracting program and assuring contractors that mistakes will be corrected expeditiously and fairly (*FAR 50.103-2(b), Correcting Mistakes*).

Under certain circumstances Contract Adjustment Boards formalize informal commitments made between the Government and contractors. The Act authorizes payment to persons or contractors who in good faith have taken action without a formal contract. The principle here is for the Government to pay for supplies or services furnished in good faith (*FAR 50.103-2(c), Formalizing Informal Commitments*).

Contractors submit requests to the contracting officer for indemnification against unusually hazardous or nuclear risks under P.L. 85-804. The contracting officer refers the request to a higher authority in the agency. A Memorandum of Decision will document the approval and become a part of the contract file. In fixed-price contracts the contracting officer will use the clause, *Indemnification Under Public Law 85-804*, at FAR 52.250-1, in the contract to show evidence of the approval. In cost-reimbursement contracts they will use *Alternate I* to the clause.

Another example of situations covered by the Act is the disbursement of advance payments to contractors. Advance payments are made before the contractor begins any of the contractual efforts. FAR 32.2, *Commercial Item Purchase Financing*, and FAR 32.4, *Advance Payments for Non-Commercial Items*, cover the procedures for advance payments. These financing functions were discussed in Chapter 13, *Contract Performance*.

FAR Part 50, *Extraordinary Contractual Actions and the Safety Act*, cites the uniform regulations for actions under Pub. L. 85-804. Requests for relief under the Act are first submitted to the contracting officer. A contractor seeking a contract adjustment that exceeds the simplified acquisition threshold, when submitting a request, must also submit a certification by a person authorized to certify the request. The certificate must state that: (1) the request is made in good faith; and (2) the supporting data are accurate and complete to the best of that person's knowledge and belief.

The CO processes all requests to the appropriate Contract Adjustment Board. The law requires that two determinations be made before relief may be granted. First, the contracting officer must have exhausted all possible remedies within the contract. Also, the Government must consider that performance by the contractor is essential to the national defense. The contracting officer's transmittal must include certain information before processing begins, such as the nature of the requested relief and the basis for determining that Pub. L. 85-804 provides the authority for the action. There must be findings of fact and conclusions based on the facts. Lastly, it must contain the CO's recommended Contract Adjustment Board action. Pub. L. 85-804 empowers the Contract Adjustment Boards to review the request from the contracting officer and consider authorizing one of the following three forms of remedial action:

- Amendments to a contract without consideration to the Government;
- Correction of mutual mistakes in a contract; and
- The formalization of informal agreements.

Unlike decisions of the Boards of Contract Appeals, contractors cannot appeal decisions of Contract Adjustment Boards. The Contract Disputes Act does not cover Contract Adjustment Board action.

# APPENDICES

# APPENDIX A

# ABBREVIATIONS AND ACRONYMS

| | |
|---|---|
| ACO | Administrative Contracting Officer |
| ADAD | After Date of Award Document |
| ADPE | Automatic Data Processing Equipment |
| ADR | Alternative Dispute Resolution |
| AFSCP | Air Force Systems Command Pamphlet |
| aka | Also known as |
| AMC | Army Materiel Command |
| AMSL | Acquisition Management Systems List |
| A-PT | Action-Phrase Topic |
| ARN | Acquisition Reform Network |
| ARO | After Receipt of Order |
| ASBCA | Armed Services Board of Contract Appeals |
| ASPM | Armed Services Pricing Manual |
| ASPR | Armed Services Procurement Regulations |
| B/A | Basic Agreement |
| BAFO | Best and Final Offer |
| BCA | Board of Contract Appeals |
| BOA | Basic Ordering Agreement |
| B&P | Bid and Proposal |
| BPA | Blanket Purchase Agreement |
| BPN | Business Partner Network |
| CAB | Contract Adjustment Board |
| CAFC | Court of Appeals for the Federal Circuit |
| CAIV | Cost as an Independent Variable |
| CAO | Contract Administration Office/Chief Acquisition Officer |
| CAS | Cost Accounting Standard |
| CASB | Cost Accounting Standards Board |
| CBD | Commerce Business Daily |
| CBO | Congressional Budget Office |
| CC | Ceiling Cost |
| CCI | Contract Capital Index |
| CCR | Central Contractor Registration |
| CDA | Contract Disputes Act |
| CDRL | Contract Data Requirements List |
| CEI | Contract End Item |

| | |
|---|---|
| CER | Cost Estimating Relationship |
| CFC | Court of Federal Claims |
| CFE | Contractor Furnished Equipment |
| CFR | Code of Federal Regulations |
| CI | Contract Item/Control Item |
| CICA | Competition in Contracting Act |
| CLIN | Contract Line Item Number |
| CO | Change Order/Contracting Officer |
| COC | Certificate of Competency |
| C.O.D. | Collect on Delivery |
| COFC | Court of Federal Claims |
| COI | Conflict of Interest |
| COM | Cost of Money |
| Comp. Gen. | Comptroller General |
| COR | Contracting Officer's Representative |
| COTR | Contracting Officer's Technical Representative |
| CP | Ceiling Price |
| CPAF | Cost-Plus-Award-Fee |
| CPARS | Contractor Performance Assessment Reporting System |
| CPFF | Cost-Plus-Fixed-Fee |
| CPIF | Cost-Plus-Incentive-Fee |
| CPO | Chief of Purchasing Office |
| CPPC | Cost-Plus-a-Percentage-of-Cost |
| CPR | Cost Performance Report |
| CPSR | Contractor Procurement System Review |
| CR | Cost-Reimbursement |
| CRC | Cost Reimbursement Contract |
| CS | Cost Sharing |
| C/SCSC | Cost/Schedule Control System Criteria |
| Ct. Cl. | Court of Claims |
| CY | Calendar Year |
| | |
| DAC | Days After Contract Award/Defense Acquisition Circular |
| DAD | Defense Acquisition Deskbook |
| DAR | Defense Acquisition Regulation |
| DCAA | Defense Contract Audit Agency |
| DCMC | Defense Contract Management Command |
| D&F | Determination and Finding |
| DFARS | Defense Federal Acquisition Regulation Supplement |
| DID | Data Item Description |
| DIPEC | Defense Industrial Plant Equipment Center |
| DLA | Defense Logistics Agency |
| DOC | Department of Commerce |

| | |
|---|---|
| DOD | Department of Defense |
| DODI | Department of Defense Instruction |
| DODISS | Department of Defense Index of Specifications and Standards |
| DOT | Department of Transportation |
| DPAS | Defense Priorities and Allocation System |
| DSA | Defense Supply Agency |
| DTC | Design-to-Cost |
| DUNS | Data Universal Numbering System |
| | |
| EC | Estimated Cost/Electronic Commerce |
| ECP | Engineering Change Proposal |
| EDI | Electronic Data Interchange |
| EEOC | Equal Employment Opportunity Commission |
| EFT | Electronic Funds Transfer |
| e.g. | For example |
| EIT | Electronic Information Technology |
| E-Mail | Electronic Mail |
| E-Sign | Electronic Signature |
| | |
| FAC | Federal Acquisition Circular |
| FACNET | Federal Acquisition Network |
| FAR | Federal Acquisition Regulation |
| FASA | Federal Acquisition Streamlining Act |
| FAX | Facsimile Transmission |
| FCCM | Facilities Capital Cost of Money |
| FED CIR | Federal Circuit |
| FED-STD | Federal Standard |
| FEMA | Federal Emergency Management Agency |
| FFP | Firm-Fixed-Price |
| FIP | Federal Information Processing |
| FIRMR | Federal Information Resources Management Regulations |
| f.o.b. | Free-on-Board |
| FP | Fixed-Price |
| FPAF | Fixed-Price Award Fee |
| FPEPA | Fixed-Price with Economic Price Adjustment |
| FPI | Fixed-Price Incentive |
| FPIF | Fixed-Price Incentive – Firm Target |
| FPIS | Fixed-Price Incentive – Successive Target |
| FPR | Federal Procurement Regulation/Fixed-Price Redeterminable |
| FPRA | Forward Pricing Rate Agreement |
| FSD | Full Scale Development |
| FSS | Federal Supply Schedule |
| FY | Fiscal Year |

| | |
|---|---|
| G&A | General and Administrative |
| GAO | Government Accountability Office |
| GFE | Government Furnished Equipment |
| GOCO | Government-Owned Contractor-Operated |
| GP | Government Property |
| GPE | Government-wide Point of Entry |
| GSA | General Services Administration |
| GSBCA | General Services Board of Contract Appeals |
| GSS | General Systems Specification |
| | |
| HUBZone | Historically Underutilized Business Zone |
| | |
| IAW | In accordance with |
| ICC | Interstate Commerce Commission |
| IDIQ | Indefinite Delivery/Indefinite Quantity |
| i.e. | That is |
| IFB | Invitation for Bids |
| Inc. | Incorporated |
| IPT | Integrated Product Team |
| IR&D | Independent Research and Development |
| IT | Information Technology |
| | |
| LCC | Life Cycle Costs |
| LCP | Letter Change Proposal |
| LH | Labor-Hour |
| LOE | Level-of-Effort |
| LRIP | Limited Rate Initial Production |
| LSA | Labor Surplus Area |
| | |
| MIL-STD | Military Standard |
| MOA | Memorandum of Agreement |
| MOB | Make-or-Buy |
| MYP | Multiyear Programs |
| | |
| NA | Not Applicable |
| NASA | National Aeronautics and Space Administration |
| NFS | NASA FAR Supplement |
| NHB | NASA Handbook |
| NMI | NASA Management Instruction |
| NOA | Notice of Award |
| NRA | NASA Research Announcement |
| NTE | Not-to-Exceed |

| | |
|---|---|
| OCI | Organizational Conflict of Interest |
| OFPP | Office of Federal Procurement Policy |
| O/H | Overhead |
| O&M | Operation and Maintenance |
| OMB | Office of Management and Budget |
| ORCA | Online Registration and Certification |
| PBP | Performance Based Payments |
| PCO | Procuring Contracting Officer |
| PDR | Preliminary Design Review |
| PII | Procurement Instrument Identification |
| PIO | Provisioned Item Order |
| PM | Program Manager |
| PMC | Program Management Codes |
| PNM | Price Negotiation Memorandum |
| PO | Purchasing Office/Purchase Order |
| PPI | Proposal Preparation Instructions/Past Performance Information |
| PRO | Plant Representative Office |
| PST | Production Special Tooling |
| PSTE | Production Special Test Equipment |
| PTA | Point of Total Assumption |
| Pub. L. | Public Law |
| QBL | Qualified Bidders List |
| QML | Qualified Manufacturers List |
| QPL | Qualified Parts List |
| R&D | Research and Development |
| RDT&E | Research, Development, Test and Evaluation |
| RFP | Request for Proposal |
| RFQ | Request for Quotation |
| RIE | Range of Incentive Effectiveness |
| ROI | Return on Investment |
| SA | Supplemental Agreement |
| SAM | System for Award Management |
| SAP | Simplified Acquisition Procedures |
| SAT | Simplified Acquisition Threshold |
| SB/SDB | Small Business/Small Disadvantaged Business |
| SBA | Small Business Administration |
| SD | Space Division |
| SEMP | Systems Engineering Management Plan |
| SF | Standard Form |

| | |
|---|---|
| SIC | Standard Industrial Classification |
| SOW | Statement of Work |
| S/R | Sharing Ratio |
| SSA | Source Selection Authority |
| SSAC | Source Selection Advisory Council |
| SSEB | Source Selection Evaluation Board |
| ST | Special Tooling |
| STAT | Statute |
| STD | Standard |
| STE | Special Test Equipment |
| | |
| TC | Target Cost |
| TCO | Termination Contracting Officer |
| T&C | Terms and Conditions |
| TF | Target Fee |
| TINA | Truth in Negotiations Act |
| T&M | Time and Materials |
| TP | Target Price/Target Profit/Technical Proposal |
| TQM | Total Quality Management |
| TWX | Teletype Message |
| | |
| UCA | Undefinitized Contract Action |
| UCC | Uniform Commercial Code |
| UPC | Unit Production Cost |
| U.S.A. | United States of America |
| USA | United States Army |
| USAF | United States Air Force |
| U.S.C. | United States Code |
| USN | United States Navy |
| | |
| VE | Value Engineering |
| VECP | Value Engineering Change Proposal |
| V-TA | Vinson-Trammel Act |
| | |
| WBS | Work Breakdown Structure |
| WGL | Weighted Guidelines |
| WGM | Weighted Guidelines Method |
| WIP | Work in Process |
| WPI | Wholesale Price Index |

# APPENDIX B

# GLOSSARY OF TERMS

**Acceptance**
The act of an authorized representative of the government by which the government assumes for itself, or as agent of another, ownership of existing and identified supplies tendered, or approves specific services rendered, as partial or complete performance of the contract on the part of the contractor.

**Accumulating Costs**
The collecting of cost data in an organized manner, such as through a system of accounts.

**Acquisition**
The acquiring by contract with appropriated funds of supplies or services (including construction) by and for the use of the Federal Government through purchase or lease, whether the supplies or services are already in existence or must be created, developed, demonstrated, and evaluated. Acquisition begins at the point when agency needs are established and includes the description of requirements to satisfy agency needs, solicitation and selection of sources, award of contracts, contract financing, contract performance, contract administration, and those technical and management functions directly related to the process of fulfilling agency needs by contract.

**Acquisition Planning**
The process by which the efforts of all personnel responsible for an acquisition are coordinated and integrated through a comprehensive plan for fulfilling the agency need in a timely manner and at a reasonable cost. It includes developing the overall strategy for managing the acquisition.

**Acquisition Streamlining**
Any effort that results in more efficient and effective use of resources to design and develop, or produce quality systems. This includes ensuring that only necessary and cost-effective requirements are included, at the most appropriate time in the acquisition cycle, in solicitations and resulting contracts for the design, development, and production of new systems, or for modifications to existing systems that involve redesign of systems or subsystems.

**Actual Costs**
Amounts determined on the basis of costs incurred, as distinguished from forecasted costs. Includes standard costs properly adjusted for applicable variances.

| | |
|---|---|
| **Allocate** | To assign an item of cost, or a group of items of cost, to one or more cost objectives. This term includes both direct assignment of cost and the reassignment of a share from the indirect cost pool. |
| **Best Value** | The expected outcome of an acquisition that, in the government's estimation, provides the greatest overall benefit in response to the requirement. |
| **Bid Guarantee** | Means a form of security accompanying a bid as assurance that the bidder will not withdraw its bid within the period specified for acceptance, and will execute a written contract and furnish such bonds as may be required within the period specified in the bid (unless a longer period is allowed) after receipt of the specified forms. |
| **Bill of Materials** | A listing of the materials and parts required to produce a given product, assembly, subassembly or part. |
| **Catalog Price** | A price included in a catalog, price list, schedule, or other form that is regularly maintained by the manufacturer or vendor, is either published or otherwise available for inspection by customers, and states prices at which sales are currently, or were last made to a significant number of buyers constituting the general public. |
| **Change Order** | A written order signed by the contracting officer, directing the contractor to make changes which the Changes clause of the contract authorizes the contracting officer to order without the consent of the contractor. |
| **Classified Contract** | Any contract that requires or will require access to classified information by the contractor or its employees in the performance of the contract. A contract may be a classified contract, even though the contract document is not classified. |
| **Commercial Item** | Any item, other than real property, that is of a type customarily used for non-governmental purposes and that: (1) has been sold, leased, or licensed to the general public; or (2) has been offered for sale, lease or license to the general public. |
| **Conflict of Interest** | Because of other activities or relationships with other persons, a person is unable or potentially unable to render impartial assistance or advice to the Government, or the person's objectivity in performing the contract work is or might be otherwise impaired, or a person has an unfair competitive advantage. |

**Contract**

All types of agreements and orders for the procurement of supplies and services. It includes awards and notices of award; contracts of a fixed-price, cost, cost-plus-a-fixed-fee, or incentive type; contracts providing for the issuance of job orders, task orders, or task letters thereunder; letter contracts, and purchase orders. It also includes supplemental agreements with respect to any of the foregoing.

**Contract Action**

Any action resulting in a contract, including contract modifications for additional supplies or services, but not including contract modifications that are within the scope and under the terms of the contract, such as contract modifications issued pursuant to the *Changes* clause, or funding and other administrative changes.

**Contract Administration Office**

The office which performs assigned functions related to the administration of contracts and assigned pre-award functions.

**Contract Inventory**

Any property acquired by and in the possession of a contractor or subcontractor under a contract where the title is vested in the government and that is in excess of the amounts needed to complete full performance under the contract. Any property which the government is obligated to or has an option to take over under any type of contract as a result either of any changes in the specifications or plans or of the termination of such contract prior to completion of the work.

**Contract Modification**

Any written alteration in the specification, delivery point, rate of delivery, contract period, price, quantity or other contract provisions of an existing contract, whether accomplished by unilateral action in accordance with a contract provision or by mutual action of the parties to the contract. It includes: (1) bilateral actions such as supplemental agreements; and (2) unilateral actions such as change orders, orders for provisioned items and notices of the exercise of a contract option.

**Contract Price**

The total amount fixed by the contract, as amended, to be paid for complete performance of the contract.

**Contract Quality Requirements**

The detailed requisites for quality incumbent on the contractor, consisting of: (1) all quality requirements contained in the contract; and (2) the detailed contractual requisites incumbent on the contractor to substantiate conformance of product or service to quality requirements of the contract.

**Contracting Officer** Any person, who either by virtue of their position or by appointment in accordance with prescribed procedures, is currently a contracting officer with the authority to enter into and administer contracts and make determinations and findings with respect thereto, or with any part of such authority. The term also includes the authorized representative of the contracting officer acting within the limits of that authority.

**Contractor** Any individual or other legal entity that: (1) directly or indirectly (e.g., through an affiliate) submits offers for or is awarded, or reasonably may be expected to submit offers for or be awarded, a government contract, including a contract for under government or commercial bills of lading, or a subcontract under a government contract; or (2) conducts business, or reasonably may be expected to conduct business, with the government as an agent or representative of another contractor.

**Contractor-Acquired Property** Property procured or otherwise provided by the contractor for the performance of a contract under whose terms title is vested in the government.

**Contractor-Furnished Property** All property, other than government property, used by the contractor in the performance of a contract.

**Cost Objective** A function, organizational subdivision, contract or other work unit for which cost data are desired and for which provision is made to accumulate and measure the cost of processes, products, jobs, capitalized projects, etc.

**Data** Recorded information regardless of form or characteristics.

**Direct Cost** Any cost which is identified specifically with a particular final cost objective. Direct costs are not limited to items which are incorporated into the end product as material or labor. Costs identified specifically with a contract are direct costs of that contract. All costs identified specifically with other final cost objectives of the contractor are direct costs of those objectives.

**Disbursing Officer** The officer or agent of the office designated as the paying office under the contract.

**Effective Date of Termination** The date upon which the notice of termination first requires the contractor to stop performance, in whole or in part, under the contract. When the termination notice is received after the date fixed for termination, the effective date is the date on which the notice is received.

**Electronic Commerce** — Electronic techniques for accomplishing business transactions; including electronic mail or messaging, World Wide Web technology, electronic bulletin boards, purchase cards, electronic funds transfer, and electronic data exchange.

**Electronic Data Interchange (EDI)** — A technique for electronically transferring and storing formatted information between computers utilizing established and published formats and codes, as authorized by the applicable Federal Information Processing Standards.

**Engineering Changes** — All changes in the physical characteristics of an item when reflected in the design, plans or specifications for the item.

**Established Supplier** — A concern which is a "source of supplies" and which has supplied the items satisfactorily to one or more government agencies or is a concern with which mobilization planning is in effect.

**Estimating Costs** — The process of forecasting a future result in terms of cost, based upon information available at the time.

**Exhibit** — A document attached to a procurement instrument referenced by its capital letter identifier in a line or subline item in the procurement instrument Schedule, which establishes deliverable requirements in the attached document as an alternative to establishing an extensive list of line or subline items in the procurement instrument Schedule.

**Expendable Property** — Property which will lose its identity or be consumed in the course of its use.

**Facilities** — Industrial property (other than material, special tooling, agency peculiar property or special test equipment) for production, maintenance, research, development or test, including real property and rights therein, buildings, structures, improvements and plant equipment.

**Facilities Contract** — A contract under which industrial facilities are provided by the government for use in connection with the performance of a contract or contracts for supplies or services.

**Final Cost Objective** — A cost objective which has allocated to it both direct and indirect costs, and, in the contractor's accumulation system, is one of the final accumulation points.

**Government-Furnished Property** — Property in the possession of or acquired directly by the government and subsequently delivered or otherwise made available to the contractor.

**Governmentwide Point of Entry (GPE)** — The single point where Government business opportunities greater than $25,000, including synopses of proposed contract actions, solicitations, and associated information, can be accessed electronically by the public. The GPE is located at http://www.fedbizopps.gov.

**Head of Procuring Activity** — The chief, commander or other official in charge of a Procuring Activity.

**Indirect Cost** — Any cost not directly identified with a single final cost objective, but identified with two or more final cost objectives or with at least one intermediate cost objective.

**Indirect Cost Pools** — Groupings of incurred costs identified with two or more cost objectives but not identified specifically with any final cost objective.

**Inspection** — The examination and testing of supplies or services (including, when appropriate, raw materials, components and intermediate assemblies) to determine whether they conform to contract requirements.

**Interested Party** — An interested party for the purpose of filing a protest means an actual or prospective offeror whose direct economic interest would be affected by the award of a contract or by the failure to be awarded a contract.

**Life-Cycle Cost** — The total cost to the Government of acquiring, operating, supporting, and (if appropriate) disposing of the items being acquired.

**Make-or-Buy** — A decision by the prime contractor to make the item or to buy it from some subcontractor.

**Material** — Property which may be incorporated into or attached to an end item to be delivered under a contract or which may be consumed or expended in the performance of a contract.

**Market Research** — Collecting and analyzing information about capabilities within the market to satisfy agency needs.

**May** — Denotes the permissive. However, the words "no person may..." means that no person is required, authorized, or permitted to do the act described.

| | |
|---|---|
| **Military Property** | Personal property peculiar to military operations which is under the cognizance of a military inventory control point. It includes weapons systems, components thereof and related support equipment, but does not include items which are consumed in the performance of a procurement contract or incorporated in the end items produced under a contract. |
| **Modular Contracting** | The use of one or more contracts to acquire information technology systems in successive, interoperable increments. |
| **Negotiate and Negotiation** | When applied to the making of purchases and contracts, refers to making purchases and contracts without sealed bidding. |
| **Negotiated Final Overhead Rates** | A percentage or dollar factor which expresses the ratios of indirect expense incurred at the close of a regularly stated period. |
| **Nonprocurement Common Rule** | The procedures used by Federal Executive Agencies to suspend, debar, or exclude individuals or entities from participating in nonprocurement transactions under Executive Order 12549. Some examples of nonprocurement transactions are: grants, cooperative agreements, scholarships, fellowships, contracts of assistance, loans, loan guarantees, subsidies, insurance, payments for specific use, and donation agreements. |
| **Nonseverable** | When related to government production and research property, nonseverable means that such property cannot be removed after erection or installation without substantial loss of value or damage thereto or to the premises where installed. |
| **Office of Administration** | The activity having overall responsibility for the administration of a contract. |
| **Partial Termination** | The termination of part, but not all, of the work which has not been completed and accepted under a contract. |
| **Paying Office** | The office which makes payments under a contract. |
| **Performance Bond** | A bond executed in connection with a contract which secures the performance and fulfillment of all the undertakings, covenants, terms, conditions and agreements contained in the contract. |
| **Plant Clearance Officer** | A representative of the termination contracting officer or administrative contracting officer authorized to settle for them all matters relating to the disposal of contractor and termination inventory. |

**Plant Equipment** — Personal property of a capital nature, such as machinery equipment, used or capable of use in the manufacture of supplies or in the performance of services or any administrative or general plant purpose.

**Potential Supplier** — A concern which is a "source of supplies" but which is not an essential supplier.

**Pricing** — The process of establishing the amount or amounts to be paid in return for goods or services.

**Procurement** — Includes purchasing, renting, leasing or otherwise obtaining supplies or services. It also includes all functions that pertain to the obtaining of supplies and services, including description (but not determination) of requirements, selection and solicitation of sources, preparation and award of a contract; and all phases of contract administration.

**Procurement Action** — Any contractual action to obtain supplies, services or construction which obligates or de-obligates funds.

**Profit Center** — The smallest organizationally independent segment of a company which has been charged by management with profit and loss responsibilities.

**Progress Payments** — Payments made to contractors as work progresses under the contract, upon the basis of costs incurred under the contract. Progress payments are divided into two main classes, customary and unusual.

**Property** — All physical property, both real and personal.

**Property Administrator** — The government representative responsible to the contract administrator for reviewing the contractor's property control procedures, examining the record of government property maintained by the contractor, making usage analysis of government property and maintaining required government property records.

**Property Records** — All records affecting the status of government property. Not restricted to stock records or other forms of an inventory record.

**Proposal** — Any offer or other submission used as a basis for pricing a contract, contract modification or termination settlement, or for securing payments thereunder.

**Provisional Overhead Rates** — A tentative overhead rate established for interim billing purposes pending negotiation of the final overhead rate.

**Purchasing Office** — The office which awards or executes a contract for supplies or services and performs post-award functions not assigned to a contract administration office.

**Quality Control Surveillance** — Determination and continuing appraisal by the government of the contractor's methods and procedures for control of its production elements effecting product quality.

**Real Property** — Lands and interests therein, leaseholds, buildings, improvements and appurtenances thereto. Also includes piers, docks, warehouses, rights-of-way and easements, and improvements permanently attached to land.

**Reporting Costs** — Provision of cost information to others. The reporting of costs involves selecting relevant cost data and presenting it in an intelligible manner for use by the recipient.

**Risk Management** — The act or practice of controlling risk. It includes risk planning, assessing risk areas, developing risk-handling options, monitoring risks to determine how risks have changed, and documenting the overall risk management program.

**Secretarial Level** — This term is limited to use in the extraordinary contractual actions to facilitate the national defense under the Act of 28 August 1958. As used there, it is an official at or above the level of assistant secretary or his deputy and a contract adjustment board established by the secretary concerned.

**Settlement Agreement** — A written agreement, in the form of an amendment to the contract, between the contractor and the government settling all or a severable portion of a settlement proposal.

**Settlement Proposal** — A termination claim submitted by a contractor or subcontractor in the form, complete with supporting data, as required by the FAR.

**Shall** — Denotes the imperative.

**Small Business Concern** — A concern that is not dominant in its field of operations and, with its affiliates, employs fewer than 500 employees or is certified as a small business concern by the Small Business Administration. A small business concern in the construction industry is a concern that is independently owned and operated, is not dominant in its field of operations, and the average annual receipts of the concern and its affiliates for the preceding three (3) years are not in excess of the amounts specified for the various types of small business.

**Small Business Set-Aside** — A method of procurement where either the total amount or a portion of a requirement is withheld from general solicitation and reserved exclusively for small business firms.

**Special Test Equipment** — Either single or multipurpose integrated test units engineered, designed, fabricated or modified to accomplish special purpose testing in the performance of the contract. Such testing units comprise electrical, electronic, hydraulic, pneumatic, mechanical or other items or assemblies of equipment, that are mechanically, electrically or electronically interconnected so as to become a new functional entity, causing the individual item or items to become interdependent and essential in the performance of special purpose testing in the development or production of particular supplies or services.

**Special Tooling** — All jigs, dies, fixtures, molds, patterns, special taps, special gages, other special equipment and manufacturing aids, acquired or manufactured by the contractor for the use in the performance of a contract, which are of such a specialized nature that without substantial modification or alteration their use is limited to the production of supplies or the performance of such services peculiar to the needs of the government.

**Specification** — A clear and accurate description of the technical requirements of a material, a product or a service, including the procedure by which it can be determined that the requirements are met.

**Subcontractor** — Any supplier, distributor, vendor or firm which furnishes supplies or services to or for a prime contractor or another subcontractor.

**Supplemental Agreement** — Any contract modification which is accomplished by the mutual action of the parties.

**Supplies** — All property except land or interest in land. It includes public works, buildings and facilities; ships, floating equipment and vessels of every character, type and description, together with parts and accessories thereto; aircraft and aircraft parts, accessories and equipment; machine tools; and the alteration or installation of any of the foregoing.

**Supporting Contract Administration** — The performance by another contract administration office of specific contract administration functions as required by the office to which the contract has been assigned for administration.

**Surplus** — Excess contractor inventory which has been screened by the various Federal agencies and is not required by them.

| | |
|---|---|
| **Technical Data** | Recorded information, regardless of form or characteristic, of a scientific or technical nature. It may, for example, document research, experimental, developmental or engineering work; or be usable or used to define a design or process or to procure, produce, support, maintain or operate material. The data may be graphic or pictorial delineations in media such as drawings or photographs; text in specifications or related performance or design type documents; or computer printouts. |
| **Terminated Portion** | That portion of a terminated contract which relates to work or end of the contract items not already completed and accepted prior to the effective date of termination and which the contractor is not to continue to perform. |
| **Termination Claim** | Any claim for compensation for termination by a contractor or subcontractor permitted by the terms of a prime contract or a subcontract thereunder. Any other claim authorized by the termination contract part of the FAR. |
| **Termination Contracting Officer** | Those contracting officers authorized to terminate contracts or to settle terminated contracts. |
| **Termination Inventory** | Any items of physical property purchased, supplied, manufactured, furnished or otherwise acquired for performance of the terminated contract and properly allocated to the terminated contract or to the terminated portion of the contract. |
| **Testing** | An element of inspection and generally denoting the determination by technical means, the properties or elements of supplies, or components thereof, and involves the application of established scientific principles and procedures. |
| **Warranty** | A promise or affirmation given by a seller to a purchaser regarding the nature, usefulness or condition of the supplies or performance of services to be furnished. |

# APPENDIX C

# CONTRACT ADMINISTRATION OFFICE FUNCTIONS

The contracting officer normally delegates the following contract administration functions to a contract administration office (CAO). The contracting officer may retain any of these functions, except those in (5), (9), (11) and (12) below, unless the cognizant Federal agency (see FAR 2.101) has designated the contracting officer to perform these functions.

(1) Review the contractor's compensation structure.

(2) Review the contractor's insurance plans.

(3) Conduct post-award orientation conferences.

(4) Review and evaluate contractors' proposals under FAR Subpart 15.4 and, when negotiation will be accomplished by the contracting officer, furnish comments and recommendations to that officer.

(5) Negotiate forward pricing rate agreements (see FAR 15.407-3).

(6) Negotiate advance agreements applicable to treatment of costs under contracts currently assigned for administration (see FAR 31.109).

(7) Determine the allowability of costs suspended or disapproved as required (see Subpart 42.8), direct the suspension or disapproval of costs when there is reason to believe they should be suspended or disapproved, and approve final vouchers.

(8) Issue Notices of Intent to Disallow or not Recognize Costs (see FAR Subpart 42.8).

(9) Establish final indirect cost rates and billing rates for those contractors meeting the criteria for contracting officer determination in FAR Subpart 42.7.

(10) Attempt to resolve issues in controversy, using ADR procedures when appropriate (see FAR Subpart 33.2); prepare findings of fact and issue decisions under the Disputes clause on matters in which the administrative contracting officer (ACO) has the authority to take definitive action.

(11) In connection with Cost Accounting Standards (see FAR 30.601 and 48 CFR Chapter 99 (FAR Appendix)):

- (i) Determine the adequacy of the contractor's disclosure statements;
- (ii) Determine whether disclosure statements are in compliance with Cost Accounting Standards and FAR Part 31;
- (iii) Determine the contractor's compliance with Cost Accounting Standards and disclosure statements, if applicable; and
- (iv) Negotiate price adjustments and execute supplemental agreements under the Cost Accounting Standards clauses at FAR 52.230-2, 52.230-3, 52.230-4, 52.230-5, and 52.230-6.

(12) Determine the adequacy of the contractor's accounting system. The contractor's accounting system should be adequate during the entire period of contract performance. The adequacy of the contractor's accounting system and its associated internal control system, as well as contractor compliance with the Cost Accounting Standards (CAS), affect the quality and validity of the contractor data upon which the Government must rely for its management oversight of the contractor and contract performance.

(13) Review and approve or disapprove the contractor's requests for payments under the progress payments or performance-based payments clauses.
(14) Make payments on assigned contracts when prescribed in agency acquisition regulations.
(15) Manage special bank accounts.
(16) Ensure timely notification by the contractor of any anticipated overrun or underrun of the estimated cost under cost-reimbursement contracts.
(17) Monitor the contractor's financial condition and advise the contracting officer when it jeopardizes contract performance.
(18) Analyze quarterly limitation on payments statements and take action in accordance with FAR Subpart 32.6 to recover overpayments from the contractor.
(19) Issue tax exemption forms.
(20) Ensure processing and execution of duty-free entry certificates.
(21) For classified contracts, administer those portions of the applicable industrial security program delegated to the CAO (see FAR Subpart 4.4).
(22) Issue work requests under maintenance, overhaul, and modification contracts.
(23) Negotiate prices and execute supplemental agreements for spare parts and other items selected through provisioning procedures when prescribed by agency acquisition regulations.
(24) Negotiate and execute contractual documents for settlement of partial and complete contract terminations for convenience, except as otherwise prescribed by FAR Part 49.
(25) Negotiate and execute contractual documents settling cancellation charges under multiyear contracts.
(26) Process and execute novation and change of name agreements under FAR Subpart 42.12.
(27) Perform property administration (see FAR Part 45).
(28) Perform necessary screening, redistribution, and disposal of contractor inventory.
(29) Issue contract modifications requiring the contractor to provide packing, crating, and handling services on excess Government property. When the ACO determines it to be in the Government's interests, the services may be secured from a contractor other than the contractor in possession of the property.
(30) When contractors request Government property:
    (i) Evaluate the contractor's requests for Government property and for changes to existing Government property and provide appropriate recommendations to the contracting officer;
    (ii) Ensure required screening of Government property before acquisition by the contractor;
    (iii) Evaluate the use of Government property on a non-interference basis in accordance with the clause at FAR 52.245-9;
    (iv) Ensure payment by the contractor of any rental due; and
    (v) Modify contracts to reflect the addition of Government-furnished property and ensure appropriate consideration.
(31) Perform production support, surveillance, and status reporting, including timely reporting of potential and actual slippages in contract delivery schedules.
(32) Perform preaward surveys (see FAR Subpart 9.1).

(33) Advise and assist contractors regarding their priorities and allocations responsibilities and assist contracting offices in processing requests for special assistance and for priority ratings for privately owned capital equipment.
(34) Monitor contractor industrial labor relations matters under the contract; apprise the contracting officer and, if designated by the agency, the cognizant labor relations advisor, of actual or potential labor disputes; and coordinate the removal of urgently required material from the strikebound contractor's plant upon instruction from, and authorization of, the contracting officer.
(35) Perform traffic management services, including issuance and control of Government bills of lading and other transportation documents.
(36) Review the adequacy of the contractor's traffic operations.
(37) Review and evaluate preservation, packaging, and packing.
(38) Ensure contractor compliance with contractual quality assurance requirements (see FAR Part 46).
(39) Ensure contractor compliance with contractual safety requirements.
(40) Perform engineering surveillance to assess compliance with contractual terms for schedule, cost, and technical performance in the areas of design, development, and production.
(41) Evaluate for adequacy and perform surveillance of contractor engineering efforts and management systems that relate to design, development, production, engineering changes, subcontractors, tests, management of engineering resources, reliability and maintainability, data control systems, configuration management, and independent research and development.
(42) Review and evaluate for technical adequacy the contractor's logistics support, maintenance, and modification programs.
(43) Report to the contracting office any inadequacies noted in specifications.
(44) Perform engineering analyses of contractor cost proposals.
(45) Review and analyze contractor-proposed engineering and design studies and submit comments and recommendations to the contracting office, as required.
(46) Review engineering change proposals for proper classification, and when required, for need, technical adequacy of design, producibility, and impact on quality, reliability, schedule, and cost; submit comments to the contracting office.
(47) Assist in evaluating and make recommendations for acceptance or rejection of waivers and deviations.
(48) Evaluate and monitor the contractor's procedures for complying with procedures regarding restrictive markings on data.
(49) Monitor the contractor's value engineering program.
(50) Review, approve or disapprove, and maintain surveillance of the contractor's purchasing system (see FAR Part 44).
(51) Consent to the placement of subcontracts.
(52) Review, evaluate, and approve plant or divisionwide small, small disadvantaged, women-owned, veteran-owned, HUBZone, and service-disabled veteran-owned small business master subcontracting plans.
(53) Obtain the contractor's currently approved company- or division-wide plans for small, small disadvantaged, women-owned, veteran-owned, HUBZone, and service-disabled veteran-owned small business subcontracting for its commercial products, or, if there is no currently approved plan, assist the contracting officer in evaluating the plans for those products.

(54) Assist the contracting officer, upon request, in evaluating an offeror's proposed small, small disadvantaged women-owned, veteran-owned, HUBZone, and service-disabled veteran-owned small business subcontracting plans, including documentation of compliance with similar plans under prior contracts.
(55) By periodic surveillance, ensure the contractor's compliance with small, small disadvantaged, women-owned, veteran-owned, HUBZone, and service-disabled veteran-owned small business subcontracting plans and any labor surplus area contractual requirements; maintain documentation of the contractor's performance under and compliance with these plans and requirements; and provide advice and assistance to the firms involved, as appropriate.
(56) Maintain surveillance of flight operations.
(57) Assign and perform supporting contract administration.
(58) Ensure timely submission of required reports.
(59) Issue administrative changes, correcting errors or omissions in typing, contractor address, facility or activity code, remittance address, computations which do not require additional contract funds, and other such changes (see FAR 43.101).
(60) Cause release of shipments from contractor's plants according to the shipping instructions. When applicable, the order of assigned priority shall be followed; shipments within the same priority shall be determined by date of the instruction.
(61) Obtain contractor proposals for any contract price adjustments resulting from amended shipping instructions. Review all amended shipping instructions on a periodic, consolidated basis to ensure that adjustments are timely made. Except when the ACO has settlement authority, the ACO shall forward the proposal to the contracting officer for contract modification. The ACO shall not delay shipments pending completion and formalization of negotiations of revised shipping instructions.
(62) Negotiate and/or execute supplemental agreements, as required, making changes in packaging subcontractors or contract shipping points.
(63) Cancel unilateral purchase orders when notified of nonacceptance by the contractor. The CAO shall notify the contracting officer when the purchase order is canceled.
(64) Negotiate and execute one-time supplemental agreements providing for the extension of contract delivery schedules up to 90 days on contracts with an assigned Criticality Designator of C (see FAR 42.1105). Notification that the contract delivery schedule is being extended shall be provided to the contracting office. Subsequent extensions on any individual contract shall be authorized only upon concurrence of the contracting office.
(65) Accomplish administrative closeout procedures (see FAR 4.804-5).
(66) Determine that the contractor has a drug-free workplace program and drug-free awareness program (see FAR Subpart 23.5).
(67) Support the program, product, and project offices regarding program reviews, program status, program performance and actual or anticipated program problems.
(68) Monitor the contractor's environmental practices for adverse impact on contract performance or contract cost, and for compliance with environmental requirements specified in the contract. ACO responsibilities include:
    (i) Requesting environmental technical assistance, if needed;
    (ii) Monitoring contractor compliance with specifications or other contractual requirements requiring the delivery or use of environmentally preferable products, energy-efficient products, products containing recovered materials, and biobased products. This must occur as part of the quality assurance procedures set forth in FAR Part 46; and

(iii) As required in the contract, ensuring that the contractor complies with the reporting requirements relating to recovered material content utilized in contract performance (see FAR Subpart 23.4).

(69) Administer commercial financing provisions and monitor contractor security to ensure its continued adequacy to cover outstanding payments, when on-site review is required.

(70) Deobligate excess funds after final price determination.

(71) Ensure that the contractor has implemented the requirements of FAR 52.203-13, *Contractor Code of Business Ethics and Conduct.*

The CAO shall perform the following functions only when and to the extent specifically authorized by the contracting office:

(1) Negotiate or negotiate and execute supplemental agreements incorporating contractor proposals resulting from change orders issued under the Changes clause. Before completing negotiations, coordinate any delivery schedule change with the contracting office.

(2) Negotiate prices and execute priced exhibits for unpriced orders issued by the contracting officer under basic ordering agreements.

(3) Negotiate or negotiate and execute supplemental agreements changing contract delivery schedules.

(4) Negotiate or negotiate and execute supplemental agreements providing for the deobligation of unexpended dollar balances considered excess to known contract requirements.

(5) Issue amended shipping instructions and, when necessary, negotiate and execute supplemental agreements incorporating contractor proposals resulting from these instructions.

(6) Negotiate changes to interim billing prices.

(7) Negotiate and definitize adjustments to contract prices resulting from exercise of an economic price adjustment clause (see FAR Subpart 16.2).

(8) Issue change orders and negotiate and execute resulting supplemental agreements under contracts for ship construction, conversion, and repair.

(9) Execute supplemental agreements on firm-fixed-price supply contracts to reduce required contract line item quantities and deobligate excess funds when notified by the contractor of an inconsequential delivery shortage, and it is determined that such action is in the best interests of the Government, notwithstanding the default provisions of the contract. Such action will be taken only upon the written request of the contractor and, in no event, shall the total downward contract price adjustment resulting from an inconsequential delivery shortage exceed $250.00 or 5 percent of the contract price, whichever is less.

(10) Execute supplemental agreements to permit a change in place of inspection at origin specified in firm-fixed-price supply contracts awarded to nonmanufacturers, as deemed necessary to protect the Government's interests.

(11) Prepare evaluations of contractor performance in accordance with FAR Subpart 42.15.

Any additional contract administration functions not listed above, or not otherwise delegated, remain the responsibility of the contracting office.

(Source: FAR 42.3, *Contract Administration Office Functions*)

# APPENDIX D

# LIST OF ILLUSTRATIONS